Abortion Bibliography

for 1983

Abortion Bibliography

for 1983

compiled by

Polly T. Goode

The Whitston Publishing Company
Troy, New York
1986

TABLE OF CONTENTS

The Bibliography is divided into two sections: a title section in alphabetical order; and a subject section. Thus, if the researcher does not wish to observe the subject heads of the complier, he can use the title section exclusively. The subject heads have been allowed to issue from the nature of the material indexed rather than being imposed from Library of Congress subject heads or other standard lists.

The Book section includes Government Publications and Monographs.

The Subject Head Index includes page numbers.

Polly T. Goode
Troy, New York

PREFACE

Abortion Bibliography for 1983 is the fourteenth annual list of books and articles surrounding the subject of abortion in the preceding year. It appears serially each fall as a contribution toward documenting in one place as comprehensively as possible the literature of one of our central social issues. It is an attempt at a comprehensive world bibliography.

Searches in compiling this material have covered the following sources: *Abstracts on Criminology and Penology; Abstracts on Police Science; Access; Air University Library Index to Military Periodicals; America: History and Life; American Humanities Index; American Reference Books Annual; Applied Science and Technology Index; Bibliographic Index; Biological Abstracts; Biological and Agricultural Index; British Humanities Index; Business Periodicals Index; Canadian Education Index; Canadian Periodical Index; Catholic Periodical and Literature Index; Communication Abstracts; College Student Personnel Abstracts; Criminal Justice Abstracts; Criminal Justice Periodical Index; Cumulative Book Index; Cumulative Index to Nursing and Allied Health Literature; Current Index to Journals in Education; Dissertation Abstracts International: A. Social Sciences and Humanities; Dissertation Abstracts International: B. Physical Sciences and Engineering; Education Index; Environment Abstracts; Essay and General Literature Index; Hospital Literature Index; Human Resources Abstracts; Humanities Index; Index Medicus; Index to Jewish Periodicals; Index to Legal Periodicals; International Nursing Index; Media Review Digest; Music Index; PAIS; PAIS Foreign Language Index; Philosopher's Index; Popular Periodical Index; Psychological Abstracts; Readers Guide to Periodical Literature; Religion Index One: Periodicals; Religious and Theological Abstracts; Sage Family Studies Abstracts; Sage Urban Studies Abstracts; Social Sciences Index; Social Work Research and Abstracts; Sociological Abstracts; Studies on Women's Abstracts* and *Women's Studies Abstracts.*

LIST OF JOURNALS CITED

AORN Journal: Association of Operating Room Nurses
Acta Europaea Fertilitatis
Acta Obstetricia et Gynecologica Scandinavica
Acta Obstetricia et Gynecologica Scandinavica, Supplement
Acta Paediatrica Scandinavica
Actas Luso-Espanolas de Neurologia y Psiquiatria y Ciencias Afines
Activitas Nervosa Superior
Ad Forum
Administration and Society
Administration in Social Work
Adolescence
Advance Data
Advertising Age
Africa
Aggressive Behavior
Akusherstvo I Ginekologiia
Alaska Law Review
Albany Law Review
Alberta Report
Alternative Lifestyles
America
American Bar Association Journal
American Economic Review
American Journal of Community Psychology
American Journal of Epidemiology
American Journal of Human Genetics
American Journal of Industrial Medicine
American Journal of Law and Medicine
American Journal of Maternal Child Nursing
American Journal of Medical Genetics
American Journal of Medical Technology

American Journal of Nursing
American Journal of Obstetrics and Gynecology
American Journal of Pathology
American Journal of Primatology
American Journal of Public Health
American Journal of Reproductive Immunology
American Journal of Veterinary Research
American Nurse
American Sociological Review
Anales de la Real Academia Nacionale de Medicina
Anatomischer Anzeiger
Andrologia
Anesthesiology
Annales de Pathologie
Annales Medico-Psychologiques
Annali di Ostetricia Ginecologia, Medicina Perinatale
Annals of the Academy of Medicine, Singapore
Annals of Emergency Medicine
Annals of Human Biology
Annals of Human Genetics
Annual Review of Public Health
Annual Survey of American Law
Anthropological Quarterly
Appetite
Archives of Andrology
Archives of Sexual Behavior
Archivio di Ostetricia e Ginecologia
Arizona Law Review
Arizona Medicine
Asian Journal of Psychology and Education
Asian Outlook
Asia-Oceania Journal of Obstetrics and Gynaecology
The Atlantic Advocate
Atlantic Insight
Audubon
Australian and New Zealand Journal of Obstetrics and Gynaecology
Australian and New Zealand Journal of Psychiatry
The Australian and New Zealand Journal of Sociology
Australian and New Zealand Journal of Surgery
Australian Family Physician
Australian Foreign Affairs Record
Australian Journal of Sex, Marriage and Family

Australian Journal of Social Issues
Australasian Nurses Journal

Behaviour
Behaviour Research and Therapy
Beijing Review
Beitraege zur Gerichtlichen Medizin
BioScience
Booklist
Boston
Bratislavske Lekarske Listy
British Journal of Anaesthesia
British Journal of Family Planning
British Journal of Hospital Medicine
British Journal of Industrial Medicine
British Journal of Obstetrics and Gynaecology
British Journal of Urology
British Journal of Venereal Diseases
British Medical Journal
Buffalo Law Review
Bulletin of Entomological Research
Bulletin of the British Psychological Society
Bulletin of the Pan American Health Organization
Bulletin of the World Health Organization
Business Insurance
Business Japan
Business Week

CHAC Review
Cahiers de Droit
Canada and the World
Canada's Mental Health
Canadian Consumer
Canadian Journal of Genetics and Cytology
Canadian Journal of Psychiatry
Canadian Journal of Public Health
Canadian Journal of Surgery
Canadian Journal of Zoology
Canadian Labour
Canadian Medical Association Journal
Canadian Nurse
Casopis Lekaru Ceskych

Catholic Digest
Catholic Lawyer
Catholic Worker
Center Journal
Central African Journal of Medicine
Ceskoslovenska Gynekologie
Ceskoslovenska Pediatrie
Ceylon Medical Journal
Changing Times
Chatelaine
Chemistry and Industry
Child Care, Health and Development
Child Psychiatry and Human Development
Children Today
Christian Century
Christianity and Crisis
Christianity Today
Chung Hua Shen Ching Ching Shen Ko Tsa Chih
Chung Hua Wai Ko Tsa Chih
Chung Kuo I Hsueh Ko Hsueh Yuan Hsueh Pao
Chung Yao Tung Pao
Clinical and Experimental Obstetrics and Gynecology
Clinical Immunology and Immunopathology
Clinical Obstetrics and Gynecology
Columbia
Columbia Human Rights Law Review
Commonweal
Community Medicine
Compte Rendue des Seances de L'Academie des Sciences
Congressional Quarterly Weekly Report
Connecticut Medicine
Contemporary Review
Contraception
Consultant
Consumers' Research Magazine
Copie Zero
Crime and Social Justice
Criminal Justice Newsletter
Criminal Law Reporter: Court Decisions and Proceedings
The Criminal Law Reporter: Text Section
Culture, Medicine and Psychiatry
Cumberland Law Review

Curationis
Current History
Cytogenetics and Cell Genetics

Daily Telegraph
Democracy
Demography
Department of State Bulletin
Development and Change
Developmental Psychobiology
Diabetes Educator
Dialogue
Dickinson Law Review
Discover
Dissertation Abstracts International: A. Humanities and Social
    Sciences
Dissertation Abstracts International: B. Physical Sciences and
    Engineering
La Documentation Catholique

Early Human Development
Ecological Entomology
Econometrica
Economic and Political Weekly
Economic Development and Cultural Change
The Economist
Ecumenist
Editorial Research Reports
Educational Horizon's
Emergency Medicine
Endocrinologia Japonica
Endokrinologie
Engage/Social Action
Entomological Review
Environment
Environmental Research
Epidemiologic Reviews
Esquire
Essence
Ethos
European Journal of Obstetrics and Gynecology
European Journal of Obstetrics, Gynecology and Reproductive
    Biology

FDA Consumer
The Family Law Reporter: Court Opinions
The Family Law Reporter: Text No. 1
The Family Law Reporter: Text No. 5
Family Planning Perspectives
Family Relations
Far Eastern Economic Review
Fel'dsher I Akusherka
Fertility and Sterility
Finance and Development
Folia Morphologica
Forbes
Free Inquiry
Frontiers

Geburtshilfe und Frauenheilkunde
Geographical Magazine
Georgetown Law Journal
Ginecologia y Obsetricia de Mexico
Ginekologia Polska
Glamour
Golden State University Law Review
Good Housekeeping
Guardian
Gynakologe
Gynaekologische Rundschau
Gynecologic and Obstetric Investigation

Hadassah Magazine
Haematologia
Harefuah
Harper's Bazaar
Harvard Journal of Law and Public Policy
Harvard Women's Law Journal
Hastings Center Report
Health
Health and Medicine
Health and Population: Perspectives and Issues
Health Education
Health Visitor
High School Journal
Histoire Social-Social History

History of European Ideas
Home Magazine
Homiletic and Pastoral Review
Horizons
Hormones and Behavior
Hospital and Community Psychiatry
Hospital Medicine
Hospital Practice
Hospital Progress
Hospitals
Houston Law Review
Human Events
Human Genetics
Human Organization
Human Rights
Humanist
Humanity and Society

Illinois Teacher of Home Economics
Indian Journal of Experimental Biology
Indian Journal of Medical Research
Indian Journal of Pathology and Microbiology
Indian Journal of Public Health
Indian Journal of Social Work
Infirmiere Canadienne
Infirmiere Francaise
Information
International and Comparative Law Quarterly
International Archives of Occupational and Environmental Health
International Family Planning Perspectives
International Journal of Biological Research in Pregnancy
International Journal of Epidemiology
International Journal of Fertility
International Journal of Gynaecology and Obstetrics
International Journal of Gynaecological Pathology
International Journal of Law and Psychiatry
International Journal of Psychoanalysis
International Journal of Women's Studies
International Planned Parenthood Federation Medical Bulletin
International Surgery
Irish Medical Journal
Israel Journal of Psychiatry and Related Sciences

JOGN Nursing: Journal of Obstetric, Gynecologic and Neonatal
  Nursing
Japanese Journal of Fertility and Sterility
Jinrui Idengaku Zasshi
Jordemodern
Journal de Gynecologie, Obstetrique et Biologie de la Reproduction
Journal of Adolescent Health Care
Journal of African Law
Journal of Ambulatory Care Management
Journal of the American Academy of Child Psychiatry
Journal of the American College Health Association
Journal of the American Dietetic Association
Journal of the American Medical Association
Journal of the American Medical Women's Association
Journal of the American Osteopathic Association
Journal of Applied Developmental Psychology
Journal of Applied Physiology
Journal of Applied Social Psychology
Journal of the Arkansas Medical Society
Journal of Biosocial Science
Journal of Black Studies
Journal of Comparative and Physiological Psychology
Journal of Developmental and Behavioral Pediatrics
Journal of Economic Entomology
Journal of Epidemiology and Community Health
Journal of Ethnopharmacology
Journal of Experimental Zoology
Journal of Family History
Journal of Family Issues
Journal of Family Practice
Journal of Family Welfare
Journal of Home Economics
Journal of the Indian Medical Association
Journal of the Indiana State Medical Association
Journal of Interdisciplinary History
Journal of Legal Medicine
Journal of Mammalogy
Journal of Marriage and the Family
Journal of the Medical Association of Thailand
Journal of Medical Ethics

Journal of Medicinal Chemistry
Journal of Medicine and Philosophy
Journal of Mental Deficiency Research
Journal of Modern African Studies
Journal of the National Medical Association
Journal of Nurse-Midwifery
Journal of Personality and Social Psychology
Journal of Pharmacology and Experimental Therapeutics
Journal of Politics
Journal of Postgraduate Medicine
Journal of Preventive Psychology
Journal of Public Health Policy
Journal of Religion and Health
Journal of Reproductive Immunology
Journal of Reproductive Medicine
Journal of Research in Science Teaching
Journal of the Royal Society of Medicine
Journal of School Health
Journal of Sex Research
Journal of Social Psychology
Journal of Theoretical Biology
Journal of Tropical Pediatrics
Journal of Urology
Journal of Value Inquiry
Journal of Youth and Adolescence
Jugoslavenska Ginekologija I Opstetricija
Jurist
Juvenile and Family Law Digest

Katilolehti
Kentucky Law Journal
Klinische Monatsblaetter fur Augenheilkunde
Krankenpflege

LARC Medical
Lakartiningen
Lamp
Lancet
Lander's Herald
Laval Theologique et Philosophique
Law and Philosophy
Law, Medicine and Health Care

Legal Medical Quarterly
Life and Health
Liguorian
Linacre Quarterly
Logos
Loyola Law Review
Lutheran Forum

MMW: Muenchener Medizinishe Wochenschrift
MMWR: Morbidity and Mortality Weekly Report
Macleans
Mademoiselle
Marine Corps Gazette
Maturitas
McCalls
Medecine Tropicale
Medical Journal of Australia
Medical Journal of Malaysia
Medical Journal of Zambia
Medical World News
Medicinal Research Reviews
Medicine, Science and Law
Medycyna Doswiadczalna I Mikrobiologia
Metaphilosophy
Michigan Hospitals
Midwife, Health Visitor and Community Nurse
Milbank Memorial Fund Quarterly
Minerva Chirurgica
Minerva Ginecologia
Minerva Medica
Minerva Pediatrica
Minerva Urologica
Missouri Nurse
Mobius
Money
Montana Law Review
Month
Mother Earth News
Ms Magazine

Nation
National Catholic Reporter

National Review
National Survey of Family Growth
Nature
Nebraska Medical Journal
Nederlands Tijdschrift voor Geneeskunde
Neurobehavioral Toxicology and Teratology
New Covenant
New Directions for Women
New England Journal of Medicine
New Republic
New Scientist
New Statesman
New York State Journal of Medicine
New York Times
New Zealand Medical Journal
Newsette
Newsweek
Nippon Sanka Fujinka Gakkai Zasshi
North Carolina Medical Journal
Nouvelle Presse Medicale
Nurse Practitioner
Nurses Drug Alert
Nursing
Nursing Clinics of North America
Nursing Forum
Nursing Journal of India
Nursing Management
Nursing Mirror and Midwive's Journal
Nursing Times

Observer
Obstetrics and Gynecology
Occupational Health
Off Our Backs
Oklahoma Observer
Omni
Ontario History
Origins
Orvosi Hetilap
L'Osservatore Romano
Our Sunday Visitor
Oxford Review of Education

Pacific Affairs
Pastoral Psychology
Patient Care
Patient Counseling and Health Education
Pediatric Nursing
People
People Weekly
Perspectives in Psychological Researches
Perspectives Psychiatriques
Pharmacology, Biochemistry and Behavior
Philosophical Quarterly
Philosophy
Physiology and Behavior
Pielegniarka I Polozna
Policy Studies Review
Political Theory
Polski Tygodnik Lekarski
Population
Population Bulletin
Population and Environment
Population and Environment: Behavioral and Social Issues
Population Index
Population Reports
Population Reports Series L
Population Research and Policy Review
Population Studies
Populi
Postgraduate Medical Journal
Practitioner
Praxis der Kinderpsychologie und Kinderpsychiatrie
Prenatal Diagnosis
Priest
Primary Care
Proceedings of the American Catholic Philosophical Association
Professional Geographer
Progress in Clinical and Biological Research
Progressive
Prostaglandins
Prostaglandins Leukotrienes and Medicine
Psyche
Psychiatric Journal of the University of Ottawa
Psychiatry

Psychological Reports
Psychology Today
Psychoneuroendocrinology
Public Health Reports
Public Health Reviews
Public Opinion Quarterly

Quest

RN
Radiology
Reader's Digest
Reason
Redbook
Reformed Journal
Register
Religious Humanism
Research in Community and Mental Health
Research in Social Problems and Public Policy
Resources for Feminist Research
Respiration
Review of Radical Political Economy
Review of Religious Research
Revista de Enfermagen
Revista de Investigacion Clinica
Revista de Medicina Interna, Neurologie, Psihiatrie, Neurochirurgie,
    Demato-Venerologie, Seria: Medicina Interna
Revista Medica de Chile
Revue de L'Institut de Sociologie
Revue Francaise de Sociologie
Revue Internationale de Sociologie
Rivista Italiana di Ginecologia

San Diego Law Review
Scandinavian Journal of Social Medicine
Scandinavian Journal of Urology and Nephrology
Scandinavian Journal of Work, Environment and Health
School Counselor
Science
Science Digest
Science News
Seton Hall Law Review

Seventeen
Sex Roles
Signs
Simon Greenleaf Law Review
Simulation and Games
Social Biology
Social Casework
Social History
Social Indicators Research
Social Justice Review
Social Problems
Social Psychology Quarterly
Social Research
Social Science and Medicine
Social Science Quarterly
Social Work, Research and Abstracts
Society
Sociological Perspectives
Sociological Quarterly
Sociology
Sociology and Social Research
Sound
South African Medical Journal
Southern Journal of Philosophy
Southern Medical Journal
Southwest Philosophical Studies
Spectator
Srpski Arhiv za Celokupno Lekarstvo
Stetson Law Review
Studies
Studies in Comparative International Development
Studies in Family Planning
Sunday Times
Surgery, Gynecology and Obstetrics
Syracuse Law Review

Tablet
Teratogenesis, Carcinogenesis and Mutagenesis
Texas Hospitals
Texas Medicine
Theological Studies
This Magazine

Thought
Tidsskrift for den Norske Laegeforening
Tijdschrift von Ziekenverpleging
Time
Times (London)
Times Higher Education Supplement
Toronto Life
Transfusion
Transplantation
Trial
Tropical Doctor
Tsitol I Genetika

UCLA Law Review
UN Chronicle
U. S. Catholic
U. S. News and World Report
Ugeskrift for Laeger
United States Naval Institute Proceedings
University of Cincinnati Law Review
Urban Anthropology
Urology

Venture
Verhandlungen der Deutschen Gesellschaft fur Pathologie
Vermont Law Review
Veterinary Clinics of North America
Veterinary Record
The Village Voice
Virginia Medical
Vital Health Statistics
Vogue

Wall Street Journal
Washburn Law Journal
Washington and Lee Law Review
Washington University Law Quarterly
Wayne Law Review
West Virginia Law Review
West Virginia Medical Journal
Western Journal of Medicine
Western Political Quarterly

Westinghouse Health Systems Report
Who Chronicles
Wiadomosci Lekarskie
Wisconsin Law Review
Women and Health
Women's Rights Law Reporter
Women's Studies International Forum
World Bank Research News
World Development
World Health
World Press Review

Yale Journal of Biology and Medicine
Yao Hsueh Hsueh Pao
Youth and Society

Zeitschrift fuer Hautkrankheiten H und G
Zeitschrift fur Aerztliche Fortbildung
Zeitschrift fur Psychosomatische Medizin und Psychoanalyse
Zeitschrift fur Urologies und Nephrologie
Zentralblatt fur Gynaekologie
Zuchthygiene

SUBJECT HEADING INDEX

BOOKS GOVERNMENT PUBLICATIONS, AND MONOGRAPHS

ABORTION BIBLIOGRAPHY FOR 1980. Troy, New York: Whitston, 1982.

ABORTION BIBLIOGRAPHY FOR 1981. Troy, New York: Whitston, 1983.

Anker, R. REPRODUCTIVE BEHAVIOUR IN HOUSEHOLDS OF RURAL GUJARAT. Concept, 1982.

Arras, J., et al. ETHICAL ISSUES IN MODERN MEDICINE, 2nd ed. Palo Alto: Mayfield, 1983.

Batchelor, Edward Jr., editor. ABORTION: THE MORAL ISSUES. New York: Pilgrim Press, 1982.

Berent, Jerzy. FAMILY PLANNING IN EUROPE AND USA IN THE 1970'S. International Statistics Institute, 1982.

Bondeson, William B. ABORTION AND THE STATUS OF THE FETUS. Dordrecht Reidel, 1983.

Callahan, Daniel. "Ethics and reproductive biology" in WHO DECIDES by Nora K. Bell. Clifton: Humana Press, 1982, p. 169-178.

Coleman, S. FAMILY PLANNING IN JAPANESE SOCIETY. Princeton: Princeton University Press, 1983.

Committee for Abortion Rights and Against Sterilization Abuse. STERILIZATION: IT'S NOT AS SIMPLE AS "TYING YOUR TUBES." New York: Carasa, 1982.

ABORTION CONTROVERSY. Boston: Atheneum, 1983.

Milnor, Susan. ABORTION IN NORTH CAROLINA: CURRENT LAW AND PROSPECTS. Chapel Hill: Institute of Government, University of North Carolina, 1982.

Mirthy, Nirmala, editor. FAMILY PLANNTING PROGRAMME IN THE ORGANIZED SECTOR; CASE STUDIES. New York: Sterling Pubs., 1983.

Morgentaler, Henry. ABORTION AND CONTRACEPTION. New York: General Publishing Company, 1982.

NEW TRENDS IN FEMALE STERILIZATION. Year Book Medical Publications, 1983.

Norback, Judith. SOURCEBOOK OF SEX THERAPY, COUNSEL-ING AND FAMILY PLANNING. New York: Nostrand Reinhold, 1983.

Odell, C. THE FIRST HUMAN RIGHT. Huntington, Indiana: Our Sunday Visitor, 1983.

Paige, C. THE RIGHT TO LIFERS. New York: Summit Books, 1983.

POPULATION EDUCATION AS INTEGRATED INTO DEVELOP-MENT PROGRAMMES; A NON-FORMAL APPROACH. Population education clearing house, UNESCO regional office for education in Asia and Oceania, 1980.

POPULATION POLICY AND COMPULSION IN FAMILY PLANNING. Poona, India: Continental Prakashan, 1981.

Porter, C. W. CONTRACEPTION. New York: Grune & Stratton, 1983.

THE PROBLEM OF ABORTION, 2nd ed. Belmont, California: Wadsworth Publishing Company, 1984.

Ramirez de Arellano, Annette B. and Conrad Seipp. COLONIALISM, CATHOLICISM, AND CONTRACEPTION: A HISTORY OF BIRTH CONTROL IN PUERTO RICO. Chapel Hill: University of

North Carolina Press, 1983.

Rashiduzzaman, M. RURAL LEADERSHIP AND POPULATION CONTROL IN BANGLADESH. University Press of America, 1982.

Richards, A. WHAT TO DO IF YOU OR SOMEONE YOU KNOW IS UNDER 18 AND PREGNANT. New York: Lothrop, Lee & Shepard Books, 1983.

SECOND TRIMESTER PREGNANCY TERMINATION. Leiden: Leiden University Press, 1982.

Smetana, Judith G. CONCEPTS OF SELF AND MORALITY; WOMEN'S REASONING ABOUT ABORTION. New York: Praeger, 1982.

Soloway, Richard Allen. BIRTH CONTROL AND THE POPULA- TION QUESTION IN ENGLAND. Chapel Hill: University of North Carolina Press, 1982.

THE ABORTION DISPUTE AND THE AMERICAN SYSTEM. Washington, D. C.: Brookings Institution, 1983.

Tarcher, J. P. IT'S YOUR CHOICE. New York: Irvington Pubs., 1982.

Tooley, Michael. ABORTION AND INFANTICIDE. Oxford: Clarendon Press, 1983.

U. N. Educational, Scientific, and Cultural Organization Regional Office for Education in Asia and the Pacific. POPULATION EDUCATION IN ASIA AND THE PACIFIC. New York: The organization, 1982.

United States. House. Committee on Foreign Affairs. Subcommittee On Inter-American Affairs. POPULATION AND DEVELOPMENT IN LATIN AMERICA AND THE CARIBBEAN: HEARING SEPTEMBER 8, 1982. Washington: GPO, 1982.

United States. House. Committee on Post Office and Civil Service. Subcommittee on Census and Population. NATIONAL POPULA- TION POLICY: HEARINGS, MARCH 10-11, 1982, ON H. R.

907, A BILL TO ESTABLISH A NATIONAL POPULATION POLICY AND TO ESTABLISH AN OFFICE OF POPULA- TION POLICY. Washington: GPO, 1982.

United States. Senate. Committee on the Judiciary. Subcommittee on the Constitution. CONSTITUTIONAL AMENDMENTS RE- LATING TO ABORTION: HEARINGS, OCTOBER 5-DECEMBER 16, 1981, ON S. J. RES. 17 [AND OTHER] BILLS PROPOSING A CONSTITUTIONAL AMENDMENT WITH RESPECT TO ABORTION. Washington: GPO, 1983.

United States. National Center for Health Statistics Division of Health Care Statistics. BASIC DATA ON VISITS TO FAMILY PLANNING SERVICES SITES: UNITED STATES, 1980. Washington: GPO, 1982.

Warwick, Donald P. BITTER PILLS: POPULATION POLICIES AND THEIR IMPLEMENTATION IN EIGHT DEVELOPING COUNTRIES. Cambridge: Cambridge University Press, 1982.

Yates, W. FAMILY PLANNING ON A CROWDED PLANET. West- port, Connecticut: Greenwoon Press, 1983.

Zeitlin, Marian F., et al. NUTRITION AND POPULATION GROWTH: THE DELICATE BALANCE. Boston: Oelgeschlager, 1982.

Zimmerman, M. SHOULD I KEEP MY BABY? Minneapolis: Bethany House, 1983.

PERIODICAL LITERATURE

TITLE INDEX

The aborted abortion counselor, by A. Benz. PSYCHE 37(5):470-473, May 1983.

Aborted fetus as source of information about the reproduction prospects of the family and population, by J. Dejmek, et al. CASOPIS LEKARU CESKYCH 121(48):1485-1489, December 1982.

The abortifacient effect of synthetic androstane derivatives in the baboon, by V. Z. Pope, et al. CONTRACEPTION 27(2):201-210, February 1983.

Abortifacient effects of the roots of Momordica angustisepala, by C. N. Aguwa, et al. JOURNAL OF ETHNOPHARMACOLOGY 7(2):169-173, March 1983.

Abortion, THE FAMILY LAW REPORTER: TEXT NO. 5 9:33, p. 3047-3075, June 21, 1983.

Abortion, by A. Menke, PIELEGNIARKA I POLOZNA (10):5-6, 1982.

Abortion [letter], by A. Simpson, et al. NEBRASKA MEDICAL JOURNAL 96(727):184-185, March 9, 1983.

Abortion after Akron: The contradictions are showing, by Richard John Neuhaus. COMMONWEAL 110:388, July 15, 1983.

Abortion amendment moves toward Senate showdown, by Russell Burnham Shaw. OUR SUNDAY VISITOR 71:8, February 27, 1983.

Abortion and adoption: Fetal value beyond the personhood debate, by M. S. Gregory. DISSERTATION ABSTRACTS INTERNATIONAL: A 7(43), January 1983.

Abortion and argument by analogy, by Lisa Sowle Cahill. HORIZONS 9:271-287, Fall 1982.

Abortion and the bomb—life-related issues; Presidential address to the National Conference of Catholic Bishops, by John Robert Roach. PRIEST 39:12-14, February 1983.

Abortion and cloning, by Eric R. Kraemer. SOUTHERN JOURNAL OF PHILOSOPHY (21):537-546, Winter 1983.

Abortion and the control of human bodies, by J. Stone. JOURNAL OF VALUE INQUIRY 17:77-85, 1983.

Abortion and the doctors, by Mary Kenny. TABLET 237:942-943, October 1, 1983.

Abortion and fertility in economic perspective: A theoretical and empirical analysis with special reference to New York City, by M. J. Kramer. DISSERTATION ABSTRACTS INTERNATIONAL: A 43:9, March 1983.

Abortion and honesty [discussion of September 14-21, 1983 article, Abortion: a question of Catholic honesty], by D. C. Maguire. CHRISTIAN CENTURY 100:1136-1138, December 7, 1983.

Abortion and M. T. P. cases—a study of hospital admissions from 1971 to 1979, by B. Mehta, et al. INDIAN JOURNAL OF PUBLIC HEALTH 26(1):38-42, January-March 1982.

Abortion and Maternal Morality 1968-1978, by Annik Houel, et al. REVUE FRANÇAISE DE SOCIOLOGIE 23:3, 487-502, July-September 1982.

Abortion and Morality, by R. Taylor, et al. FREE INQUIRY 2:33, Fall 1982.

Abortion and national policymaking; reflections on the Congress reversing the rule of Roe v. Wade and Doe v. Bolton, by Stephen M. Krason. SOCIAL JUSTICE REVIEW 74:35-44, March-April 1983.

Abortion and physical dependence, by D. Geuras, et al. SOUTH-WEST PHILOSOPHICAL STUDIES 7:124-130, April 1984.

Abortion and the Pursuit of happiness, by P. Rossi. LOGOS (USA) 3:61-77, 1982.

Abortion and the Supreme Court, and interview with C. H. Smith, by W. McGurn. REGISTER 59:1, September 4, 1983.

The abortion arena: recent activity, by L. S. Goldstein, et al. LEGAL MEDICAL QUARTERLY 213-226, 1982.

Abortion as a mixed good, by M. Kohl. FREE INQUIRY 3:42, Winter 1982-1983.

Abortion attitude scale, by L. A. Sloan. HEALTH EDUCATION 14:41-42, May-June 1983.

Abortion attitudes in medical students, by J. W. Bonar, et al. JOURNAL OF THE AMERICAN MEDICAL WOMEN'S ASSOCIATION 38(2):43-45, March-April 1983.

Abortion: autonomy or isolation, by M. O'Brien Steinfels. CHRISTIANITY AND CRISIS 43:192-194, May 16, 1983.

Abortion—children's rights—constitutional rights. THE FAMILY LAW REPORTER: COURT OPINIONS 9(14):2219, February 8, 1983.

Abortion choice and the law in Vermont: a recent study. VERMONT LAW REVIEW 7:281-313, Fall 1982.

Abortion, contraception, infanticide, by P. E. Devine. PHILOSOPHY 58:513-520, October 1983.

The abortion debate, by M. Jones. WORLD HEALTH, 6-9, November 1982.

Abortion: the debate continues. ENGAGE/SOCIAL ACTION FORUM 91(11):9-40, March 1983.

The abortion debate in the Republic of Ireland, by T. P. O'Mahoney. AMERICA 148:110-112, February 12, 1983.

The abortion debate . . . obtaining statistics in Latin American
   countries is enormously difficult, by M. Jones. WORLD
   HEALTH. November 1982, p. 6-9.

Abortion: decade of debate [since the 1973 U.S. Supreme Court
   ruling making abortion legal] , by M. Leepson. EDITORAL RE-
   SEARCH REPORTS, p. 27-44, January 14, 1983.

Abortion. Doctors, pro and/or con. REVISTA DE ENFERMAGEN
   6(58-59):28-31, May-June 1983.

Abortion—Education—Registration Fees—Religion. THE FAMILY
   LAW REPORTER: COURT OPINIONS 9:1, p. 2011, November
   2, 1982.

Abortion examined, by M. Kenny. TABLET 237:578-579, June
   18, 1983; 602-603, June 25, 1983; 627-628, July 2, 1983.

Abortion explained by a nurse, by M. A. Bastit i Costa. REVISTA DE
   ENFERMAGEN 6(58-59):36-39, May-June 1983.

Abortion following the immigration of an adult male baboon (papio
   cynocephalus), by M. E. Pereira. AMERICAN JOURNAL OF
   PRIMATOLOGY 4(1):93-98, 1983.

Abortion from the legal viewpoint for the physician, by H. D.
   Hiersche. GYNAKOLOGE 15(2):72-79, June 1982.

Abortion funding restrictions: state constitutional protections
   exceed federal safeguards. WASHINGTON & LEE LAW REVIEW
   46(13):1469-1489, Fall 1982.

Abortion: Getting the Ethics straight, by K. Lebacqz. LOGOS (USA)
   3:47-60, 1982.

Abortion goes to trial, by R. D. Eisler. MACLEAN'S 96:50, May
   23, 1983.

Abortion—husband's consent—jurisdiction and procedure—mootness.
   THE FAMILY LAW REPORTER: COURT OPINIONS 9(17):
   2267, March 1, 1983.

Abortion in America: ABC's of a raging battle; come January 22, it will be a decade since the Supreme Court's landmark ruling [question-and-answer format], by T. Gest. US NEWS AND WORLD REPORT 94:47-49, January 24, 1983.

Abortion: in congress: repeal Roe to senate floor, by M. B. Welch. OFF OUR BACKS 13:9, June 1983.

Abortion in the '80s: confrontation and crisis, by R. Collison. CHATELAINE 56:47+, July 1983.

Abortion in Greece, by S. Ginger. CONTEMPORARY REVIEW 243:253-255, November 1983.

Abortion in Japan; interview with Anthony Zimmerman, by M. Meehan. REGISTER 59:1+, January 23, 1983.

Abortion in mice induced by intravenous injections of antibodies to type IV collagen or laminin, by J. M. Foidart, et al. AMERICAN JOURNAL OF PATHOLOGY 110(3):346-357, March 1983.

Abortion in sows and the isolation of pasteurella ureae, by J. D. Corkish, et al. VETERINARY RECORD 110:582, June 19, 1982.

Abortion in tumor patients from a legal viewpoint, by W. Spann. MUENCHENER MEDIZINISCHE WOCHENSCHRIFT 124 (44):957-958, November 5, 1982.

Abortion: Ireland divided once more, by R. Ford. TIMES, August 26, 1983, p. 6.

Abortion issue still raging after 10 years, by N. Thimmesch. HEALTH EDUCATION 43:16, February 26, 1983.

Abortion: justice Harry A. Blackman and the Roe v. Wade decision, by J. A. La Rue. SIMON GREENLEAF LAW REVIEW 2:122-145, 1982-1983.

Abortion laws in African commonwealth countries, by R. J. Cook, et al. JOURNAL OF AFRICAN LAW 25:60-79, Autumn 1981.

Abortion laws will bend under new medical, social pressures, by D. J. Horan, et al. HOSPITAL PROGRESS 63(12):48-52, December 1982.

Abortion legislation [letter]. JOURNAL OF THE AMERICAN MEDICAL ASSOCIATION 249(4):472-473, January 28, 1983.

Abortion legislation [letter], by C. A. Winterling. JOURNAL OF THE AMERICAN MEDICAL ASSOCIATION 249(23):3173-3174, June 17, 1983.

Abortion: a look at our Christian roots, by E. K. Jesaitis. NATIONAL CATHOLIC REPORTER 19:7, January 21, 1983.

The abortion mess in Los Angeles [controversy over disposition of dead fetuses found at defunct private pathology lab], by D. W. Pawley. CHRISTIANITY TODAY 26:46+, September 17, 1982.

Abortion: methods and sequelae, by W. Savage, et al. BRITISH JOURNAL OF HOSPITAL MEDICINE 28(4):364, 369-372+, October 1982.

Abortion mortality [letter], by K. Augensen, et al. AMERICAN JOURNAL OF OBSTETRICS AND GYNECOLOGY 144(6):740-741, November 15, 1982.

Abortion: the mourning after, by C. L. Mithers. MADEMOISELLE 89:66, September 1983.

Abortion: a national security issue, by S. D. Mumford. HUMANIST 42:12-13+, September-October 1982.

Abortion 1982: the supreme court once again, by J. M. Healey. CONNECTICUT MEDICINE 46(11):681, November 1982.

Abortion—notice to husband. THE FAMILY LAW REPORTER: TEXT NO. 1 9(6):3001-3026, December 7, 1982.

Abortion on back burner?, by J. F. Hitchcock. REGISTER 59:1+, June 19, 1983.

Abortion: the pendulum swings to the right, by D. Folster, et al.

ATLANTIC INSIGHT 4:52, November 1982.

Abortion pioneer now a top pro-life advocate: interview with Bernard Nathanson. HEALTH EDUCATION 43:13, May 7, 1983.

Abortion policymaking a decade after Roe, by J. K. Boles. POLICY STUDIES REVIEW 2(1):133-135, 1982.

Abortion politics and public policy, by P. R. Lee, et al. MOBIUS 2(4):66-74, October 1982.

Abortion: a question of Catholic honesty, by D. C. Maguire. CHRISTIAN CENTURY 100:803-807, September 14-21, 1983.

Abortion rate in pregnancies following ovulation induced by human menopausal gonadotropin/human chorionic gonadotropin, by Z. Ben-Rafael, et al. FERTILITY AND STERILITY 39(2):157-161, February 1983.

Abortion—restrictions. THE CRIMINAL LAW REPORTER: SUPREME COURT PROCEEDINGS 32(10):4115-4121, December 8, 1982.

Abortion rights, by R. Copelon. MS 12:146, October 1983.

Abortion rights rescued: the triumph of coalition politics, by S. Caudle. MS 11:40+, January 1983.

Abortion ruling eyed, by M. Meehan. REGISTER 59:1+, July 3, 1983.

Abortion. Spain: the keys to the controversy. REVISTA DE ENFERMAGEN 6(58-59):34-35, May-June 1983.

Abortion surveillance: preliminary analysis, 1979-1980 United States. MORBIDITY AND MORTALITY WEEKLY REPORT 32(5):62-64, February 11, 1983.

Abortion ten years later. COMMONWEAL 110:35-37, January 28, 1983.

Abortion ten years later, by J. T. Beifuss. NATIONAL CATHOLIC REPORTER 19:1+, January 21, 1983.

Abortion trial tests limit of necessity defense, by J. Orso. REGISTER 59:1+, February 13, 1983.

Abortion—waiting period—hospitalization—insurance. THE FAMILY LAW REPORTER: COURT OPINIONS 9(10):2150, January 11, 1983.

Abortions to black teens helped stem increase in out-of-wedlock births. FAMILY PLANNING PERSPECTIVES 15:84-85, March-April 1983.

Acceptance of family planning practice among rural women clientele, by G. Kaur, et al. INDIAN JOURNAL OF PUBLIC HEALTH 26(3):194-199, July-September 1982.

Acceptability of medroxyprogesterone acetate among medical and paramedical personnel in family planning, by A. Cervantes, et al. GINECOLOGIA Y OBSTETRICIA DE MEXICO 50(300):85-88, April 1982.

Achievements in preventing the premature termination of pregnancy, by V. I. Bodiazhina. AKUSHERSTVO I GINEKOLOGIIA (12):12-16, 1982.

Acquaintance with the private clinic. Study of the use of a lay center, by G. Remotti, et al. ANNALI DI OSTETRICIA GINECOLOGIA, MEDICINA PERINATALE 103(3):237-240, May-June 1982.

Action mechanisms of gossypol as a male contraceptive agent: In vitro study (leydig cell of rats), by H. Hoshiai, et al. JAPANESE JOURNAL OF FERTILITY AND STERILITY 27(2):156-160.

Active duty pregnancy, by N. S. Stewart. MARINE CORPS GAZETTE 67:19-20, February 1983.

Acupuncture reflexotherapy in abortion, by A. I. Liubimova, et al. AKUSHERSTVO I GINEKOLOGIIA (12):31-34, 1982.

Acute collapse after administration of prostaglandin F2-alpha for induction of missed abortion, by O. Okland, et al. TIDSSKRIFT FOR DEN NORSKE LAEGEFORENING 102(34-36):1855-1857, December 10, 1982.

Adolescent autonomy and minors' legal rights: contraception and abortion, by H. Rodman, et al. JOURNAL OF APPLIED DEVELOPMENTAL PSYCHOLOGY 3(4):307-317, October-December 1982.

Adolescent development and its effects on sexual and contraceptive behavior: development and evaluation of a training design for health professionals, by C. D. Brindis. DISSERTATION ABSTRACTS INTERNATIONAL: A. 43(8), February 1983.

Adolescent family life program as a prevention measure, by M. E. Mecklenburg, et al. PUBLIC HEALTH REPORTS 98:21-29, January-February 1983.

Adolescent sexuality, contraceptive and fertility decisions, by K. M. Charnowski. DISSERTATION ABSTRACTS INTERNATIONAL: A. 43(7), January 1983.

Adolescents and abortion: a theoretical framework for decision making, by M. A. Brown. JOURNAL OF OBSTETRIC GYNECOLOGIC AND NEONATAL NURSING 12(4):241-247, July-August 1983.

Advice to pro-lifers—treasure life after birth as well as before, by T. Unsworth. NATIONAL CATHOLIC REPORTER 20:13, December 23, 1983.

Advising women on sterilization options, by C. B. Demarest. PATIENT CARE 17(9):128-131; 134-135; 139-143+, May 15, 1983.

After 15 years humanae vitae called prophetic, by Sister M. A. Walsh. OUR SUNDAY VISITOR 72:3, July 24, 1983.

After ten years pro-lifers know how to win but are not sure they can win, by R. B. Shaw. OUR SUNDAY VISITOR 71:4-5, January 16, 1983.

Age at menarche and fertility in Haiti, by J. Allman. HUMAN ORGANIZATION 41:350-354, Winter 1982.

Age at menarche and unsuccessful pregnancy outcome, by G. Wyshak. ANNALS OF HUMAN BIOLOGY 10(1):69-73, January-February 1983.

Age of consent. ECONOMIST 288:22, August 6, 1983.

All life is blessed, by J. Sammon. CATHOLIC WORKER 50:1-2, January-February 1983.

All people are shocked by the birth control policy calamity: the Chinese communists are facing an impasse of the problem of population, by J. Wang. ASIAN OUTLOOK 18:25-30, April 1983.

Ambulatory sterilization by minilaparotomy, by S. Melander. LAKARTIDNINGEN 79(38):3310-3314, September 22, 1982.

American childbirth educators in China: a transcultural exchange, by D. Williamson, et al. JOURNAL OF NURSE-MIDWIFERY 27(5):15-22, September-October 1982.

An analysis of access to contraceptive care in western Pennsylvania, by S. E. Milligan, et al. SOCIAL WORK RESEARCH AND ABSTRACTS 20:3, Fall 1984.

An analysis of factors affecting traditional family expectations and perceptions of ideal fertility, by W. J. Scott, et al. SEX ROLES 9:901-914, August 1983.

Analysis of failure of microsurgical anastomosis after mid-segment, non-coagulation tubal ligation, by A. H. DeCherney, et al. FERTILITY AND STERILITY 39(5):618-22, May 1983.

Analysis of multiple birth rates in Japan. VII. Rates of spontaneous and induced terminations of pregnancy in twins, by Y. Imaizumi, et al. JINRUI IDENGAKU ZASSHI 27(3):235-242, September 1982.

Analysis of official permissions for medically indicated pregnancy interruptions, by E. Czeizel. ORVOSI HETILAP. 124(22):1297-1302, May 29, 1983.

Analysis of pathological outcome of pregnancy, by J. Olsen, et al. SCANDINAVIAN JOURNAL OF SOCIAL MEDICINE. 11(1):3-6, 1983.

An analysis of variations in U. S. fertility and female labor force participation trends, by B. Devaney. DEMOGRAPHY. 20:147-162, May 1983.

Anti-Jk B alloimmunization and abortion, by G. Noia, et al. HAEMATOLOGICA. 67(5):775-780, October 1982.

Anti-PP1Pk and early abortion, by G. Cantin, et al. TRANSFUSION. 23(4):350-351, July-August 1983.

The anti-abortion movement and symbolic crusades: reappraisal of a popular theory, by P. J. Leahy, et al. ALTERNATIVE LIFE-STYLES. 6(1):27-47, Fall 1983.

Antiserum to LH reverses the abortifacient effect of Bromergocryptine treatment in early rat pregnancy, by M. Tabarelli, et al. JOURNAL OF REPRODUCTIVE IMMUNOLOGY. 4(6):325-335, December 1982.

Anxieties of the castrator, by G. Devereux. ETHOS. 10(3):279-297, Fall 1982.

The application of law 194/1978 in our hospital. Study of its use in the first 5 semesters, by P. Tellini, et al. RIVISTA ITALIANA DI GINECOLOGIA. 59 suppl:3-68, 1980.

An approach to family planning for Indochinese refugee women, by N. J. Presswell. AUSTRALIAN FAMILY PHYSICIAN. 11(8):644-645, August 1982.

Archbishop and the abortions: the pro-life turn their fire on the catholic establishment, by V. Byfield. ALBERTA REPORT. 9:50, October 25, 1982.

Archbishop calls for nun's resignation from state post, by E. C. Szoka. ORIGINS. 12:621-622, March 10, 1983.

Archbishop Szoka announces his decision, by E. C. Szoka. OUR SUNDAY VISITOR. 71:5, March 13, 1983.

Are Catholic hospitals morally responsible for surgical practices in associated office buildings? HOSPITAL PROGRESS. 64(5):61-62, May 1983.

The arguments in favor of abortion are strong, by L. B. Smedes. CHRISTIANITY TODAY. 27:62, July 15, 1983.

Arrested 15 times, this mother fights for unborn, by M. Meehan. REGISTER. 59:1+, May 8, 1983.

Artifical insemination with fresh donor semen using the cervical cap technique: A review of 278 cases, by C. A. Bergquist, et al. OBSTETRICS ND GYNECOLOGY. 60(2):195-199, 1982.

Aryl 4-guanidinobenzoates as inhibitors of human acrosin and human trypsin and as potential vaginal contraceptive agents, by J. M. Kaminiski. DISSERTATION ABSTRACTS INTER-NATIONAL: B. 44(5), November 1983.

As I see it . . . parents', teenagers' rights clash in 'squeal' rule, by R. Mortimer, et al. AMERICAN NURSE. 15(6):5.

Aspects of the pathophysiology of the first trimester of pregnancy, by H. Fox. GINEKOLOGIA POLSKA. 53(9):585-592, 1982.

Assessing the impact of copayment on family planning services: a preliminary analysis in California, by B. M. Aved, et al. AMERICAN JOURNAL OF PUBLIC HEALTH. 73(7):763-765, July 1983.

Assessment of methods and results of reproductive occupational epidemiology: spontaneous abortions and malformations in the offspring of working women, by K. Hemminki, et al. AMERICAN JOURNAL OF INDUSTRIAL MEDICINE.

4(1-2):293-307, 1983.

Assessment of reproductive knowledge in an inner-city clinic, by
S. M. Johnson, et al. SOCIAL SCIENCE AND MEDICINE.
16(19):1657-1662, 1982.

Attack directed by groups of male mice towards lactating intruders:
involvement of hormones and neurotransmitters, by M. Haug,
et al. AGGRESSIVE BEHAVIOR. 8(2):188-190, 1982.

Attacks on innocent life continue: abortion and infanticide at
record levels, by W. Murchison. CATHOLIC DIGEST. 9:56,
March 1983.

The attack on women's rights, by L. Cooper. CRIME AND SOCIAL
JUSTICE. 15:39-41, Summer 1981.

Attitude extremism in the abortion controversy: a test of social
judgment, cognitive dissonance, and attribution theories, by S.
L. Goettsch. DISSERTATION ABSTRACTS INTERNATIONAL:
A. 44(3), September 1983.

Attitude of the university student to contraceptive methods, by
G. Escarcega Rivera, et al. GINECOLOGIA Y OBSTETRICA DE
MEXICO. 50(304):205-212, 1982.

Attitudes of abortion counselors and their work role, by A. M. Jones.
DISSERTATION ABSTRACTS INTERNATIONAL: A. 43(7),
January 1983.

Attitudes of college males toward parenthood timing, by D. B.
Eversoll, et al. JOURNAL OF HOME ECONOMICS. 74(4):25-29+,
Winter 1983.

Attitudes toward abortion among Catholic Mexican-American women:
the effects of religiosity and education, by S. Rosenhouse-Persson,
et al. DEMOGRAPHY. 20:87-98, Fall 1983.

Attitudes toward abortion in a provincial area of New Zealand:
differentials and determinants, by P. Perry, et al. THE
AUSTRALIAN AND NEW ZEALAND JOURNAL OF
SOCIOLOGY. 18(3):399-416, 1982.

Australian attitudes towards abortion: recent complementary surveys, by S. E. Fraser, et al. AUSTRALIAN JOURNAL OF SEX, MARRIAGE AND FAMILY. 3(4):171-180, November 1982.

Australian family planning surveys: some problems of comparability, by D. J. Lucas. JOURNAL OF BIOSOCIAL SCIENCE. 15(3):357:366, July 1983.

Awkward questions about IUCDs, by E. Trimmer. MIDWIFE HEALTH VISITOR AND COMMUNITY NURSE. 19(2):66, February 1983.

B, T and null lymphocytes in threatened abortion, by T. Bartoszewicz, et al. GINEKOLOGIA POLSKA. 53(5-6):307-310, 1982.

A bacterial mutagenicity study of rivanol, an acridine derivative used as an abortifacient, by M. Wugmeister, et al. YALE JOURNAL OF BIOLOGY AND MEDICINE. 56(1):9-13, January-February 1983.

The bacteriology of septic abortion, by W. S. Callahan. AMERICAN JOURNAL OF MEDICAL TECHNOLOGY. 45(4):161-171, July-August 1983.

Barrenness against nature: recourse to abortion in pre-industrial England, by A. McLaren. JOURNAL OF SEX RESEARCH. 17(3):224-237, August 1981.

Basal body temperature [letter], by E. F. Keefe. FERTILITY AND STERILITY. 38(4):502-503, October 1982.

Basic data on women who use family planning clinics: United States, 1980, by B. Bloom. VITAL HEALTH STATISTICS. 13(67):1-46, September 1982.

Battle in the scholarly world, by E. McGrath. TIME. 121:72, March 14, 1983.

Battle of the bulge, by D. Bonavia, et al. FAR EASTERN ECONOMIC REVIEW. 117:18-19, July 9-15, 1982.

Battle of the bulge is no easy fight, by V. G. Kulkarni. FAR
    EASTERN ECONOMIC REVIEW. 120:50-1, April 28, 1983.

The battle over abortion, by G. Kopecky. GLAMOUR. 81:218-19+,
    June 1983.

Before the velvet curtain: the Connecticut contraceptive cases as
    a study in constitutional law and supreme court behavior, by
    R. J. Fiseus. DISSERTATION ABSTRACTS INTERNATIONAL:
    A. 43(12), June 1983.

The beginning of personhood: a Thomistic perspective, by P. A.
    Smith. LAVAL THEOLOGIQUE ET PHILOSOPHIQUE.
    39:195-214, June 1983.

Behavioural patterns in women requesting postcoital contraception,
    by S. Rowlands, et al. JOURNAL OF BIOSOCIAL SCIENCE.
    15:145-152, April 1983.

Behavioral tests in monkey infants exposed embryonically to an
    oral contraceptive, by M. S. Golub, et al. NEUROBEHAVIORAL
    TOXICOLOGY AND TERATOLOGY. 5(3):301-304, May-
    June 1983.

Benefits of the pill, by N. Mallory. HOME MAGAZINE. 18:92BB,
    May 1983.

Bernadette. COPIE ZERO. 12:19, 1982.

Better late than never? Post-coital contraception, by J. Naughton.
    OBSERVER, May 15, 1983, p. 25.

Beyond the abortion charges, by P. Carlyle-Gordge. MACLEANS.
    96:17, September 12, 1983.

A bibliography of publications based on the U. S. national survey
    of family growth [on fertility, birth control and family
    formation]. POPULATION INDEX. 49:14-19, Spring 1983.

Big-boss government. ECONOMIST. (286):35, January 29, 1983.

Bilateral tubal pregnancy with vaginal delivery, by H. M. Foster.

OBSTETRICS AND GYNECOLOGY. 60(5):664-666, November 1982.

Bill may ban abortion in unemployed health coverage. OUR SUNDAY VISITOR. 72:8, June 12, 1983.

Biophysical studies on molecular mechanisms of abortifacient action of prostaglandins. V. CNDO/2 estimation of the relative affinities of the cations Na+, Mg2+, and Ca2+ to the carboxylic group, by V. Kothekar, et al. JOURNAL OF THEORETICAL BIOLOGY. 101(2):225-231, March 21, 1983.

—. VI. Conformation energy calculation on PGE2, PGF2 alpha and 15-(s)-methyl PGF2 alpha, by V. Kothekar. JOURNAL OF THEORETICAL BIOLOGY. 101(2):233-240, March 21, 1983.

Biosynthesis of platelet lipids in relation to aggregation in women using oral contraceptives, by M. Ciavatti, et al. CONTRACEPTION. 25(6):629-638, 1982.

Birth control, by M. McAdoo. MS. 11:113-114, May, 1983.

Birth control and disease, by S. Katz. CHATELAINE. 56:20, January 1983.

Birth control decisions, by J. Lederer. PSYCHOLOGY TODAY. 17:32-8, June 1983.

Birth control: different conceptions, by R. V. Wells. JOURNAL OF INTERDISCIPLINARY HISTORY. 10(3):511-516, 1979.

Birth control is not the main issue: parental notification (federal funding and delivery of birth control devices is an illegitimate function of the government), by W. E. Williams. HUMAN EVENTS. 43:6+, March 12, 1983.

Birth control movie, by E. Mandell. BOOKLIST. 79(6):45, November 15, 1982.

Birth control movie. LANDER'S HERALD. 27(2):53, November-December 1982.

Birth control myths and facts, by K. McCoy. SEVENTEEN.
42:52+, October 1983.

Birth control overseas, by J. C. Cazenave, et al. MEDECINE
TROPICALE. 43(1):93-97, January-February 1983.

Birth control rule: clinics ponder effects, by N. Brozan. NEW
YORK TIMES, January 29, 1983, p. 11.

Birth control update. HARPERS BAZAAR. 116:208+, October
1983.

Birth order, maternal age and spontaneous abortion [letter], by W.
H. James. EARLY HUMAN DEVELOPMENT. 8(2):179-180,
July 1983.

Birth rate status. Number of children desired and actual situation,
by M. Ritamies. KATILOLEHTI. 88(4):85-89, April 1983.

Birth rights in Ireland, by S. Hoggart. OBSERVER, January 23,
1983, p. 43.

Bishop's pawns. ECONOMIST. 287:46+, April 9, 1983.

Blacks, whites, and attitudes toward abortion, by M. W. Combs,
et al. PUBLIC OPINION QUARTERLY. 46:510-520, Winter
1982.

Boll weevil (Coleoptera: Curculionidae); field competitiveness of
diflubenzuron-fed, irradiated males—1980, 1981, by E. J.
Villavaso. JOURNAL OF ECONOMIC ENTOMOLOGY.
75:662-664, August 1982.

Breast cancer and spontaneous abortion [letter], by W. H. James.
AMERICAN JOURNAL OF EPIDEMIOLOGY. 117(5):641-642,
May 1983.

Breastfeeding and family planning: meaningful integration of
services, by E. C. Baer. STUDIES IN FAMILY PLANNING.
12(4):164-166, April 1981.

Breastfeeding and fertility control, by C. W. Tyler, Jr. AMERICAN

JOURNAL OF PUBLIC HEALTH. 73:364-365, April 1983.

Britain bites the bullet over depo-provera. NEW SCIENTIST. 98:136, April 21, 1983.

Bungled. ECONOMIST. 287:38, May 7-13, 1983.

Buyer beware. CANADIAN NURSE. 79:62, June 1983.

By justified means, a life ends. REGISTER. 59:3, September 11, 1983.

CLC affirms women's right to abortion. CANADIAN LABOUR. 28:7, May 7, 1983.

CMA abortion survey. CANADIAN MEDICAL ASSOCIATION JOURNAL. 129(3):262-272, August 1, 1983.

Calculator for birth control, by S. Katz. CHATELAINE. 56:22, April 1983.

California conservator's petition to sterilize incompetent ward denied. THE FAMILY LAW REPORTER: COURT OPINIONS. 9(31):2471-2472, June 7, 1983.

A California scientist remodels a perpetual problem's ancient solution: the contraceptive sponge, by M. A. Fischer. PEOPLE WEEKLY. 19:57-58, May 2, 1983.

Calling for prolife unity. REGISTER. 59:1+, January 23, 1983.

Campaign to overturn ban on abortion funding begun, by N. Cohodas. CONGRESSIONAL QUARTERLY WEEKLY REPORT. 41:1689-1693, August 20, 1983.

Campylobacter sp. isolated from the cervix during septic abortion, case report, by S. E. West, et al. BRITISH JOURNAL OF OBSTETRICS AND GYNAECOLOGY. 89(9):771-772, September 1982.

Can congress settle the abortion issue?, by M. C. Segers. HASTINGS CENTER REPORT. 12:20-8, June 1982.

Canada court helps, hurts prolife cause, by J. Rasmussen. REGISTER. 59:1+, October 30, 1983.

Canada's abortion dispute escalating, by J. Rasmussen. REGISTER. 59:1+, May 29, 1983.

The Canadian birth control movement on trial, 1936-37, by D. Dodd. HISTOIRE SOCIALE—SOCIAL HISTORY. 16(32):411-428, 1983.

Cardiovascular disease: risks and prognosis for women as compared with men, by S. R. Winternitz, et al. CONSULTANT. 23(2):118-120, 123, 126-127+, February 1983.

The careless streetwalker [failure of prostitutes to use contraceptives], by J. C. Horn. PSYCHOLOGY TODAY. 17:69, March 1983.

Carter holdover promotes foreign abortions, by D. Lambro. CATHOLIC DIGEST. 9:6, March 1983.

A case for concern? . . . depo-provera, by A. Gartland. NURSING TIMES. 79(18):10-11, May 4-10, 1983.

Case report of a termination of pregnancy in a severely subnormal epileptic and the problems which arose, by P. Beynon. COMMUNITY MEDICINE. 4(4):280-283, November 1982.

Case studies of indigenous abortion practitioners in rural Bangladesh, by S. Islam. STUDIES IN FAMILY PLANNING. 13(3):86-93, March 1982.

Case study of the reproductive experience of women who have had three or more induced abortions, by E. Lincoln. DISSERTATION ABSTRACTS INTERNATIONAL: A. 44(4), October 1983.

Castration, clinging, shame: three Hermannian models, by B. Dalle, et al. PERSPECTIVES PSYCHIATRIQUES. 19(4):291-295, 1981.

Castration or incarceration?, by M. S. Serrill. TIME. 122:70, December 12, 1983.

Catamnestic examinations performed after the utilization of two
different sterilization techniques, by H. H. Riedel, et al.
GYNECOLOGIC AND OBSTETRIC INVESTIGATION.
15(2):119-126, 1983.

The catholic church and social justice issues, by S. Mumford.
HUMANIST. 43:5-14, July-August 1983.

Catholic doctor who fought for the pill (John Rock), by L.
McLaughlin. DISCOVER. 4:82+, February 1982.

Catholic hospitals in today's Canada, by E. J. MacNeil. CHAC
REVIEW. 10(4-5):12-15, July-October 1982.

Catholics waver on abortion, by C. Hayes, et al. ALBERTA
REPORT. 10:21, May 30, 1983.

Cellular immunity factors in the physiological course of pregnancy
and abortion, by P. I. Fogel. AKUSHERSTVO I GINE-
KOLOGIIA. (12):28-30, 1982.

Cephalothin prophylaxis for midtrimester abortion, by M. R.
Spence, et al. OBSTETRICS AND GYNECOLOGY. 60(4):502-
505, October 1982.

Cervical and serum IgA and serum IgG antibodies in Chlamydia
trachomatis and herpes simplex virus in threatened abortion:
a prospective study, by M, Grönroos, et al. BRITISH JOURNAL
OF OBSTETRICS AND GYNAECOLOGY. 90(2):167-170,
February 1983.

The cervical cap: a barrier contraceptive, by M. T. Hastings-Tolsma.
AMERCIAN JOURNAL OF MATERNAL CHILD NURSING.
7(6):382-386, November-December 1982.

The cervical cap: effectiveness as a contraceptive, by D. Boehm.
JOURNAL OF NURSE-MIDWIFERY. 28(1):3-6, January-
February 1983.

Cervical cerclage: an aggressive approach to threatened or recurrent
pregnancy wastage, by W. R. Crombleholme, et al. AMERICAN

JOURNAL OF OBSTETRICS AND GYNECOLOGY. 146(2):168-174, May 15, 1983.

Cervical injury during first-trimester abortion reduced with laminaria. FAMILY PLANNING PERSPECTIVES. 15:136-137, May-June 1983.

Cervical resistance in patients with previous spontaneous mid-trimester abortion, by G. S. Anthony, et al. BRITISH JOURNAL OF OBSTETRICS AND GYNAECOLOGY. 89(12):1046-1049, December 1982.

Ces choix qui font de nous ce que nous sommes, by J. R. Roach. LA DOCUMENTATION CATHOLIQUE. 80:99-102, January 16, 1983.

Challenging the teenage regulations: the legal battle, by P. Donovan. FAMILY PLANNING PERSPECTIVES. 15:126-130, May-June 1983.

Changes in attitudes toward contraceptive concomitant with instructional activities in physiology, by I. Owie. JOURNAL OF RESEARCH IN SCIENCE TEACHING. 20(6):571-575, September 1983.

Changes in the blood level of alpha-fetoprotein in threatened abortion, by D. Berlingieri, et al. ARCHIVIO DI OBSTETRICIA E GINECOLOGIA. 87(1-2):21-32, January-April 1982.

Changes in intraocular pressure during prostaglandin-induced abortion, by M. Ober, et al. KLINISCHE MONATSBLAETTER FUR AUGENHEILKUNDE. 180(3):230-231, 1982.

Changes in menstrual blood loss and libido after different methods of tubal ligation, by A. Neri, et al. INTERNATIONAL SURGERY. 67(4 suppl):527-528, October-December 1982.

Changes in physiological, electroencephalographic and psychological parameters in women during the spontaneous menstrual cycle and following oral contraceptives, by D. Becker, et al. PSYCHONEUROENDOCRINOLOGY. 7(1):75-90, 1982.

Changes in sexual desire after voluntary sterilization, by F. D. Bean, et al. SOCIAL BIOLOGY. 27:186-193, Fall 1980.

Changes in uterine phosphatase levels in mice treated with aristolic acid during early pregnancy, by A. Pakrashi, et al. CONTRA-CEPTION. 26(6):635-643, December 1982.

Changing conceptions of family regulation among the Hindu East Indians in rural Trinidad, by J. Nevadomsky. ANTHRO-POLOGICAL QUARTERLY. 55:189-198, October 1982.

Characteristics and follow-up of sterilized women, by R. Molina, et al. REVISTA MEDICA DE CHILE. 110(2):175-180, February 1982.

Characteristics of abortion patients in the United States, 1979 and 1980, by S. K. Henshaw, et al. FAMILY PLANNING PER-SPECTIVES. 15:5-15, January-February 1983.

Characteristics of two samples of women seeking abortion in Queensland, by A. S. Bourne, et al. AUSTRALIAN JOURNAL OF SOCIAL ISSUES. 17(3):207-219, 1982.

Chemical sterilization in the male part I: rats, by M. S. Fahim, et al. ARCHIVES OF ANDROLOGY. 9(3):261-265, November 1982.

Chick's in the male, by D. Lessem. BOSTON. 74:19, October 1982.

Child psychiatry and the law: developmental rights to privacy and independent decisionmaking, by M. J. Guyer, et al. JOURNAL OF THE AMERICAN ACADEMY OF CHILD PSYCHIATRY. 21:298-302, May 1982.

Child support—birth control. THE FAMILY LAW REPORTER: COURT OPINIONS. 9(30):2462-2463, May 31, 1983.

Childlessness and partner selection, by V. J. Callan. JOURNAL OF MARRIAGE AND THE FAMILY. 45:181-186, February 1983.

Childlessness in a transitional population: the United States at the turn of the century, by S. E. Tolnay, et al. JOURNAL OF FAMILY HISTORY. 7:200-219, Summer 1982.

Children by choice, not chance. FAMILY RELATIONS. 31(1):165, January 1982.

The China solution, by L. Lader. SCIENCE DIGEST. 91:78, April 1983.

China: two's a crowd and it's illegal. ECONOMIST. 268:31+, January 29, 1983.

China's population crisis, by P. R. Ehrlich, et al. MOTHER EARTH NEWS. 81:150-151, May-June 1983.

China's population policy, by I. K. Chen. CURRENT HISTORY. 81:251+, September 1982.

China's she-baby cull. ECONOMIST. 287:36, April 16, 1983.

Choice decision [senate turns down Hatch amendment]. TIME. 122:21, July 11, 1983.

Choice of sterilization procedure [letter], by R. L. Anderson. JOURNAL OF FAMILY PRACTICE. 16(2):238, February 1983.

Christian action: third approach to abortion, by. G. B. Wilson. NATIONAL CATHOLIC REPORTER. 19:4, January 21, 1983.

Chromosome anomalies in spontaneous abortions, by M. Tsancheva. AKUSHERSTVO I GINEKOLOGIIA. 22(1):7-13, 1983.

Chromosome heteromorphism in couples with repeated spontaneous abortions, by P. K. Ghosh, et al. INDIAN JOURNAL OF MEDICAL RESEARCH. 77:272-277, April 1983.

Chronic schizophrenic women's attitudes toward sex, pregnancy, birth control, and childrearing, by J. P. McEvoy, et al. HOSPITAL AND COMMUNITY PSYCHIATRY. 34(6):536-539, June 1983.

Chronicle of life and death: nobody wants an abortion, by M. B. Gordon. COMMONWEAL. 110:557-558, October 21, 1983.

Church and state: a Protestant backlash against next month's referendum on abortion, by M. Holland. NEW STATESMAN. May 13, 1983, p. 16-17.

Church-state cases, by W. R. Caron. CATHOLIC LAWYER. 27:197-204, Summer 1982.

Civil law and common law traditions: judicial review and legislative supremacy in West Germany and Canada, by S. G. Mezey. INTERNATIONAL AND COMPARATIVE LAW QUARTERLY. 32:689-707, July 1983.

Civil liberties: big-boss government. ECONOMIST. 286:21, January 29, 1983.

Clinical applications of prostaglandins in obstetrics and gynaecology, by S. M. Karim. ANNALS OF THE ACADEMY OF MEDICINE, SINGAPORE. 11(4):493-502, October 1982.

Clinical efficacy of extracts of radix teichosanthis and wikstroemia chamaedaphne meisn on mid-term labor induction—analysis of 248 cases, by M. Z. Wu, et al. CHUNG KUO I HSUEH KO HSUEH YUAN HSUEH PAO. 4(4):241-242, August 1982.

Clinical immunology of vasectomy and vasovasostomy, by L. Linnet. UROLOGY. 22(2):101-114, August 1983.

Clinical research work of the institute for family planning in the area of intrauterine contraception from 1964 to 1980, by M. Kožuh-Novak. JUGOSLAVENSKA GINEKOLOGIJA I OPSTETRICIJA. 21(1-2):54-57, January-April 1981.

Clinical significance of the determination of the plasma concentration of progesterone in threatened abortions during the first half of pregnancy, by I. Mišinger, et al. CESKOSLOVENSKA GYNEKOLOGIE. 48(1):18-21, February 1983.

Clinical test for placenta in 300 consecutive menstrual aspirations,

by R. A. Munsick. OBSTETRICS AND GYNECOLOGY.
60(6):738-741, December 1982.

The coathanger and the rose, by D. Granberg, et al. SOCIETY.
19(4):39-46, 1982.

Coagulation studies following mid-trimester intra-amniotic urea
injection, by M. A. Deshmukh, et al. JOURNAL OF POST-
GRADUATE MEDICINE. 28(4):210-213, 1982.

Coercion in a soft state: the family planning program of India,
by M. Vicziany. PACIFIC AFFAIRS. 55:373-402, Fall
1982-1983; 557-592, Winter 1982-1983.

Cohort fertility of Czech and Slovak women since 1930, by Y.
Lesney. POPULATION. 38:267-282, March-April 1983.

College students' attitudes toward shared responsibility in
decisions about abortion: implications for counseling, by
I. J. Ryan, et al. JOURNAL OF THE AMERICAN COLLEGE
HEALTH ASSOCIATION. 31(6):231-235, June 1983.

Commentary from Coeur d'Alene: one baby-or two?, by E. R.
Fox. WESTERN JOURNAL OF MEDICINE. 138(6):894-895,
June 1983.

Commentary on making up her mind: consent, pregnancy and
mental handicap, by M. Lockwood. JOURNAL OF MEDICAL
ETHICS. 9:224-226, December 1983.

Committee cautions on misuse of conscience, by D. Goldkamp.
REGISTER. 59:2, March 6, 1983.

Committee to defend reproductive rights v. Myers: procreative
choice guaranteed for all women. GOLDEN GATE UNIVERSITY
LAW REVIEW. 12:619-716, Summer 1982.

Communication factors and their influence on family planning
behaviour among non-adopters, by M. M. Reddy. JOURNAL
OF FAMILY WELFARE. 29:12-20, March 1983.

Community-based health and family planning. POPULATION REPORTS SERIES L. (3), 1982.

Community family planning clinics. An evaluation, by K. E. Schöpflin. PRACTITIONER. 227(1379):829-831, May 1983.

Community forum. 1. Family planning. Palaces of advice, by J. Bunting. NURSING MIRROR AND MIDWIVE'S JOURNAL. 156(3):34-36, January 19, 1983.

Community study of spontaneous abortions: relation to occupation and air pollution by sulfur dioxide, hydrogen sulfide, and carbon disulfide, by K. Hemminki, et al. INTERNATIONAL ARCHIVES OF OCCUPATIONAL AND ENVIRONMENTAL HEALTH. 51(1):55-63, 1982.

Comparative effects of castration and chlorpromazine in the arcuate nucleus of the hypothalamus of the rat, by A. Ledesma-Jimeno, et al. ACTAS LUSO-ESPAÑOLAS DE NEUROLOGIA Y PSIQUIATRÎA Y CIENCIAS AFINES. 10(6):351-358, November-December 1982.

Comparative effects of the oral contraceptive combinations 0.150 milligram desogestrel plus 0.030 milligram ethynylestradiol and 0.150 milligram levonorgestrel plus 0.030 milligram ethynylestradiol on lipid and lipoprotein metabolism in healthy female volunteers, by G. Samsioe. CONTRACEPTION. 25(5):487-504, 1982.

Comparative study of the attitude of married and unmarried women towards religion, equality of women and birth control in relation to their adjustment, by M. A. Shah, et al. ASIAN JOURNAL OF PSYCHOLOGY AND EDUCATION. 9(1):15-20, January 1982.

A comparative study of the effectiveness of the lippes loop, the copper-t-200 and the nova-t intrauterine contraceptive devices in Lagos, Nigeria, by M. A. Oyediran, et al. INTERNATIONAL JOURNAL OF FERTILITY. 27(2):109-112, 1982.

A comparison of definable traits in women requesting reversal of
sterilization and women satisfied with sterilization, by A.
Leader, et al. AMERICAN JOURNAL OF OBSTETRICS
AND GYNECOLOGY. 145(2):198-202, January 15, 1983.

A comparison of different laparoscopic sterilization occlusion
techniques in 24,439 procedures, by P. P. Bhiwandiwala, et al.
AMERICAN JOURNAL OF OBSTETRICS AND GYNECOLOGY.
144(3):319-331, October 1, 1982.

Comparison of members of pro and anti-abortion organizations
in Missouri, by D. Granberg. SOCIAL BIOLOGY. 28(3-4):239-
252, Fall-Winter 1981.

Comparison of natural and synthetic prostaglandin E2 tablets in
labour induction, by E. R. Luther, et al. CANADIAN MEDICAL
ASSOCIATION JOURNAL. 128(10):1189-1191, May 15,
1983.

Comparison of pro-choice and pro-life activists: their values,
attitudes, and beliefs [Missouri], by D. Granberg. POPULATION
AND ENVIRONMENT. 5:75-94, Summer 1982.

A comparison of responses to adolescent-oriented and traditional
contraceptive programs, by S. G. Philliber, et al. JOURNAL OF
AMBULATORY CARE MANAGEMENT. 6(2):32-42, May
1983.

Comparison of results of contraceptive prevalence surveys in five
countries with particular emphasis on knowledge, use and
availability, by T. Wardlaw, et al. WESTINGHOUSE HEALTH
SYSTEMS REPORT. 2(35), March 1982.

Comparison of serum and urine hCG levels with SP1 and PAPP-A
levels in patients with first-trimester vaginal bleeding, by G. M.
Masson, et al. OBSTETRICS AND GYNECOLOGY. 61(2):223-
226, February 1983.

Comparison of three subcutaneous modes of prostaglandin F2 alpha
administration for pregnancy termination in the hamster, by J.
W. Wilks. PROSTAGLANDINS. 24(6):837-842, December 1982.

Complications after abdominal and vaginal sterilization operation, by J. Misra. JOURNAL OF THE INDIAN MEDICAL ASSOCIATION. 80(2):25-27, January 16, 1983.

Complications of interval laparoscopic tubal sterilization, by F. Destefano, et al. OBSTETRICS AND GYNECOLOGY. 61(2):153-158, February 1983.

Complications of laparoscopie sterilization, by B. Gonik, et al. JOURNAL OF REPRODUCTIVE MEDICINE. 27(8):471-473, August 1982.

Complications of sickle cell disease, by I. Walters, et al. NURSING CLINICS OF NORTH AMERICA. 18(1):139-184, March 1983.

Components of period fertility in the Irish republic, 1962-77, by K. Wilson-Davis. JOURNAL OF BIOSOCIAL SCIENCE. 15:95-106, January 1983.

Compulsory birth control and fertility measures in India, by S. S. Halli. SIMULATION AND GAMES. 14(4):429-444, December 1983.

Compulsory sterilization statutes: public sentiment and public policy, by R. A. Cohen, et al. RESEARCH IN COMMUNITY AND MENTAL HEALTH. 2:327-357, 1981.

Conception and the concept of harm, by E. H. Morreim. JOURNAL OF MEDICINE AND PHILOSOPHY. 8:137-157, May 1983.

Conditions for abortion, by J. Finch. NURSING MIRROR. 156(7):38, April 27, 1983.

Congressional withdrawal of jurisdiction from federal courts: a reply to professor Uddo, by M. Vitiello. LOYOLA LAW REVIEW. 28:61-76, Winter 1982.

Conservatism, attitude to abortion, and Maccoby's biophilia, by J. J. Ray, et al. JOURNAL OF SOCIAL PSYCHOLOGY. 118(1):143-144, October 1982.

Conservative vs. surgical management of septic abortion with renal failure, by P. C. Singhal, et al. INTERNATIONAL JOURNAL OF GYNAECOLOGY AND OBSTETRICS. 20(3):189-194, June 1982.

A consideration of abortion survivors, by P. G. Ney. CHILD PSYCHIATRY AND HUMAN DEVELOPMENT. 13:168-179, September 1983.

Considering abortion: measuring the distances between the law, social reality and personal morality, by A. Collins. TORONTO LIFE. December 1983, p. 107-112.

Consistency, welfare rights and abortion: a reply to Perry, by J. P. Sterba. METAPHILOSOPHY. 14:162-165, April, 1983.

Consitution and the anomaly of the pregnant teenager, by E. Buchanan. ARIZONA LAW REVIEW. 24:553-610, 1982.

Constitutional law—abortion—court focuses on husband's interest regarding spousal notification requirements to procure abortion. Scheinberg v. Smith. CUMBERLAND LAW REVIEW. 13:143-159, 1982-1983.

Constitutional law—equal protection—abortion funding—state constitution requires New Jersey to fund health preserving but not elective abortions—Right to choose v. Byrne. SETON HALL LAW REVIEW. 13:779-802, 1983.

Constitutional law—a minor's abortion right under a parental notice statute. WAYNE LAW REVIEW. 28:1901-1928, Summer 1982.

Constitutionality of the human life bill. WASHINGTON UNIVER-SITY LAW QUARTERLY. 61:219-252, Spring 1983.

Consumer demand and household production: the relationship between fertility and child morality, by M. R. Rosenszeig, et al. AMERICAN ECONOMIC REVIEW. 73:38-42, May 1983.

Continuous extra-amniotic intracavitary application of prostaglandin

F2 alpha for medicamentous induction of labour in high-risk cases of pregnancy interruption, by E. Ehrig, et al. ZENTRAL-BLATT FUR GYNAEKOLOGIE. 104(13):769-776, 1982.

Contraception, by H. Herbert. NURSING. 2(14):405, 408-409, 412-414, June 1983.

Contraception and community in Egypt: a preliminary evaluation of the population/development mix, by J. M. Stycos, et al. STUDIES IN FAMILY PLANNING. 13(12):365, December 1982.

Contraception and fertility in the Netherlands, by E. Ketting. FAMILY PLANNING PERSPECTIVES. 15(1):19-25, January-February 1983.

Contraception and fertility in the Netherlands, by E. Ketting. INTERNATIONAL JOURNAL OF FAMILY PLANNING. 8:141-147, December 1982.

Contraception and prescriptive infallibility, by G. L. Hallett. THEOLOGICAL STUDIES. 43:629-650, December 1982.

Contraception and the rejection of God, by L. Ciccone. L'OSSERVATORE ROMANO. 50(813):9-10, December 12, 1983.

Contraception and the rhythm method, by P. Clifion. RELIGIOUS HUMANISM. 17:36-39, Winter 1983.

Contraception—are women getting a fair deal?, by J. Spray. HEALTH VISITOR. 56(5):163-164, May 1983.

Contraception in ethnic minority groups in Bedford, by P. Beard. HEALTH VISITOR. 55(8):417-421, August 1982.

Contraception is less risky for teenagers than is pregnancy, world-wide study finds. FAMILY PLANNING PERSPECTIVES. 14(5):274-276, September-October 1982.

Contraception, marital fertility and breast-feeding in the Yemen

Arab republic, by H. I. Goldberg, et al. JOURNAL OF BIOSOCIAL SCIENCE. 15:67-82, January 1983.

Contraception: yes, but at what cost?, by D. Grenon-Plante. INFIRMIERE CANADIENNE. 24(10):27-31, November 1982.

Contraception: yes, but at what price?, by D. Grenon-Plante. KRANKENPFLEGE. (5):38-41, May 1983.

Contraceptive choices for lactating women: suggestions for post-partum family planning, by V. H. Laukaran. STUDIES IN FAMILY PLANNING. 12(4):156-163, April 1981.

Contraceptive choices may soon include convenient OTC sponge . . .; . . . but animal cancers still hold up FDA approval of depo-provera. MEDICAL WORLD NEWS. 24:24-26, February 14, 1983.

Contraceptive failure and continuation among married women in the United States, by W. R. Grady, et al. STUDIES IN FAMILY PLANNING. 14:9-19, January 1983.

The contraceptive mentality, by D. T. De Marco. HOMILETIC AND PASTORAL REVIEW. 83:56-63, July 1983.

Contraceptive practices of teenage mothers, by A. C. Washington, et al. JOURNAL OF THE NATIONAL MEDICAL ASSOCIATION. 75(11):1059-1063, November 1983.

Contraceptive sponges. CANADIAN CONSUMER. 13:3, September 1983.

Contraceptive sterilization: a comparison of Mexican-Americans and Anglos living in U. S. countries bordering Mexico, by C. W. Warren, et al. SOCIAL BIOLOGY. 28(3-4):265-280, Fall-Winter 1981.

Contraceptive use and perceptions of chance and ability of conceiving in women electing abortion, by P. M. Klein. JOURNAL OF OBSTETRIC, GYNECOLOGIC AND NEONATAL NURSING. 12(3):167-171, May-June 1983.

Contraceptive use by college dating couples: a comparison of
men's and women's reports, by C. Hill, et al. POPULATION
AND ENVIRONMENT: BEHAVIORIAL AND SOCIAL
ISSUES. 6(1):60-69, Spring 1983.

Contraceptive use high in Norway, where IUD is most popular
method. FAMILY PLANNING PERSPECTIVES. 15:87-88,
March-April 1983.

Contraceptive users in rural Bangladesh: a time trend analysis,
by S. Bhatia. STUDIES IN FAMILY PLANNING. 14:20-28,
January 1983.

Contraceptive versus pregnancy risks, by P. M. Layde, et al.
SCIENCE NEWS. 121:375, June 5, 1982.

Controversial appointment, CHRISTIAN CENTURY. 100:266-
267, March 23-30, 1983.

Conventional versus laser reanastomosis of rabbit ligated uterine
horns, by J. K. Choe, et al. OBSTETRICS AND GYNECOLOGY.
61(6):689-694, June 1983.

Conversion disorder following termination of pregnancy, by G. D.
Tollefson, et al. JOURNAL OF FAMILY PRACTICE.
16(1):73-77, January 1983.

Coping with fertility in Israel: a case study of culture clash, by
E. Basker. CULTURE, MEDICINE AND PSYCHIATRY.
7(2):199-211, June 1983.

Correcting contraceptive failure rates for sample composition
and sample selection bias, by J. Trussell, et al. SOCIAL BIOLOGY.
28:293-298, Fall-Winter 1981.

Correlation between hormonal levels and ultrasound in patients
with threatened abortion, by R. Dessaive, et al. GYNECOLOGIC
AND OBSTETRIC INVESTIGATION. 14(1):65-78, 1982.

The costs of contraception, by A. Torres, et al. FAMILY PLANNING
PERSPECTIVES. 15:70-72, March-April 1983.

Counting on condoms . . . a CAC test. CANADIAN CONSUMER. November 1982, p. 116A-116B, 116D+.

Couple computerizes NFP. REGISTER. 59:2, August 28, 1983.

Couple to couple league, hospitals cooperate in teaching NFP. HOSPITAL PROGRESS. 64:57+, March 1983.

Court decision fuels abortion controversy: is Hatch amendment a remedy? HEALTH EDUCATION. 43:3, June 25, 1983.

Court unmoved. ECONOMIST. 287:42-43, June 25, 1983.

The court stands by abortion, by A. Press, et al. NEWSWEEK. 101(26):62-63, June 27, 1983.

The covenant theology of sex, by J. F. Kippley. HOMILETIC AND PASTORAL REVIEW. 83:22-32, August-September 1983.

Criminal abortion as seen in the university teaching hospital, Lusaka, by J. N. Narone, et al. MEDICAL JOURNAL OF ZAMBIA. 15(3):80-84, May-July 1981.

A critique of abortion rights, by R. Stith. DEMOCRACY. 3:60-70, Fall 1983.

A critique of focus group and survey research: the machismo case, by J. M. Stycos. STUDIES IN FAMILY PLANNING. 12(12 pt 1):450-456, December 1981.

A cross-national comparison of contraception and abortion laws, by I. M. Wasserman. SOCIAL INDICATORS RESEARCH. 13(3):281-309, October 1983.

Crushing freedom in the name of life, by N. Dorsen. HUMAN RIGHTS. 10:18-21+, Spring 1982.

Cryocauterization of the vas deferens, by P. L. Dias. JOURNAL OF THE ROYAL SOCIETY OF MEDICINE. 75(11):868-870, November 1982.

Cumulative prevalence rates and corrected incidence rates of

surgical sterilization among women in the United States, 1971-
1978, by T. F. Nolan, et al. AMERICAN JOURNAL OF
EPIDEMIOLOGY. 116(5):776-781, November 1982.

Current concepts in vasectomy reversal, by E. F. Lizza, et al.
WEST VIRGINIA MEDICAL JOURNAL. 78(11):283-285,
November 1982.

Current legal trends regarding abortions for minors: a dilemma
for counselors, by L. C. Talbutt. SCHOOL COUNSELOR.
31(2):120-124, November 1983.

Cutting the umbilical cord: can family planning clinics survive
without government funding?, by L. A. Villadsen. REASON.
14:21-26, Fall 1983.

Cytogenetic investigations on patients with difficulties in reproducing,
by S. Adzic, et al. JOURNAL DE GYNECOLOGIE,
OBSTETRIQUE ET BIOLOGIE DE LA REPRODUCTION.
11(3):371-374, 1982.

Cytogenetic studies in couples with multiple spontaneous abortions,
by S. Schwartz. DISSERTATION ABSTRACTS INTER-
NATIONAL: B. 43(9), March 1983.

Cytogenetic surveillance of spontaneous abortions, by N. E. Morton,
et al. CYTOGENETICS AND CELL GENETICS. 33(3):232-
239, 1982.

Cytotoxicity of anti-PP1Pk antibodies and possible relationship
with early abortions of p mothers, by M. Lopez, et al. CLINICAL
IMMUNOLOGY AND IMMUNOPATHOLOGY. 28(2):296-303,
August 1983.

D and E midtrimester abortion: a medical innovation, by S. Lewit.
WOMEN & HEALTH. 7(1):49-55, Spring 1982.

D. C. federal district court enjoins enforcement of HHS "squeal
rule." THE FAMILY LAW REPORTER: COURT OPINIONS.
9(18):2282, March 8, 1983.

Dalkon shield class action overturned, by S. Sherwood. BUSINESS

INSURANCE. 16:1+, June 28, 1982.

Dalkon shield warning. FDA CONSUMER. 17:2, July-August 1983.

Damages for the birth of a child—some possible policy barriers, by G. Robertson. MEDICINE, SCIENCE AND LAW. 23(1):2-4, January 1983.

Damages for wrongful birth, life and death, by A. H. Bernstein. HOSPITALS. 57(1):67, 70-72, January 1983.

The day I faced the reality of abortion, by E. Q. Vich. RN. 46(8):50, 52, August 1983.

Dearth of contraception fuels world abortion debate. NATIONAL PERSPECTIVES. 15(2):78, March-April 1983.

Deaths attributable to tubal sterilization in the United States, 1977 to 1981, by H. B. Peterson, et al. AMERICAN JOURNAL OF OBSTETRICS AND GYNECOLOGY. 146(2):131-136, May 15, 1983.

Deaths attributable to tubal sterilization—United States, 1977-1981. MORBIDITY AND MORALITY WEEKLY REPORT. 32(19):249-250, May 20, 1983.

Deaths from contraceptive sterilization in Bangladesh: rates, causes, and prevention, by D. A. Grimes, et al. OBSTETRICS AND GYNECOLOGY. 60(5):635-640, November 1982.

Decisions, decisions [South Carolina judge sentences rapists to choice of thirty years in prison or castration]. NEW REPUBLIC. 189:4+, December 26, 1983.

The decline in the birth rate and its consequences for planning in different sectors in developed capitalized countries, by J. C. Chesnais. POPULATION. 37:1133-1158, November-December 1982.

The decline of marital fertility in the late nineteenth century: the case of England and Wales, by R. Woods, et al. POPULATION STUDIES. 37:207-225, July 1983.

Defining battle lines; rules for debate, by K. Himes. NATIONAL CATHOLIC REPORTER. 19:7, January 21, 1983.

Deletion of confidential information from official public records, by D. E. Bruns. WASHBURN LAW JOURNAL. 22(2):364-370, 1983.

A delicate balance: not everything goes in the marketing of unmentionables [condoms], by J. Alter. ADVERTISING AGE. 53(sec 2):M2-M3+, July 12, 1982.

Demographic characteristics, wish and intent to procreate, and the use of contraception in a group of women in Mexico City, by E. Casanueva, et al. REVISTA DE INVESTIGACION CLINICA. 35(1):21-26, January-March 1983.

Demographic consequences, client satisfaction, and reasons for selecting sterilization among vasectomy and tubectomy clients in Bangladesh, by I. Swenson, et al. CONTRACEPTION. 25(6):573-590, June 1982.

Demographic data for the Czechoslovak Soviet socialist republic (Bohemia and Slovakia) for the years 1980 and 1981. CESKOSLOVENSKA PEDIATRIE. 37(8):477-480, August 1982.

Demographic implications of the biological determinants of female fecundity, by R. E. Frisch. SOCIAL BIOLOGY. 29:187, Spring-Summer 1982.

The depo-provera debate, by M. Clark, et al. NEWSWEEK. 101(4):70, January 24, 1983.

Depo-provera: a drug on trial, by J. Bryan. TIMES. April 13, 1983, p. 8.

Depo-provera: FDA hearings raise questions, by J. Skurnik. OFF OUR BACKS. 13:5-6, February 1983.

Depo-provera: the jury still out, by G. Rachel. FAMILY PLANNING PERSPECTIVES. 15(2):78, March-April 1983.

Depo-provera: a new offensive [issues in the marketing for human use of this long-acting, injectable contraceptive and in its possible approval for use in the United States], by J. Norsigian. HEALTH AND MEDICINE. 1:3-5, Winter-Spring 1983.

Depo-provera: on trial again [injectable contraceptive, Britain]. ECONOMIST. 287:116, April 30, 1983.

Depo-provera under scrutiny, by A. Chen. SCIENCE NEWS. 123(8):122, February 19, 1983.

Descriptive study of the attitudes of males involved in abortion, by D. A. Cornelio. DISSERTATION ABSTRACTS INTER-NATIONAL: A. 44(5), November 1983.

Determinants of national family planning effort, by W. R. Kelly, et al. POPULATION RESEARCH AND POLICY. 2(2):111-130, May 1983.

Determination of essential content as the basis for development of a curriculum model on care of the induced abortion patient for baccalaureate nursing faculty, by M. L. Olsen. DISSERTATION ABSTRACTS INTERNATIONAL: A. 43(12), June 1983.

Determination of 15-methyl prostaglandin F2a by derivatization high pressure liquid chromatography, by Z. S. Wang, et al. YAO HSUEH HSUEH PAO. 17(8):603-608, August 1982.

The development of fertility in Romania: a longitudinal study, by V. Ghetau. POPULATION. 38:247-266, March-April 1983.

The development of the institute for family planning in Ljubljana, by Z. Ograjensek. JUGOSLAVENSKA GINEKOLOGIJA I OPSTETRICIJA. 21(1-2):50-53, January-April 1981.

Development of tolerance to the effects of morphine on luteinizing hormone secretion as a function of castration in the male rat, by T. J. Cicero, et al. JOURNAL OF PHARMACOLOGY AND EXPERIMENTAL THERAPEUTICS. 223(3):784-789, December 1983.

Developmental disability and human sexuality, by M. J. Krajicek. NURSING CLINICS OF NORTH AMERICA. 17(3):377-386, September 1982.

Developmental issues for adolescent parents and their children, by V. Washington, et al. EDUCATIONAL HORIZONS. 61(4):195-199, Summer 1983.

Diagnosis and treatment of missed abortion, by M. A. Omarov, et al. AKUSHERSTVO I GINEKOLOGIIA. (5):57-59, May 1983.

Differences in the pregnancy-terminating effectiveness of an LH-RH analogue by subcutaneous, vaginal, rectal, and nasal routes in rats, by I. Yamazaki. ENDOCRINOLOGIA JAPONICA. 29(4):415-421, August 1982.

Differential childlessness by color: a further examination, by J. E. Veevers. SOCIAL BIOLOGY. 29:180-186, Spring-Summer 1982.

Differentials in the planning status of most recent live births to Mexican Americans and Anglos, by C. W. Warren, et al. PUBLIC HEALTH REPORTS. 98(2):152-160, March-April 1983.

Dignity of life developments, by D. J. Horan. CATHOLIC LAWYER. 27:239-245, Summer 1982.

Dilatation and evacuation [letter], by W. M. Hern. OBSTETRICS AND GYNECOLOGY. 60(5):667-668, November 1982.

The dilemma of an anti-abortion democrat, by D. R. Carlin, Jr. COMMONWEAL. 110:626-628, November 18, 1983.

Dilemmas in prenatal diagnosis: a case study, by W. J. Fibison, et al. ISSUES IN HEALTH CARE OF WOMEN. 4(1):57-67, January-February 1983.

Dispositions—Indiana. JUVENILE AND FAMILY LAW DIGEST. 15(5):183-186, May 1983.

Dispositions—Maryland. JUVENILE AND FAMILY LAW DIGEST. 14(12):395-398, December 1982.

Disseminated intravascular coagulation following midtrimester abortions, by P. F. White, et al. ANESTHESIOLOGY. 58(1):99-101, January 1983.

Dissenting catholics take pro-choice stand, by B. Yuill. NATIONAL CATHOLIC REPORTER. 19:25, February 11, 1983.

Distribution of down's syndrome, by S. G. Read. JOURNAL OF MENTAL DEFICIENCY RESEARCH. 26(4):215-227, December 1982.

Do couples make fertility plans one birth at a time?, by J. R. Udry. DEMOGRAPHY. 20(2):117-128, May 1983.

Do we need a domiciliary family planning service?, by A. Arnheim. HEALTH VISITOR. 56(5):162-163, May 1983.

A doctoral student says Chinese force women to have abortions, by S. W. Mosher. CHRISTIANITY TODAY. 27(36), October 21, 1983.

Doctors and abortion, by J. Van Dusen. MACLEANS. 96:43, August 8, 1983.

The doctors defy antiabortion tides [abortions resume at Moncton hospital, N.B.], by D. Folster. MACLEANS. 96:15, January 10, 1983.

Doctors' dilemma, by D. Gollob. NEW STATESMAN. February 4, 1983, p. 18.

Does prolactin influence first trimester abortion? A preliminary clinical observation, by E. Peer, et al. GYNECOLOGIC AND OBSTETRIC INVESTIGATION. 15(6):362-364, 1983.

The doing and undoing of surgical sterilization: a psychosocial profile of the tubal reimplantation patient, by J. Ballou, et al. PSYCHIATRY. 46(2):161-171, May 1983.

Don't take a chance on love: the latest and safest in birth control. MADEMOISELLE. 89:38-39+, November 1983.

Down's syndrome, by R. Brandon. OBSERVER. June 12, 1983, p. 26.

Dr. Rock's magic pill, by S. Davidson. ESQUIRE. 100:100+, December 1983.

Dressed to over kill, by M. Musto. VILLAGE VOICE. 28:27, March 8, 1983.

A drug on trial, by E. Potter, et al. SUNDAY TIMES. April 10, 1983, p. 17.

Drug treatment of retained abortion, intrauterine death of the fetus and of vesicular mole with 15-ME-PGF2 alpha, by D. Granese, et al. MINERVA GINECOLOGIA. 34(6):467-474, June 1982.

Dynamic evaluation of the incidence of hereditary pathology by an accounting of spontaneous abortions and congenital developmental defects, by N. P. Bochkov, et al. TSITOL I GENETIKA. 16(6):33-37, November-December 1982.

Dyserythropoiesis in the fetal liver as an indicator of the intensity of stress caused by abortion, by A. Pajor, et al. ORVOSI HETILIP. 124(11):619-622, March 13, 1983.

Early complication risks of legal abortions, Canada, 1975-1980, by S. Wadhera. CANADIAN JOURNAL OF PUBLIC HEALTH. 73(6):396-400, November-December 1982.

Early complications and effectiveness of abortion induction with PG F2 alpha, by G. Koinzer. ZENTRALBLATT FUR GYNAEKOLOGIE. 104(16):1009-1019, 1982.

Early midtrimester pregnancy termination: A comparison of dilatation and evacuation and intravaginal prostaglandin E2, by J. Robins, et al. JOURNAL OF REPRODUCTIVE MEDICINE. 27(7):415-419, 1982.

Early miscarriage: are we too quick to dismiss the pain?, by T. M. Stephany. RN. 45(11):89, November 1982.

Early office termination of pregnancy by soft cannula vacuum aspiration, by J. H. Meyer, Jr. AMERICAN JOURNAL OF OBSTETRICS AND BYNECOLOGY. 147(2):202-207, September 15, 1983.

Early postnatal sterilization, by R. Ichnovský, et al. CESKOSLOVENSKA BYNEKOLOGIE. 48(2):117-118, March 1983.

Ecological analysis of the socioeconomic status of women having abortions in Manhattan, by R. M. Pierce. SOCIAL SCIENCE AND MEDICINE. 15D(2):277-286, May 1981.

Economic analyses of the spacing of births, by J. L. Newman. AMERICAN ECONOMIC REVIEW. 73:33-37, May 1983.

Economic issues, not abortion, are the primary concern of the electorate. FAMILY PLANNING PERSPECTIVES. 15:35-36, January-February 1983.

Economic model of fertility, sex and contraception, by H. Brunborg. DISSERTATION ABSTRACTS INTERNATIONAL: A. 44(6), December 1983.

Ectopic pregnancies: rising incidence rates in northern California, by P. H. Shiono, et al. AMERICAN JOURNAL OF PUBLIC HEALTH. 72:173-175, February 1982.

Ectopic pregnancy after sterilization [letter] by A. McCausland. OBSTETRICS AND GYNECOLOGY. 61(6):766, June 1983.

Ectopic pregnancy after tubal sterilization, by I. T. Jones. MEDICAL JOURNAL OF AUSTRALIA. 1(6):279-280, March 19, 1983.

Ectopic pregnancy after tubal sterilization: mechanism of re-canalization: a case, by P. Rimdusit. JOURNAL OF THE MEDICAL ASSOCIATION OF THAILAND. 65(2):101-105, 1982.

Ectopic pregnancy and prior induced abortion, by A. A. Levin, et al. AMERICAN JOURNAL OF PUBLIC HEALTH. 72:253-256, March 1982.

Ectopic pregnancy following tubal sterilization, by E. Qvigstad, et al. INTERNATIONAL JOURNAL OF GYNAECOLOGY AND OBSTETRICS. 20(4):279-281, August 1982.

Ecumenical approach to abortion, by R. Evans. ECUMENIST. 21:64-67, May-June, July-August 1983.

The effect of administration family planning policy on maternal and child health, by L. S. Zabin. JOURNAL OF PUBLIC HEALTH POLICY. 4:268-278, September 1983.

Effect of anesthesia and surgery on the pre-s-phase cell cycle kinetics of mitogen-stimulated lymphocytes of previously healthy people, by A. J. Robertson, et al. BRITISH JOURNAL OF ANAESTHESIOLOGY. 55(4):339-347, April 1983.

Effect of centchroman on ovarian responsiveness to exogenous gonadotropins in immature female rats, by M. M. Singh, et al. INDIAN JOURNAL OF EXPERIMENTAL BIOLOGY. 20(6):448-451, 1982.

Effect of child mortality on contraceptive use and fertility in Columbia, Costa Rica and Korea, by B. S. Mensch. DIS-SERTATION ABSTRACTS INTERNATIONAL: A. 44(3), September 1983.

The effect of chromosome constitution on growth in culture of human spontaneous abortions, by T. Hassold, et al. HUMAN GENETICS. 63(2):166-170, 1983.

The effect of fecundity of pill acceptance during postpartum amenorrhea: a comment, by R. Gray, et al. STUDIES IN FAMILY PLANNING. 14(5):150-155, May 1983.

Effect of 15-me-prostaglandin F2 alpha on the release of endogenous prostaglandin F2 alpha and the concentration of estrogen and progesterone receptors in the human endometrium, by I. A. Manuilova, et al. AKUSHERSTVO I GINEKOLOGIIA. (1):54-55, 1983.

Effect of influenza on pregnancy, the fetus and the newborn, by

V. Arnaudova, et al. AKUSHERSTVO I GINEKOLOGIIA.
21(4):278-284, 1982.

Effect of supply source on oral contraceptive use in Mexico, by
J. Bailey, et al. STUDIES IN FAMILY PLANNING. 13(11):343,
November 1982.

Effect of the toxic agents of pseudomonas aeruginosa culture on
the course of pregnancy and fetal development in porton mice,
by M. Bilinska, et al. MEDYCYNA DOSWIADCZALNA I
MIKROBIOLOGIA. 34(3-4):145-148, 1982.

Effective, but how safe? TIME. 121(4):67, January 24, 1983.

Effectiveness and complications of interrupting pregnancy during
the 2d trimester with the Hungarian preparation ensaprost F,
by Ts. Despodova, et al. AKUSHERSTVO I GINEKOLOGIIA.
21(5):373-377, 1982.

The effectiveness of various arguments for the humanity of the
unborn, by J. V. Wagner. PROCEEDINGS OF THE AMERICAN
CATHOLIC PHILOSOPHICAL ASSOCIATION. 56:146-153,
1982.

Effects of androgen treatment of full-grown puberally castrated rats
upon male sexual behavior, intermale aggressive behavior and
the sequential patterning of aggressive interactions, by B. Bermond.
BEHAVIOUR. 80(3-4):143-173, 1982.

The effects of an antiprogesterone steroid in women: interruption
of the menstrual cycle and of early pregnancy, by W. Herrmann,
et al. COMPTE RENDUE DES SEANCES DE L'ACADEMIE
DES SCIENCES. 294(18):933-938, May 17, 1982.

Effects of benzylphenol and benzyl-1,3- benzodioxole derivatives
on fertility and longevity of the yellow fever mosquito (diptera:
culicidae), by F. R. S. Nelson, et al. JOURNAL OF ECONOMIC
ENTOMOLOGY. 75:877-878, October 1982.

Effects of breastfeeding on IUD performance, by L. Cole, et al.
AMERICAN JOURNAL OF PUBLIC HEALTH. 73:384-388,
April 1983.

Effects of carbon monoxide exposure on pregnant sows and their fetuses, by M. A. Dominick, et al. AMERICAN JOURNAL OF VETERINARY RESEARCH. 44:35-40, January 1983.

Effects of castration on aggressive and defensiye-escape components of agonistic behaviour in male mice, by A. Sulcová, et al. ACTIVITAS NERVOSA SUPERIOR. 23(4):317-318, December 1981.

Effects of delta-9-THC and castration on behavior and plasma hormone levels in male mice, by S. L. Dalterio, et al. PHARMACOLOGY, BIOCHEMISTRY AND BEHAVIOR. 18(1):81-86, January 1983.

Effects of desogestrel and levonorgestrel in low-dose estrogen oral contraceptives on serum lipoproteins, by E. W. Bergink, et al. CONTRACEPTION. 25(5):477-486, 1982.

Effects of hysterectomy on sexual receptivity, food intake, running wheel activity and hypothalanic ostrogen and progestin receptors in rats, by H. B. Ahdieh, et al. JOURNAL OF COMPARATIVE AND PHYSIOLOGICAL PSYCHOLOGY. 96(6):886-892, December 1982.

The effects of induced abortion on subsequent reproduction, by C. J. Hogue, et al. EPIDEMIOLOGIC REVIEWS. 4:66-94, 1982.

Effects of intracervical PGE2-gel on myometrial activity and cervical state in first trimester pregnancy, by A. Forman, et al. PROSTAGLANDINS. 24(3):303-312, September 1982.

Effects of marking with preputial gland material on the attack directed towards long-term castrates by isolated males, by M. H. Homady, et al. AGGRESSIVE BEHAVIOR. 8(2):137-140, 1982.

Effects of own attitude on polarization of judgment, by D. Romer. JOURNAL OF PERSONALITY AND SOCIAL PSYCHOLOGY. 44:273-284, February 1983.

The effects of sperm antibodies on fertility after vasectomy reversal,

by J. M. Parslow, et al. AMERICAN JOURNAL OF RE-
PRODUCTIVE IMMUNOLOGY. 3(1):28-31, January-
February 1983.

Efficacy of antibotic therapy in preventing spontaneous pregnancy
loss among couples colonized with genital mycoplasmas, by
P. A. Quinn, et al. AMERICAN JOURNAL OF OBSTETRICS
AND GYNECOLOGY. 145(2):239-244, January 15, 1983.

Efficacy on the Billings' method, by W. Fijalkowski. PIELEGNIARKA
I POLOZNA. (6):6-7, 1982.

Eleven million sterilizations from 1971 to 1981, but rate is now
declining. FAMILY PLANNING PERSPECTIVES. 15:89-90,
March-April 1983.

Elimination of medieval birth control and the witch trials of modern
times, by G. Heinsohn, et al. INTERNATIONAL JOURNAL OF
WOMEN'S STUDIES. 5(3):193-214, 1982.

Emotional consequences of sterilization. Clinical comments on the
methodology of psychological studies, by P. Petersen.
GEBURTSHILFE UND FRAYENHEILKUNDE. 43(4):253-
258, April 1983.

Empty cradles, by C. MacDonald. CANADA AND THE WORLD.
49:18-20, October 1983.

Endocrinological aspects of rehabilitating women following induced
abortion, by G. P. Koreneva, et al. AKUSHERSTVO I
GINEKOLOGIIA. (12):45-48, 1982.

Endoscopy and pelvic infection, by S. L. Corson. CLINICAL
OBSTETRICS AND GYNECOLOGY. 26(2):334-338, June
1983.

Englehardt on the abortion and euthansia of defective infants, by
G. E. Jones. LINACRE QUARTERLY. 50:172-181, May 1983.

Epididymo-deferens anastomosis. Experimental study in the rat, by
P. Hacker, et al. JOURNAL OF UROLOGY. 89(3):193-199, 1983.

An 'epidemic' of spontaneous abortion: psychosocial factors, by M. Kaffman, et al. ISRAEL JOURNAL OF PSYCHIATRY AND RELATED SCIENCES. 19(3):239-246, 1982.

An equal-opportunity destroyer, by J. McGowan. US CATHOLIC. 48:27-29, April 1983.

Error patterns in the prediction of fertility behavior, by A. R. Davidson, et al. JOURNAL OF APPLIED SOCIAL PSYCHOLOGY. 11:475-488, November-December 1981.

Estroprogestative contraception, by A. Harlay. INFIRMIERE FRANCAISE. (244):20, April 1983.

Ethical considerations concerning adolescents consulting for contraceptive services, by T. J. Silber. JOURNAL OF FAMILY PRACTICE. 15(5):909-911, November 1982.

The ethics of anthropology, by J. Lincoln. NATION. 237:226, September 24, 1983.

Ethnic variation in adolescent use of a contraceptive service, by P. B. Namerow, et al. JOURNAL OF ADOLESCENT HEALTH CARE. 3(3):165-172, December 1982.

Eugenic sterilization in Virginia: Aubrey Strode and the case of Buck vs. Bell, by P. A. Lombardo. DISSERTATION ABSTRACTS INTERNATIONAL: A. 43(10), April 1983.

Europe and the USA: abortion throughout the world. REVISTA DE ENFERMAGEN. 6(58-59):32-33, May-June 1983.

Evaluating DMPA [medroxyprogesterone acetate], by A. Henry. OFF OUR BACKS. 13:7+, February 1983.

Evaluation of the abortus and stillborn infant, by M. Barr, Jr., et al. JOURNAL OF REPRODUCTIVE MEDICINE. 27(9):601-603, September 1982.

Evaluation of a continuing education program in sex therapy, by P. M. Sarrel, et al. AMERICAN JOURNAL OF PUBLIC HEALTH.

72(8):839-843, 1982.

An evaluation of the declaration method of eligibility determination, by G. T. Berns. ADMINISTRATION IN SOCIAL WORK. 7(2):23-36, Summer 1983.

Evaluation of female pelvic pain part 2, by K. C. Edelin. HOSPITAL MEDICINE. 19(2):37-39, 42-44, 46+, February 1983.

Evaluation of intramuscular 15 (S) 15 methyl prostaglandin F2 alpha for menstrual regulation and preoperative cervical dilatation, by S. Jain, et al. INDIAN JOURNAL OF MEDICAL RESEARCH. 77:49-53, January 1983.

Evaluation of ovarian function after tubal sterilization, by E. Radwanska, et al. JOURNAL OF REPRODUCTIVE MEDICINE. 27(7):376-384, July 1982.

Evaluation the sterile male method on red-winged blackbirds; effects of the chemosterilant thiotepa on the reproduction of clinically treated birds under field conditions, by N. Potvin, et al. CANADIAN JOURNAL OF ZOOLOGY. 60:2337-2343, October 1982.

Everybody wants in, by J. Merwin. FORBES. 132:52-53, July 4, 1983.

The evolution of a constitutional right to an abortion: fashioned in the 1970's and secured in the 1980's, by N. Ford. JOURNAL OF LEGAL MEDICINE. 4:271-322, September 1983.

Examinations of various coagulation techniques, by H. H. Riedel, et al. PROGRESS IN CLINICAL AND BIOLOGICAL RESEARCH. 112(pt B):119-126, 1982.

Excommunication over abortion, by R. Lee, et al. ALBERTA REPORT. 10:42-43, July 11, 1983.

Expectation—threshold model of reproductive decision making, by L. R. Beach, et al. POPULATION AND ENVIRONMENT: BEHAVIORAL AND SOCIAL ISSUES. 5(2):95-108, Summer 1982.

Expelled, for giving the facts on abortions, by J. Mirsky. TIMES. April 9, 1983, p. 6.

Experience with prostaglandins for therapeutic abortion in Norway. Their need and their benefits, by P. Fylling, et al. ACTA OBSTETRICIA ET GYNECOLOGICA SCANDINAVICA, SUPPLEMENT. 113:113-116, 1983.

Experience with 16-phenoxy-omega-tetranor-PGE2-methylsulfona-mide (sulprostone) for termination of second trimester pregnancy, by P. Fylling. CONTRACEPTION. 26(3):279-283, September 1982.

Experiences from a sex-counseling and birth control practice for adolescents, by H. J. Ahrendt. ZEITSCHRIFT FUR ARZTLICHE FORTBILDUNG. 77(5):201-205, 1983.

Experiences in the treatment of childless couples in a family service institute with special reference to andrologic problems, by I. Aszodi. ZEITSCHRIFT FUR HAUTKRANKHEITEN H UND G. 58(7):456-459, April 1, 1983.

Experiences with sulproston for cervical priming in pregnancy termination in the 1st trimester, by S. Heinzl, et al. GYNAEKOLOGISCHE RUNDSCHAU. 22(4):233-240, 1982.

An explanatory model of contraceptive use among young single women, by E. S. Herold, et al. JOURNAL OF SEX RESEARCH. 18:289-304, November 1982.

Exposure to anaesthetic gases and spontaneous abortion: response bias in a postal questionnaire study, by G. Axelsson, et al. INTERNATIONAL JOURNAL OF EPIDEMIOLOGY. 11(3):250-256, September 1982.

The extent of contraceptive use and the social paradigm of modern demography, by G. S. Douglas. SOCIOLOGY. 17:380-387, August 1983.

Extra-amniotic prostaglandin gel in the management of fetal death and fetal abnormality, by M. A. Quinn, et al. AUSTRALIAN AND NEW ZEALAND JOURNAL OF OBSTETRICS AND GYNAE-

COLOGY. 22(2):76-77, May 1982.

FDA assails safety of depo-provera, by R. J. Smith. SCIENCE. 219:371, January 28, 1983.

Factor structure of the menstrual symptom questionnaire: relationship to oral contraceptives, neuroticism and life stress, by L. A. Stephenson, et al. BEHAVIOUR RESEARCH AND THERAPY. 21(2):129-135.

Factors affecting the association of oral contraceptives and ovarian cancer, by D. W. Cramer, et al. NEW ENGLAND JOURNAL OF MEDICINE. 307:1047-1051, October 21, 1982.

Factors affecting early and late deciders of voluntary childlessness, by V. J. Callan. JOURNAL OF SOCIAL PSYCHOLOGY. 119:261-268, April 1983.

Factors affecting perception of pregnancy risk-in the adolescent, by P. B. Smith, et al. JOURNAL OF YOUTH AND ADOLESCENCE. 11(3):207-215, June 1982.

Factors affecting sexual and contraceptive attitudes and behaviors among adolescents, by R. S. Sterns. DISSERTATION ABSTRACTS INTERNATIONAL: A. 43(10), April 1983.

Factors influencing choice of contraceptive method among married fecund women who intend no additional births: health belief model and economic perspectives, by N. M. MacDowell, Jr. DISSERTATION ABSTRACTS INTERNATIONAL: B. 43(11), May 1983.

Factors influencing the outcome of microsurgical tubal ligation reversals, by J. C. Seiler. AMERICAN JOURNAL OF OBSTETRICS AND GYNECOLOGY. 146(3):292-298, June 1, 1983.

Factors related to effective contraceptive use in adolescent women, by D. M. Morrison. DISSERTATION ABSTRACTS INTER-NATIONAL: B. 43(12), June 1983.

Failures of laparoscopic sterilization by hulka-clemens clips, by A. Tadjerouni, et al. EUROPEAN JOURNAL OF OBSTETRICS,

GYNECOLOGY AND REPRODUCTIVE BIOLOGY. 14(6):393-398, March 1983.

Faith, reason popularize natural family planning, by A. Jones. NATIONAL CATHOLIC REPORTER. 19:1+, October 22, 1982.

The fallacy of legalized abortion as a lesser evil, by C. De Celles. SOCIAL JUSTICE REVIEW. 74:3-5, January-February 1983.

Fallopian tube microsurgery, by B. G. Bateman, et al. VIRGINIA MEDICAL. 110(3):171-173, 176, March 1983.

Fallopian tube occlusion rings: a consideration in the differential diagnosis of ureteral calculi, by D. B. Spring. RADIOLOGY. 145(1):51-52, October 1982.

A family affair [regulation requiring facilities receiving federal funding to notify parents after supplying contraceptive devices to minor children]. AMERICA. 148:102-103, February 12, 1983.

Family formation, desire for children and birth control of Swiss married couples—results of a representative survey. II. Contraception in Switzerland—knowledge and practice of Swiss married couples, by F. Kuhne, et al. GYNAEKOLOGISCHE RUNDSCHAU. 23(2):77-87, 1983.

Family health by women's health corps (WHC) in Iran, by S. Amidi. JOURNAL OF TROPICAL PEDIATRICS. 28(3):149-152, June 1982.

Family lifeline—an aid for family life planning, by S. F. Weis. ILLINOIS TEACHER OF HOME ECONOMICS. 26(1):29-30, September-October 1982.

Family plan [squeal law providing for notification of parents when children receive contraceptives from clinics]. TIME. 121:41, February 7, 1983.

Family planning among the urban poor: sexual politics and social policy, by M. Cummings, et al. FAMILY RELATIONS.

Family planning and female sterilization in the United States, by T. M. Shapiro, et al. SOCIAL SCIENCE AND MEDICINE. 17(23):1847-1855, 1983.

Family planning and the handicapped, by C. Welman. CURATIONIS. 5(3):54-56, September 1982.

Family planning and health: the Narangwal experiment, by R. Faruqee. FINANCE AND DEVELOPMENT. 20(2):43-46, June 1983.

The family planning association. HEALTH VISITOR. 56(5):165-166, May 1983.

Family planning clinic services in the United States, 1981, by A. Torres, et al. FAMILY PLANNING PERSPECTIVES. 15(6):272-278, November-December 1983.

Family planning, cost benefits and the nursing role, by A. Leathard. MIDWIFE, HEALTH VISITOR AND COMMUNITY NURSE. 18(12):526-527, 536, December 1982.

Family planning education, by M. V. Hamburg. JOURNAL OF SCHOOL HEALTH. 53(2):108-111, February 1983.

Family-planning education in Michigan schools, by K. Sung. PUBLIC HEALTH REVIEWS. 10(2):199-212, April-June 1982.

Family planning field research projects: balancing internal against external validity, by A. Fisher, et al. STUDIES IN FAMILY PLANNING. 14(1):3, January 1983.

Family planning incentives in developing nations and western Europe, by N. Fincancioglu, et al. PEOPLE. 9(4):3, 1982.

Family planning perspectives, by O. J. Sikes. POPULI. 9(2):25, 1982.

The family planning program and cuts in federal spending. Initial effects on the provision of services part 2, by A. Torres. FAMILY PLANNING PERSPECTIVES. 15(4):184-188,

191, July-August 1983.

The family planning service, by K. Arger. MIDWIFE, HEALTH VISITOR AND COMMUNITY NURSE. 19(1):14-15, January 1983.

Family planning [Shanghai] , by Z. Wis-sen, et al. AMERICAN JOURNAL OF PUBLIC HEALTH. 72:24-25, September 1982.

A family planning study in Kuala Pilah, Peninsular Malaysia, by V. Thambypillai. MEDICAL JOURNAL OF MALAYSIA. 37(4):326-335, December 1982.

Family planning update, by H. Martins. HEALTH VISITOR. 56(5):166-169, May 1983.

Family planning, wish for children and birth control of Swiss couples—results of a representative survey. I. Family planning and wish for children, by F. Hopflinger, et al. GYNAE-KOLOGISCHE RUNDSCHAU. 23(1):25-34, 1983.

Family size and contraceptive use among Mormons: 1965-1975, by T. B. Heaton, et al. REVIEW OF RELIGIOUS RESEARCH. 25(2):102-113, 1983.

Family welfare as health need in Indian population policy, by S. Bergstrom. TROPICAL DOCTOR. 12(4 pt 1):182-184, October 1982.

Female employment and fertility in the Dominican republic: a dynamic perspective, by D. T. Gurak, et al. AMERICAN SOCIOLOGICAL REVIEW. 47:810-818, December 1982.

Female sterilization with hulka clips—initial experience at the University Hospital, Kuala Lumpur, by A. A. Rahman, et al. MEDICAL JOURNAL OF MALAYSIA. 37(3):276-280, September 1982.

Feminists against abortion: the prolife movement is broadening, by B. Spring. CHRISTIANITY TODAY. 27:35-36, April 22, 1983.

Fertility and acquisition of property, by C. Bonvalet. POPULATION.

58

37:1198-1204, November-December 1982.

Fertility and family planning behaviour among Muslims: a study in a village in Andhra Pradesh. HEALTH AND POPULATION: PERSPECTIVES AND ISSUES. 4(3):151-162, July-September 1981.

Fertility and family planning in the 1970's, by W. D. Mosher. NATIONAL SURVEY OF FAMILY GROWTH. 14(6):314-319, November-December 1982.

Fertility awareness: the University of California/Berkeley experience, by G. Kramer. JOURNAL OF THE AMERICAN COLLEGE HEALTH ASSOCIATION. 31(4):166-167, February 1983.

Fertility control, by M. J. Harper. MEDICINAL RESEARCH REVIEWS. 2(4):403-432, October-December 1982.

Fertility could plummet, if. UN CHRONICLE. 19:81-82, July 1982.

Fertility, development and family planning, by S. Menard. STUDIES IN COMPARATIVE INTERNATIONAL DEVELOP-MENT. 17(3):77-100, Fall 1983.

Fertility following reversal of male and female sterilization, by E. Weisberg, et al. CONTRACEPTION. 26(4):361-371, October 1982.

Fertility rate slows in 1980, but large increases continue among older mothers, unmarried women. FAMILY PLANNING PERSPECTIVES. 15:38-39, January-February 1983.

Fertility-related state laws enacted in 1982, by D. Bush. FAMILY PLANNING PERSPECTIVES. 15:111-116, May-June 1983.

Fertilizing capacity and sperm antibodies in vasovasostomized men, by E. Requeda, et al. FERTILITY AND STERILITY. 39(2):197-203, February 1983.

Fetal alcohol syndrome; other effects of alcohol on pregnancy, by A. S. Lele. NEW YORK STATE JOURNAL OF MEDICINE. 82(8):1225-1227, July 1982.

Fetal anatomical abnormalities and other associated factors in middle-trimester abortion and their relevance to patient counselling, by M. J. Haxton, et al. BRITISH JOURNAL OF OBSTETRICS AND GYNAECOLOGY. 90(6):501-506, June 1983.

Fetal indication for the termination of pregnancy from an ethical viewpoint, by A. Auer. GEBURTSHILFE UND FRAUENHEILKUNDE. 43(1):51-56, January 1983.

Fetal Rh blood determination in pregnancy termination by dilatation and evacuation, by J. J. LaFerla, et al. TRANSFUSION. 23(1):67-68, January-February 1983.

Fetus as organ donor [using pancreas from aborted fetuses; work of Josiah Brown and Kevin Lafferty]. SCIENCE DIGEST. 91:85, June 1983.

The fetus as a patient: emerging rights as a person?, by J. L. Lenow. AMERICAN JOURNAL OF LAW AND MEDICINE. 9:1-29, Spring 1983.

The fetus between abortion and protection of life, by H. Ostendorf. BEITRAEGE ZUR GERICHTLICHEN MEDIZIN. 40:29-33, 1982.

A field evaluation of the sexual competitiveness of sterile melon flies, dacus (zeugodacus) cucurbitae, by O. Iwahashi, et al. ECOLOGICAL ENTOMOLOGY. 8:43-48, February 1983.

Fifteen million lives snuffed out; President Ronald Reagan reports, by R. W. Reagan. COLUMBIA. 63:4-9, August 1983.

The first human right: a pro-life primer; excerpts from the first human right: a pro-life primer, by C. M. Odell, et al. OUR SUNDAY VISITOR. 71:1+, January 16, 1983.

First intercourse among young Americans, by M. Zelnik, et al. FAMILY PLANNING PERSPECTIVES. 15(2):64-70, March-April 1983.

A five-year clinical trial of levonorgestrel silastic implants (Norplant), by S. Diaz, et al. CONTRACEPTION. 25(5):447-456, 1982.

A five year experience with laparoscopic falope ring sterilization, by J. H. Meyer, Jr. INTERNATIONAL JOURNAL OF GYNAECOLOGY AND OBSTETRICS. 20(3):183-187, June 1982.

Foetus papyraceus, by U. Thakkar, et al. MEDICAL JOURNAL OF ZAMBIA. 15(3):72-74, May-July 1981.

A foetus papyraceus in twin birth at term, by H. Göcke, et al. GEBURTSHILFE UND FRAUENHEILKUNDE. 42(80):605-608, August 1982.

Foetuses, famous violinists, and the right to continued aid, by M. Davis. PHILOSOPHICAL QUARTERLY. 33:259-278, July 1983.

Follow-up of adolescent family planning clinic users, by P. B. Namerow, et al. FAMILY PLANNING PERSPECTIVES. 15(4):172-176, July-August 1983.

Food and drug administration approves vaginal sponge, by D. Kafka, et al. FAMILY PLANNING PERSPECTIVES. 15(3):146-148, May-June 1983.

For recognizing one's fertile period: Bioself. KRANKENPFLEGE. (5):42, May 1983.

For safety and efficacy, most methods of tubal sterilization are similar (statistics). FAMILY PLANNING PERSPECTIVES. 15(3):141-142, May-June 1983.

Forgiveness for abortion, by Sister M. A. Walsh. CATHOLIC DIGEST. 47:83-84, July 1983.

Formation of kidney stones in mummified extrauterine pregnancy, by H. J. Hertkens. ZEITSCHRIFT FUR UROLOGIE UND NEPHROLOGIE. 75(7):501-502, July 1982.

Fraud between partners regarding the use of contraceptives, by D. M. Carlton. KENTUCKY LAW JOURNAL. 71(3):593-615, 1982-1983.

Freedom of choice is immoral, by B. Amiel. MACLEANS. 96:17, November 21, 1983.

From the courts to congress. AMERICA. 149:2, June 25-July 2, 1983.

From discussion to normalization: the counselor's role in the interview prior to a voluntary interruption of pregnancy, by A. M. Devreux. REVUE FRANCAISE DE SOCIOLOGIE. 23(3):455-471, July-September 1982.

From judge Dooling's decision [national conference of Catholic Bishops' pro-life organizing campaign], by J. Dooling. HUMANIST. 43:10-11, July-August 1983.

Frozen embryo aborts, by V. Sarma. NATURE. 304(5924):301, July 28-August 3, 1983.

Genetic decision making and pastoral care. Clergy involvement, by R. C. Baumiller. HOSPITAL PRACTICE. 18(4):38A, 38D-38F, April 1983.

Genetic polymorphisms and human reproduction: a study of phosphoglucomutase in spontaneous abortion, by M. Nicotra, et al. INTERNATIONAL JOURNAL OF FERTILITY. 27(4):229-233, 1982.

Genito-urinary symptoms and signs in women using different contraceptive methods, by N. B. Loudon, et al. BRITISH JOURNAL OF FAMILY PLANNING. 8(1):3-6, 1982.

Genocide fears in a rural black community: an empirical examination, by W. C. Farrell, Jr. JOURNAL OF BLACK STUDIES. 14(1):49-67, September 1983.

Getting the message across [combining family planning and parasite control], by M. Jones. WORLD HEALTH. February-March 1983, p. 22-24.

Glimpses of health programs in the people's republic of China: family planning education, by M. V. Hamburg. JOURNAL OF SCHOOL HEALTH. 53:108-111, February 1983.

Glycohemoglobin (hemoglobin A_1) levels in oral contraceptive users, by M. Blum, et al. EUROPEAN JOURNAL OF OBSTETRICS AND GYNECOLOGY. 15(2):97-102, 1983.

The goods [visit to the Trojan manufacturing plant], by B. Greene. ESQUIRE. 100:24+, July 1983.

Gossypol, an effective male contraceptive, was not mutagenic in sperm head abnormality assay in mice, by S. K. Majumdar, et al. CANADIAN JOURNAL OF GENETICS AND CYTOLOGY. 24(6):777-780, 1982.

Government funding for surgical reversal of voluntary female sterilization. Ethical points of reference, by B. Freedman, et al. JOURNAL OF REPRODUCTIVE MEDICINE. 27(6):339-344, June 1982.

The greater immorality. STUDIES. 72:1-5, Spring 1983.

Grieving after termination of pregnancy [letter], by M. Ryan, et al. MEDICAL JOURNAL OF AUSTRALIA. 1(4):155, February 19, 1983.

Growing conservatism in the United States? An examination of trends in political opinion between 1972 and 1980, by J. Saltzman-Chafetz, et al. SOCIOLOGICAL PERSPECTIVES. 26(3):275-298, 1983.

HCG and SP-1 in normal pregnancy and in high-risk early pregnancy, by K. Vetter, et al. GEBURTSHILFE UND FRAUNHEILKUNDE. 42(12):868-870, December 1982.

HLA system antigens in abortion, by V. V. Grigor'eva, et al. AKUSHERSTVO I GINEKOLOGIIA. (12):26-28, 1982.

Half our pregnancies are unintentional. NEWSWEEK. 102:37, October 10, 1983.

Hamilton birth control clinic of the 1930's, by D. Dodd. ONTARIO HISTORY. 75:71-86, March 1983.

Harsh days at the high court: abortion decision devastates right-to-life movement, by B. Spring. CHRISTIANITY TODAY. 27:30-31, July 15, 1983.

Hatch amendment and the new federalism, by J. T. Noonan, Jr. HARVARD JOURNAL OF LAW AND PUBLIC POLICY. 6:93-102, Spring 1982.

Haughey placed, FitzGerald nobbled. ECONOMIST. 286:58-59, February 19, 1983.

The health belief model: can it help us to understand contraceptive use among adolescents?, by E. S. Herold. JOURNAL OF SCHOOL HEALTH. 53:19-21, January 1983.

Health practices: family planning and sex education, by C. Bailey. NURSING. 2(2):32-33, June 1982.

The health visitor, family planning and personal relationships . . . methods used to teach professional people, by H. Martins. HEALTH VISITOR. 56(5):161-162, May 1983.

Helms strung by NCCB staff memo, by M. Meehan. REGISTER. 59:1+, August 21, 1983.

Henry Hyde on new prolife legislation; interview with Henry John Hyde, by M. Meehan. REGISTER. 59:6, March 6, 1983.

The hidden grief of abortion, by J. Upton. PASTORAL PSYCHOLOGY. 31:19-25, Fall 1982.

High court clears up any doubts on abortion; justice disallow limit on contraceptive ads, by L. Greenhouse. NEW YORK TIMES. June 19, 1983, news section 4, p. E7.

High court ruling bad news, good news for pro-lifers, by W. A. Ryan. OUR SUNDAY VISITOR. 72:8, July 3, 1983.

High court strikes down Akron abortion ordinance. OUR SUNDAY VISITOR. 72:8, June 26, 1983.

A highly emotional decision . . . abortion, by J. Thompson. NURSING MIRROR AND MIDWIVE'S JOURNAL. 157(4):41, July 27, 1983.

Histopathologic changes in fallopian tubes subsequent to sterilization procedures, by R. J. Stock. INTERNATIONAL JOURNAL OF GYNECOLOGICAL PATHOLOGY. 2(1):13-27, 1983.

Hoechst conceives new birth control drug. CHEMISTRY AND INDUSTRY. January 3, 1983, p. 4.

Hormonal contraception for men: acceptability and effects on sexuality. STUDIES IN FAMILY PLANNING. 13(11):328, November 1982.

Hormonal profile on the second trimester of normal and pathologic pregnancies, by D. Tsenov, et al. AKUSHERSTVO I GINEKOLOGIIA. 21(3):184-188, 1982.

Hormone treatments for sex offenders. CRIMINAL JUSTICE NEWSLETTER. 14(7):3, March 28, 1983.

Hospitalization requirements for second trimester abortions: for the purpose of health or hindrance?, by M. C. Foley. THE GEORGETOWN LAW JOURNAL. 71(3):991-1021, 1983.

A household study of the pattern of utilization of mother and child health services in rural Greece and variation by socio-economic status, by C. G. Tzoumaka-Bakoula, et al. CHILD CARE, HEALTH AND DEVELOPMENT. 9(2):85-95, March-April 1983.

How startups buck the odds in birth control, by M. McAdoo. VENTURE. 4:56+, October 1982.

How to curb the fertility of the unfit: the feeble-minded in Edwardian Britain, by D. Barker. OXFORD REVIEW OF EDUCATION. 9(3):197-211, 223-225, 1983.

Human life federalism amendment: 1. legal aspects; 2. legislative update, by W. R. Caron, et al. CATHOLIC LAWYER. 28:111-128, Spring 1983.

Human placental lactogen, pregnancy-specific beta-1-glycoprotein and alpha-fetoprotein in serum in threatened abortion, by J. B.

Hertz, et al. INTERNATIONAL JOURNAL OF GYNAECOLOGY AND OBSTETRICS. 21(2):111-117, April 1983.

Humanae vitae, fifteen years later, by R. Bautch. REGISTER. 59:1+, July 24, 1983.

Husband or wife?: a multivariate analysis of decision making for voluntary sterilization, by M. D. Clark, et al. JOURNAL OF FAMILY ISSUES. 3(3):341-360, September 1982.

Husband-wife communciation, wife's employment and the decision for male or female sterilization, by F. D. Bean, et al. JOURNAL OF MARRIAGE AND THE FAMILY. 45:395-404, May 1983.

Hypertonic saline as an abortifacient in a select group of patients, by J. A. Garbaciak, Jr., et al. OBSTETRICS AND GYNECOLOGY. 61(1):37-41, January 1983.

Hysterectomy and sexual counseling, by J. Ananth. PSYCHIATRIC JOURNAL OF THE UNIVERSITY OF OTTAWA. 8(4):213-217, December 1983.

Hysterectomy and sterilization rates. Regional variations, by W. Savage. PRACTITIONER. 227(1379):839-845, May 1983.

Hysterectomy following sterilization, by A. A. Templeton, et al. BRITISH JOURNAL OF OBSTETRICS AND GYNAECOLOGY. 89(10):845-848, October 1982.

Hysterectomy in six European countries, by P. A. Van Keep, et al. MATURITAS. 5(2):69-76, 1983.

Hysteroscopic findings in 100 women requesting reversal of a previously performed voluntary tubal sterilization, by J. L. Goerzen, et al. FERTILITY AND STERILITY. 39(1):103-104, January 1983.

Hysteroscopic sterilization: silicone elastic plugs, by T. P. Reed. CLINICAL OBSTETRICS AND GYNECOLOGY. 26(2):313-320, June 1983.

Hysteroscopic tubal occlusion with formed-in-place silicone plugs,

by R. M. Houck, et al. OBSTETRICS AND GYNECOLOGY.
60(5):641-648, November 1982.

Hysteroscopic tubal occlusion with silicone rubber, by T. P.
Reed, III, et al. OBSTETRICS AND GYNECOLOGY.
61(3):388-392, March 1983.

IUD dangers: are you a potential victim?, by M. Engle. GLAMOUR.
81:254, November 1983.

IUD insertion following spontaneous abortion: a clinical trial of
the TCu 220C, liuppes loop D, and copper 7. STUDIES IN
FAMILY PLANNING. 14(4):109-114, April 1983.

IUD's and ectopic pregnancy, by I. Sivin. STUDIES IN FAMILY
PLANNING. 14(2):57, February 1983.

IUD's: an appropriate contraceptive for many women. POPULATION
REPORTS. 10(4), July 1982

Idiopathic spontaneous abortions, by W. P. Faulk. AMERICAN
JOURNAL OF REPRODUCTIVE IMMUNOLOGY. 3(1):48-49,
January-February 1983.

If not abortion, what then [three articles], by S. Reed, et al.
CHRISTIANITY TODAY. 27:14-23, May 20, 1983.

"If you prick us, do we not bleed?": of Shylock, fetuses, and
the concept of person in the law, by C. H. Baron. LAW,
MEDICINE AND HEALTH CARE. 11(2):52-63, 81, April
1983.

Illegal abortions take toll in Portugal, by P. Kassell. NEW
DIRECTIONS FOR WOMEN. 11:9, May-June 1983.

Immediate postabortal insertion of a levonorgestrel-releasing IUD,
by M. Heikkilä, et al. CONTRACEPTION. 26(3):245-259,
September 1982.

Immune reactivity among women on oral contraceptives, by H. D.
Zane. DISSERTATION ABSTRACTS INTERNATIONAL: B.
44(4), October 1983.

Immunogenetics of spontaneous abortions in humans, by T. J. Gill, 3rd. TRANSPLANTATION. 35(1):1-6, January 1983.

Immunoglobulin in seminal fluid of fertile, infertile, vasectomy and vasectomy reversal patients, by J. E. Fowler, Jr, et al. JOURNAL OF UROLOGY. 129(4):869-872, April 1983.

Immunohistochemical study of SP1, HPL and HCG in chorionic tissue with early spontaneous and induced abortions, by M. Ito, et al. NIPPON SANKA FUJINKA GAKKAI ZASSHI. 34(12):2115-2122, December 1982.

The impact of legal termination of pregnancy and of prenatal diagnosis on the birth prevalence of Down syndrome in Denmark, by M. Mikkelsen, et al. ANNALS OF HUMAN GENETICS. 47(pt 2):123-131, May 1983.

Impact of vacuum aspiration abortion on future childbearing: a review, by C. J. Rowland Hogue, et al. FAMILY PLANNING PERSPECTIVES. 15:119-125, May-June 1983.

Implantation of dihydrotestosterone propionate into the lateral septum or medial amygdala facilitates copulation in castrated male rats given estradiol systemically, by M. J. Baum, et al. HORMONES AND BEHAVIOR. 16(2):208-223, June 1982.

In the decade since Roe v. Wade; symposium, part 1. HOSPITAL PROGRESS. 63:37-69, December 1982.

—. part 2. HOSPITAL PROGRESS. 63:70-83, December 1982.

In defense of the pill. EMERGENCY MEDICINE. 14(17):205, October 15, 1982.

In re guardianship of Eberhardy (Wis): the sterilization of the mentally retarded. WISCONSIN LAW REVIEW. 1982, p. 1199-1227.

In search of constituency for the new religious right, by C. Mueller. PUBLIC OPINION QUARTERLY. 47(2):213-229, 1983.

In utero selection against fetuses with trisomy [letter], by D.

Warburton, et al. AMERICAN JOURNAL OF HUMAN GENETICS. 35(5):1059-1064, September 1983.

In vitro fertilization system of the rat: influence of rat spermatozoal antibodies: an experiment in the allogenic system, by L. Mettler, et al. ZUCHTHYGIENE. 17(1):19-28, 1982.

The incidence of intrauterine adhesions following spontaneous abortion, by A. Adoni, et al. INTERNATIONAL JOURNAL OF FERTILITY. 27(2):117-118, 1982.

Incidence of legal abortions in 1978 in Serbia proper, excluding autonomous environs, by J. Ananijevic-Pandej. SRPSKI ARHIV ZA CELOKUPNO LEKARSTVO. 110(2):177-184, February 1982.

Incidence of obstetrical-risk pregnancies in the Wloclawek region - prenatal and intrapartum risk and the state of the newborn infant, by B. Bilyk, et al. GINEKOLOGIA POLSKOL. 53(12):869-873, December 1982.

Incomplete and inevitable abortion: treatment by suction curettage in the emergency department, by R. G. Farrell, et al. ANNALS OF EMERGENCY MEDICINE. 11(12):652-658, December 1982.

Increasing the effectiveness of community workers through training of spouses: a family planning experiment in Guatemala, by M. A. Pineda, et al. PUBLIC HEALTH REPORTS. 98(3):273-277, May-June 1983.

Indicators of contraceptive policy for nations at three levels of development [comparison of the use of condoms, birth control pills, and intrauterine devices], by I. M. Wasserman, et al. SOCIAL INDICATORS RESEARCH. 12:153-168, February 1983.

Induced abortion and social factors in wild horses, by J. Berger. NATURE. 303(5912):59-61, May 1983.

Induced abortion in Belgium: clinical experience and psychosocial observations, by M. Vekemans, et al. STUDIES IN FAMILY PLANNING. 13(pt 1):355-364, December 1982.

Induced abortion in fertility regulation, by L. Andolsek, et al. JUGOSLAVENSKA GINEKOLOGIJA I OPSTETRICIJA. 21(1-2):57-61, January-April 1981.

Induction of abortion during the second pregnancy trimester by intra-amniotic administration of PGF2 alpha, by A. Pajor, et al. ORVOSI HETLIAP. 124(28):1671-1674, July 10, 1983.

Induction of female sexual behavior by GTP in ovariectomized estrogen primed rats, by C. Beyer, et al. PHYSIOLOGY AND BEHAVIOR. 28(6):1073-1076, June 1982.

Induction of internal abortion and vesicular mole with intra-muscular administration of 15(S)15-methyl-prostaglandin F2 alpha, by A. Nasi, et al. MINERVA GINECOLOGIA. 34(6):461-466, June 1982.

Induction of therapeutic abortion by intra-amniotic and intravenous administration of prostaglandin F2-alpha in the second trimester of pregnancy, by A. Otoka, et al. WIADOMOSCI LEKARSKIE. 35(15-16):969-972, September 15, 1982.

Infant and child survival and contraceptive use in the closed pregnancy interval, by B. Janowitz, et al. SOCIAL SCIENCE AND MEDICINE. 17(2):113-118, 1983.

The infanticide tragedy in China, by J. Mirsky. NATION. 237:12-14, July 2, 1983.

Inferior epigasttic haemorrhage, an avoidable complication of laparoscopic clip sterilization, by D. W. Pring. BRITISH JOURNAL OF OBSTETRICS AND GYNAECOLOGY. 90(5):480-482, May 1983.

Infertility in bitches induced by active immunization with porcine zonae pellucidae, by C. A. Mahi-Brown, et al. JOURNAL OF EXPERIMENTAL ZOOLOGY. 222:89-95, July 20, 1982.

Influence of background and programme factors on the family planning programme in India, by K. B. Pathak, et al. JOURNAL OF FAMILY WELFARE. 29:3-11, March 1983.

Inhibition of human placental progesterone synthesis and aromatase activity by synthetic steroidogenic inhibitors in vitro, by T. Rabe, et al. FERTILITY AND STERILITY. 39(6):829-835, June 1983.

Initial results on spontaneous abortion from July 1976 to June 1978 in TCDD-polluted area of Seveso, by G. Remotti, et al. ANNALI DI OSTETRICIA GINECOLOGIA, MEDICINA PERINATALE. 103(4):249-253, July-August 1982.

Innovative approaches for reaching young people in health and family planning programs, by E. Vadies. BULLETIN OF THE PAN AMERICAN HEALTH ORGANIZATION. 16(4):323-328, 1982.

Institutional factors affecting teenagers' choice and reasons for delay in attending a family planning clinic , by L. Schwab Zabin, et al. FAMILY PLANNING PERSPECTIVES. 15:25-29, January-February 1983.

Intake of estroprogestins in pregnancy and hypospadias, by S. Milia, et al. MINERVA GINECOLOGIA. 34(12):1023-1027, December 1982.

An interactive model program of care for diabetic women before and during pregnancy part 2, by D. L. McCoy, et al. DIABETES EDUCATOR. 9(2):suppl: 11S-20S, Summer 1983.

Intermediate variables and educational differentials in ferility in Korea and the Philippines, by L. Bumpass, et al. DEMOGRAPHY. 19:241-260, May 1982.

Interruptions of pregnancy, by H. Zakut, et al. HAREFUAH. 102(8):350-352, April 15, 1982.

Interval IUD insertion in parous women: a randomized multicentre comparative trial of the lippes loop D, TCu220c and the copper 7. CONTRACEPTION. 26(1):1-22, July 1982.

Interval sterilizations. A substitute for postpartum procedures, an example from Southeast Brazil, by B. Janowitz, et al. SOCIAL SCIENCE AND MEDICINE. 16(22):1979-1983, 1982.

Intraamniotic injection of ethacridine for second-trimester induction of labor, by K. H. Tien. OBSTETRICS AND GYNECOLOGY. 61(6):733-766, June 1983.

Intraoperative observations during vasovasostomy in 334 patients, by A. M. Belker, et al. JOURNAL OF UROLOGY. 129(3):524-527, March 1983.

Inversion of the uterus following abortion, by A. S. Gupta, et al. JOURNAL OF THE INDIAN MEDICAL ASSOCIATION. 79(8):123-126, October 16, 1982.

Investigation of the relationship between sex role orientation, level of assertiveness, affective orientation to sexuality and a model of contraceptive behavior, by M. J. Hynes. DISSERTATION ABSTRACTS INTERNATIONAL: B. 43(9), March 1983.

Involuntary sterilization in Germany from 1933 to 1945 and some consequences for today, by F. Pfafflin, et al. INTERNATIONAL JOURNAL OF LAW AND PSYCHIATRY. 5(3-4):419-423, 1983.

Involuntary sterilization standard of evidence spelled out by court. THE FAMILY LAW REPORTER: COURT OPINIONS. 9(41):2623-2625, August 23, 1983.

Ireland: bungled (abortion referendum). ECONOMIST. 287:38, May 7, 1983.

Ireland debates abortion, by L. McRedmond. TABLET. 237:346-347, April 16, 1983.

Ireland: a referendum to abort Fine Gael? ECONOMIST. 284:39+, August 7, 1982.

Ireland's abortion vote: the bishops and the press, by T. P. O'Mahony. AMERICA. 149:329-330, November 26, 1983.

Irish abortion bill criticized. REGISTER. 59:3, April 17, 1983.

Irish voters and their new antiabortion amendment, by J. P. McCarthy. AMERICA. 149:209-211, October 15, 1983.

The Irish will vote for life or death on September 7, by L. H.
Pumphrey. OUR SUNDAY VISITOR. 72:5, September 4,
1983.

Is abortion morally justifiable?, by S. K. Bell. NURSING FORUM.
20(3):288-295, 1981.

Is a sociology of abortion possible?, by F. A. Isambert. REVUE
FRANCAISE DE SOCIOLOGIE. 23(3):359-381, July-September 1982.

Is this drug dangerous? [depo-provera]. ESSENCE. 14:42,
July 1983.

Is tubal sterilization with the tupla-clip a reversible method?, by
B. Henkel, et al. GEBURTSHILFE UND FRAUENHEILKUNDE.
43(2):127-130, February 1983.

Isolation of leptospira interrogans serovar hardjo from aborted
bovine fetuses in England, by S. C. Hathaway, et al. VETERINARY
RECORD. 111:58, July 17, 1982.

The issue that won't go away, by M. Beck. NEWSWEEK. 101:31,
January 31, 1983.

It happens to us. LANDERS HERALD. 26(4):153, March-April 1982.

It's an ill wind. . . ECONOMIST. 286:60-61, February 5, 1983.

Japanese ceremonies show private doubts over use of abortion,
by U. C. Lehner. WALL STREET JOURNAL. January 6, 1983,
p. 1.

Jesse Helms in the dock, by B. Spring. CHRISTIANITY TODAY.
27:78+, March 4, 1983.

The judicial portrayal of the physician in abortion and sterilization
decisions: the use and abuse of medical discretion, by A. Asaro.
HARVARD WOMEN'S LAW JOURNAL. 6:51-102, Spring 1983.

Jurisdiction: the superior court possesses jurisdiction over petitions
for sterilization of incompetents—in the matter of C.D.M.
ALASKA LAW REVIEW. 11:213-221, Spring 1982.

Justice O'Connor's dissent in the Akron abortion case, by S. D. O'Connor. ORIGINS. 13:159-164, July 21, 1983.

Justification of the monitoring of early pregnancy under conditions of restricted fertility, by W. Gromadzki, et al. GINEKOLOGIA POLSKA. 53(5-6):311-320, 1982.

Kentucky's new abortion law: searching for the outer limits of permissible regulation, by K. Moorman. KENTUCKY LAW JOURNAL. 1982-1983, p. 617-646.

Killing makes me uneasy, by R. A. Hanley. NEW COVENENT. 12:17-18, June 1983.

Know your organizations: the birth control trust, by J. Roe. HEALTH VISITOR. 55(4):179, April 1982.

Know your organizations: British pregnancy advisory service, by D. Munday. HEALTH VISITOR. 55(4):179, April 1982.

Know your organizations: the Brook advisory centres. HEALTH VISITOR. 55(4):177-178, April 1982.

Knowing abortion firsthand, by M. Meehan. REGISTER. 59:1+, July 31, 1983.

LHRH and rat avoidance behavior: influence of castration and testosterone, by S. Mora, et al. PHYSIOLOGY AND BEHAVIOR. 30(1):19-22, January 1983.

LHRH found to inhibit ovulation successfully with few side effects. FAMILY PLANNING PERSPECTIVES. 15:32-34, January-February 1983.

Landmarks during the first forty-two days of gestation demonstrated by the beta-subunit of human chorionic gonadotropin and ultrasound, by F. R. Batzer, et al. AMERICAN JOURNAL OF OBSTETRICS AND GYNECOLOGY. 146(8):973-979, August 15, 1983.

Laparoscopic sterilization of women, by O. H. Jensen, et al. TIDSSKRIFT FOR DEN NORSKE LAEGEFORENING.

102(19-21):1008-1009, July 10, 1982.

Laparoscopic sterilization with the falope-ring. Preoperative and late complications, method safety and a randomized investigation of immediate postoperative abdominal pain, by K. E. Larsen, et al. ACTA OBSTETRICIA ET GYNECOLOGICA SCANDINAVICA. 62(2):125-130, 1983.

Laparoscopic sterilisation with the filshie clip under local anaesthesia, by P. Paterson. MEDICAL JOURNAL OF AUSTRALIA. 2(10):476-477, November 13, 1982.

Laparoscopic sterilizations (16,803) without vaginal manipulation, by P. V. Mehta. INTERNATIONAL JOURNAL OF GYNAE-KOLOGY AND OBSTETRICS. 20(4):323-325, August 1982.

Laparoscopic tubal coagulation—technic and follow-up results, by H. Hopp, et al. ZENTRALBLATT FUR GYNAEKOLOGIE. 105(1): 19-25, 1983.

Laparoscopic tubal sterilisation using Yoon's rings. The technique and psychological effects, by M. Dubois, et al. JOURNAL DE GYNECOLOGIE, OBSTETRIQUE ET BIOLOGIE DE LA REPRODUCTION. 11(5):611-618, 1982.

Late sequelae of sterilization in women, by E. Garner, et al. UGESKRIFT FOR LAEGER. 144(40):2935-2938, October 4, 1982.

Law and the life sciences (Roe v. Wade reaffirmed), by G. J. Annas. HASTINGS CENTER REPORT. 13:21-22, August 1983.

Law. Conditions for abortion, by J. Finch. NURSING MIRROR. 156(17):38, April 27, 1983.

The law on abortion: chronology of events and positions taken, by A. M. Devreux, et al. REVUE FRANCAISE DE SOCIOLOGIE. 23(3):503-518, July-September 1982.

Law: wrongful birth, by H. Creighton. NURSING MANAGEMENT. 14(7):41-42, July 1983.

Leads from the MMWR. Tubal sterilization—related deaths in US,

1977-1981. JOURNAL OF THE AMERICAN MEDICAL ASSOCIATION. 249(22):3011, June 10, 1983.

Learning from Roe v. Wade, by A. Verhey. REFORMED JOURNAL. 33(4):3-4, April 1983.

Legal abortion in Italy, 1978-1980 [letter to the editor], by T. Landucci, et al. THE NEW ENGLAND JOURNAL OF MEDICINE. 308(1):51-52, 1982.

Legalized abortion ten years later, by C. Schweich. MCCALLS. 110:61, January 1983.

Lesbian feminism and the pro-choice movement, by W. Kolasinska. RESOURCES FOR FEMINIST RESEARCH. 12:61-62, March 1983.

The liberal position on abortion and welfare rights, by C. Perry. METAPHILOSOPHY. 14:12-18, January 1983.

Life table analysis of birth intervals for Bangladesh, by M. Kabir, et al. JOURNAL OF FAMILY WELFARE. 29:21-32, March 1983.

Linking cancer with the pill [oral contraceptives containing synthetic progesterone]. NEWSWEEK. 102:78, October 31, 1983.

Literary but technical abortion. REVISTA DE ENFERMAGEN. 6(58-59):40-41, May-June 1983.

Lobbying for life, by C. Hays. REGISTER. 59:9, February 6, 1983.

Local application of prostaglandin F2 alpha to primigravid inter-ruption patients in first trimester, by M. Heinz, et al. ZENTRAL-BLATT FUR GYNAEKOLOGIE. 104(13):784-790, 1982.

Locus of control and the use of contraception among unmarried black adolescent fathers and their controls: a preliminary report, by L. E. Hendricks, et al. JOURNAL OF YOUTH AND ADOLESCENCE. 12:225-233, June 1983.

Long-term effects of tubal sterilization [letter], by P. A. Poma. AMERICAN JOURNAL OF OBSTETRICS AND GYNECOLOGY.

76

146(1):119-120, May 1, 1983.

Long-term oral contraceptive use and the risk of breast cancer: the centers for disease control cancer and steroid hormone study. JOURNAL OF THE AMERICAN MEDICAL ASSOCIATION. 249:1591-1595, March 25, 1983.

Long-term study of the incidence of the birth of premature fetuses in Czechoslovakia, by I. Pfeifer, et al. CESKOSLOVENSKA GYNEKOLOGIE. 48(2):83-88, March 1983.

Lore Maier's fight against abortion is real war story, by G. Pakulski. OUR SUNDAY VISITOR. 72:3, July 31, 1983.

The loss of baby Elizabeth . . . how Mary—a girl with Down's syndrome—coped with the loss of her baby, by H. Hughes, et al. NURSING MIRROR. 155(12):67-68, September 22, 1982.

Low fertility in Europe: a report from the 1981 IUSSP meeting [International Union for the Scientific Study of Population], by D. Wulf. FAMILY PLANNING PERSPECTIVES. 14:264-270, September-October 1982.

Macroscopic and microscopic changes in the fallopian tube after bipolar cauterization, by K. D. Gunston, et al. SOUTH AFRICAN MEDICAL JOURNAL. 63(14):518-519, April 2, 1983.

Maintenance of mating-induced, regulatory patterns in castrated, testosterone-treated male rats, by F. A. Weizenbaum, et al. APPETITE. 3(3):191-202, September 1982.

Make them all wanted children, by N. Mallory. HOME MAGAZINE. 18:62, 64, April 1983.

Male adolescent psychosexual development: the influence of significant others on contraceptive behavior, by D. D. Cohen. DISSERTATION ABSTRACTS INTERNATIONAL: A. 43(11), May 1983.

Male contraceptive in stomach salve, by S. Steinberg. SCIENCE NEWS. 124:117, August 20, 1983.

The male role in contraception: implications for health education, by C. L. Chng. JOURNAL OF SCHOOL HEALTH. 53:197-201, March 1983.

Male utopias or nightmares, by D. Kumar. ECONOMIC AND POLITICAL WEEKLY. 18(3):61-64, 1983.

Malthusianism, socialism and feminism in the United States, by L. Gordon. HISTORY OF EUROPEAN IDEAS. 4:203-214, 1983.

The man who would be anthropologist [S. Mosher dismissed from Stanford for article on birth control], by W. Herbert. SCIENCE NEWS. 123:252-253, April 16, 1983.

Management of missed abortion by intramuscular administration of 15(S) 15 methyl prostaglandin F2 alpha, by M. K. Mapa, et al. ASIA-OCEANIA JOURNAL OF OBSTETRICS AND GYNAE-COLOGY. 8(4):369-372, December 1982.

Managing drug interactions with oral contraceptives, by G. P. Stoehr, et al. JOURNAL OF OBSTETRIC GYNECOLOGIC AND NEONATAL NURSING. 12(5):327-331, September-October 1983.

March for life gears up for anniversary, by M. Meehan. REGISTER. 59:1+, January 16, 1983.

"March for life" marks tenth anniversary (anti-abortion demon-stration). HEALTH EDUCATION. 43(5):26, February 5, 1983.

Marital sexual relationships and birth spacing among two Yoruba sub-groups, by L. A. Adeokun. AFRICA. 52(4):1-14, 1982.

Marketing anti-abortion as pro-life. NATIONAL CATHOLIC REPORTER. 19:3, January 21, 1983.

Marriage, fertility, and family planning: summary of the major findings of the Egyptian rural fertility survey 1979. POPULA-TION STUDIES. 9:37-49, January-March 1982.

Marriage, sexuality, and contraception in the British middle class, 1918-1939. The correspondence of Marie Stopes, by E. M.

Holtzman. DISSERTATION ABSTRACTS INTERNATIONAL: A. 43(10), April 1983.

Marriage: the vision of humanae vitae, by G. D. Coleman. THOUGHT. 58:18-34, March 1983.

Marxism and Chinese population policies, by R. Wiltgen, et al. REVIEW OF RADICAL POLITICAL ECONOMY. 14:18-28, Winter 1982.

Masculinity-femininity and the desire for sexual intercourse after vasectomy: a longitudinal study, by D. Williams, et al. SOCIAL PSYCHOLOGY QUARTERLY. 43(3):347-352, September 1980.

Mass communication, cosmopolite channels, and family planning among villagers in Mexico, by F. Korzenny, et al. DEVELOPMENT AND CHANGE. 14(2):237-253, April 1983.

Maternal deaths associated with antepartum fetal death in utero, United States, 1972 to 1978, by S. F. Dorfman, et al. SOUTHERN MEDICAL JOURNAL. 76(7):838-843, July 1983.

Maternal smoking and trisomy among spontaneously aborted conceptions, by J. Kline, et al. AMERICAN JOURNAL OF HUMAN GENETICS. 35(3):421-431, May 1983.

Mating competitiveness of irradiation-substerilized males of the tobacco moth, by J. H. Brower. JOURNAL OF ECONOMIC ENTOMOLOGY. 75:454-457, June 1982.

Matters of conscience: the morning after, the night before, by B. Bardsley. NURSING MIRROR. 156(21):12-13, May 25, 1983.

Maybe you should think twice about your contraceptive. REDBOOK. 159:58+, May 1982.

The meaning and implications of "unlawful" in Canada's abortion law, by P. J. Micallef. CAHIERS DE DROIT. 88:1029-1046, December 1982.

Measuring the unmet need for contraception to space and limit births: the findings suggest a sizable unsaturated market for contraceptive services and supplies [developing countries], by D. L. Nortman. INTERNATIONAL FAMILY PLANNING PERSPECTIVES. 8:125-134, December 1982.

Medical aspects of tubal sterilization in modern planning of human reproduction, by B. M. Beric. JUGOSLAVENSKA GINE-KOLOGIJA I OPSTETRICIJA. 21(1-2):45-50, January-April 1981.

Medical association is involved, by H. Vorse. OKLAHOMA OBSERVER. 15:9, October 10, 1983.

Medical motives for induced abortion in hospital, by G. Spaziante. ANNALI DI OSTETRICIA GINECOLOGIA, MEDICINA PERINATALE. 104(1):5-30, January-February 1983.

Medical practices—abortion—Down's syndrome. THE FAMILY LAW REPORTER: COURT OPINIONS. 8(48):2733, October 12, 1982.

Medical-social aspects of the voluntary interruption of pregnancy: reflections on the routine data of an outpatient clinic, by C. Humblet, et al. REVUE DE L'INSTITUT DE SOCIOLOGIE. (3-4):477-507, 1982.

Medical termination of pregnancy act—1971—the purported and perceived purpose [India], by T. R. Sati, et al. JOURNAL OF FAMILY WELFARE. 29:33-38, March 1983.

Medical update on the pill, by M. B. Gardner. GOOD HOUSE-KEEPING. 196:89-92, June 1983.

Medicalization and social control of abortion: the issues behind the law, by M. Ferrand-Picard. REVUE FRANCAISE DE SOCIOLOGIE. 23(3):383-396, July-September 1982.

Medicalized killing in Auschwitz, by R. J. Lifton. PSYCHIATRY. 45(4):283-297, November 1982.

Medicinal plants used for abortion and childbirth in eastern Africa, by G. D. Yu. CHUNG YAO TUNG PAO. 7(5):6-7, September 1982.

Medicine and the law. The postcoital pill and intrauterine device: contraceptive or abortifacient?, by D. Brahams. LANCET. 1(8332):1039, May 7, 1983.

Medico-legal aspects of abortion, by B. Piga Sanchez-Morate. ANALES DE LA REAL ACADEMIA NACIONALE DE MEDICINA. 99(1):51-70, 1982.

Men and abortion: three neglected ethical aspects, by A. B. Shostak. HUMANITY AND SOCIETY. 7(1):66-85, February 1983.

Menarcheal age and miscarriage, by E. J. Martin, et al. AMERICAN JOURNAL OF EPIDEMIOLOGY. 117(5):634-636, May 1983.

Menarcheal age and spontaneous abortion: a casual connection? [letter], by M. J. Mayaux, et al. AMERICAN JOURNAL OF EPIDEMIOLOGY. 117(3):377-378, March 1983.

Menses induction and second-trimester pregnancy termination using a polymeric controlled release vaginal delivery system containing 15(S) 15-methyl PGF2 alpha methyl ester, by M. Bygdeman, et al. CONTRACEPTION. 27(2):141-151, February 1983.

Menstrual bleeding expectations and short-term contraceptive discontinuation in Mexico, by G. Zetina-Lozano. STUDIES IN FAMILY PLANNING. 14(5):127, May 1983.

Menstrual induction with sulproston, by A. I. Csapo, et al. PROSTAGLANDINS. 24(5):657-665, November 1982.

Menstrual pattern changes following laparoscopic sterilization [letter], by P. A. Poma. JOURNAL OF REPRODUCTIVE MEDICINE. 28(3):115-116, March 1983.

Menstrual pattern changes following laparoscopic sterilization with different occlusion techniques: a review of 10,004 cases, by P. P. Bhiwandiwala, et al. AMERICAN JOURNAL OF OBSTETRICS AND GYNECOLOGY. 145(6):684-694, March 15, 1983.

Method of predicting obstetrical complications, by G. A. Ushakova, et al. AKUSHERSTVO I GINEKOLOGIIA. (9):45-47, September 1982.

Method of sterilization using surgery of the fallopian tubes, by M. Kh. Iakhv'iaeva-Urunova. AKUSHERSTVO I GINEKOLOGIIA. (11):25-26, November 1982.

Methylmercury toxicity: in vivo evaluation of teratogenesis and cytogenetic changes, by D. C. Curle, et al. ANATOMISCHER ANZIEGER. 153(1):69-82, 1983.

Metrorrhagia after sterilization, by C. Nickelsen, et al. UGESKRIFT FOR LAEGER. 144(40):2938-2940, October 4, 1982.

Microscopic tubal reversal, by C. Fleming, et al. ASSOCIATION OF OPERATING ROOM NURSES JOURNAL. 37(2):199-204, February 1983.

Microsurgical repair of the fallopian tubes, by B. M. O'Brien, et al. AUSTRALIAN AND NEW ZEALAND JOURNAL OF SURGERY. 53(2):161-167, April 1983.

Microsurgical reversal in a patient vasectomized ten years previously, by A. L. Gaspari, et al. MINERVA UROLOGICA. 35(1):49-52, March 1983.

Microsurgical reversal of sterilization: experiences and results in 119 cases, by H. W. Schlosser, et al. GEBURTSHILFE UND FRAUENHEILKUNDE. 43(4):213-216, April 1983.

Microsurgical reversal of tubal sterilization: a review, by N. Perone. TEXAS MEDICINE. 78(11):47-54, November 1982.

Microsurgical tubal reanastomosis in a community hospital: report of a three-year study, by A. C. Wittich. JOURNAL OF THE AMERICAN OSTEOPATHIC ASSOCIATION. 82(suppl 9):695-703, May 1983.

Microsurgical vasovasostomy: an outpatient procedure under local anesthesia, by K. W. Kaye, et al. JOURNAL OF UROLOGY. 129(5):992-994, May 1983.

Micro-vasovasotomy: report of seven cases, by X. Li. CHUNG HUA
WAI KO TSA CHIH. 21(3):180, March 1983.

Midtrimester abortion by ethacridine lactate, by B. K. Goswami,
et al. JOURNAL OF THE INDIAN MEDICAL ASSOCIATION.
79(1-2):7-9, July 1982.

Midtrimester abortion by hypertonic saline instillation experience
in Ramathibodi hospital, by S. Suthutvoravut, et al. JOURNAL
OF THE MEDICAL ASSOCIATION OF THAILAND. 66(3):176-
182, March 1983.

Mid-trimester abortions: a decade in review, by M. C. Martin, et al.
CANADIAN JOURNAL OF SURGERY. 25(6):641-643,
November 1982.

Midtrimester pregnancy termination by intravaginal administration
of prostaglandin E2, by E. J. Surrago, et al. CONTRACEPTION.
26(3):285-294, September 1982.

Mini-incision for post-partum sterilization of women: a multicentred,
multinational prospective study. CONTRACEPTION. 26(5):495-
503, November 1982.

Minilaparatomy sterilization by Valtchev's uterine mobilization, by
S. Grunstein, et al. HAREFUAH. 102(7):275-276, April 1, 1982.

Minor complications relevant to anaesthetic technique following
bilateral tubal ligation, by J. P. Jayasuriya, et al. CEYLON
MEDICAL JOURNAL. 26(2):71-76, June 1981.

Minor's right to abortion, by S. McCarthy, et al. ALBERTA REPORT.
10:38, November 14, 1983.

Misbegotten referendum. ECONOMIST. 288:13, September 3, 1983.

Miscarriage: a diagnostic dilemma, by B. A. Buehler. NEBRASKA
MEDICAL JOURNAL. 68(5):143-144, May 1983.

Miscarriages and abortions affect breast-cancer risks, by S. Katz.
CHATELAINE. 56:18, July 1983.

83

Misuse of MTP, by N. Ghose. JOURNAL OF THE INDIAN MEDICAL ASSOCIATION. 80(2):32-33, January 16, 1983.

A model of fertility control in a Puerto Rican community, by S. L. Schensul, et al. URBAN ANTHROPOLOGY. 11(1):81-99, Spring 1982.

A model of premarital coitus and contraceptive behavior among female adolescents, by W. M. Strahle. ARCHIVES OF SEXUAL BEHAVIOR. 12:67, February 1983.

Modern and traditional fertility regulation in a Mexican community: the process of decision making, by M. G. Shedlin, et al. STUDIES IN FAMILY PLANNING. 12(6-7):278-296, June-July 1981.

Modernity and fertility preference in Taiwan, by K. Yamanaka, et al. SOCIOLOGICAL QUARTERLY. 23:539-552, August 1982.

Modernity value orientations, fertility and family planning, by K. P. Singh. JOURNAL OF FAMILY WELFARE. 29:84, December 1982.

Monthly birth control? [synthetic inhibitory analog of luteinizing hormone-releasing hormone]. SCIENCE DIGEST. 91:89, July 1983.

A moral dilemma for the doctors, by R. Butt. TIMES. September 29, 1983, p. 14.

Moral dilemmas that are acute within a religious tradition. A Jewish perspective, by I. Franck. HOSPITAL PRACTICE. 18(7):192-196, July 1983.

The moral disarmament of Betty Coed [reprint from September 1962 issue], by G. Steinem. ESQUIRE. 99:243+, June 1983.

Morality of contraception, by H. Rodrigues. AUSTRALASIAN NURSES JOURNAL. 11(6):28-29, July 1982.

More reading, less breeding. ECONOMIST. 284:30, August 28-September 3, 1982.

The Morgentaler file, by E. Hillen. MACLEANS. 96:44, July 18, 1983.

Morgentaler manifesto, by K. Govier. QUEST. 12:cover, 22+, October 1983.

Morgentaler moves west [abortion clinic in Winnipeg], by P. Carlyle-Gordge. MACLEANS. 96:42-43, May 16, 1983.

Morgentaler's crusade moves east [Toronto clinic opens], by C. Bruman. MACLEANS. 96:44, June 27, 1983.

The morning after . . . the night before . . . postcoital contraception, by B. Bardsley. NURSING MIRROR AND MIDWIVE'S JOURNAL. 156(21):12-13, May 25, 1983.

Morphologic and cytogenetic findings in early abortions, by H. Gocke, et al. VERHANDLUNGEN DER DEUTSCHEN GESELLSCHAFT FUR PATHOLOGIE. 66:141-146, 1982.

Morphologic changes of the vas deferens after vasectomy and vasovasostomy in dogs, by A. Hamidinia, et al. SURGERY, GYNECOLOGY AND OBSTETRICS. 156(6):737-742, June 1983.

Morphological evaluation of human fetal kidneys from spontaneous abortions, by T. Kozielec, et al. FOLIA MORPHOLOGICA. 40(2):113-121, 1981.

Mortality associated with fertility and fertility control—1983, by H. W. Ory. FAMILY PLANNING PERSPECTIVES. 15:57-63, March-April 1983.

Mortality from abortion and childbirth [letter], by A. R. Hansen. JOURNAL OF THE AMERICAN MEDICAL ASSOCIATION. 249(2):194, January 14, 1983.

Mortality from abortion and childbirth [letter], by M. J. Lanska, et al. JOURNAL OF THE AMERICAN MEDICAL ASSOCIATION. 250(3):361-362, July 15, 1983.

Mortality rates, mortality events and the number of births, by R. J.

Olsen. AMERICAN ECONOMIC REVIEW. 73:29-32, May 1983.

Mosaic trisomies in human spontaneous abortions, by T. Hassold. HUMAN GENETICS. 61(1):31-35, 1982.

Mosher's expulsion from Stanford [discussion of May 13, 1983 article, the mysterious expulsion of Steven Mosher]. SCIENCE. 220:1334+, June 24, 1983.

Moving the tubing: "parking" the fallopian tubes in the pelvic membrane makes for reversible sterilization, by V. Hewitt. HEALTH. 15(6):14, June 1983.

The Mumford affair [firing of population control researcher from family health international for anti-Catholic criticism]. HUMANIST. 43:5-10, November-December 1983.

A mutation in the mechanisms of social control: the case of abortion, by C. Horellou-Lafarge. REVUE FRANCAISE DE SOCIOLOGIE. 23(3):397-416, July-September 1982.

My two daughters' abortions, by N. Hunt. MS. 12:21-24, August 1983.

My visit to an abortion clinic, by A. Von Stamwitz. LIGUORIAN. 71:26-31, August 1983.

Mycoplasma hominis and spontaneous abortion, by E. Damianova, et al. AKUSHERSTVO I GINEKOLOGIIA. 21(6):447-451, 1982.

The mysterious expulsion of Steven Mosher [dismissal from Stanford University for article on birth control], by M. Sun. SCIENCE. 220:692-694, May 13, 1983.

NFP center reaches couples, teens, physicians, parents; St. Francis Regional Medical Center, Inc., Wichita, KS. HOSPITAL PROGRESS. 64:28+, April 1983.

NFP services in Catholic hospitals, by J. T. McHugh. LINACRE QUARTERLY. 50:246-250, August 1983.

N. Y. federal district court enjoins enforcement of HHS "squeal rule." THE FAMILY LAW REPORTER: COURT OPINIONS. 9(18):2281, March 8, 1983.

Nation's new agony over abortion, by S. Riley. MACLEANS. 96:cover, 32-35, July 25, 1983.

Natural family planning, by C. Bourdillon. CENTRAL AFRICAN JOURNAL OF MEDICINE. 28(11):284-287, November 1982.

Natural family planning: a birth control alternative, by N. Matis. JOURNAL OF NURSE-MIDWIFERY. 28(1):7-16, January-February 1983.

Natural family planning. An interview with Phyllis Jones, by G. Erlandson. REGISTER. 59:1+, July 24, 1983.

Natural family planning requires sexual maturity, by P. Cullen. OUR SUNDAY VISITOR. 72:5, November 6, 1983.

Natural means of birth control, by L. Dumas. INFIRMIERE CANADIENNE. 24(9):19-30, October 1982.

Natural or hormone-induced sexual and social behaviors in the female brown lemming (lemmus trimucronatus), by W. U. Huck, et al. HORMONES AND BEHAVIOR. 16(2):199-207, June 1982.

The need for family planning in psychiatric hospitals, by G. Holloway. NURSING TIMES. 78(49):2087-2088, December 8-14, 1982.

Need to care. INFORMATION. 5(6):111, 1982.

The need to know: recalled adolescent sources of sexual and contraceptive information and sexual behavior, by D. J. Kallen, et al. JOURNAL OF SEX RESEARCH. 19(2):137-159, May 1983.

Needle point debate: abortion referendum, by M. Holland. NEW STATESMAN. February 25, 1983, p. 11.

Never give up Helms says, as struggle for the unborn intensifies, by
   M. Meehan. REGISTER. 59:8, February 6, 1983.

Never-pregnant teenagers more effective users of contraceptives than
   those previously pregnant. FAMILY PLANNING PERSPECTIVES.
   15(3):137-138, May-June 1983.

The new biology and the question of personhood: implications
   for abortion, by T. H. Milby. AMERICAN JOURNAL OF LAW
   AND MEDICINE. 9:31-41, Spring 1983.

New Brunswick: the doctors defy antiabortion tides, by D. Folster.
   MACLEANS. 96:15, January 10, 1983.

A new class of nonhormonal pregnancy-terminating agents. Synthesis
   and contragestational activity of 3,5-diaryl-s-triazoles, by A.
   Omodei-Sale, et al. JOURNAL OF MEDICINAL CHEMISTRY.
   26(8):1187-1192, August 1983.

A new contraceptive borrows an ancient idea. BUSINESS WEEK.
   April 18, 1983, p. 42.

The new contraceptive sponge, by J. Ralston. MCCALLS. 110:48+,
   July 1983.

The new contraceptives [triphasic pill and sponge], by L. J. Sarrel,
   et al. REDBOOK. 161:20, August 1983.

New data on reproductive deaths. SCIENCE DIGEST. 91:91,
   March 1983.

New guidelines on counseling in family planning. KATILOLEHIT.
   87(7-8):249-251, August 1982.

New insurance law could mandate abortion coverage. OUR SUNDAY
   VISITOR. 72:8, May 29, 1983.

New Jersey limit on medicaid for abortions is held unconstitutional.
   THE FAMILY LAW REPORTER: COURT OPINIONS.
   8(44):2660-2661, September 14, 1982.

New look at happiness. BEIJING REVIEW. 26:27-28, February 14,
   1983.

New male contraceptive, by S. Katz. CHATELAINE. 56:18, December 1983.

New oral contraceptive [triphasil] , by S. Katz. CHATELAINE. 56:16, June 1983.

New population policies, by L. R. Brown. ENVIRONMENT. 25:32-33, July-August 1983.

New problems in congress for the antiabortions, by B. Spring. CHRISTIANITY TODAY. 27:60-61+, February 4, 1983.

New prolife initiatives, by M. Meehan. REGISTER. 59:1+, February 20, 1983.

New prospects for luteinising hormone releasing hormone as a contraceptive and therapeutic agent, by H. M. Fraser. BRITISH MEDICAL JOURNAL. 6347:990-991, October 9, 1982.

New row looms over birth jab, by F. Lesser, et al. NEW SCIENTIST. 99:256, July 28, 1983.

A new squeal rule, by C. Leslie. NEWSWEEK. 101:24, February 7, 1983.

New synthetic laminaria, by M. Chvapil, et al. OBSTETRICS AND GYNECOLOGY. 60(6):729-733, December 1982.

New technique for microscopic vasovasostomy, by S. A. Leonard, et al. UROLOGY. 22(2):188-189, August 1983.

New vaginal [suppository] contraceptive, by S. Katz. CHATELAINE. 56:16, May 1983.

New version of Hatch amendment clears first hurdle. OUR SUNDAY VISITOR. 71:8, April 10, 1983.

1980 synod: about birth control, some compassion, by P. Hebblethwaite. NATIONAL CATHOLIC REPORTER. 20:18, October 28, 1983.

Nobody wants an abortion, by M. B. Gordon. COMMONWEAL.

110:557-558, October 21, 1983.

A nonsurgical method for sterilization [plastic-like plug], by D. Winston. VENTURE. 5:19+, September 1983.

Normal pregnancy with circulating anticoagulant after spontaneous abortion. Soulier - Boffa syndrome [letter], by J. H. Cohen, et al. NOUVELLE PRESSE MEDICALE. 11(51):3795, December 18, 1982.

Normative boundaries and abortion policy: the politics of morality, by S. L. Markson. RESEARCH IN SOCIAL PROBLEMS AND PUBLIC POLICY. 2:21-33, 1982.

Not tonight, by H. M. White. INFORMATION. 1:16, 1982.

Note of desired family size and contraceptive use in rural Egypt, by C. S. Stokes, et al. JOURNAL OF BIOSOCIAL SCIENCES. 15(1):59-65, January 1983.

Notice to parents not required when minors seek contraceptives. THE FAMILY LAW REPORT: COURT OPINIONS. 9(37):2552, July 28, 1983.

Nun defended as head of agency funding abortions, by T. Ewald. OUR SUNDAY VISITOR. 71:8, January 30, 1982.

The nuns' revolt: Sister Agnes Mary Mansour: her vow to the people, by M. K. Blakely. MS. 12:54+, September 1983.

The nurse-midwife in a contraceptive program for adolescents, by G. Callender-Green, et al. JOURNAL OF AMBULATORY CARE MANAGEMENT. 6(2):57-65, May 1983.

Nutritional status of women attending family planning clinics, by D. A. Roe, et al. JOURNAL OF THE AMERICAN DIETETIC ASSOCIATION. 81(6):682-687, December 1982.

Obey or leave [A. Mansour leaves Sister of Mercy in order to remain director of Michigan's Dept. of Social Serivces]. TIME. 121:57, May 23, 1983.

Obstetric histories of women occupationally exposed to styrene, by H. Harkonen, et al. SCANDINAVIAN JOURNAL OF WORK, ENVIRONMENT AND HEALTH. 8(1):74-77, March 1982.

Occurrence of IgM antibodies against cytomegalovirus-induced late antigens in women with imminent abortion in comparison to women with normal pregnancy, by L. Gartner, et al. ZENTRALBLATT FUR GYNAEKOLOGIE. 104(16):1005-1008, 1982.

Oh, those filthy spots (laws banning advertising of contraceptives on television). PROGRESSIVE. 46:9-10, April 1982.

Old age pensions and fertility in rural areas of less developed countries: some evidence from Mexico, by J. B. Nugent, et al. ECONOMIC DEVELOPMENT AND CULTURAL CHANGE. 31:809-829, July 1983.

On aborting the constitution [senate vote on Hatch amendment], by W. F. Buckley. NATIONAL REVIEW. 35:960, August 5, 1983.

On abortion, by B. Greenberg. HADASSAH MAGAZINE. 64:19-21+, October 1982.

On abortion: sorting out the questions - a Lutheran contribution to the public policy debate, by R. W. Jenson. LUTHERAN FORAM. 17(1):9-12+, 1983.

On Gutmann, moral philosophy and political problems, by P. Abbott. POLITICAL THEORY. 10:606-609, November 1982.

On trial again. Depo-provera. ECONOMIST. 287:110, April 30, 1983.

On trial: nursing, by A. J. Kellett. MISSOURI NURSE. 51(3):2-3, June-July 1982.

One day you will understand . . . having an abortion. NURSING MIRROR AND MIDWIVE'S JOURNAL. 157(8): midwifery forum 8:xi-xii, August 24, 1983.

One-fourth of the world is large enough. BEIJING REVIEW. 25:8, December 6, 1982.

One from Egypt [disposable contraceptive sponge]. TIME. 121:48-49, March 28, 1983.

One shot too many [depo-provera]. PROGRESSIVE. 47:11-12, March 1983.

One's good, two's enough, by S. Fraser. FAR EASTERN ECONOMIC REVIEW. 117:18-19, July 9-15, 1982.

Ontario law on family planning classes causes uproar. OUR SUNDAY VISITOR. 71:8, March 6, 1983.

Open to debate . . . abortion . . . nurses should be involved in open debate, by A. Webber. NURSING MIRROR AND MIDWIVE'S JOURNAL. 157(4):38-40, July 27, 1983.

Operating on the fetus, by W. Ruddick, et al. HASTINGS CENTER REPORT. 12:10-14, October 1982.

Opinions of the United States supreme court: abortion. THE CRIMINAL LAW REPORTER: TEXT NO. 10. 33(11):3143-3159, June 15, 1983.

Opposition should not gloat, Hyde tells pro-lifers. OUR SUNDAY VISITOR. 72:8, July 24, 1983.

Opting for adoption—dispelling the myths, by B. Maschinot. NATIONAL CATHOLIC REPORTER. 19:2, January 21, 1983.

Oral contraception, coital frequency and the time required to conceive, by C. F. Westoff, et al. SOCIAL BIOLOGY. 29:157-167, Spring-Summer 1982.

Oral contraception: selection and management, by J. C. Bartosch. NURSE PRACTITIONER. 8(5):56-63, 79, May 1983.

Oral contraceptive medication in prevention of psychotic exacerbations associated with phases of the menstrual cycle, by A. R. Felthons, et al. JOURNAL OF PREVENTIVE PSYCHOLOGY.

1(1):5-15, 1981.

The oral contraceptive pill: use, user satisfaction, side effects and fears among Manawatu women, by A. D. Trlin, et al. NEW ZEALAND MEDICAL JOURNAL. 95(717):700-703, October 13, 1982.

Oral contraceptive use and the risk of endometrial cancer: the centers for disease control cancer and steroid hormone study, by B. S. Hulka. JOURNAL OF THE AMERICAN MEDICAL ASSOCIATION. 249:1600-1604, March 25, 1983.

Oral contraceptive use and the risk of ovarian cancer: the centers for disease control cancer and steroid hormone study. JOURNAL OF THE AMERICAN MEDICAL ASSOCIATION. 249:1596-1599, March 25, 1983.

Oral contraceptives and fibrinolysis among female cyclists before and after exercise, by I. A. Huisveld, et al. JOURNAL OF APPLIED PHYSIOLOGY. 53:330-334, August 1982.

Oral contraceptives and rheumatoid arthritis: further epidemiologic evidence for a protective effect, by J. P. Vandenbroncke. DISSERTATION ABSTRACTS INTERNATIONAL: B. 44(1), July 1983.

Oral contraceptives can increase the potency of diazepam. NURSES DRUG ALERT. 7(3):17, March 1983.

Oral contraceptives: the good news. JOURNAL OF THE AMERICAN MEDICAL ASSOCIATION. 249:1624-1625, March 25, 1983.

Oral contraceptives: the latest facts on their benefits and risks, by D. R. Mishell, Jr. CONSULTANT. 23(4):139-143, April 1983.

Oregon rule permitting state funding of only some abortions found invalid. THE FAMILY LAW REPORTER: COURT OPINIONS. 9(32):2488-2489, June 14, 1983.

Orientations toward voluntary childlessness, by F. E. Baum. JOURNAL OF BIOSOCIAL SCIENCE. 15:153-164, April 1983.

An original method of reversible surgical sterilization of women: salpingodeviation, by I. Terzi, et al. MINERVA GINECOLOGICA. 34(10):797-802, October 1982.

Other milestones [letter], by L. G. Keith, et al. FERTILITY AND STERILITY. 40(2):272-273, August 1983.

Our experiences with early vacuum aspiration (miniinterruption), by K Poradovsky, et al. BRATISLAVSKE LEKARSKE LISTY. 78(1):74-78, July 1982.

Outcrossings in Caucasians and fetal loss, by J. B. Bresler. SOCIAL BIOLOGY. 29(1-2):121-130, Spring-Summer 1982.

Oxidative deamination of different amines in the placenta in spontaneous abortions and premature labor, by N. I. Miskevich, et al. AKUSHERSTVO I GINEKOLOGIIA. (3):41-43, 1983.

POP . . . progestogen-only pill, by L. Pyle, et al. NURSING TIMES. 79(4):64-66, January 26-February 1, 1983.

Palaces of advice . . . results of a survey on where people obtain family planning advice and reasons for their choice, by J. Bunting. NURSING MIRROR AND MIDWIVE'S JOURNAL. 156(3):community forum 1:34-36, January 19, 1983.

Panel upholds dismissal of Mosher [alleged misconduct while conducting field research], by M. Sun. SCIENCE. 221:348, July 22, 1983.

A paracentric chromosomal inversion associated with repeated early pregnancy wastage, by G. Stetten, et al. FERTILITY AND STERILITY. 40(1):124-126, July 1983.

Parental notification and abortion: a review and recommendation to West Virginia's legislature. WEST VIRGINIA LAW REVIEW. 85:943-968, Summer 1983.

Parental origin of chromosome abnormalities in spontaneous abortions, by G. H. Meulenbroek, et al. HUMAN GENETICS. 62(2):129-133, 1982.

Parents must be notified after minors receive birth control pills or devices. THE FAMILY LAW REPORTER: COURT OPINIONS. 9(14):2223-2224, February 8, 1983.

Parents', teenagers' rights clash in "squeal" rule, by R. Mortimer, et al. AMERICAN NURSE. 15(6):5, 19, June 1983.

Participate or not? . . . how nurses have become increasingly involved in carrying out pregnancy terminations, by J. Finch. NURSING MIRROR AND MIDWIVE'S JOURNAL. 156(18):38, May 4, 1983.

Patient, physician, society: whose rights control life issues?, by R. A. Carlson. HOSPITAL PROGRESS. 63(12):53-59, December 1982.

Patient profile, national reporting system for family planning services: United States, 1978, by J. E. Foster. ADVANCE DATA. (73):1-6, June 24, 1981.

Patterns of contraceptive use in Kingston and St. Andrew, Jamaica, 1970-1977, by W. Bailey, et al. SOCIAL SCIENCE AND MEDICINE. 16(19):1675-1683, 1982.

Patterns of contraceptive use among female adolescents: method consistency in a clinic setting, by M. Gorosh. JOURNAL OF ADOLESCENT HEALTH CARE. 3(2):96-102, September 1982.

Pelivc inflammatory disease associated with chlamydia trachomatis infection after therapeutic abortion. A prospective study, by E. Qvigstad, et al. BRITISH JOURNAL OF VENEREAL DISEASE. 59(3):189-192, June 1983.

Pennsylvania anti-abortion law in court, by T. Dejanikus. OFF OUR BACKS. 13:18, February 1983.

People and resources: a reappraisal, by A. Nevett. MONTH. 16:163-167, May 1983.

Perceptions of family planning among rural Kenyan women, by T. E. Dow, et al. STUDIES IN FAMILY PLANNING. 14:35-42, February 1983.

Perforation risk greater when IUD's are inserted in breastfeeding women. FAMILY PLANNING PERSPECTIVES. 15(3):138-140, May-June 1983.

Pericentric inversion of chromosome 6 in women with spontaneous abortions, by A. Andreev, et al. AKUSHERSTVO I GINE-KOLOGIIA. 22(1):14-16, 1983.

Perinatal mortality: changes in the diagnostic panorama 1974-1980, by O. Lofgren, et al. ACTA PAEDIATRICA SCANDINAVICA. 72(3):327-332, May 1983.

Personal conscience and abortion, by J. W. Baker. SOCIAL JUSTICE REVIEW. 74:63, March-April 1983.

Personality factors, self-concept, and family variables related to first time and repeat abortion seeking behavior in adolescent women, by M. B. Deutsch. DISSERTATION ABSTRACTS INTERNATIONAL: A. 43(10), April 1983.

Personhood and the contraceptive right. INDIANA LAW JOURNAL. 57:579-604, Fall 1982.

Personhood, property rights and the permissibility of abortion, by P. A. Roth. LAW AND PHILOSOPHY. 2:163-192, August 1983.

Perspectives on family and fertility in developing countries, by M. Cain. POPULATION STUDIES. 36(2):159, July 1982.

Pharmacokinetics and pharmacodynamics of local analgesia for laparoscopic tubal ligations, by F. J. Spielman, et al. AMERICAN JOURNAL OF OBSTETRICS AND GYNECOLOGY. 146(7):821-824, August 1, 1983.

The Philippine population program. NEWSETTE. 21(4):18-20, October-December 1981.

Phone book discounts for abortion raise pro-life ire. OUR SUNDAY VISITOR. 71:8, December 5, 1982.

Physicians vs. auxiliary nurse-midwives as providers of IUD services—a study in Turkey and the Philippines, by N. Eren, et al. STUDIES

IN FAMILY PLANNING. 14:43-47, February 1983.

The pill: a closer look, by J. Dickerson. AMERICAN JOURNAL OF NURSING. 83(10):1392-1398, October 1983.

Pill cuts arthritis, ovarian cancer risk, doesn't cause gallbladder disease, raises stroke risk slightly. FAMILY PLANNING PERSPECTIVES. 15:36-37, January-February 1983.

The pill for men: bad news, good news—or no news?, by J. Kelly. MADEMOISELLE. 89:210+, September 1983.

The pill in various countries, by P. D. Bardis. REVUE INTERNATIONALE DE SOCIOLOGIE. 18(1-3):128-135, April-December 1982.

The pill revisited: new cancer link?, by J. Silberner. SCIENCE NEWS. 124:279, October 29, 1983.

The "pill scare" and fertility in England and Wales, by M. Bone. INTERNATIONAL PLANNED PARENTHOOD FEDERATION MEDICAL BULLETIN. 16(4):2, August 1982.

The pill: what's a woman to do?, by M. Wallace, et al. SUNDAY TIMES. October 23, 1983, p. 15, 18.

Planned fertility of one-couple/one-child policy in the people's republic of China, by L. J. Huang. JOURNAL OF MARRIAGE AND THE FAMILY. 44:775-784, August 1982.

Planned parenthood affiliates served 1.5 million in 1981. FAMILY PLANNING PERSPECTIVES. 15(3):136, May-June 1983.

Planned parenthood attacks a parent's need to know, by K. S. Kantzer. CHRISTIANITY TODAY. 27:11-13, May 20, 1983.

Planned parenthood, Shandong style. BEIJING REVIEW. 26:24-26, February 14, 1983.

Planning for people, by R. Lawton. GEOGRAPHICAL MAGAZINE. 55:390-392, August 1983.

Plasma creatine kinase and myoglobin levels, before and after abortion, in human fetuses at risk for Duchenne muscular dystrophy, by R. J. Edwards, et al. AMERICAN JOURNAL OF MEDICAL GENETICS. 15(3):475-482, July 1983.

Plasma levels of 9-deoxo-16, 16-dimethyl-9-methylene-PGE2 in connection with its development as an abortifacient, by K. Green, et al. PROSTAGLANDINS. 24(4):451-466, October 1982.

Plasma lidocaine levels following paracervical infiltration for aspiration abortion, by L. J. Blanco, et al. OBSTETRICS AND GYNECOLOGY. 60(4):506-508, October 1982.

Policy analysis of fertility and contraceptive behavior in Bangladesh. WORLD BANK RESEARCH NEWS. 4(1):24-25, Spring 1983.

Policy implementation and community linkages: hospital abortion services after Roe v. Wade, by C. A. Johnson, et al. WESTERN POLITICAL QUARTERLY. 35(3):385-405, September 1982.

Policy implementation and responsiveness in nongovernmental institutions: hospital abortion services after Roe v. Wade, by C. A. Johnson, et al. WESTERN POLITICAL QUARTERLY. 35:385-405, September 1982.

Politics of abortion: a Morgentaler invitation embitters Calgary aldermen, by C. Hayes, et al. ALBERTA REPORT. 10:11, 13, April 11, 1983.

Pope's role in Mansour case tied to abortion issue. OUR SUNDAY VISITOR. 72:8, May 29, 1983.

Population and family planning in Mexico: progress and problems, by D. Wulf. INTERNATIONAL FAMILY PLANNING PERSPECTIVES. 8:135-140, December 1982.

Population growth and the policy of nations [developing countries; emphasis on India], by R. E. Benedick. DEPARTMENT OF STATE BULLETIN. 82:53-56, December 1982.

Population lid: China cajoles families and offers incentives to reduce birth rate; but one-child policy stirs resistance, hasn't ended the preference for sons, by A. Bennett. WALL STREET JOURNAL. 202:1+, July 6, 1983.

Population reports. Community-based health and family planning, by A. J. Kols, et al. POPULATION REPORTS SERIES L. (3):77-111, November-December 1982.

Post-abortion counselling, by G. Cooper. NURSING MIRROR AND MIDWIVE'S JOURNAL. 157(8):Midwifery forum 8:i-xi, August 24, 1983.

Post-cesarean ovarian transposition as a method of reversible sterilization: initial study, by V. Ruiz Velasco, et al. GINE-COLOGIA Y OBSTETRICIA DE MEXICO. 50(297):1-3, January 1982.

Postcoital antifertility effect on piperine, by P. Piyachaturawat, et al. CONTRACEPTION. 26(6):625-633, December 1982.

Postcoital contraception or abortion? [letter]. LANCET. 2(8343): 223, July 23, 1983.

Post-election reflections [November 2, 1982], by J. Sobran. CENTER JOURNAL. 2(1):115-120, Winter 1982.

Post-hysterectomy adaptation: a review and report of two follow-up studies, by B. Singh, et al. AUSTRALIAN AND NEW ZEALAND JOURNAL OF PSYCHIATRY. 17:227-236, September 1983.

Postpartum lactational amenorrhoea as a means of family planning in the Sudan: a study of 500 cases, by A. D. Adnan, et al. JOURNAL OF BIOSOCIAL SCIENCE. 15:9-24, January 1983.

Postpartum tubal ligation by nurse—midwives in Thailand: a field trial, by S. Satyapan, et al. STUDIES IN FAMILY PLANNING. 14(4):115-118, April 1983.

Postsalpingectomy endometriosis: a reassessment, by R. J. Stock. OBSTETRICS AND GYNECOLOGY. 60(5):560-570, November 1982.

Practical contribution of examination of the products of abortion, by E. Philippe. ANNALES DE PATHOLOGIE. 3(1):73-78, 1983.

Prairie storm, by E. Mandell. BOOKLIST. 79(5):398, November 1, 1982.

Predicted senate loss may bring final pro-life win closer, by R. B. Shaw. OUR SUNDAY VISITOR. 72:5, June 19, 1983.

Predictors of abortion attitudes in the federal republic of Germany, by J. S. Legge, Jr. JOURNAL OF POLITICS. 45(3):759-766, August 1983.

Pregnancy after tubal occlusion. A five-year study, by K. D. Gunston, et al. SOUTH AFRICAN MEDICAL JOURNAL. 63(14):517-518, April 2, 1983.

Pregnancy-associated plasma protein A in the prediction of early pregnancy failure, by J. G. Westergaard, et al. AMERICAN JOURNAL OF OBSTETRICS AND GYNECOLOGY. 145(1):67-69, January 1, 1983.

Pregnancy complicated by periarteritis nodosa: induced abortion as an alternative, by D. A. Nagey, et al. AMERICAN JOURNAL OF OBSTETRICS AND GYNECOLOGY. 147(1):103-105, September 1, 1983.

Pregnancy failure in the red-backed vole, clethrionomys gapperi, by F. V. Clulow, et al. JOURNAL OF MAMMALOGY. 63:499-500, August 1982.

Pregnancy in early and late adolescence, by D. de Anda. JOURNAL OF YOUTH AND ADOLESCENCE. 12:33-42, February 1983.

Pregnancy in teenagers-a comparative study, by D. Krishnamoni, et al. PSYCHIATRIC JOURNAL OF THE UNIVERSITY OF OTTAWA. 8(4):202-207, December 1983.

Pregnancy interception with a combination of prostaglandins: studies in monkeys, by J. W. Wilks. SCIENCE. 221:1407-1409, September 30, 1983.

Pregnancy interruption from the pediatric viewpoint, by A. Rett. GEBURTSHILFE UND FRAUENHEILKUNDE. 43(4):259-262, April 1983.

Pregnancy maintenance after early luteectomy by 17-hydroxy-progesterone-capronate, by M. O. Pulkkinen. ACTA OBSTETRICIA ET GYNECOLOGICA SCANDINAVICA. 61(4):347-349, 1982.

Pregnancy-terminating action of a luteinizing hormone-releasing hormone agonist D-Ser(But)6desGly10ProEA in baboons, by C. Das, et al. FERTILITY AND STERILITY. 39(2):218-223, February 1983.

Pregnancy termination by prostaglandin F_{2a} stimulates maternal behavior in the rat, by J. F. Rodriguez-Sierva, et al. HORMONES AND BEHAVIOR. 16(3):343-351, September 1982.

Pregnant? No thanks! . . . nine women discuss their experiences. NURSING MIRROR AND MIDWIVE'S JOURNAL. 156(4): Clinical forum 1:33-37, January 26, 1983.

Pregnant women's attitudes toward the abortion of defective fetuses, by R. Faden, et al. POPULATION AND ENVIRONMENT. 6(4):197-209, 1983.

Prenatal testing for Tay-Sachs disease in the light of Jewish views regarding abortion, by J. Baskin. ISSUES IN HEALTH CARE OF WOMEN. 4(1):41-56, January-February 1983.

Preoperative cervical dilatation by vaginal pessaries containing prostaglandin E1 analogue, by J. K. Chen, et al. OBSTETRICS AND GYNECOLOGY. 62(3):339-342, September 1983.

Pre-operative cervical dilatation in termination of first trimester pregnancies using 16, 16-dimethyl-trans-delta 2 PGE1 methyl ester vaginal pessaries, by P. C. Ho, et al. CONTRACEPTION. 27(4):339-346, April 1983.

A prescription for concern: depo-provera. GUARDIAN. April 29, 1983, p. 15.

President Reagan authors anti-abortion article. CHRISTIANITY

TODAY. 27:42-43, June 17, 1983.

Presidential pen [R. Reagan's anti-abortion article published in Human Life Review]. TIME. 121:36, May 9, 1983.

Prevention of unwanted pregnancy, by M. Gerrard, et al. AMERICAN JOURNAL OF COMMUNITY PSYCHOLOGY. 11(2):153-167, April 1983.

Priests and politics, by M. Holland. NEW STATESMAN. September 2, 1983, p. 13-14.

Primary health care and community-based family planning. POPULATION REPORTS. (3):79, November-December 1982.

Principles in conflict [appointment of Sister A. Mansour to the Dept. of Social Services in Michigan]. AMERICA. 148:409-410, May 28, 1983.

Principles of examination and treatment in missed abortion, missed labor, by L. V. Timoshenko, et al. AKUSHERSTVO I GINE-KOLOGIIA. (1):56-57, 1983.

Principles to be considered in fertility control, by E. Donache. AUSTRALASIAN NURSES JOURNAL. 11(7):1, August 1982.

Prior contraceptive attempts among pregnant black adolescents, by B. H. Wade. DISSERTATION ABSTRACTS INTERNATIONAL: A. 44(6), December 1983.

Priorities in relation to abortion [letter], by S. R. Belton. AMERICAN JOURNAL OF OBSTETRICS AND GYNECOLOGY. 144(6):736-738, November 15, 1982.

Probability of another child in Costa Rica, by M. P. Shiedls, et al. ECONOMIC DEVELOPMENT AND CULTURAL CHANGE. 31:787-807, July 1983.

The problem of abortion in patients with heart surgery, by E. Revelli, et al. MINERVA MEDICA. 73(44):3163-3167, November 17, 1982.

Problem of unmarried mothers (a study of sociopsychological aspects of 100 women seeking MTP), by K. T. Mandal. JOURNAL OF THE INDIAN MEDICAL ASSOCIATION. 79(5-6):81-86, September 1982.

Problems in indications for abortion in psychiatry, by J. Pogady, et al. BRATISLAVSKE LEKARSKE LISTY. 79(3):353-359, 1983.

Production versus reproduction: a threat to China's development strategy, by E. J. Croll. WORLD DEVELOPMENT. 11:467-481, June 1983.

Progestereone and testosterone: contraceptive and immunosuppressive effects in mice, by Z. Pokorna, et al. ENDOKRINOLOGIE. 79(2):185-189, 1982.

Progesterone levels before and after laparoscopic tubal sterilization using endotherm coagulation, by G. Helm, et al. ACTA OBSTETRICIA ET GYNECOLOGICA SCANDINAVICA. 62(1):63-66, 1983.

Progestogen implicated in slight blood pressure rise among pill users. FAMILY PLANNING PERSPECTIVES. 15:88-89, March-April 1983.

Prognostic value of plasma progesterone-R. I. A. in threatened abortion, by D. Marchesoni, et al. CLINICAL AND EXPER-IMENTAL OBSTETRICS AND GYNECOLOGY. 9(1):42-45, 1982.

Project redirection results in better method use, fewer 2nd pregnancies among teenage parents. FAMILY PLANNING PERSPECTIVES. 14(6):335-336, November-December 1982.

The prolife agenda: converts or convicts?, by R. E. Burns. US CATHOLIC. 48:2, April 1983.

Prolife bill moves ahead, by M. Meehan. REGISTER. 59:1+, May 22, 1983.

Prolife clause heats ERA debate. REGISTER. 59:2, September 4, 1983.

Prolife compassion or crusade?, by J. Evans. AMERICA. 147:373-374, December 11, 1982.

Pro-life groups plan for 1984, by J. T. Beifuss. NATIONAL CATHOLIC REPORTER. 19:8, July 15, 1983.

Pro-life or pro-choice? CANADA AND THE WORLD. 48:7-9, May 1983.

Prolife, prochoice groups claim midterm election victories, by J. Castelli. HOSPITAL PROGRESS. 63:18-19, December 1982.

Pro-life, pro-uniformity, by M. Holland. NEW STATESMAN. 103:12-13, May 21, 1982.

Prolifers facing stiffer jail terms, by D. Goldkamp. REGISTER. 59:1+, June 19, 1983.

The pro-lifers fight on, by J. G. Deedy. TABLET. 237:747-748, August 6, 1983.

Pro-lifers, foes clash at fair, by C. Fugere. NATIONAL CATHOLIC REPORTER. 20:4, November 11, 1983.

Prolifers react to Hatch, by R. Bautch. REGISTER. 59:10, July 17, 1983.

Prolifers will accept heckler, by C. Hays. REGISTER. 59:1+, February 27, 1983.

Promotion of birth spacing on Idjwi Island, Zaire, by M. Carael, et al. STUDIES IN FAMILY PLANNING. 14(5):134-142, May 1983.

Prospects for autosterilisation of tsetse flies, glossina ssp (diptera: glossinidae), using sex pheromone and bisazir in the field, by P. A. Langley, et al. BULLETIN OF ENTOMOLOGICAL RESEARCH. 72:319-327, June 1982.

Prospects of pregnancy following induced and spontaneous abortion of primigravidae and assessment of fertility, by G. Schott, et al. ZENTRALBLATT FUR GYNAEKOLOGIE. 104(7):397-404, 1982.

Prostitutes and contraceptives. SOCIETY. 20:2-3, May-June 1983.

Protection of the unborn child . . . legal principles which relate to the preservation of human life, by J. Finch. NURSING MIRROR AND MIDWIVE'S JOURNAL. 156(16):33, April 20, 1983.

Providing maternal and child health-family planning services to a large rural population: results of the Bohol project, Philippines, by N. E. Williamson, et al. AMERICAN JOURNAL OF PUBLIC HEALTH. 73(1):62-71, January 1983.

The provision of birth control services to unwed minors: a national survey of physician attitudes and practices, by E. D. Boldt, et al. CANADIAN JOURNAL OF PUBLIC HEALTH. 73(6):392-395, November-December 1982.

Psychic disorders following induced abortion, by D. Langer. POLSKI TYGODNIK LEKARSKI. 37(11):305-308, May 10, 1982.

Psychodynamics of the desire for refertilization in women after sexual sterilization, by S. Davies-Osterkamp, et al. GEBURTSHILFE UND FRAUENHEILKUNDE. 43(5):313-320, May 1983.

Psychologic approach to voluntary termination of pregnancy, by M. T. Aussilloux, et al. ANNALES MEDICO-PSYCHOLOGIQUES. 140(8):896-923, September-October 1982.

Psychological aspects of family planning, by K. D. Bledin. MIDWIFE, HEALTH VISITOR AND COMMUNITY NURSE. 18(12):518, 522-523, December 1982.

Psychological aspects of miscarriage, by G. B. Bjork. KATILOLEHTI. 88(3):108-111, March 1983.

Psychological conditions in pregnancy and the puerperium and their relevance to postpartum sterilization: a review, by K. D. Bledin, et al. BULLETIN OF THE WORLD HEALTH ORGANIZATION. 61(3):533-544, 1983.

Psychological correlates of contraceptive behavior in late adolescent women, by R. J. Ma. DISSERTATION ABSTRACTS INTER-

NATIONAL: B. 44(5), November 1983.

Psychological issues arising from the development of new male contraceptives, by A. E. Reading, et al. BULLETIN OF THE BRITISH PSYCHOLOGICAL SOCIETY. 35:369-371, October 1982.

Psychological issues in contraceptive sterilisation, by K. D. Bledin. MIDWIFE, HEALTH VISITOR AND COMMUNITY NURSE. 19(1):6, 10-11, January 1983.

Psychological problems of pregnant women under special medical care, by M. Beisert, et al. GINEKOLOGIA POLSKA. 53(11):721-732, 1982.

Psychological sequelae from induced abortion: a follow-up study of women who seek postabortion counseling, by M. K. Hendricks-Matthews. DISSERTATION ABSTRACTS INTERNATIONAL: B. 44(5), November 1983.

Psychopathologic dynamics following abortion, or the Niobe syndrome of modern times, by R. Peltonen, et al. PRAXIS DER KINDERPSYCHOLOGIE UND KINDERPSYCHIATRIE. 32(4): 125-128, May-June 1983.

Psychosocial determinants of abortion attitudes among Mexican American women, by A. Hortensia de Los Angeles. DISSER-TATION ABSTRACTS INTERNATIONAL: B. 43(10), April 1983.

Public attitudes toward life and death, by D. O. Sawyer. PUBLIC OPINION QUARTERLY. 46(4):521-533, Winter 1982.

The public health implications of abortion, by C. W. Tyler, Jr. ANNUAL REVIEW OF PUBLIC HEALTH. 4:223-258, 1983.

Public opinion reflects secularization, rationalization, by W. J. Monahan. HOSPITAL PROGRESS. 63(12):65-69, December 1982.

Public policies and family outcomes: empirical evidence or theology?, by S. L. Zimmerman. SOCIAL CASEWORK. 64(3):138-146,1983.

Public policy and female sterilization in Costa Rica, by M. Gomez Barrantes, et al. STUDIES IN FAMILY PLANNING. 14(10): 246-252, 1983.

Public views abortion, by J. Mann. OKLAHOMA OBSERVER. 14:3, November 10, 1982.

Publicizing abortion: more knowledge, more controversy, by N. Kwan. OFF OUR BACKS. 13:10-11, July 1983.

Pyrrhic victory: the Irish abortion referendum, by O. O'Leary. SPECTATOR. September 17, 1983, p. 12, 14.

Progress in controlling population growth in Asia, by G. Jones. AUSTRALIAN FOREIGN AFFAIRS RECORD. 53:760-763, December 1982.

A pyrrhic victory; disarray over abortion, by P. Kirby. COMMON-WEAL. 110:517-519, October 7, 1983.

Quality of object relations in abortion seeking, in teleo-cyesis and never-pregnant adolescents, by E. D. Hibbs. DISSERTATION ABSTRACTS INTERNATIONAL: B. 44(3), September 1983.

Quantitative effect of family planning programme in India (1965-1976), by A. S. Mohammad, et al. INDIAN JOURNAL OF PUBLIC HEALTH. 25(3):111-116, July-September 1981.

The quest for the male pill, by J. Langone. DISCOVER. 3(10):26, October 1982.

The quest for the male pill, by G. Youcha. SCIENCE DIGEST. 90:33+, March 1982.

Question and answers about female sterilization . . . patient education aid. PATIENT CARE. 17(9):147-148, May 15, 1983.

Question: I've recently heard that you can buy condoms coated with spermicide. CANADIAN CONSUMER. 13:6, May 1983.

Questioning the ideal [depo-provera]. CONSUMER'S RESEARCH MAGAZINE. 66:4, March 1983.

Questions women ask about birth control, by L. J. Sarrel, et al. REDBOOK. 161:35, June 1983.

Rabbit oviduct microvascular architecture after tubal ligation, by C. J. Verco, et al. FERTILITY AND STERILITY. 40(1):127-130, July 1983.

Race-specific patterns of abortion use by American teenagers, by N. V. Ezzard, et al. AMERICAN JOURNAL OF PUBLIC HEALTH. 72:809-814, August 1982.

Racism and sexism in Nazi Germany: motherhood, compulsory sterilization and the state, by G. Bock. SIGNS. 8(3):400-421, 1983.

A raid in the abortion war [H. Morgentaler's clinic in Winnipeg], by V. Ross. MACLEANS. 96:21, June 13, 1983.

Randomized comparative study of culdoscopy and minilaparotomy for surgical contraception in women. CONTRACEPTION. 26(6):587-593, December 1982.

Rape and abortion in America [dismissal of teacher and rape victim J. Eckmann for deciding to keep her baby in McHenry county, Ill], by L. M. Delloff. CHRISTIAN CENTURY. 99:1037-1038, October 20, 1982.

A rare complication following the insertion of a bleier-secu-clip, by W. Behrendt. GEBURTSHILFE UND FRAUENHEILKUNDE. 43(4):248-249, April 1983.

Rationalizing the abortion debate: legal rhetoric and the abortion controversy, by E. Chemerinsky. BUFFALO LAW REVIEW. 31(1):107-164, 1982.

Reanastomosis of the vas deferens: techniques and results, by S. S. Schmidt. CLINICAL OBSTETRICS AND GYNECOLOGY. 25(3):533-540, September 1982.

Reagan addresses religious broadcasters, condemns abortion. REGISTER. 59:2, February 13, 1983.

Reagan appoints an ardent prolifer to a cabinet position [M. Heckler at Health and Human services]. CHRISTIANITY TODAY. 27:48-50, April 8, 1983.

Reagan wants parents to be told when teens get contraceptives. CHRISTIANITY TODAY. 26:41, April 23, 1982.

The real abortion issue, by S. G. Cole. THIS MAGAZINE. 17:4-8, June 1983.

Recent changes in predictors of abortion attitudes, by S. N. Barnett, et al. SOCIOLOGY AND SOCIAL RESEARCH. 66(3):320-334, April 1982.

Reciprocal translocations in couples with spontaneous abortions, by P. Alicata, et al. ACTA EUROPAEA FERTILITATIS. 13(2): 73-78, June 1982.

Recovery of fertility following vasovasotomy, by S. R. Plymate, et al. ANDROLOGIA. 15(3):279-281, May-June 1983.

Redefining risks: the good news about the pill [cancer risks], by M. Weber. VOGUE. 173:414, September 1983.

Reduction of teenage pregnancy as a rationale for sex education: a position paper, by P. Dunn. JOURNAL OF SCHOOL HEALTH. 52(10):611-613, December 1982.

Re-evaluation of measurements of maternal serum hCG, hPL and progesterone as prognostic markers of abortion in early pregnancy, by N. Sugita, et al. ASIA-OCEANIA JOURNAL OF OBSTETRICS AND GYNAECOLOGY. 9(1):49-54, March 1983.

Re-examining Roe vs. Wade, by C. De Celles. REGISTER. 59:1+, January 23, 1983; 59:1+, January 30, 1983.

Referendum to abort Fine Gael? ECONOMIST. 284:39+, August 7-13, 1982.

Refusing the pill "no argument to those who want or need it", by J. Gomez. DAILY TELEGRAPH. August 17, 1983, p. 11.

Regional dimensions of abortion-facility services, by N. F. Henry. PROFESSIONAL GEOGRAPHER. 34:65-70, February 1982.

Relationship between psychological characteristics and contraceptive behaviors among university women, by C. N. Roper. DISSER-TATION ABSTRACTS INTERNATIONAL: B. 44(4), October 1983.

Relationship between socio-economic-status and attitude towards family planning, by Mrs. S. Pratap, et al. PERSPECTIVES IN PSYCHOLOGICAL RESEARCHES. 5(2):31, October 1982.

The relationship between spontaneous and induced abortion and the occurrence of second-trimester abortion in subsequent pregnancies, by J. L. Puyenbroek, et al. EUROPEAN JOURNAL OF OBSTETRICS, GYNECOLOGY AND REPRODUCTIVE MEDICINE. 14(5):299-309, February 1983.

The relationship of contraceptive availability to contraceptive use [based on a study of seven developing countries], by A. R. Pebley, et al. INTERNATIONAL FAMILY PLANNING PERSPECTIVES. 8:84-92, September 1982.

The relationship of endometriosis to spontaneous abortion, by J. M. Wheeler, et al. FERTILITY AND STERILITY. 39(5):656-660, May 1983.

Relationship of weight change to required size of vaginal diaphragm, by K. Fiscella. NURSE PRACTITIONER. 7(7):21, 25, July-August 1982.

Relationships of selected variables to the use/nonuse of contraceptives among undergraduate college and university students, by C. A. S. Ellis. DISSERTATION ABSTRACTS INTERNATIONAL: A. 43(9), March 1983.

Relative body weight as a factor in the decision to abort, by T. H. Thelen, et al. PSYCHOLOGICAL REPORTS. 52:763-775, June 1983.

Relative weight, smoking and contraceptive pills: interrelations to blood pressure in students, by A. Lehtonen. JOURNAL OF THE

AMERICAN COLLEGE HEALTH ASSOCIATION. 31(3):105-108, December 1982.

Relevance of early psychic development to pregnancy and abortion, by D. Pines. INTERNATIONAL JOURNAL OF PSYCHO-ANALYSIS. 63(3):311-319, 1982.

Religion, beliefs about human life and the abortion decision, by D. G. Williams. REVIEW OF RELIGIOUS RESEARCH. 24(1):40-48, September 1982.

Religion, law and public policy in America, by C. E. Curran. JURIST. 42:14-28, 1982.

Religiosity, sexual behavior and contraceptive use of college females, by M. Young. JOURNAL OF THE AMERICAN COLLEGE HEALTH ASSOCIATION. 30:216-220, April 1982.

Religious identity and attitudes toward contraceptives among university students in Nigeria, by I. Owie. SOCIAL BIOLOGY. 30(1):101-105, Spring 1983.

Renal functional recovery after acute postabortal renal insufficiency, by N. Manescu, et al. REVISTA DE MEDICINA INTERNA, NEUROLOGIE, PSIHIATRIE, NEUROCHIRURGIE, DEMATO-VENEROLOGIE, SERIA: MEDICINA INTERNA. 34(6):553-560, November-December 1982.

Reopening of the tubes after surgical sterilization, by B. Lanciaux, et al. LARC MEDICAL. 2(11):927-931, December 1982.

"Repeal Roe" measure proposed [U.S. Congress] : state legislators attempt to limit abortion; nun will administer state medicaid for abortions [Michigan]. OFF OUR BACKS. 13:2+, April 1983.

Repeat abortion in the United States: new insights, by C. Tietze, et al. STUDIES IN FAMILY PLANNING. 13(12):373, December 1982.

Repeat abortion-seeking behaviour in Queensland, Australia: knowledge and use of contraception and reasons for terminating the pregnancy, by V. J. Callan. JOURNAL OF BIOSOCIAL SCIENCE.

15(1):1-8, January 1983.

Repeat and first abortion seekers: single women in Brisbane, Australia, by V. J. Callan. JOURNAL OF BIOSOCIAL SCIENCE. 15:217-222, April 1983.

Repeat pregnancies among metropolitan-area teenagers: 1971-1979, by M. A. Koenig, et al. FAMILY PLANNING PERSPECTIVES. 14(6):341-344, November-December 1982.

Reproductive decisions: adolescents with down syndrome, by J. K. Williams. PEDIATRIC NURSING. 9(1):43-44, 58, January-February 1983.

Reproductive hazards in the workplace: bearing the burden of fetal risk, by R. Bayer. MILBANK MEDICAL FUND QUARTERLY. 60(4):633-656, Fall 1982.

Reproductive losses and chromosomal anomaiies, by V. I. Alipov, et al. AKUSHERSTVO I GINEKILOGIIA. (1):38-41, 1983.

Reproductive rights 1983: an international survey, by S. L. Isaacs. COLUMBIA HUMAN RIGHTS LAW REVIEW. 311: 353, Fall-Winter 1982-1983.

Reproductive state modulates ethanol intake in rats: effects of ovariectomys ethanol concentration, estrous cycle and pregnancy, by N. G. Forger, et al. PHARMACOLOGY, BIOCHEMISTRY AND BEHAVIOR. 17(2):323-331, August 1982.

Research in the area of family planning from the aspect of public health, by C. C. Standley, et al. JUGOSLAVENSKA GINE-KOLOGIJA I OPSTETRICIJA. 21(1-2):3-5, January-April 1981.

Research in family planning: 1. WHO CHRONICLES. 36(4):153-155, 1982.

Research in family planning: 2. WHO CHRONICLES. 36(5):179, 1982.

Researchers confirm induced abortion to be safer for women than childbirth: refute claims of critics. FAMILY PLANNING

112

PERSPECTIVES. 14:271-272, September-October 1982.

Respecting life and painting dragons, by T. C. Fox. NATIONAL
CATHOLIC REPORTER. 18:2, October 15, 1982.

Response to requests for abortion: the influence of guilt and
knowledge, by A. R. Allgeier, et al. JOURNAL OF APPLIED
SOCIAL PSYCHOLOGY. 12(4):281-291, 1982.

Responsibility and moral maturity in the control of fertility—or,
a woman's place is in the wrong, by M. A. O'Loughlin.
SOCIAL RESEARCH. 50(3):556-575, 1983.

Restricting federal funds for abortion: another look, by P. M.
Sommers, et al. SOCIAL SCIENCE QUARTERLY. 64:340-
346, June 1983.

Restricting or prohibiting abortion by constitutional amendment.
Some health implications, by D. H. Huber. JOURNAL OF
REPRODUCTIVE MEDICINE. 27(12):729-736, December
1982.

Results of ten years of performing abortions at the gynecologic
clinic of the Dresden medical academy, by F. Rossel, et al.
ZENTRALBLATT FUR GYNAEKOLOGIE. 105(11):700-
709, 1983.

Retardation and sterilization, by B. M. Dickens. INTERNATIONAL
JOURNAL OF LAW AND PSYCHIATRY. 5(3-4):295-318, 1983.

Rethinking pro-life issues. NATIONAL CATHOLIC REPORTER.
19:12, January 21, 1983.

Reversal of female sterilization by magnification lens, by S.
Srivannaboon. JOURNAL OF THE MEDICAL ASSOCIATION
OF THAILAND. 66(1):7-9, January 1983.

Reversal of female sterilization: a review, by G. P. Wood. JOURNAL
OF THE ARKANSAS MEDICAL SOCIETY. 79(12):443-444,
May 1983.

Reversal of vasectomy [letter], by O. N. Mehrotra. NEW ZEALAND

MEDICAL JOURNAL. 95(717):710, October 13, 1982.

Reversibility of clip sterilizations [letter], by J. F. Hulka, et al.
LANCET. 2(8304):927, October 23, 1982.

Reversible methods of sterilization [letter], by G. W. Rosemann,
et al. SOUTH AFRICAN MEDICAL JOURNAL. 62(18):635,
October 23, 1982.

Right of the adolescent to health protection according to Italian
legislation, by T. L. Schwarzenberg. MINERVA PEDIATRICA.
35(8):363-371, April 30, 1983.

The right of minors to confidential access to contraceptives, by A.
L. Morano. ALBANY LAW REVIEW. 47(1):214-240, 1982.

Right to abortion limited: the supreme court upholds the
constitutionality of parental notification statutes. LOYOLA
LAW REVIEW. 28:281-296, Winter 1982.

Rights for the unborn. ECONOMIST. 288:55-56, September 3, 1983.

Rise in antiabortion terrorism [tactics of right to life groups], by L.
C. Wohl. MS. 11:19, November 1982.

Risk factors for complications of interval tubal sterilization by
laparotomy, by P. M. Layde, et al. OBSTETRICS AND GYNE-
COLOGY. 62(2):180-184, August 1983.

Risk of ectopic pregnancy following tubal sterilization, by F.
DeStefano, et al. OBSTETRICS AND GYNECOLOGY.
60(3):326-330, September 1982.

Risk of hysterectomy after sterilization [letter], by P. J. Cooper.
LANCET. 1(8314-8315):59, January 1, 1983.

The risk of premarital first pregnancy among metropolitan-area
teenagers: 1976 and 1979, by M. A. Koenig, et al. FAMILY
PLANNING PERSPECTIVES. 14(5):239-241, 243-247,
September-October 1982.

Risk of wound and pelvic infection after laparoscopic tubal

sterilization: instrument disinfection versus sterilization, by C. M. Huezo, et al. OBSTETRICS AND GYNECOLOGY. 61(5): 598-602, May 1983.

Roe v. Wade reaffirmed [Akron v. Akron center for reproductive health], by G. J. Annas. HASTINGS CENTER REPORT. 13:21-22, August 1983.

Role of abortion on demand and contraception in the reproductive process in a population, by I. Dimitrov. AKUSHERSTVO I GINEKOLOGIIA. 21(3):234-238, 1982.

Role of genetic anomalies in the etiology of spontaneous abortion, by B. Stambolov, et al. AKUSHERSTVO I GINEKOLOGIIA. 21(5):371-373, 1982.

The role of the midwife in permanent contraception, by J. K. Gall, et al. JOURNAL OF NURSE-MIDWIFERY. 28(4):13-17, July-August 1983.

The role of minor chromosomal aberrations in reproduction disorders. A report on three new cases of satellites on chromosome 17, by D. Ioan, et al. ENDOCRINOLOGIE. 20(3):199-202, July-September 1982.

Rubella vaccine does not mandate abortion. NURSES DRUG ALERT. 7(1):3, January 1983.

Safety: anaesthetic hazard in operating theatres, by S. Barnes, et al. OCCUPATIONAL HEALTH. 34(8):370-372, August 1982.

The safety and efficacy of tubal sterilization: an international overview, by H. B. Peterson, et al. INTERNATIONAL JOURNAL OF GYNAECOLOGY AND OBSTETRICS. 21(2):139-144, April 1983.

Safety of fertility control, by C. W. Tyler, Jr., et al. JUGO-SLAVENSKA GINEKOLOGIJA I OPSTETRICIJA. 21(1-2): 27-34, January-April 1981.

Saving the babies, by J. Hensley. NEW COVENANT. 12:15-17, June 1983.

Scholarship report of a 1982 study trip in western and middle Turkey, by A. L. Ericsson. JORDEMODERN. 95(10):337-340, October 1982.

Second-trimester abortion by dilatation and evacuation: an analysis of 11,747 cases, by W. F. Peterson, et al. OBSTETRICS AND GYNECOLOGY. 62(2):185-190, August 1983.

Second victory of Anthony Comstock, by R. Polenberg. SOCIETY. 19(4):32-38, 1982.

Seeking unity to save lives, by M. Meehan, et al. REGISTER. 59:1+, July 17, 1983.

Selected family planning and general health profiles in a teen health clinic, by P. B. Smith, et al. JOURNAL OF ADOLESCENT HEALTH CARE. 2(4):267-272, June 1982.

Self-care/health maintenance and contraceptive use, information needs, and knowledge of a selected group of university women, by J. W. Hawkins, et al. ISSUES IN HEALTH CARE OF WOMEN. 3(5-6):287-305, September-December 1981.

Self-help birth control study, by T. Land. TIMES HIGHER EDUCATIONAL SUPPLEMENT. 498:7, May 21, 1982.

Self-sustaining clinics: innovation or retreat?, by L. C. Landman. FAMILY PLANNING PERSPECTIVES. 15(5):218-223, September-October 1983.

Senate nixes Hatch, by M. Meehan. REGISTER. 59:1+, July 10, 1983.

The senate threat to our lives [Hatch amendment], by L. C. Wohl. MS. 10:21, June 1982.

Septic abortion in an IUCD user [letter], by C. J. Conaghan, et al. NEW ZEALAND MEDICAL JOURNAL. 95(720):826-827, November 24, 1982.

Septic induced abortion—a report of 100 cases in Sarawak, by M. Teo Yu Keng, et al. MEDICAL JOURNAL OF MALAYSIA.

37(4):322-325, December 1982.

Septic shock in obstetrics, by B. V. Molodkin. FEL'DSHER I
AKUSHERKA. 48(3):23-27, 1983.

Serenely silent no longer, two angry nuns battle their bishops
over the issue of abortion [opposition to Hatch amendment].
PEOPLE WEEKLY. 18:90, August 16, 1982.

Serologic evidence of ureaplasma urealyticum infection in
women with spontaneous pregnancy loss, by P. A. Quinn, et al.
AMERICAN JOURNAL OF OBSTETRICS AND GYNECOLOGY.
145(2):245-250, January 15, 1983.

Serum copper and ceruloplasmin as an index of foetal well being in
abortions, by A. Singhal, et al. INDIAN JOURNAL OF
PATHOLOGY AND MICROBIOLOGY. 25(4):242-244,
October 1982.

Serum levels of polychlorinated biphenyls and some organochlorine
insecticides in women with recent and former missed abortions,
by B. Bercovici, et al. ENVIRONMENTAL RESEARCH.
30(1):169-174, February 1983.

Service offers alternatives. NATIONAL CATHOLIC REPORTER.
18:19, October 15, 1982.

Setting up the project . . . to determine a patient's need after an
abortion, by S. Anthony. NURSING MIRROR AND MIDWIVE'S
JOURNAL. 156(4):Clinical forum 1:32, January 26, 1983.

Seventeenth century midwifery: the treatment of miscarriage, by
R. K. Marshall. NURSING MIRROR AND MIDWIVE'S JOURNAL.
155(24):31-36, December 15, 1982.

Sex and sympathy: contraceptive advice for under-16-year olds, by
F. Hutchinson. SUNDAY TIMES. July 31, 1983, p. 16.

Sex discrimination: title VII burdens of proof, comparable worth,
and sexual harassment; abortion funding and notice and consent
requirements. ANNUAL SURVEY OF AMERICAN LAW.
December 1982, p. 1-47.

Sex education, abortion views of Mexican Americans typical of U. S. beliefs. FAMILY PLANNING PERSPECTIVES. 15:197, July-August 1983.

Sex education and contraceptive education in U. S. public high schools, by M. T. Orr. FAMILY PLANNING PERSPECTIVES. 14:304+, November-December 1982.

The sex police [law requiring birth-control clinics to notify parents]. NATION. 236:164-165, February 12, 1983.

Sex ratio in spontaneous abortions, by T. Hassold, et al. ANNALS OF HUMAN GENETICS. 47(pt 1):39-47, January 1983.

Sex, sex guilt, and contraceptive use, by M. Gerrard. JOURNAL OF PERSONALITY AND SOCIAL PSYCHOLOGY. 42:153-158, January 1982.

Sexual imprinting in male Japanese quail: effects of castration at hatching, by R. E. Hutchinson, et al. DEVELOPMENTAL PSYCHOBIOLOGY. 15(5):471-477, September 1982.

Sexual practice and the use of contraception, by J. Bell. HIGH SCHOOL JOURNAL. 65:241-244, April 1982.

Sexuality, fertility and fertility control, by A. Woodhouse. WOMEN'S STUDIES INTERNATIONAL FORUM. 5(1):1-15, 1982.

Sexually active but not pregnant: a comparison of teens who risk and teens who plan, by J. B. Jones, et al. JOURNAL OF YOUTH AND ADOLESCENCE. 12:235-251, June 1983.

Sexually active teenager, by S. J. Emans. JOURNAL OF DEVELOP-MENTAL AND BEHAVIORAL PEDIATRICS. 4(1):37-42, March 1983.

Sharing the pain of abortion [impact on men], by J. Leo. TIME. 122:78, September 26, 1983.

Should courts curb mail they consider too direct [prophylactics], by T. J. McGrew. AD FORUM. 4:41, February 1983.

Should a doctor tell? TABLET. 237:743, August 6, 1983.

Should parents be told when teens get contraceptives? CHRISTIAN-
ITY TODAY. 27:22, March 18, 1983.

Side effects and early complications following cervical priming with
prostaglandin F2 alpha (PGF2 alpha) in inducing abortion in
young women in their first pregnancy, by B. Seifert, et al.
ZENTRALBLATT FUR GYNAEKOLOGIE. 105(11):710-714,
1983.

Sidewalk counselors are voice of the unborn, by S. Settle. REGISTER.
59:1+, September 11, 1983.

The silent holocaust: step II, by J. Blattner. NEW COVENANT.
13:16-20, September 1983.

Simultaneity in the birth rate equation: the effects of education,
labor force participation, income and health, by D. J. Conger,
et al. ECONOMETRICA. 46:631-641, May 1978.

—. Discussion. ECONOMETRICA. 50:1585-1590, November 1982.

The Sino-Stanford scandal [dismissal of S. Mosher for article on
mandatory birth control], by A. Dubro. SCIENCE DIGEST.
91:98-101, August 1983.

Sister Mansour is not alone [appointment to Michigan Dept. of
Social Services], by M. Kolbenschlag. COMMONWEAL. 110:
359-264, June 17, 1983.

Six in ten Americans now support medicaid fuding of abortions.
FAMILY PLANNING PERSPECTIVES. 15:201, July-August
1983.

Sixteen thousand, five hundred fetuses intensify fight in which they
have no stake, by P. Edmonds. NATIONAL CATHOLIC RE-
PORTER. 19:1, January 21, 1983.

Slaughter of the innocents still goes on [China], by V. G. Kulkarni.
FAR EASTERN ECONOMIC REVIEW. 120:50-53, April 28,
1983.

Slow-release contraceptive systems [implants that release levonor-gestrel] . SCIENCE NEWS. 123:236, April 9, 1983.

Smoking and the occurrence of congenital malformations and spontaneous abortions: multivariate analysis, by K. Hemminki, et al. AMERICAN JOURNAL OF OBSTETRICS AND GYNECOLOGY. 145(1):61-66, January 1, 1983.

Smooth muscle antibodies in complicated early pregnancies, by I. Pietarinen, et al. AMERICAN JOURNAL OF REPRODUCTIVE IMMUNOLOGY. 3(1):43-45, January-February 1983.

Social, spatial and political determinants of U. S. abortion rates, by N. F. Henry, et al. SOCIAL SCIENCE AND MEDICINE. 16(9):987-996, 1982.

Socialization for sexual and contraceptive behavior: moral absolutes versus relative consequences, by E. Thompson. YOUTH AND SOCIETY. 14(1):103-128, September 1982.

Society anxiety, sexual behavior and contraceptive use, by M. R. Leary, et al. JOURNAL OF PERSONALITY AND SOCIAL PSYCHOLOGY. 45:1347-1354, December 1983.

Socio-demographic correlates of the decision process for medical termination of pregnancy and family planning, by A. R. Chaurasia, et al. INDIAN JOURNAL OF PUBLIC HEALTH. 26(1):4-9, January-March 1982.

Socioeconomic determinants of fertility, by G. Arora. JOURNAL OF FAMILY WELFARE. 29:39-52, March 1983.

Some areas of the law relevant to family planning in medical practice: an analysis from a comparative perspective, by D. C. Jayasuriya. CEYLON MEDICAL JOURNAL. 24(3-4):58-64, September-December 1979.

Some basic facts about abortion, by D. S. Gluckin, et al. MADEMOISELLE. 89:166+, October 1983.

Some biological insights into abortion, by G. Hardin. BIOSCIENCE. 32:720+, October 1982.

Some effects of ovariectomy and estrogen replacement on body composition in the rat, by R. G. Clark, et al. PHYSIOLOGY AND BEHAVIOR. 28(6):963-969, June 1982.

Some good news about the pill [cancer risks disputed]. NEWSWEEK. 101:84, April 4, 1983.

Some questions of identity: late miscarriage, stillbirth and perinatal loss, by A. Lovell. SOCIAL SCIENCE AND MEDICINE. 17(11): 755-761, 1983.

Some thoughts on the ethics of abortion on demand, by R. L. Cleary. DIALOGUE. 25:60-68, April 1983.

Sooner or later? Nagging question for some, by A. S. Kasper. NEW DIRECTIONS FOR WOMEN. 11:4, May-June 1983.

Sources of population and family planning assistance. POPULATION REPORTS. (26):J621-655, January-February 1983.

Spain: the abortion battle. REVISTA DE ENFERMAGEN. 6(58-59): 22-27, May-June 1983.

Spain's abortion controversy, by R. Plaza. WORLD PRESS REVIEW. 30:56, April 1983.

Spanish women still struggle in "Paradise", by A. Dermansky. NEW DIRECTIONS FOR WOMEN. 12:4, July-August 1983.

A spatial autocorrelation model of the effects of population density on fertility, by C. Loftin, et al. AMERICAN SOCIOLOGICAL REVIEW. 48:121-128, February 1983.

Spermicide effect on unborn in question. SCIENCE NEWS. 121: 326, May 15, 1982.

The sponge, by K. Freifeld, et al. HEALTH. 15(7):56, July 1983.

A sponge contraceptive, by C. A. Helwick. HEALTH. 14:13, April 1982.

Sponge gets OK. SCIENCE NEWS. 123:261, April 23, 1983.

Spontaneous abortion and birth order [letter], by W. H. James. EARLY HUMAN DEVELOPMENT. 7(2):195, November 1982.

Spontaneous abortion and diabetes mellitus, by A. D. Wright, et al. POSTGRADUATE MEDICAL JOURNAL. 59(691):295-298, May 1983.

Spontaneous abortion and ectopic pregnancy, by R. F. Avant. PRIMARY CARE. 10(2):161-172, June 1983.

Spontaneous abortion and induced abortion: an adjustment for the presence of induced abortion when estimating the rate of spontaneous abortion from cross-sectional studies, by E. Susser. AMERICAN JOURNAL OF EPIDEMIOLOGY. 117(3):305-308, March 1983.

Spontaneous abortion and subsequent down syndrome livebirth, by E. B. Hook, et al. HUMAN GENETICS. 64(3):267-270, 1983.

Spontaneous abortion incidence in the treatment of infertility: addendum on in vitro fertilization [letter], by R. P. Jansen. AMERICAN JOURNAL OF OBSTETRICS AND GYNECOLOGY. 144(6):738-739, November 15, 1982.

Spontaneous abortion: the role of heterogeneous risk and selective fertility, by A. J. Wilcox, et al. EARLY HUMAN DEVELOPMENT. 7(2):165-178, November 1982.

Spontaneous abortions after the Three Mile Island nuclear accident: a life table analysis, by M. K. Goldhaber, et al. AMERICAN JOURNAL OF PUBLIC HEALTH. 73(7):752-759, July 1983.

Spontaneous abortions and reproductive selection mechanisms in the rubber and leather industry in Finland, by K. Hemminki, et al. BRITISH JOURNAL OF INDUSTRIAL MEDICINE. 40(1): 81-86, February 1983.

Spontaneous abortions in hospital staff engaged in sterilising instruments with chemical agents, by K. Hemminki, et al. BRITISH MEDICAL JOURNAL. 285(6353):1461-1463, November 20, 1982.

Spontaneous abortions in hospital sterilising staff [letter]. BRITISH MEDICAL JOURNAL. 286(6382):1976-1977, June 18, 1983.

Spontaneous abortions in an industrialized community in Finland, by K. Hemminki, et al. AMERICAN JOURNAL OF PUBLIC HEALTH. 73(1):32-37, January 1983.

Spray a day keeps babies away. NEW SCIENTIST. 96:293, November 4, 1982.

Spring clip technique for sterilization [letter], by J. F. Hulka. OBSTETRICS AND GYNECOLOGY. 60(6):760, December 1982.

Spousal notice—weighing the burden on a woman's abortion decision: Scheinberg vs. Smith. STETSON LAW REVIEW. 12:250-264, Fall 1982.

Spousal notification and consent in abortion situations: Scheinberg vs. Smith. HOUSTON LAW REVIEW. 19:1025-1039, July 1982.

The squeal rule and Lolita rights, by D. R. Carlin, Jr. COMMON-WEAL. 110:465-467, September 9, 1983.

The squeal rule: halt! [federal regulation that would require health clinics to notify parents of any girl who applied for prescription contraceptives]. NEWSWEEK. 101:17, February 28, 1983.

State can't prohibit first-trimester, nonlifesaving abortion on incompetent. THE FAMILY LAW REPORTER: COURT OPINIONS. 8(48):2728-2729, October 12, 1982.

State of the world population [trends and family planning programs], by R. M. Salas. POPULI. 9(2):3-12, 1982.

State statutes regulating abortion leave unresolved issues, by J. S. Showalter, et al. HOSPITAL PROGRESS. 63(12):60-64, December 1982.

Sterilization acceptance in China, by H. Y. Tien. STUDIES IN FAMILY PLANNING. 13:287-292, October 1982.

Sterilization and the mentally handicapped person, by R. McManus.

NORTH CAROLINA MEDICAL JOURNAL. 44(2):92-93,
February 1983.

Sterilization and the mentally retarded, by K. L. Dickin, et al.
CANADA'S MENTAL HEALTH. 31(1):4-8, March 1983.

Sterilization by laparoscopy, by P. C. Pelland. CLINICAL
OBSTETRICS AND GYNECOLOGY. 26(2):321-333, June 1983.

Sterilization by vas occlusion without transection does not reduce
postvasectomy sperm-agglutinating antibodies in serum. A
randomized trial of vas occlusion versus vasectomy, by T. C.
Gerstenberg, et al. SCANDINAVIAN JOURNAL OF UROLOGY
AND NEPHROLOGY. 17(2):149-151, 1983.

Sterilization: contraception for both men and women, by T. P.
Reed, III. CONSULTANT. 22(10):240-242, 247, 250, October
1982.

Sterilization—forbidden by Rome, pushed by U. S., by R. J. McClory.
NATIONAL CATHOLIC REPORTER. 20:1+, November 11, 1983.

Sterilization in Bangladesh: mortality, morbidity, and risk factors,
by M. J. Rosenberg, et al. INTERNATIONAL JOURNAL OF
GYNAECOLOGY AND OBSTETRICS. 20(4):283-291, August
1982.

Sterilization in Quebec, by N. Marcil-Gratton, et al. FAMILY
PLANNING PERSPECTIVES. 15:73-77, March-April 1983.

Sterilization—medical practices—life-endangering conditions. THE
FAMILY LAW REPORTER: COURT OPINIONS. 8(47):2717,
October 5, 1982.

Sterilization of the mentally retarded, by C. D. Davis. TEXAS
HOSPITALS. 38(4):48-49, September 1982.

Sterilization of mentally retarded women, by W. Heidenreich, et al.
GEBURTSHILFE UND FRAUENHEILKUNDE. 42(7):554-557,
July 1982.

Sterilization of the retarded: a break in the impasse?, by H. C. Moss,

JOURNAL OF THE INDIANA STATE MEDICAL ASSOCIATION. 75(7):458-459, July 1982.

Sterilization of Salvadorans promoted by U. S. agency, by C. Hedges. NATIONAL CATHOLIC REPORTER. 20:1, November 11, 1983.

Sterlisation of women: prevalence and outcome, by A. F. Wright. BRITISH MEDICAL JOURNAL. 285(6342):609-611, August 28, 1982.

Sterilization performed at the time of a probably fertilized but not yet nidated ovum, by K. D. Skyggebjerg, et al. UGESKRIFT FOR LAEGER. 145(27):2096, July 4, 1983.

Sterilization petitions: developing judicial guidelines. MONTANA LAW REVIEW. 44:127-136, Winter 1983.

Sterilization without surgery has promise, by N. Brozan. NEW YORK TIMES. September 6, 1982, p. 38.

Sterilization without surgery . . . several methods for plugging the fallopian tubes, by M. Klitsch. FAMILY PLANNING PER-SPECTIVES. 14(6):324-327, November-December 1982.

Sterilising effects of benzyl-1,3-benzodioxoles on the tsetse fly glossina morsitans morsitans Westwood (diptera: glossinidae), by P. A. Langley, et al. ENTOMOLOGICAL REVIEW. 72:473-481, September 1982.

Sterilizing effects of tepa, hempa., and N,N'-hexamethylenebis (1-aziridinecarboxamide) on the smaller European elm bark beetle, by W. N. Cannon, Jr.. JOURNAL OF ECONOMIC ENTOMOLOGY. 75:535-537, June 1982.

Steven Mosher and the politics of cultural exchange, by J. Lincoln. NATION. 237:176+, September 3-10, 1983.

Stifled squeal [injunction blocking requirement that federally funded clinics notify parents if their teenagers receive contra-ceptives]. TIME. 121:24, February 28, 1983.

Stop signs and detours in the way of abortion, by L. McQuaig. MACLEANS. 96:36-37, July 25, 1983.

Strategy, please? NATIONAL REVIEW. 35:856-857, July 22, 1983.

Struggling for the soul of social science [case of S. Mosher], by I. L. Horowitz. SOCIETY. 20:4-15, July-August 1983.

Student refusal to pay abortion-related fees—a first amendment right? SAN DIEGO LAW REVIEW. 20:837-857, August 1983.

Studies on the agent of bovine chlamydial abortion: serology, microbiology and cell culture, by T. Homma. DISSERTATION ABSTRACTS INTERNATIONAL: B. 44(5), November 1983.

Study finds no rise in atherosclerosis symptoms in men vasectomized an average of 15 years ago. FAMILY PLANNING PERSPECTIVES. 15(1):30-31, January-February 1983.

Study of Bleier tubal clip for fertility control, by C. S. Vear. AUSTRALIAN AND NEW ZEALAND JOURNAL OF OBSTETRICS AND GYNAECOLOGY. 22(4):234-236, November, 1982.

A study on the use of contraceptives by adolescents, by M. A. Requillart. REVUE FRANCAISE DE SOCIOLOGIE. 24:81-96, January-March 1983.

Subclinical abortions in patients treated with clomiphene citrate, by P. C. Ho, et al. INTERNATIONAL JOURNAL OF GYNAE-COLOGY AND OBSTETRICS. 20(5):379-382, October 1982.

Subsidized family planning services in Texas, by L. W. Mondy. TEXAS MEDICINE. 78(11):58-62, November 1982.

Subsidized family planning services in Texas credited with averting 56,000 pregnancies, saving 30 million dollars. FAMILY PLANNING PERSPECTIVES. 15:86-87, March-April 1983.

Successful family planning based on humanistic approach, by C. Kunii. BUSINESS JAPAN. 27:69-70, November 1982.

Suction curettage for incomplete and inevitable abortion an

emergency medicine procedure?, by M. C. Tomlanovich. ANNALS OF EMERGENCY MEDICINE. 11(12):695-696, December 1982.

Support—Ohio. JUVENILE AND FAMILY LAW DIGEST. 14(3): 122, March 1982.

Supreme court and congress on abortion: an analysis of comparative institutional capacity, by C. D. Reedy. DISSERTATION AB-STRACTS INTERNATIONAL: A. 43(11), May 1983.

Supreme court clarifies abortion rules, by A. H. Bernstein. HOSPITALS. 57(17):93, September 1, 1983.

Supreme court faces the family, by H. H. Clark, Jr. CHILDREN TODAY. 11(6):18-21, November-December 1982.

Supreme court reaffirms abortion rights [rulings on separate cases from Missouri, Virginia, and Akron, Ohio, testing the validity of state and local government efforts to regulate abortion], by E. Witt. CONGRESSIONAL QUARTERLY WEEKLY REPORT. 41:1247-1249, June 18, 1983.

Supreme court report: six justices stand firm on abortion decision, by R. L. Young. AMERICAN BAR ASSOCIATION JOURNAL. 69:1290, 1292, September 1983.

Supreme court: rulings limit nonprofit groups' lobbying . . . remove restrictions on abortion, by P. R. McGinn. NATIONAL CATHOLIC REPORTER. 19:6, July 1, 1983.

Supreme court strikes Akron abortion provisions, by F. L. Powell, Jr. ORIGINS. 13:149+, July 21, 1983.

Supreme court's abortion decisions: a critical study of the shaping of a major American public policy and a basis for change, by S. M. Krason. DISSERTATION ABSTRACTS INTERNATIONAL: A. 44(1), July 1983.

Surgical death, by J. V. Schall. LINACRE QUARTERLY. 49:305-307, November 1982.

Surgical sterilization. Analysis of 250 cases, by D. Campos Navarro,

127

et al. GINECOLOGIA Y OBSTETRICIA DE MEXICO. 50(301): 111-114, May 1982.

Surveillance of pregnancy loss in human populations, by A. J. Wilcox. AMERICAN JOURNAL OF INDUSTRIAL MEDICINE. 4(1-2): 285-291, 1983.

Survey discloses NFP practices, preferences in U. S. Catholic hospitals, by M. C. Martin, et al. HOSPITAL PROGRESS. 64:52-58, February 1983.

A survey of attitudes concerning contraception and the resolution of teenage pregnancy, by C. Rinck, et al. ADOLESCENCE. 18(72):923-929, Winter 1983.

A survey of marital status and family planning of schizophrenics, by Y. Z. Fang. CHUNG HUA SHEN CHING CHANG SHEN KO TSA CHIH. 15(4):204-206, November 1982.

The survivor, by M. Masterson. OUR SUNDAY VISITOR. 72:4-5, July 31, 1983.

Sustaining the prolife momentum: legal and political strategies, by G. D. Wendel, et al. HOSPITAL PROGRESS. 63(12):70-73, December 1982.

Systemic adverse reactions to prostaglandin F2 (PGF2 alpha, dinoprostone, prostin F2 alpha, prostalmon F, by L. Wislicki. INTERNATIONAL JOURNAL OF BIOLOGICAL RESEARCH IN PREGNANCY. 3(4):158-160, 1982.

Synthesis and antifertility activity of 13-aza 14-oxo-prostaglandins, by D. Favara, et al. PROSTAGLANDINS. 25(3):311-320, March 1983.

Szoka draws praise, by F. Lilly. REGISTER. 59:1+, March 13, 1983.

Taking the plunge and trying the sponge, by A. Diamant. REDBOOK. 161:29, September 1983.

Talking to parents about sex, birth control does not have an impact on teenagers' contraceptive use. FAMILY PLANNING PER-

SPECTIVES. 14(5):279-280, September-October 1982.

Tay-sachs and the abortion controversy, by M. Kukin. JOURNAL OF RELIGION AND HEALTH. 20(3):224-242, 1981.

Technological advances and Roe v. Wade: the need to rethink abortion law, by K. Martyn. UCLA LAW REVIEW. 29(5-6):1194-1215, June-August 1982.

Technological marvel: not tonight, dear, the computer is beeping. NATIONAL CATHOLIC REPORTER. 19:1+, April 29, 1983.

Technology and reproductive rights: how advances in technology can be used to limit women's reproductive rights [right to abortion], by S. M. Lynn. WOMEN'S RIGHTS LAW REPORTER. 7:223-227, Spring 1982.

Technology transfer aids Indonesian family planning program [Japan], by M. Tanaka. BUSINESS JAPAN. 27:61+, November 1982.

Teen sex-clinic furore [Calgary], by F. Orr. ALBERTA REPORT. 10:32-33, September 26, 1983.

Teen-agers and birth control, by G. F. Will. NEWSWEEK. 101:80, February 28, 1983.

Teenagers' assessment of reproductive health-care services, by S. W. Nenney, et al. PATIENT COUNSELLING AND HEALTH EDUCATION. 4(3):152-155, 1983.

Teenager's guide to sex safety, by A. K. Richards, et al. MS. 12:81-84, July 1983.

Ten years of abortion, by J. G. Deedy. TABLET. 237:148-150, February 19, 1983.

Termination of early first trimester pregnancy by vaginal administration of 16, 16-dimethyl-trans-delta 2-PGE1 methyl ester. ASIA-OCEANIA JOURNAL OF OBSTETRICS AND GYNAECOLOGY. 8(3):263-268, September 1982.

Termination of early gestation with 9-deoxo-16,16-dimethyl-9-methylene prostaglandin E2, by P. F. Brenner, et al. CONTRACEPTION. 26(3):261-277, September 1982.

Termination of pregnancy, by D. Krishnamoni, et al. CANADIAN JOURNAL OF PSYCHIATRY. 28(6):457-461, October 1983.

Termination of pregnancy in cases of intrauterine fetal death, missed abortion, molar and anencephalic pregnancy with intramuscular administration of 2a 2b dihomo 15(S) 15 methyl PGF2 alpha methyl ester—a multicentre study, by S. M. Karim, et al. ANNALS OF THE ACADEMY OF MEDICINE, SINGAPORE. 11(4):508-512, October 1982.

Termination of second trimester pregnancy by intramuscular injection of 16-phenoxy-omega-17,18,19,20-tetranor-PGE2 methyl sulphonylamide. INTERNATIONAL JOURNAL OF GYNAECOLOGY AND OBSTETRICS. 20(5):383-386, October 1982.

Termination of second trimester pregnancy with a long-acting vaginal pessary containing 15-methyl-PGF2 alpha methyl ester. INTERNATIONAL JOURNAL OF GYNAECOLOGY AND OBSTETRICS. 21(2):159-165, April 1983.

Termino-terminal vaso-vasostomy and spermatic granuloma. Experimental research in rats (first histological and electron microscopic results), by G. Cavallaro, et al. MINERVA CHIRURGICA. 37(23-24):2097-2103, December 15-31, 1982.

Testing a better birth-control pill, by M. Clark. NEWSWEEK. 99:85, May 3, 1982.

Testing times for women in body lab . . . depo-provera, by W. Bacon. LAMP. 40(3):38-40, May 1983.

Tests of a forgotten barrier [cervical cap]. SCIENCE NEWS. 123:236, April 9, 1983.

Tetanus complicating elective surgery. Two cases following female sterilization, by J. M. Aubert, et al. TROPICAL DOCTOR. 13(2):61-64, April 1983.

Thailand's family planning program: an Asian success story, by A. Rosenfield, et al. INTERNATIONAL FAMILY PLANNING PERSPECTIVES. 8:43-51, June 1982.

Thailand's reproductive revolution: an update, by P. Kamnuansilpa, et al. INTERNATIONAL FAMILY PLANNING PERSPECTIVES. 8:51-56, June 1982.

Theoretical framework for studying adolescent contraceptive use, by K. A. Urberg. ADOLESCENCE. 17(67):527-540, 1982.

Therapeutic abortion and chlamydial infection, by G. L. Ridgway, et al. BRITISH MEDICAL JOURNAL. 286(6376):1478-1479, May 7, 1983.

Therapeutic abortion and chlamydial infection [letter], by A. Mills. BRITISH MEDICAL JOURNAL. 286(6378):1649, May 21, 1983.

Therapeutic abortion and chlamydia trachomatis infection, by E. Qvigstad, et al. BRITISH JOURNAL OF VENEREAL DISEASE. 58(3):182-183.

Therapeutic abortion in life-threatening pregnancies [letter], by J. Aznar, et al. LANCET. 1(8336):1280-1281, June 4, 1983.

Therapeutic abortion: the medical argument, by J. F. Murphy, et al. IRISH MEDICAL JOURNAL. 75(8):304-306, August 1982.

Therapeutic abortion on psychiatric grounds. Part III. Implementing the abortion and sterilization act (1975-1981), by E. S. Nash, et al. SOUTH AFRICAN MEDICAL JOURNAL. 63(17):639-644, April 23, 1983.

There oughta be a law fantasy [regulations requiring birth control clinics to notify parents when minors receive contraceptives], by J. M. Wall. CHRISTIAN CENTURY. 100:171, March 2, 1983.

Third-trimester abortion rate inflated in Georgia; true rate is 4 per 100,000. FAMILY PLANNING PERSPECTIVES. 15:196, July-August 1983.

Third-trimester induced abortion in Georgia, 1979 and 1980, by

131

A. M. Spitz, et al. AMERICAN JOURNAL OF PUBLIC HEALTH. 73:594-595, May 1983.

Third world family planning programs: measuring the costs, by N. Yinger, et al. POPULATION BULLETIN. February 1983.

This bitter pill for parents: rules of professional secrecy over contraception, by R. Butt. TIMES. July 7, 1983, p. 12.

This is what you thought about . . . men's rights [results of survey]. GLAMOUR. 80:21, July 1982.

The threat of numbers, by R. W. Peterson. AUDUBON. 84:107, July 1982.

Three neuroleptanalgesia schedules for laparoscopic sterilization by electrocoagulation, by S. Koetsawang, et al. INTERNATIONAL JOURNAL OF GYNAECOLOGY AND OBSTETRICS. 21(2): 133-137, April 1983.

Three supreme court rulings nullify several abortion restrictions, by J. S. Showalter, et al. HOSPITAL PROGRESS. 64(7):20-21, July 1983.

A throw-away diaphragm, by R. Kall. HEALTH. 14:18, March 1982.

Time running out on death row, by M. Meehan. NATIONAL CATHOLIC REPORTER. 20:12, November 18, 1983.

The timing of entry into motherhood in Asia: a comparative perspective, by R. Rindfuss, et al. POPULATION STUDIES. 37: 253-272, July 1983.

Title X parental notification regulation—a different prognosis, by E. F. Diamond. LINACRE QUARTERLY. 50:56-63, February 1983.

To be or not to be: protecting the unborn's potentiality of life, by J. A. Parness, et al. UNIVERSITY OF CINCINNATI LAW REVIEW. 51:257-298, 1982.

To rescue the unborn: two courtroom avenues offer new hope [Alberta], by R. Dolphin, et al. ALBERTA REPORT. 9:34-35, November 8, 1982.

Today's contraceptives: what's new? What's best?, by W. S. Ross. READER'S DIGEST. 123:217+, November 1983.

Toledo doctor wages campaign against the pill, by A. Jones. NATIONAL CATHOLIC REPORTER. 18:1+, October 15, 1982.

Toward constitutional abortion control legislation: the Pennsylvania approach. DICKINSON LAW REVIEW. 87:373-406, Winter 1983.

Toward a Copernican revolution in our thinking about life's beginning and life's end, by R. M. Green. SOUND. 66:152-173, Summer 1983.

Toward a new understanding of population change in Bali, by M. Poffenberger. POPULATION STUDIES. 37:43-59, March 1983.

Towards a better service . . . women would appreciate a postabortion counselling service. NURSING MIRROR AND MIDWIVE'S JOURNAL. 156(4):Clinical forum 1:37, January 26, 1983.

Trace anesthetic gases: an unproven health hazard, by L. F. Walts. ASSOCIATION OF OPERATING ROOM NURSES. 37(4):728-729, 732, 736+, March 1983.

Transabdominal isthmic cerclage for the treatment of incompetent cervix, by S. Olsen, et al. ACTA OBSTETRICIA ET GYNE-COLOGICA SCANDINAVICA. 61(5):473-475, 1982.

The transition in Korean family planning behavior, 1935-1976: a retrospective cohort analysis, by J. R. Foreit. STUDIES IN FAMILY PLANNING. 13(8-9):227-236, 1982.

Treating early miscarriage in the ED. EMERGENCY MEDICINE. 15(13):148-152, 161, 164, July 15, 1983.

Trends in fertility, family size preferences, and family planning practice: Taiwan, 1961-1980, by M. C. Chang, et al. STUDIES IN FAMILY PLANNING. 12(5):211-228, May 1981.

Trends in induced abortion in England and Wales, by J. R. Ashton, et al. JOURNAL OF EPIDEMIOLOGY AND COMMUNITY HEALTH. 37(2):105-110, June 1983.

Trend of socio-demographic characteristics of tubectomy acceptors in a rural area of West Bengal (Singur), by S. P. Saha. INDIAN JOURNAL OF PUBLIC HEALTH. 25(3):102-110, July-September 1981.

Trials of a contraceptive [depo-provera], by A. Kerr. MACLEANS. 96:46, January 24, 1983.

Trials on mistrial. NATURE. 304(5923):198, July 21-27, 1983.

Trials with the Femcept method of female sterilization and experience with radiopaque methylcyanoacrylate, by R. S. Neuwirth, et al. AMERICAN JOURNAL OF OBSTETRICS AND GYNECOLOGY. 145(8):948-954, April 15, 1983.

Trying to slam the door [vote in favor of constitutional amendment banning abortions]. TIME. 122:42, September 19, 1983.

Trying to understand the other side, by A. Nowlan. THE ATLANTIC ADVOCATE. 73:62, January 1983.

Tubal plugs bar pregnancy [tubal occlusion: silicone plugs block Fallopian tubes]. SCIENCE DIGEST. 90:89, November 1982.

Tubal sterilization and menstrual dysfunction, by J. E. Malick, et al. JOURNAL OF THE AMERICAN OSTEOPATHIC ASSOCIATION. 82(2):103-108, October 1982.

Tubal sterilization: characteristics of women most affected by the option of reversibility, by R. N. Shain, et al. SOCIAL SCIENCE AND MEDICINE. 16(10):1067-1077, 1982.

Tubal sterilization: findings in a large prospective study, by M. Vessey, et al. BRITISH JOURNAL OF OBSTETRICS AND GYNAECOLOGY. 90(3):203-209, March 1983.

Twinning rate in spontaneous abortions, by I. A. Uchida, et al. AMERICAN JOURNAL OF HUMAN GENETICS. 35(5):987-993, September 1983.

Two-year follow-up of 3,466 sterilizations in India, by S. Pachauri, et al. JOURNAL OF REPRODUCTIVE MEDICINE. 27(8):459-463, August 1982.

Two's a crowd and it's illegal. ECONOMIST. 286:47, 50, January 29, 1983.

Typical AFDC family smaller than ten years ago: average number of children fell from three to two. FAMILY PLANNING PERSPECTIVES. 15:31-32, January-February 1983.

U. S. population policies, development, and the rural poor of Africa, by E. Green. JOURNAL OF MODERN AFRICAN STUDIES. 20:45-67, March 1982.

The U. S. supreme court 1982-1983 term: abortion. THE CRIMINAL LAW REPORTER: SUPREME COURT PROCEEDINGS. 34(1): 4024, October 5, 1983.

Ultrasonic and endocrinological aspects of first trimester miscarriage, by S. Sakamoto, et al. ASIA-OCEANIA JOURNAL OF OBSTETRICS AND GYNAECOLOGY. 8(2):105-116, June 1982.

Ultrasonic diagnosis of retained tissues after artificial abortion on demand, by K. Ilieva, et al. AKUSHERSTVO I GINEKOLOGIIA. 22(1):45-48, 1983.

Ultrasonic placental localization in relation to spontaneous abortion after mid-trimester amniocentesis, by J. A. Hill, et al. PRENATAL DIAGNOSIS. 2(4):289-295, October 1982.

An unfortunate amendment on abortion. TABLET. 237:887, September 17, 1983.

The unintended consequences of policy change: the effect of a restrictive abortion policy [on maternal deaths in Rumania], by J. S. Legge, Jr. ADMINISTRATION AND SOCIETY. 15:243-256, August 1983.

Unmarried black adolescent fathers attitudes toward abortion, contraception and sexuality: a preliminary report, by L. E. Hendricks. JOURNAL OF ADOLESCENT HEALTH CARE. 2(3):199-204, 1982.

An unpopular referendum, by L. McRedmond. TABLET. 237: 816-818, August 27, 1983.

Unwanted pregnancies amongst teenagers, by C. Francome. JOURNAL OF BIOSOCIAL SCIENCE. 15:139-144, April 1983.

The unwanted pregnancy and its termination—a possibility for unconscious introjection of grief, by A. E. Benz. PSYCHE. 37(2): 130-138, 1983.

Unwanted pregnancy: a neurotic attempt at conflict-solving? An analysis of the conflict-situations of 228 women immediately before legal abortion, by P. Goebel. ZEITSCHRIFT FUR PSYCHOSOMATISCHE MEDIZIN UND PSYCHOANALYSE. 28(3):280-299, 1982.

Update on contraceptives: what's safe? Effective? Convenient? CHANGING TIMES. 37:72+, October 1983.

Urea-prostaglandin versus hypertonic saline for instillation abortion, by N. J. Binkin, et al. AMERICAN JOURNAL OF OBSTETRICS AND GYNECOLOGY. 146(8):947-952, August 15, 1983.

Ureterouterine fistula as a complication of elective abortion, by G. T. Keegan, et al. JOURNAL OF UROLOGY. 128(1):137-138, 1982.

Use of contraceptive for delaying and spacing births in Columbia, Costa Rica and Korea, by J. S. Grigsby. DISSERTATION ABSTRACTS INTERNATIONAL: A. 44(3), September 1983.

Use of 15(S)-15-methyl PGF 2-alpha in the treatment of internal abortion and intrauterine death of the fetus, by G. B. Melis, et al. MINERVA GINECOLOGIA. 34(9):729-734, September 1982.

Use of hormonal preparations on women with threatened abortion, by R. N. Stepanova. AKUSHERSTVO I GINEKOLOGIIA. (12):40-42, 1982.

The use of prostaglandins for regulation of the estrous cycle and as an abortifacient in cattle, by J. G. Manns. VETERINARY CLINICS OF NORTH AMERICA. 5(1):169-181, March 1983.

The use of prostaglandins for termination of abnormal pregnancy,

by N. J. Christensen, et al. ACTA OBSTETRICIA ET GYNE-
COLOGICA SCANDINAVICA SUPPLEMENT. 113:153-157,
1983.

Use of quinine for self-induced abortion, by A. L. Dannenberg, et
al. SOUTHERN MEDICAL JOURNAL. 76(7):846-849, July 1983.

The use of sulprostone to induce abortion in the second trimester,
by N. Ragni, et al. PROSTAGLANDINS LEUKOTRIENES
AND MEDICINE. 9(5):483-489, November 1982.

The use of traditional and modern methods of fertility control in
Kinshasa, Zaire, by J. Bertrand, et al. POPULATION STUDIES.
37(1):129+, March 1983.

Usefulness of cytohormonal vaginal smears for monitoring threatened
early pregnancy, by M. Myskow, et al. WIADOMOSCI
LEKARSKIE. 35(15-16):973-977, September 15, 1982.

The user perspective in northern Thailand: a series of case studies,
by N. Iddhichiracharas, et al. STUDIES IN FAMILY PLANNING.
14:48-56, February 1983.

Using model projects to introduce change into family planning
programs, by M. H. Bernhart. STUDIES IN FAMILY PLANNING.
12(10):346-352, October 1981.

Using oral history to chart the course of illegal abortions in Montana,
by D. Sands. FRONTIERS. 7(1):32-37, 1983.

Uterine activity and placental histology in abortion at mid-trimester
by rivanol and catheter, by Y. Manabe, et al. ACTA OBSTETRICIA
ET GYNECOLOGICA SCANDINAVICA. 61(5):433-437, 1982.

Vacuum aspiration in therapeutic abortions, by G. Frick. ACTA
OBSTETRICIA ET GYNECOLOGICA SCANDINAVICA.
61(6):523-524, 1982.

Vaginal colonization of Escherichia coli and its relation to contraceptive methods, by A. W. Chow. CONTRACEPTION. 27(5):
497-504, 1983.

Vaginal spermicides and miscarriage seen primarily in the emergency room, by H. Jick, et al. TERATOGENESIS, CARCINOGENESIS, AND MUTAGENESIS. 2(2):205-210, 1982.

Vaginal spermicides, chromosomal abnormalities and limb reduction defects, by J. F. Cordero, et al. FAMILY PLANNING PERSPECTIVES. 15(1):16-18, January-February 1983.

Value of Schwangerschaftsprotein 1 (SP1) and pregnancy-associated plasma protein-A (PAPP-A) in the clinical management of threatened abortion, by G. M. Masson, et al. BRITISH JOURNAL OF OBSTETRICS AND GYNAECOLOGY. 90(2):146-149, February 1983.

Value scaling of family planning conditions, by B. Maspfuhl. ZENTRALBLATT FUR GYNAKOLOGIE. 104(15):980-987, 1982.

Values clarification as a technique for family planning education, by J. V. Toohey, et al. JOURNAL OF SCHOOL HEALTH. 53(2):121-125, February 1983.

Variation of fat intake with estrous cycle, ovariectomy and estradiol replacement in hamsters, by M. O. Miceli, et al. PHYSIOLOGY AND BEHAVIOR. 30(3):415-420, March 1983.

Vasectomy, by H. Brownlee, et al. JOURNAL OF FAMILY PRACTICE. 16(2):379-384, February 1983.

The vasectomy decision-making process, by S. D. Mumford. STUDIES IN FAMILY PLANNING. 14(3):83, March 1983.

Vasectomy, disease link refuted. SCIENCE NEWS. 124:377, December 10, 1983.

Vasectomy in Guatemala: a follow-up study of five-hundred acceptors, by R. Santiso, et al. SOCIAL BIOLOGY. 28(3-4): 253-264, Fall-Winter 1981.

Vasectomy: an international appraisal, by J. H. Johnson. FAMILY PLANNING PERSPECTIVES. 15:45-48, January-February 1983.

Vasectomy reversal: experience in Ramathibodi hospital, Thailand, by K. Ratana-olarn, et al. JOURNAL OF THE MEDICAL ASSOCIATION OF THAILAND. 65(5):240-245, May 1982.

Vasectomy reversal technique and results, by S. E. Denton, et al. ARIZONA MEDICINE. 40(1):33-36, January 1983.

Vasoplasty: flap operation, by H. Singh, et al. BRITISH JOURNAL OF UROLOGY. 55(2):233-234, April 1983.

Vasovasostomy in the rat. Improved technique using absorable microsuture (polyglycolic acid), by S. Lee, et al. UROLOGY. 20(4):418-421, October 1982.

Vasvasostomy: results 1975-1981 of reconstructive operations following the sterilization of males, by H. J. Ubels, et al. NEDERLANDS TIJDSCHRIFT VOOR GENEESKUNDE. 126(30):1359-1363, July 24, 1982.

The vatican and population growth control: why an American confrontation, by S. D. Mumford. THE HUMANIST. 43(5):18-24, 34, September-October 1983.

Vatican backs Szoka, by F. Lilly. REGISTER. 59:1+, April 10, 1983.

Vatican veto [appointment of nun to Michigan's Dept. of Social Services]. CHRISTIAN CENTURY. 100:337, April 13, 1983.

Ventilatory response of humans to chronic contraceptive pill administration, by C. A. Smith, et al. RESPIRATION. 43(3): 179-185, 1982.

Verbal war of morality [Ireland], by B. Keenan. MACLEANS. 96:53, September 19, 1983.

Via Dolorosa. ECONOMIST. 286:46, February 5-11, 1983.

Via Dolorosa. ECONOMIST. 286-62, February 5, 1983.

Vital aspects of nursing: the family planning component, by U. Bhandari, et al. NURSING JOURNAL OF INDIA. 73(5):

141-143, May 1982.

Voluntary sterilization for persons with mental disabilities: the need for legislation, by B. A. Burnett. SYRACUSE LAW REVIEW. 32:913-955, Fall 1981.

Voluntary sterilization in Flanders, by R. L. Cliquet, et al. JOURNAL OF BIOSOCIAL SCIENCE. 13:47-61, 1981.

Voluntary sterilization in Guatemala: a comparison of men and women, by R. Santiso, et al. STUDIES IN FAMILY PLANNING. 14(3):73-82, March 1983.

Volunteers can't support abortion. REGISTER. 59:2, June 5, 1983.

WFS survey shows that western, eastern Europe differ greatly in use of modern contraceptives. FAMILY PLANNING PERSPECTIVES. 15:82-83, March-April 1983.

Waiting times to first birth in a rural area, by L. Rosetta. ANNALS OF HUMAN BIOLOGY. 10(4):347-352, July-August 1983.

War and abortion are twin targets for this veteran Christian activist, by M. Meehan. REGISTER. 59:1+, October 23, 1983.

Water intoxication following oxytocin perfusion, by G. Borg, et al. JOURNAL DE GYNECOLOGIE, OBSTETRIQUE ET BIOLOGIE DE LA REPRODUCTION. 12(1):51-53, 1983.

"What has this to do with working class women?": birth control and the Canadian left, 1900-1939, by A. McLaren. SOCIAL HISTORY. 14(28):435-454, 1981.

What price children? [expensive years of parenthood], by C. Tuhy. MONEY. 12:77-84, March 1983.

What U. S. women think and do about contraception, by J. D. Forrest, et al. FAMILY PLANNING PERSPECTIVES. 15(4): 157-158, 160-166, July-August 1983.

What you should know about over-the-counter contraceptives, by E. Rodgers. SEVENTEEN. 42:26+, April 1983.

What's holding up the male birth-control pill?, by L. Lader. MC-CALLS. 110:158, May 1983.

What's new in female sterilization? The silicone tubal plug is, by F. D. Loffer. ARIZONA MEDICINE. 39(7):442-445, July 1982.

What's new: kiss and tell—squeal rule enjoined, by A. Ashman. AMERICAN BAR ASSOCIATION JOURNAL. 69:829-830, June 1983.

When does personhood begin, by P. Donovan. FAMILY PLANNING PERSPECTIVES. 15:40-44, January-February 1983.

When patients ask . . . about . . . the latest and safest oral contraceptive, by E. Trimmer. MIDWIFE, HEALTH VISITOR AND COMMUNITY NURSE. 18(11):484, November 1982.

When the pill is not first choice, by L. Edmunds. DAILY TELE-GRAPH. August 31, 1983, p. 13.

When rebel nuns go public [views on abortion], by A. P. Ware. MS. 12:102-104, September 1983.

Who is still afraid of the pill today? The development of hormonal contraception ('the pill') in the last 20 years. Current status, by M. van Vliet. TIJDSCHRIFT VOR ZIEKENVERPLEGING. 35(20):659-663, October 1982.

Whose life?, by M. Holland. NEW STATESMAN. 105:12-13, January 28, 1983.

Why is the number of pregnancies among teenagers decreasing?, by M. G. Powell, et al. CANADIAN MEDICAL ASSOCIATION JOURNAL. 127(6):493-495, September 1982.

Why is pro-abortion AID official still there? (J. J. Speidel), by D. Lambro. HEALTH EDUCATION. 43:16, February 12, 1983.

Why now?, by J. I. Rosoff. FAMILY PLANNING PERSPECTIVES. 14(4):180, July-August 1982.

Why teenagers get pregnant [failure to use contraceptives due to erotophobia (fear of sex), by W. A. Fisher. PSYCHOLOGY TODAY. 17:70-71, March 1983.

Why teens opt for abortion, by P. Craig. OKLAHOMA OBSERVER. 14:12, November 10, 1982.

Will a do-it-yourself abortion drug hit the market soon? [Upjohn's research on prostaglandins], by R. Frame. CHRISTIANITY TODAY. 27:71-72, October 7, 1983.

Women in the sea services: 1972-1982, by G. C. Sadler. UNITED STATES NAVEL INSTITUTE PROCEEDINGS. 109:140-155, May 1983.

Women in toxic work environments: a case study of social problem development, by D. M. Randall, et al. SOCIAL PROBLEMS. 30:410-424, April 1983.

Women who didn't have an abortion. LANDERS HERALD. 26(4): 140, March-April 1982.

Women who have had an abortion. LANDERS HERALD. 26(4): 141, March-April 1982.

Women who use barrier methods less likely to be hospitalized for PID [pelivc inflammatory disease]. FAMILY PLANNING PERSPECTIVES. 14:331-332, November-December 1982.

Women, work and reproductive hazards, by R. Bayer. HASTINGS CENTER REPORT. 12:14-19, October 1982.

The women's centre in Jamaica: an innovative project for adolescent mothers, by P. McNeil, et al. STUDIES IN FAMILY PLANNING. 14(5):143-149, May 1983.

Wrongful birth concept gains acceptance, by G. Oliver. NATIONAL CATHOLIC REPORTER. 19:2, February 4, 1983.

Wrongful birth: how much is it worth not to be born?, by E. B. Goldman. MICHIGAN HOSPITALS. 19(3):25, 27-28, March 1983.

Yes to consistent life ethic. NATIONAL CATHOLIC REPORTER. 20:12, December 16, 1983.

Young and dedicated, Ellen works for life, by V. Warner. REGISTER. 59:1-2, June 26, 1983.

Young adult women's contraceptive decision: a comparison of two predictive models of choice, by E. J. Herz. DISSERTATION ABSTRACTS INTERNATIONAL: B. 44(3), September 1983.

Your opinion [teen-age birth control squeal rule], by L. A. Sullivan, et al. SEVENTEEN. 42:42+, November 1983.

The zoapatle I—a traditional remedy from Mexico emerges to modern times, by A. J. Gallegos. CONTRACEPTION. 27(3):211-225, March 1983.

PERIODICAL LITERATURE

SUBJECT INDEX

ABORTION: GENERAL
Abortion, by A. Menke. PIELEGNIARKA I POLOZNA.
(10):5-6, 1982.

Abortion [letter], by A. Simpson, et al. NEW ZEALAND
MEDICAL JOURNAL. 96(727):184-185, March 9, 1983.

Abortion and argument by analogy, by L. S. Cahill. HORIZONS.
9:271-287, Fall 1982.

Abortion and cloning, by E. R. Kraemer. SOUTHERN JOUR-
NAL OF PHILOSOPHY. 21:537-546, Winter 1983.

Abortion and physical dependence, by D. Gueras, et al. SOUTH-
WEST PHILOSOPHICAL STUDIES. 7:124-130, April 1984.

The abortion arena: recent activity, by L. S. Goldstein, et al.
LEGAL MEDICAL QUARTERLY. 213-226, 1982.

Abortion, contraception, infanticide, by P. E. Devine. PHI-
LOSOPHY. 58:513-520, October 1983.

Abortion examined, by M. Kenny. TABLET. 237:578-579,
June 18, 1983; 602-603, June 25, 1983; 627-628, July 2,
1983.

Abortion: a national security issue, by S. D. Mumford.
HUMANIST. 42:12-13+, September-October 1982.

Aspects of the pathophysiology of the first trimester of

pregnancy, by H. Fox. GINEKOLOGIA POLSKA. 53(9): 585-592, 1982.

The attack on women's rights, by L. Cooper. CRIME AND SOCIAL JUSTICE. 15:39-41, Summer 1981.

Bernadette. COPIE ZERO. 12:19, 1982.

Bill may ban abortion in unemployed health coverage. OUR SUNDAY VISITOR. 72:8, June 12, 1983.

By justified means, a life ends. REGISTER. 59:3, September 11, 1983.

The coathanger and the rose, by D. Granberg, et al. SOCIETY. 19(4):39-46, 1982.

Contraception and prescriptive infallibility, by G. L. Hallett. THEOLOGICAL STUDIES. 43:629-650, December 1982.

A critique on abortion rights, by R. Stith. DEMOCRACY. 3:60-70, Fall 1983.

Dearth of contraception fuels world abortion rate. NATIONAL CATHOLIC REPORTER. 19:10, January 21, 1983.

Dilemmas in prenatal diagnosis: a case study, by W. J. Fibison, et al. ISSUES IN HEALTH CARE OF WOMEN. 4(1):57-67, January-February 1983.

Dressed to over kill, by M. Musto. VILLAGE VOICE. 28:27, March 8, 1983.

Fetal alcohol syndrome; other effects of alcohol on pregnancy, by A. S. Lele. NEW YORK STATE JOURNAL OF MEDICINE. 82(8):1225-1227, July 1982.

Fetus as organ donor [using pancreas aborted fetuses; work of Josiah Brown and Kevin Lafferty]. SCIENCE DIGEST. 91:85, June 1983.

If not abortion, what then, by S. Reed, et al. CHRISTIANITY TODAY. 27:14-23, May 20, 1983.

Interruption of pregnancy, by H. Zakut, et al. HAREFUAH. 102(8):350-352, April 15, 1982.

It happens to us. LANDER'S HERALD. 26(4):153, March-April 1982.

Literary but technical abortion. REVISTA DE ENFERMAGEN. 6(58-59):40-41, May-June 1983.

Medical association is involved, by H. Vorse. OKLAHOMA OBSERVER. 15:9, October 10, 1983.

Need to care. INFORMATION. 5(6):111, 1982.

New row looms over birth jab, by F. Lesser, et al. NEW SCIENTIST. 99:256, July 28, 1983.

Not tonight, by H. M. White. INFORMATION. 1:16, 1982.

On abortion, by B. Greenberg. HADASSAH MAGAZINE. 64:19-21, October 1982.

Operating on the fetus, by W. Ruddick, et al. HASTINGS CENTER REPORT. 12:10-14, October 1982.

Opting for adoption—dispelling the myths, by B. Maschinot. NATIONAL CATHOLIC REPORTER. 19:2, January 21, 1983.

Politics of abortion: a Morgentaler invitation embitters Calgary aldermen, by C. Hayes, et al. ALBERTA REPORT. 10:11, 13, April 11, 1983.

Prairie storm, by E. Mandell. BOOKLIST. 79(5):398, November 1, 1982.

Prevention of unwanted pregnancy, by M. Gerrard, et al.

AMERICAN JOURNAL OF COMMUNITY PSYCHOLOGY. 11(2):153-167, April 1983.

Relative body weight as a factor in the decision to abort, by T. H. Thelen. PSYCHOLOGICAL REPORTS. 52(3):763-775, June 1983.

Responsibility and moral maturity in the control of fertility—or, a woman's place is in the wrong, by M. A. O'Loughlin. SOCIAL RESEARCH. 50(3):556-575, 1983.

Rubella vaccine does not mandate abortion. NURSE DRUG ALERT. 7(1):3, January 1983.

Some basic facts about abortion, by D. S. Gluckin, et al. MADEMOISELLE. 89:166+, October 1983.

Some biological insights into abortion, by G. Hardin. BIO-SCIENCE. 32:720+, October 1982.

Sooner or later? Nagging question for some, by A. S. Kasper. NEW DIRECTIONS FOR WOMEN. 11:4, May-June 1983.

Surgical death, by J. V. Schall. LINACRE QUARTERLY. 49:305-307, November 1982.

Surveillance of pregnancy loss in human populations, by A. J. Wilcos. AMERICAN JOURNAL OF INDUSTRIAL MEDICINE. 4(1-2):285-291, 1983.

Szoka draws praise, by F. Lilly. REGISTER. 59:1+, March 13, 1983.

Technology and reproductive rights: how advances in technology can be used to limit women's reproductive rights [right to abortion], by S. M. Lynn. WOMEN'S RIGHTS LAW RE-PORTER. 7:223-227, Spring 1982.

Termination of pregnancy, by D. Krishnamoni, et al.

CANADIAN JOURNAL OF PSYCHIATRY. 28(6):457-461, October 1983.

Time running out on death row, by M. Meehan. NATIONAL CATHOLIC REPORTER. 20:12, November 18, 1983.

To be or not to be: protecting the unborn's potentiality of live, by J. A. Parness, et al. UNIVERSITY OF CINCINNATI LAW REVIEW. 51:257-298, 1982.

Women who didn't have an abortion. LANDERS HERALD. 26(4):140, March-April 1982.

Women who have had an abortion. LANDERS HERALD. 26(4):141, March-April 1982.

Wrongful birth concept gains acceptance, by G. Oliver. NATIONAL CATHOLIC REPORTER. 19:2, February 4, 1983.

AFRICA
Medicinal plants used for abortion and childbirth in eastern Africa, by G. D. Yu. CHUNG YAO TUNG PAO. 7(5):6-7, September 1982.

AUSTRALIA
Australian attitudes towards abortion: recent complementary surveys, by S. E. Fraser, et al. AUSTRALIAN JOURNAL OF SEX, MARRIAGE AND FAMILY. 3(4):171-180, November 1982.

Characteristics of two samples of women seeking abortion in Queensland, by A. S. Bourne, et al. AUSTRALIAN JOURNAL OF SOCIAL ISSUES. 17(3):207-219, 1982.

Conservatism, attitude to abortion, and Maccoby's biophilia, by J. J. Ray, et al. JOURNAL OF SOCIAL PSYCHOLOGY. 118:143-144, October 1982.

Repeat abortion-seeking behaviour in Queensland, Australia: knowledge and use of contraception and reasons for terminating the pregnancy, by V. J. Callan. JOURNAL OF BIOSOCIAL SCIENCE. 15:1-8, January 1983.

Repeat and first abortion seekers: single women in Brisbane, Australia, by V. J. Callan. JOURNAL OF BIOSOCIAL SCIENCE. 15:217-222, April 1983.

BANGLADESH
Case studies of indigenous abortion practitioners in rural Bangladesh, by S. Islam. STUDIES IN FAMILY PLANNING. 13(3):86-93, March 1982.

BELGIUM
Induced abortion in Belgium: clinical experience and psychosocial observations, by M. Vekemans, et al. STUDIES IN FAMILY PLANNING. 13(pt 1):355-364, December 1982.

CANADA
Beyond the abortion charges, by P. Carlyle-Gordge. MACLEANS. 96:17, September 12, 1983.

Canada's abortion dispute escalating, by J. Rasmussen. REGISTER. 59:1+, May 29, 1983.

Doctors and abortion, by J. Van Dusen. MACLEANS. 96:43, August 8, 1983.

Early complication risks of legal abortions, Canada, 1975-1980, by S. Wadhera. CANADIAN JOURNAL OF PUBLIC HEALTH. 73(6):396-400, November-December 1982.

Morgentaler moves west [abortion clinic in Winnipeg], by P. Carlyle-Gordge. MACLEANS. 96:42-43, May 16, 1983.

Morgentaler's crusade moves east [Toronto clinic opens], by C. Bruman. MACLEANS. 96:44, June 27, 1983.

A raid in the abortion war [H. Morgentaler's clinic in Winnipeg], by V. Ross. MACLEANS. 96:21, June 13, 1983.

CHINA
Expelled, for giving the facts on abortions, by J. Mirsky.
TIMES. April 9, 1983, p. 6.

CZECHOSLOVAKIA
Demographic data for the Czechoslovak Soviet Socialist Republic
(Bohemia and Slovakia) for the years 1980 and 1981.
CESKOSLOVENSKA PEDIATRIE. 37(8):477-480,
August 1982.

Long-term study of the incidence of the birth of premature
fetuses in Czechoslovakia, by I. Pfeifer, et al.
CESKOSLOVENSKA GYNEKOLOGIE. 48(2):83-88,
March 1983.

FINLAND
Spontaneous abortions and reproductive selection mechanisms
in the rubber and leather industry in Finland, by K.
Hemminiki, et al. BRITISH JOURNAL OF INDUSTRIAL
MEDICINE. 40(1):81-86, February 1983.

Spontaneous abortions in an industrialized community in
Finland, by K. Hemminki, et al. AMERICAN JOURNAL OF
PUBLIC HEALTH. 73(1):32-37, January 1983.

FRANCE
Is a sociology of abortion possible?, by F. A. Isambert. REVUE
FRANCAISE DE SOCIOLOGIE. 23(3):359-381, July-
September 1982.

GERMANY
Predictors of abortion attitudes in the federal republic of
Germany, by J. S. Legge, Jr. JOURNAL OF POLITICS.
45(3):759-766, August 1983.

GREAT BRITAIN
Barrenness against nature: recourse to abortion in pre-industrial
England, by A. McLaren. JOURNAL OF SEX RESEARCH.

17(3):224-237, August 1981.

Trends in induced abortion in England and Wales, by J. R. Ashton, et al. JOURNAL OF EPIDEMIOLOGY AND COMMUNITY HEALTH. 37(2):105-110, June 1983.

GREECE
Abortion in Greece, by S. Ginger. CONTEMPORARY RE-VIEW. 243:253-255, November 1983.

INDIA
An equal-opportunity destroyer, by J. McGowan. US CATHOLIC. 48:27-29, April 1983.

IRELAND
The abortion debate, by M. Jones. WORLD HEALTH. November 1982, p. 6-9.

The abortion debate in the republic of Ireland, by T. P. O'Mahoney. AMERICA. 148:110-112, February 12, 1983.

Bishop's pawns. ECONOMIST. 287:46+, April 9, 1983.

Church and state: a Protestant backlash against next month's referendum on abortion, by M. Holland. NEW STATESMAN. May 13, 1983, p. 16-17.

The greater immorality. STUDIES. 72:1-5, Spring 1983.

Haughey placed, FitzGerald nobbled. ECONOMIST. 286:58-59, February 19, 1983.

Ireland: a referendum to abort Fine Gael? ECONOMIST. 284:39+, August 7, 1982.

Ireland debates abortion, by L. McRedmond. TABLET. 237:346-347, April 16, 1983.

It's an ill wind . . . ECONOMIST. 286:60-61, February 5, 1983.

ABORTION: GENERAL (continued)

Needle point debate: referendum, by M. Holland. NEW
STATESMAN. February 25, 1983, p. 11.

Pro-life, pro-uniformity, by M. Holland. NEW STATESMAN.
103:12-13, May 21, 1982.

Whose life?, by M. Holland. NEW STATESMAN. 105:12-13,
January 28, 1983.

ITALY
Legal abortion in Italy, 1978-1980 [letter], by S. L. Tosi, et al.
NEW ENGLAND JOURNAL OF MEDICINE. 308(1):51-52,
January 6, 1983.

JAPAN
Analysis of multiple birth rates in Japan. VII. Rates spontaneous
and induced terminations of pregnancy in twins, by Y.
Imaizumi, et al. JINRUI IDENGAKU ZASSHI. 27(3):235-
242, September 1982.

LATIN AMERICA
The abortion debate . . . obtaining statistics in Latin American
countries is enormously difficult, by M. Jones. WORLD
HEALTH. November 1982, p. 6-9.

MEXICO
Psychosocial determinants of abortion attitudes among Mexican
American women, by A. Hortensia de Los Angeles. DIS-
SERTATION ABSTRACTS INTERNATIONAL: B. 43(10),
April 1983.

The zoapatle I—a traditional remedy from Mexico emerges to
modern times, by A. J. Gallegos. CONTRACEPTION. 27(3):
211-225, March 1983.

NEW ZEALAND
Attitudes toward abortion in a provincial area of New Zealand:
differentials and determinants, by P. Perry, et al. THE
AUSTRALIAN AND NEW ZEALAND JOURNAL OF
SOCIOLOGY. 18(3):399-416, 1982.

NORWAY

Experience with prostaglandins for therapeutic abortion in Norway. Their need and their benefits, by P. Fylling, et al. ACTA OBSTETRICIA ET GYNECOLOGICA SCANDINAVICA, SUPPLEMENT. 113:113-116, 1983.

PORTUGAL

Illegal abortions take toll in Portugal, by P. Kassell. NEW DIRECTIONS FOR WOMEN. 11:9, May-June 1983.

SPAIN

Abortion. Spain: the keys to the controversy. REVISTA DE ENFERMAGEN. 6(58-59):34-35, May-June 1983.

Doctors' dilemma, by D. Gollob. NEW STATESMAN. February 4, 1983, p. 18.

Spain: the abortion battle. REVISTA DE ENFERMAGEN. 6(58-59):22-27, May-June 1983.

Spain's abortion controversy, by R. Plaza. WORLD PRESS REVIEW. 30:56, April 1983.

Via Dolorosa. ECONOMIST. 286:46, February 5-11, 1983.

UNITED STATES

Abortion and fertility in economic perspective: a theoretical and empirical analysis with special reference to New York City, 1969-1972, by M. J. Kramer. DISSERTATION ABSTRACTS INTERNATIONAL: A. 43(9), March 1983.

Attitudes toward abortion among Catholic Mexican-American women: the effects of religiosity and education, by S. Rosenhouse-Persson, et al. DEMOGRAPHY. 20:87-98, February 1983.

Characteristics of abortion patients in the United States, 1979 and 1980, by S. K. Henshaw, et al. FAMILY PLANNING PERSPECTIVES. 15:5-15, January-February 1983.

ABORTION: GENERAL (continued)

Comparison of members of pro- and anti-abortion organizations in Missouri, by D. Granberg. SOCIAL BIOLOGY. 28(3-4): 239-252, Fall-Winter 1981.

Ecological analysis of the socioeconomic status of women having abortions in Manhattan, by R. M. Pierce. SOCIAL SCIENCE AND MEDICINE. 15D(2):277-286, May 1981.

Europe and the USA: abortion throughout the world. REVISTA DE ENFERMAGEN. 6(58-59):32-33, May-June 1983.

Repeat abortion in the United States: new insights, by C. Tietze, et al. STUDIES IN FAMILY PLANNING. 13(12):373, December 1982.

Sex education, abortion views of Mexican Americans typical of U. S. beliefs. FAMILY PLANNING PERSPECTIVES. 15:197, July-August 1983.

Third-trimester abortion rate inflated in Georgia; true rate is 4 per 100,000. FAMILY PLANNING PERSPECTIVES. 15:196, July-August 1983.

Third-trimester induced abortion in Georgia, 1979 and 1980, by A. M. Spitz, et al. AMERICAN JOURNAL OF PUBLIC HEALTH. 73:594-595, May 1983.

Using oral history to chart the course of illegal abortions in Montana, by D. Sands. FRONTIERS. 7(1):32-37, 1983.

ABORTION: ATTITUDES

Abortion and adoption: fetal value beyond the personhood debate, by M. S. Gregory. DISSERTATION ABSTRACTS INTERNATIONAL: A. 43(7), January 1983.

Abortion and the control of human bodies, by J. Stone. JOURNAL OF VALUE INQUIRY. 17:77-85, 1983.

Abortion and maternal morality 1968-1978, by A. Houel, et al.

REVUE FRANCAISE DE SOCIOLOGIE. 23(3):487-502, July-September 1982.

Abortion and morality, by R. Taylor, et al. FREE INQUIRY. 2:33, Fall 1982.

Abortion and the pursuit of happiness, by D. Rossi. LOGOS (USA). 3:61-67, 1982.

Abortion as a mixed good, by M. Kohl. FREE INQUIRY. 3:42, Winter 1982-1983.

Abortion attitude scale, by L. A. Sloan. HEALTH EDUCATION. 14:41-42, May-June 1983.

Abortion attitudes in medical students, by J. W. Bonar, et al. JOURNAL OF THE AMERICAN MEDICAL WOMEN'S ASSOCIATION. 38(2):43-45, March-April 1983.

Abortion: getting the ethics straight, by K. Lebacqz. LOGOS (USA). 3:47-60, 1982.

Abortion: the pendulum swings to the right, by D. Folster, et al. ATLANTIC INSIGHT. 4:52, November 1982.

Advice to pro-lifers—treasure life after birth as well as before, by T. Unsworth. NATIONAL CATHOLIC REPORTER. 20:13, December 23, 1983.

The antiabortion movement and symbolic crusades: re-appraisal of a popular theory, by P. J. Leahy, et al. ALTERNATIVE LIFESTYLES. 6(1):27-47, Fall 1983.

The arguments in favor of abortion are strong, by L. B. Smedes. CHRISTIANITY TODAY. 27:62, July 15, 1983.

Arrested 15 times, this mother fights for unborn, by M. Meehan. REGISTER. 59:1+, May 8, 1983.

Attacks on innocent life continue: abortion and infanticide at record levels, by W. Murchison. CATHOLIC DIGEST. 9:56, March 1983.

Attitudes of abortion counselors and their work role, by A. M. Jones. DISSERTATION ABSTRACTS INTERNATIONAL: A. 43(7), January 1983.

Attitudes toward abortion among Catholic Mexican-American women: the effects of religiosity and education, by S. Rosenhouse-Persson, et al. DEMOGRAPHY. 20:87-98, February 1983.

Attitudes toward abortion in a provincal area of New Zealand: differentials and determinants, by P. Perry, et al. THE AUSTRALIAN AND NEW ZEALAND JOURNAL OF SOCIOLOGY. 18(3):399-416, November 1982.

Australian attitudes towards abortion: recent complementary surveys, by S. E. Fraser, et al. AUSTRALIAN JOURNAL OF SEX, MARRIAGE AND FAMILY. 3(4):171-180, November 1982.

Basic data on visits to family planning services sites: United States, 1980, by B. L. Hudson. VITAL HEALTH STATISTICS. 68:1-32, July 1982.

The beginning of personhood: a Thomistic perspective, by P. A. Smith. LAVAL THEOLOGIQUE ET PHILOSOPHIQUE. 39:195-214, June 1983.

Blacks, whites, and attitudes toward abortion, by M. W. Combs, et al. PUBLIC OPINION QUARTERLY. 46:510-520, Winter 1982.

CLC affirms women's right to abortion. CANADIAN LABOUR. 28:7, May 1983.

Chronicle of life and death: nobody wants an abortion, by M. B. Gordon. COMMONWEAL. 110:557-558, October 21, 1983.

College students' attitudes toward shared responsibility in decisions about abortion: implications for counseling, by I. J. Ryan, et al. JOURNAL OF THE AMERICAN COLLEGE HEALTH ASSOCIATION. 31(6):231-235, June 1983.

Comparison of members of pro- and anti-abortion organizations in Missouri, by D. Granberg. SOCIAL BIOLOGY. 28(3-4):239-252, Fall-Winter 1981.

Comparison of pro-choice and pro-life activists: their values, attitudes, and beliefs [Missouri], by D. Granberg. POPULATION AND ENVIRONMENT. 5:75-94, Summer 1982.

Conservatism, attitude to abortion, and Maccoby's biophilia, by J. J. Ray, et al. JOURNAL OF SOCIAL PSYCHOLOGY. 118(1):143-144, October 1982.

Considering abortion: measuring the distances between the law, social reality and personal morality, by A. Collins. TORONTO LIFE. December 1983, p. 107-112.

Contraceptive use and perceptions of chance and ability of conceiving in women electing abortion, by P. M. Klein. JOURNAL OF OBSTETRIC, GYNECOLOGIC AND NEONATAL NURSING. 12(3):167-171, May-June 1983.

The day I faced the reality of abortion, by E. Q. Vich. RN. 46(8):50, 52, August 1983.

Defining battle lines; rules for debate, by K. Himes. NATIONAL CATHOLIC REPORTER. 19:7, January 21, 1983.

Dignity of life developments, by D. J. Horan. CATHOLIC LAWYER. 27:239-245, Summer 1982.

Ecumenical approach to abortion, by R. Evans. ECUMENIST. 21:64-67, May-June, July-August 1983.

The effectiveness of various arguments for the humanity of

the unborn, by J. V. Wagner. PROCEEDINGS OF THE
AMERICAN CATHOLIC PHILOSOPHICAL ASSOCIATION.
56:146-153, 1982.

Englehardt on the abortion and euthanasia of defective infants,
by G. E. Jones. LINACRE QUARTERLY. 50:172-181,
May 1983.

An equal-opportunity destroyer, by J. McGowan. US
CATHOLIC. 48:27-29, April 1983.

Fetal indication for the termination of pregnancy from an
ethical viewpoint, by A. Auer. GEBURTSHILFE UND
FRAUENHEILKUNDE. 43(1):51-56, January 1983.

The fetus as a patient: emerging rights as a person?, by J. L.
Lenow. AMERICAN JOURNAL OF LAW AND MEDICINE.
9:1-29, Spring 1983.

The first human right: a pro-life primer; excerpts from the
first human right: a pro-life primer, by C. M. Odell, et al.
OUR SUNDAY VISITOR. 71:1+, January 16, 1983.

Foetuses, famous violinists, and the right to continued aid, by
M. Davis. PHILOSOPHICAL QUARTERLY. 33:259-278,
July 1983.

The hidden grief of abortion, by J. Upton. PASTORAL PSYCHOL-
OGY. 31:19-25, Fall 1982.

A highly emotional decision . . . abortion, by J. Thompson.
NURSING MIRROR AND MIDWIVE'S JOURNAL. 157(4):
41, July 27, 1983.

"If you prick us, do we not bleed?": of Shylock, fetuses, and
the concept of person in the law, by C. H. Baron. LAW,
MEDICINE AND HEALTH CARE. 11(2):52-63, April 1983.

Is abortion morally justifiable?, by S. K. Bell. NURSING
FORUM. 20(3):288-295, 1981.

Killing makes me uneasy, by R. A. Hanley. NEW COVENANT. 12:17-18, June 1983.

Knowing abortion firsthand, by M. Meehan. REGISTER. 59:1+, July 31, 1983.

Make them all wanted children, by N. Mallory. HOME MAGAZINE. 18:62, 64, April 1983.

Male utopias or nightmares, by D. Kumar. ECONOMIC AND POLITICAL WEEKLY. 18(3):61-64, 1983.

March for life gears up for anniversary, by M. Meehan. REGISTER. 59:1+, January 16, 1983.

Medical-social aspects of the voluntary interruption of pregnancy: reflections on the routine data of an outpatient clinic, by C. Humblet, et al. REVUE DE L'INSTITUT DE SOCIOLOGIE. (3-4):477-507, 1982.

Method of predicting obstetrical complications, by G. A. Ushakova. AKUSHERSTVO I GINEKOLOGIIA. (9):45-47, September 1982.

Miscarriages and abortions affect breast-cancer risks, by S. Katz. CHATELAINE. 56:18, July 1983.

A mutation in the mechanisms of social control: the case of abortion, by C. Horellou-Lafarge. REVUE FRANCAISE DE SOCIOLOGIE. 23(3):397-416, July-September 1982.

My two daughters' abortions, by N. Hunt. MS. 12:21-24, August 1983.

Nation's new agony over abortion, by S. Riley. MACLEANS. 96:cover, 32-35, July 25, 1983.

Never give up Helms says, as struggle for the unborn intensifies, by M. Meehan. REGISTER. 59:8, February 6, 1983.

The new biology and the question of personhood: implications for abortion, by T. H. Milby. AMERICAN JOURNAL OF LAW AND MEDICINE. 9:31-41, Spring 1983.

New Brunswick: the doctors defy antiabortion tides, by D. Folster. MACLEANS. 96:15, January 10, 1983.

Normative boundaries and abortion policy: the politics of morality, by S. L. Markson. RESEARCH IN SOCIAL PROBLEMS AND PUBLIC POLICY. 2:21-33, 1982.

Obstetric histories of women occupationally exposed to styrene, by H. Harkonen, et al. SCANDINAVIAN JOURNAL OF WORK, ENVIRONMENT AND HEALTH. 8(1):74-77, March 1982.

One day you will understand . . . having an abortion. NURSING MIRROR AND MIDWIVE'S JOURNAL. 157(8):Midwifery forum 8:xi-xii, August 24, 1983.

Operating on the fetus, by W. Ruddick. HASTINGS CENTER REPORT. 12:10-14, October 1982.

Opinions of the United States supreme court: abortion. THE CRIMINAL LAW REPORTER: TEXT NO. 10. 33(11):3143-3159, June 15, 1983.

Personal conscience and abortion, by J. W. Baker. SOCIAL JUSTICE REVIEW. 74:63, March-April 1983.

Personhood, property rights and the permissibility of abortion, by P. A. Roth. LAW AND PHILOSOPHY. 2:163-192, August 1983.

Phone book discounts for abortion raise pro-life ire. OUR SUNDAY VISITOR. 71:8, December 5, 1982.

Post-abortion counselling, by G. Cooper. NURSING MIRROR AND MIDWIVE'S JOURNAL. 157(8):Midwifery forum 8: i-xi, August 24, 1983.

Predictors of abortion attitudes in the federal republic of Germany, by J. S. Legge, Jr. JOURNAL OF POLITICS. 45(3):759-766, August 1983.

Pregnant? No thanks! . . . nine women discuss their experiences. NURSING MIRROR AND MIDWIVE'S JOURNAL. 156(4): Clinical forum 1:33-37, January 26, 1983.

Pregnant women's attitudes toward the abortion of defective fetuses, by R. Faden, et al. POPULATION AND ENVIRON-MENT. 6(4):197-209, 1983.

Prenatal testing for tay-sachs disease in the light of Jewish views regarding abortion, by J. Baskin. ISSUES IN HEALTH CARE OF WOMEN. 4(1):41-56, January-February 1983.

The problem of abortion in patients with heart surgery, by E. Revelli, et al. MINERVA MEDICA. 73(44):3163-3167, November 17, 1982.

The prolife agenda: converts or convicts?, by R. E. Burns. US CATHOLIC. 48:2, April 1983.

Prolife compassion or crusade?, by J. Evans. AMERICA. 147:373-374, December 11, 1982.

Pro-life or pro-choice? CANADA AND THE WORLD. 48:7-9, May 1983.

Prolifers will accept heckler, by C. Hays. REGISTER. 59:1+, February 27, 1983.

Psychosocial determinants of abortion attitudes among Mexican American women, by A. Hortensia de Los Angeles. DIS-SERTATION ABSTRACTS INTERNATIONAL: B. 43(10), April 1983.

Public attitudes toward life and death, by D. O. Sawyer. PUBLIC OPINION QUARTERLY. 46(4):521-533, Winter 1982.

Public policies and family outcomes: empirical evidence or theology?, by S. L. Zimmerman. SOCIAL CASEWORK. 64(3):138-146, 1983.

Public views abortion, by J. Mann. OKLAHOMA OBSERVER. 14:3, November 10, 1982.

Rape and abortion in America [dismissal of teacher and rape victim J. Eckmann for deciding to keep her baby in McHenry County, Ill., by L. M. Delloff. CHRISTIAN CENTURY. 99:1037-1038, October 20, 1982.

Recent changes in predictors of abortion attitudes, by S. N. Barnett, et al. SOCIOLOGY AND SOCIAL RESEARCH. 66(3):320-334, April 1982.

Respecting life and painting dragons, by T. C. Fox. NATIONAL CATHOLIC REPORTER. 18:2, October 15, 1982.

Response to requests for abortion: the influence of guilt and knowledge, by A. R. Allgeier, et al. JOURNAL OF APPLIED SOCIAL PSYCHOLOGY. 12(4):281-291, 1982.

Rethinking pro-life issues. NATIONAL CATHOLIC REPORTER. 19:12, January 21, 1983.

Rise in antiabortion terrorism [tactics of right to life groups], by L. C. Wohl. MS. 11:19, November 1982.

Saving the babies, by J. Hensley. NEW COVENANT. 12:15-17, June 1983.

Setting up the project . . . to determine a patient's needs after an abortion, by S. Anthony. NURSING MIRROR AND MIDWIVE'S JOURNAL. 156(4):Clinical forum 1:32, January 26, 1983.

The silent holocaust: step II, by J. Blattner. NEW COVENANT. 13:16-20, September 1983.

Sixteen thousand fetuses intensify fight in which they have no stake, by P. Edmonds. NATIONAL CATHOLIC RE-PORTER. 19:1, January 21, 1983.

Socialization for sexual and contraceptive behavior: moral absolutes versus relative consequences, by E. Thomson. YOUTH AND SOCIETY. 14(1):103-128, September 1982.

Some thoughts on the ethics of abortion on demand, by R. L. Cleary. DIALOGUE. 25:60-68, April 1983.

Spanish women still struggle in "Paradise", by A. Dermansky. NEW DIRECTIONS FOR WOMEN. 12:4, July-August 1983.

Tay-sachs and the abortion controversy, by M. Kukin. JOURNAL OF RELIGION AND HEALTH. 20(3):224-242, 1981.

Toward a Copernican revolution in our thinking about life's beginning and life's end, by R. M. Green. SOUND. 66:152-173, Summer 1983.

Unmarried black adolescent fathers attitudes toward abortion, contraception and sexuality: a preliminary report, by L. E. Hendricks. JOURNAL OF ADOLESCENT HEALTH CARE. 2(3):199-204, 1982.

A verbal war of morality, by B. Keenan. MACLEANS. 96:53, September 19, 1983.

Volunteers can't support abortion. REGISTER. 59:2, June 5, 1983.

When does personhood begin, by P. Donovan. FAMILY PLANNING PERSPECTIVES. 15:40-44, January-February 1983.

Whose life?, by M. Holland. NEW STATESMAN. January 28, 1983, p. 12-13.

ABORTION: ATTITUDES (continued)

Wrongful birth concept gains acceptance, by G. Oliver. NATIONAL CATHOLIC REPORTER. 19:2, February 4, 1983.

Yes, to consistent life ethic. NATIONAL CATHOLIC REPORTER. 20:12, December 16, 1983.

ABORTION: COMPLICATIONS

Achievements in preventing the premature termination of pregnancy, by V. I. Bodiazhina. AKUSHERSTVO I GINEKOLOGIIA. (12):12-16, 1982.

Analysis of pathological outcome of pregnancy, by J. Olsen, et al. SCANDINAVIAN JOURNAL OF SOCIAL MEDICINE. 11(1):3-6, 1983.

Cervical injury during first-trimester abortion reduced with laminaria. FAMILY PLANNING PERSPECTIVES. 15:136-137, May-June 1983.

Contraceptive use and perceptions of chance and ability of conceiving in women electing abortion, by P. M. Klein. JOURNAL OF OBSTETRIC, GYNECOLOGIC AND NEONATAL NURSING. 12(3):167-171, May-June 1983.

Conversion disorder following termination of pregnancy, by G. D. Tollefson, et al. JOURNAL OF FAMILY PRACTICE. 16(1):73-77, January 1983.

Drug treatment of retained abortion, intrauterine death of the fetus and of vesicular mole with 15-ME-PGF2-alpha, by D. Granese, et al. MINERVA GINECOLOGIA. 34(6):467-474, June 1982.

Dyserythropoiesis in the fetal liver as an indicator of the intensity of stress caused by abortion, by A. Pajor, et al. ORVOSI HETILIP. 124(11):619-622, March 13, 1983.

Evaluation of the abortus and stillborn infant, by M. Barr, Jr.,

et al. JOURNAL OF REPRODUCTIVE MEDICINE.
27(9):601-603, September 1982.

Evaluation of female pelvic pain part 2, by K. C. Edelin.
HOSPITAL MEDICINE. 19(2):37-39, 42-44, 46+, February
1983.

Freedom of choice is immoral, by B. Amiel. MACLEANS.
96:17, November 21, 1983.

Impact of vacuum aspiration abortion on future childbear: a
review. FAMILY PLANNING PERSPECTIVES. 15:119-
125, May-June 1983.

Inversion of the uterus following abortion, by A. S. Gupta,
et al. JOURNAL OF THE INDIAN MEDICAL ASSOCIATION.
79(8):123-126, October 16, 1982.

Medical practices—abortion—down's syndrome. THE FAMILY
LAW REPORTER: COURT OPINIONS. 8(48):2733,
October 12, 1982.

Outcrossings in Caucasians and fetal loss, by J. B. Bresler.
SOCIAL BIOLOGY. 29(1-2):121-130, Spring-Summer 1982.

Pregnancy maintenance after early luteectomy by 17-
hydroxyprogesterone-capronate, by M. O. Pulkkinen. ACTA
OBSTETRICIA ET GYNECOLOGICA SCANDINAVICA.
61(4):347-349, 1982.

Relative body weight as a factor in the decision to abort, by
T. H. Thelen, et al. PSYCHOLOGICAL REPORTS. 52:
763-765, June 1983.

Renal functional recovery after acute postabortal renal in-
sufficiency, by N. Manescu, et al. REVISTA DE MEDICINA
INTERNA, NEUROLOGIE, PSIHIATRIE, NEURO-
CHIRURGIE, DEMATO-VENEROLOGIE, SERIA:
MEDICINA INTERNA. 34(6):553-560, November-December
1982.

Reproductive losses and chromosomal anomalies, by V. I. Alipov, et al. AKUSHERSTVO I GINEKOLOGIIA. (1): 38-41, 1983.

The role of minor chromosomal aberrations in reproduction disorders. A report on three new cases of satellites on chromosome 17, by D. Ioan, et al. ENDOCRINOLOGIE. 20(3):199-202, July-September 1982.

Side effects and early complications following cervical priming with prostaglandin F2 alpha (PGF2 alpha) in inducing abortion in young women in their first pregnancy, by B. Seifert, et al. ZENTRALBLATT FUR GYNAE-KOLOGIE. 105(11):710-714, 1983.

Smooth muscle antibodies in complicated early pregnancies, by I. Pietarinen, et al. AMERICAN JOURNAL OF REPRODUCTIVE IMMUNOLOGY. 3(1):43-45, January-February 1983.

Subclinical abortions in patients treated with clomiphene citrate, by P. C. Ho, et al. INTERNATIONAL JOURNAL OF GYNAECOLOGY AND OBSTETRICS. 20(5):379-382, October 1982.

Transabdominal isthmic cerclage for the treatment of in-competent cervix, by S. Olsen, et al. ACTA OBSTETRICIA ET GYNECOLOGICA SCANDINAVICA. 61(5):473-475, 1982.

Ureterouterine fistula as a complication of elective abortion, by G. T. Keegan, et al. JOURNAL OF UROLOGY. 128(1): 137-138, 1982.

ABORTION: COMPLICATIONS: PSYCHOLOGICAL

Factors affecting early and late deciders of voluntary childless-ness, by V. J. Callan. JOURNAL OF SOCIAL PSYCHOLOGY. 119:261-268, April 1983.

ABORTION: HISTORY

Abortion ten years later—1.5 million yearly; backers, foes
polarized, by J. T. Beifuss. NATIONAL CATHOLIC
REPORTER. 19:1+, January 21, 1983.

Second victory of Anthony Comstock, by R. Polenberg.
SOCIETY. 19(4):32-38, 1982.

Seventeenth century midwifery: the treatment of miscarriage,
by R. K. Marshall. NURSING MIRROR. 155(24):31-36,
December 15, 1982.

ABORTION: ILLEGAL

Illegal abortions take toll in Portugal, by P. Kassell. NEW
DIRECTIONS FOR WOMEN. 11:9, May-June 1983.

Using oral history to chart the course of illegal abortion in
Montana, by D. Sands. FRONTIERS. 7(1):32-37, 1983.

ABORTION: INCOMPLETE

Incomplete and inevitable abortion: treatment by suction
curettage in the emergency department, by R. G. Farrell,
et al. ANNALS OF EMERGENCY MEDICINE. 11(12):
652-658, December 1982.

ABORTION: INDUCED

Analysis of multiple birth rates in Japan. VII. Rates of
spontaneous and induced terminations of pregnancy in
twins, by Y. Imaizumi, et al. JINRUI IDENGAKU
ZASSHI. 27(3):235-242, September 1982.

Changes in intraocular pressure during prostaglandin-induced
abortion, by M. Ober, et al. KLINISCHE MONATS-
BLAETTER FUR AUGENHEILKUNDE. 180(3):230-
231, 1982.

Clinical efficacy of extracts of radix teichosanthis and

wikstroemia chamaedaphne meisn on mid-term labor induction—analysis of 248 cases, by M. Z. Wu, et al. CHUNG KUO I HSUEH KO HSUEH YUAN HSUEH PAO. 4(4):241-242, August 1982.

Determination of essential content as the basis for development of a curriculum model on care of the induced abortion patient for baccalaureate nursing faculty, by M. L. Olson. DISSERTATION ABSTRACTS INTERNATIONAL: A. 43(12), June 1983.

The effects of induced abortion on subsequent reproduction, by C. J. Hogue, et al. EPIDEMIOLOGIC REVIEWS. 4: 66-94, 1982.

Endocrinological aspects of rehabilitating women following induced abortion, by G. P. Koreneva, et al. AKUSHERSTVO I GINEKOLOGIIA. (12):45-48, 1982.

Induced abortion and social factors in wild horses, by J. Berger. NATURE. 303(5912):59-61, May 1983.

Induced abortion in Belgium: clinical experience and psychosocial observations, by M. Vekemans, et al. STUDIES IN FAMILY PLANNING. 13(12):355, December 1982.

Induced abortion in fertility regulation, by L. Andolsek, et al. JUGOSLAVENSKA GINEKOLOGIJA I OPSTETRICIJA. 21(1-2):57-61, January-April 1981.

Induction of abortion during the second pregnancy trimester by intra-amniotic administration of PGF2 alpha, by A. Pajor, et al. ORVOSI HETILAP. 124(28):1671-1674, July 10, 1983.

Intraamniotic injection of ethacridine for second-trimester induction of labor, by K. H. Tien. OBSTETRICS AND GYNECOLOGY. 61(6):733-736, June 1983.

Medical motives for induced abortion in hospital, by G.

Spaziante. ANNALI DI OSTETRICIA GINECOLOGIA, MEDICINA PERINATALE. 104(1):5-30, January-February 1983.

Menstrual induction with sulproston, by A. I. Csapo, et al. PROSTAGLANDINS. 24(5):657-665, November 1982.

Prospects of pregnancy following induced and spontaneous abortion of primigravidae and assessment of fertility, by G. Schott, et al. ZENTRALBLATT FUR GYNAEKOLOGIE. 104(7):397-404, 1982.

The relationship between spontaneous and induced abortion and the occurrence of second-trimester abortion in subsequent pregnancies, by J. I. Puyenbrock, et al. EUROPEAN JOURNAL OF OBSTETRICS, GYNECOLOGY AND REPRODUCTIVE MEDICINE. 14(5):299-309, February 1983.

Researchers confirm induced abortion to be safer for women than childbirth: refute claims of critics. FAMILY PLANNING PERSPECTIVE. 14(5):271-272, September-October 1982.

Spontaneous abortion and induced abortion: an adjustment for the presence of induced abortion when estimating the rate of spontaneous abortion from cross-sectional studies, by E. Susser. AMERICAN JOURNAL OF EPIDEMIOLOGY. 117(3):305-308, March 1983.

Use of quinine for self-induced abortion, by A. L. Dannenberg, et al. SOUTHERN MEDICAL JOURNAL. 76(7):846-849, July 1983.

The use of sulprostone to induce abortion in the second trimester, by N. Ragni, et al. PROSTAGLANDINS LEUKOTRIENES AND MEDICINE. 9(5):483-489, November 1982.

ABORTION: INDUCED: COMPLICATIONS

Abortion rate in pregnancies following ovulation induced
by human menopausal gonadotropin/human chorionic
gonadotropin, by Z. Ben-Rafael, et al. FERTILITY AND
STERILITY. 39(2):157-161, February 1983.

Case study of the reproductive experience of women who
have had three or more induced abortions, by E. Lincoln.
DISSERTATION ABSTRACTS INTERNATIONAL: A.
44(4), October 1983.

Early complications and effectiveness of abortion induction
with PG F2 alpha, by G. Koinzer. ZENTRALBLATT FUR
GYNAEKOLOGIE. 104(16):1009-1019, 1982.

Ectopic pregnancy and prior induced abortion, by A. A.
Levin, et al. AMERICAN JOURNAL OF PUBLIC HEALTH.
72:253-256, March 1982.

Immunohistochemical study of SP1, HPL and HCG in
chroionic tissue with early spontaneous and induced
abortions, by M. Ito, et al. NIPPON SANKA FUJINKA
GAKKAI ZASSHI. 34(12)2115-2122, December 1982.

Psychological sequelae from induced abortion: a follow-up
study of women who seek postabortion counseling, by
M. K. Hendricks-Matthews. DISSERTATION ABSTRACTS
INTERNATIONAL: B. 44(5), November 1983.

ABORTION: JOURNALISM

Publicizing abortion: more knowledge, more controversy, by
N. Kwan. OFF OUR BACKS. 13:10-11, July 1983.

ABORTION: LAWS AND LEGISLATION: GENERAL

Abortion. THE FAMILY LAW REPORTER: TEXT NO. 5.
9(33):3047-3075, June 21, 1983.

Abortion: decade of debate [since the 1973 U. S. supreme

court ruling making abortion legal] , by M. Leepson.
EDITORIAL RESEARCH REPORTS. January 14, 1983,
p. 27-44.

Abortion after Akron: the contradictions are showing, by
R. J. Neuhaus. COMMWEAL. 110:388, July 15, 1983.

Abortion amendment moves toward senate showdown, by
R. B. Shaw. OUR SUNDAY VISITOR. 71:8, February 27,
1983.

Abortion and M. T. P. cases—a study of hospital admissions
from 1971 to 1979, by B. Mehta, et al. INDIAN JOURNAL
OF PUBLIC HEALTH. 26(1):38-42, January-March 1982.

Abortion and national policymaking; reflections on the congress
reversing the rule of Roe v. Wade and Doe v. Bolton, by
S. M. Krason. SOCIAL JUSTICE REVIEW. 74:35-44,
March-April 1983.

Abortion and the supreme court; an interview with C. H.
Smith, by W. McGurn. REGISTER. 59:1+, September 4,
1983.

Abortion—children's rights—constitutional rights. THE
FAMILY LAW REPORTER: COURT OPINIONS. 9(14):
2219, February 8, 1983.

Abortion—education—registration fees—religion. THE
FAMILY LAW REPORTER: COURT OPINIONS. 9(1):
2011, November 2, 1982.

Abortion from the legal viewpoint for the physician, by H.
D. Hiersche. GYNAKOLOGE. 15(2):72-79, June 1982.

Abortion—husband's consent—jurisdiction and procedure—
mootness. THE FAMILY LAW REPORTER: COURT
OPINIONS. 9(17):2267, March 1, 1983.

Abortion: In congress: repeal Roe to senate floor, by M. B. Welch.
OFF OUR BACKS. 13:9, June 1983.

Abortion in tumor patients from a legal viewpoint, by W.
Spann. MUENCHENER MEDIZINISHE WOCHENSCHRIFT.
124(44):957-958, November 5, 1982.

Abortion: justice Harry A. Blackman and the Roe v. Wade
decision, by J. A. La Rue. SIMON GREENLEAF LAW
REVIEW. 2:122-145, 1982-1983.

Abortion laws will bend under new medical, social pressures,
by D. J. Horan, et al. HOSPITAL PROGRESS. 63(12):
48-52, December 1982.

Abortion legislation [letter]. JOURNAL OF THE AMERICAN
MEDICAL ASSOCIATION. 249(4):472-473, January 28,
1983.

Abortion legislation [letter], by C. A. Winterling. JOURNAL
OF THE AMERICAN MEDICAL ASSOCIATION. 249(23):
3173-3174, June 17, 1983.

Abortion: methods and sequelae, by W. Savage, et al. BRITISH
JOURNAL OF HOSPITAL MEDICINE. 28(4):364, 369-
372+, October 1982.

Abortion 1982: the supreme court once again, by J. M. Healey.
CONNECTICUT MEDICINE. 46(11):681, November 1982.

Abortion—notice to husband. THE FAMILY LAW REPORTER:
TEXT NO. 1. 9(6):3001-3026, December 7, 1982.

Abortion on back burner?, by J. F. Hitchcock. REGISTER.
59:1+, June 19, 1983.

Abortion policymaking a decade after Roe, by J. K. Boles.
POLICY STUDIES REVIEW. 2(1):133-135, 1982.

Abortion—restrictions. THE CRIMINAL LAW REPORTER: SUPREME COURT PROCEEDINGS. 32(10):4115-4121, December 8, 1982.

Abortion rights, by R. Copelon. MS. 12:146, October 1983.

Abortion rights rescued: the triumph of coalition politics, by S. Caudel. MS. 11:40+, January 1983.

Abortion ruling eyed, by M. Meehan. REGISTER. 59:1+, July 3, 1983.

Abortion ten years later. COMMONWEAL. 110:35-37, January 28, 1983.

Abortion ten years later, by J. T. Beifuss. NATIONAL CATHOLIC REPORTER. 19:1+, January 21, 1983.

Abortion—waiting period—hospitalization—insurance. THE FAMILY LAW REPORTER: COURT OPINIONS. 9(10): 2150, January 11, 1983.

Adolescent autonomy and minors' legal rights: contraception and abortion, by H. Rodman, et al. JOURNAL OF APPLIED DEVELOPMENTAL PSYCHOLOGY. 3(4):307-317, October-December 1982.

After ten years pro-lifers know how to win but are not sure they can win, by R. B. Shaw. OUR SUNDAY VISITOR. 71:4-5, January 16, 1983.

Analysis of official permission for medically indicated pregnancy interruptions, by E. Czeizel. ORVOSI HETILAP. 124(22): 1297-1302, May 29, 1983.

The application of law 194/1978 in our hospital. Study of its use in the first five semesters, by P. Tellini, et al. REVISTA ITALIANA DI GINECOLOGIA. 59 suppl:3-68, 1980.

Case report of a termination of pregnancy in a severely subnormal epileptic and the problems which arose, by P.
Beynon. COMMUNITY MEDICINE. 4(4):280-283, November
1982.

Child psychiatry and the law; developmental rights to privacy
and independent decisionmaking, by M. J. Guyer, et al.
JOURNAL OF THE AMERICAN ADADEMY OF CHILD
PSYCHIATRY. 21:298-302, May 1982.

Choice decision [senate turns down Hatch amendment]. TIME.
122:21, July 11, 1983.

Committee cautions on misuse of conscience, by D. Goldkamp.
REGISTER. 59:2, March 6, 1983.

Committee to defend reproductive rights v. Myers: procreative
choice guaranteed for all women. GOLDEN GATE
UNIVERSITY LAW REVIEW. 12:691-716, Summer 1982.

Congressional withdrawal of jurisdiction from federal courts:
a reply to Professor Uddo, by M. Vitiello. LOYOLA LAW
REVIEW. 28:61-76, Winter 1982.

Constitution and the anomaly of the pregnant teenager, by
E. Buchanan. ARIZONA LAW REVIEW. 24:553-610,
1982.

Constitutional law—abortion—court focuses on husband's
interest regarding spousal notification requirements to
procure abortion. Scheinberg v. Smith. CUMBERLAND
LAW REVIEW. 13:143-159, 1982-1983.

Constitutional law—equal protection—abortion funding—state
constitution requires New Jersey to fund health preserving
but not elective abortions—Right to Choose v. Byrne.
SETON HALL LAW REVIEW. 13:779-802, 1983.

Constitutional law—a minor's abortion right under a parental

notice statute. WAYNE LAW REVIEW. 28:1901-1928,
Summer 1982.

Constitutionality of the human life bill. WASHINGTON
UNIVERSITY LAW QUARTERLY. 61:219-252, Spring
1983.

Court decision fuels abortion controversy: is Hatch amendment
a remedy? HEALTH EDUCATION. 43:3, June 25, 1983.

The court stands by abortion, by A. Press, et al. NEWSWEEK.
101(26):62-63, June 27, 1983.

A cross-national comparison of contraception and abortion
laws, by I. M. Wasserman. SOCIAL INDICATORS RE-
SEARCH. 13(3):281-309, October 1983.

Crushing freedom in the name of life, by N. Dorsen. HUMAN
RIGHTS. 10:18+, Spring 1982.

Current legal trends regarding abortions for minors: a dilemma
for counselors, by L. C. Talbutt. SCHOOL COUNSELOR.
31(2):120-124, November 1983.

Deletion of confidential information from official public
records, by D. E. Bruns. WASHBURN LAW JOURNAL.
22(2):364-370, 1983.

Effects of own attitude on polarization of judgment, by D.
Romer. JOURNAL OF PERSONALITY AND SOCIAL
PSYCHOLOGY. 44:723-284, February 1983.

The evolution of a constitutional right to an abortion:
fashioned in the 1970's and secured in the 1980's, by
N. Ford. JOURNAL OF LEGAL MEDICINE. 4:271-
322, September 1983.

Fetal indication for termination of pregnancy—from the
legal view, by W. Weissauer. GERBURTSHILFE UND
FRAUNHEILKUNDE. 43(3):193-196, March 1983.

The fetus between abortion and protection of life, by H.
Ostendorf. BEITRAEGE ZUR GERICHTLICHEN MEDIZIN.
40:29-33, 1982.

From the courts to congress. AMERICA. 149:2, June 25-July 2,
1983.

Growing conservatism in the United States? An examination
of trends in political opinion between 1972 and 1980, by
J. Saltzman-Chafetz, et al. SOCIOLOGICAL PERSPECTIVES.
26(3):275-298, 1983.

Harsh days at the high court: abortion decision devastates right-
to-life movement, by B. Spring. CHRISTIANITY TODAY.
27:30-31, July 15, 1983.

Hatch amendment and the new federalism, by J. T. Noonan, Jr.
HARVARD JOURNAL OF LAW AND PUBLIC POLICY.
6:93-102, 1982.

Helms stung by NCCB staff memo, by M. Meehan. REGISTER.
59:1+, August 21, 1983.

Henry Hyde on new prolife legislation; interview with H. J.
Hyde, by M. Meehan. REGISTER. 59:6, March 6, 1983.

High court clears up any doubts on abortion; justices disallow
limit on contraceptive ads, by L. Greenhouse. NEW YORK
TIMES. June 19, 1983, news section 4, pg. E7.

High court ruling bad news, good news for pro-lifers, by W. A.
Ryan. OUR SUNDAY VISITOR. 72:8, July 3, 1983.

High court strikes down Akron abortion ordinance. OUR
SUNDAY VISITOR. 72:8, June 26, 1983.

"If you prick us, do we not bleed?": of Shylock, fetuses, and
the concept of person in the law, by C. H. Baron. LAW,
MEDICINE AND HEALTH CARE. 11(2):52-63, April
1983.

Immediate postabortal insertion of levonorgestrel-releasing IUD, by M. Heikkila, et al. CONTRACEPTION. 26(3): 245-259, September 1982.

In the decade since Roe v. Wade; symposium, part 1. HOSPITAL PROGRESS. 63:37-69, December 1982.

—. part 2. HOSPITAL PROGRESS. 63:70-83, December 1982.

Incidence of legal abortions in 1978 in Serbia proper, excluding autunomous environs, by J. Ananijevic-Pandej. SRPSKI ARCHIV ZA CELOKUPNO LEKARSTVO. 110(2):177-184, February 1982.

The issue that won't go away, by M. Beck. NEWSWEEK. 101: 31, January 31, 1983.

Jesse Helms in the dock, by B. Spring. CHRISTIANITY TODAY. 27:78+, March 4, 1983.

Justice O'Connor's dissent in the Akron abortion case, by S. D. O'Connor. ORIGINS. 13:159-164, July 21, 1983.

Law and the life sciences (Roe v. Wade reaffirmed), by G. J. Annas. HASTINGS CENTER REPORT. 13:21-22, August 1983.

Law. Conditions for abortion, by J. Finch. NURSING MIRROR. 156(17):38, April 27, 1983.

The law on abortion: chronology of events and positions taken, by A. M. Devreux, et al. REVUE FRANCAISE DE SOCIOLOGIE. 23(3):503-518, July-September 1982.

Learning from Roe v. Wade, by A. Verhey. REFORMED JOURNAL. 33(4):3-4, April 1983.

Legalized abortion ten years later, by C. Schweich. MCCALLS. 110:61, January 1983.

Medical termination of pregnancy act—1971—the purported and perceived purpose [India], by T. R. Sati, et al. JOURNAL OF FAMILY WELFARE. 29:33-38, March 1983.

Medicalization and social control of abortion: the issues behind the law, by M. Ferrand-Picard. REVUE FRANCAISE DE SOCIOLOGIE. 23(3):383-396, July-September 1982.

Medicine and the law. The postcoital pill and intrauterine device: contraceptive or abortifacient?, by D. Brahams. LANCET. 1(8332):1039, May 7, 1983.

Medico-legal aspects of abortion, by B. Piga Sanchez-Morate. ANALES DE LA REAL ACADEMIA NACIONALE DE MEDICINA. 99(1):51-70, 1982.

Misuse of MTP, by N. Ghose. JOURNAL OF THE INDIAN MEDICAL ASSOCIATION. 80(2):32-33, January 16, 1983.

Morgentaler file, by E. Hillen. MACLEANS. 96:44, July 18, 1983.

Morgentaler manifesto, by K. Govier. QUEST. 12:cover, 22+, October 1983.

The nation's new agony over abortion. MACLEANS. 96(2): 32-38, July 25, 1983.

New problems in congress for the antiabortionists, by B. Spring. CHRISTIANITY TODAY. 27:60+, February 4, 1983.

New version of Hatch amendment clears first hurdle. OUR SUNDAY VISITOR. 71:8, April 10, 1983.

On aborting the constitution [senate vote on Hatch amendment], by W. F. Buckley. NATIONAL REVIEW. 35:960, August 5, 1983.

Opinions of the United States supreme court: abortion. THE
CRIMINAL LAW REPORTER: TEXT NO. 10. 33(11):
3143-3159, June 15, 1983.

Opposition should not gloat, Hyde tells pro-lifers. OUR
SUNDAY VISITOR. 72:8, July 24, 1983.

Oregon rule permitting state funding of only some abortions
found invalid. THE FAMILY LAW REPORTER: COURT
OPINIONS. 9(32):2488-2489, June 14, 1983.

Pennsylvania anti-abortion law in court, by T. Dejanikus. OFF
OUR BACKS. 13:18, February 1983.

Policy implementation and community linkages: hospital
abortion services after Roe v. Wade, by C. A. Johnson, et al.
WESTERN POLITICAL QUARTERLY. 35(3):385-405,
1982.

Policy implementation and responsiveness in nongovernmental
institutions: hospital abortion services after Roe v. Wade, by
C. A. Johnson, et al. WESTERN POLITICAL QUARTERLY.
35:385-405, September 1982.

Postcoital contraception or abortion? [letter]. LANCET.
2(8343):223, July 23, 1983.

Predicted senate loss may bring final pro-life win closer, by
R. B. Shaw. OUR SUNDAY VISITOR. 72:5, June 19, 1983.

Priorities in relation to abortion [letter], by S. R. Belton.
AMERICAN JOURNAL OF OBSTETRICS AND GYNE-
COLOGY. 144(6):736-738, November 15, 1982.

Prolife bill moves ahead, by M. Meehan. REGISTER. 59:1+,
May 22, 1983.

Pro-life groups plan for 1984, by J. T. Beifuss. NATIONAL
CATHOLIC REPORTER. 19:8, July 15, 1983.

ABORTION: LAWS AND LEGISLATION: GENERAL (continued)

Prolifers facing stiffer jail terms, by D. Goldkamp. REGISTER.
59:1+, June 19, 1983.

The pro-lifers fight on, by J. G. Deedy. TABLET. 237:747-
748, August 6, 1983.

Prolifers react to Hatch, by R. Bautch. REGISTER. 59:10,
July 17, 1983.

The public health implications of abortion, by C. W. Tyler, Jr.
ANNUAL REVIEW OF PUBLIC HEALTH. 4:223-258, 1983.

Rationalizing the abortion debate: legal rhetoric and the
abortion controversy, by E. Chemerinsky. BUFFALO LAW
REVIEW. 31(1):107-164, 1982.

The Real abortion issue, by S. G. Cole. THIS MAGAZINE.
17:4-8, June 1983.

"Repeal Roe" measure proposed [U. S. Congress] ; state
legislature attempt to limit abortion; Nun will administer
state medicaid for abortions [Michigan], by T. Dejanikus.
OFF OUR BACKS. 13:2+, April 1983.

Restricting or prohibiting abortion by constitutional amend-
ment. Some health implications, by D. H. Huber. JOURNAL
OF REPRODUCTIVE MEDICINE. 27(12):729-736,
December 1982.

Roe v. Wade reaffirmed [Akron v. Akron center for reproductive
health], by G. J. Annas. HASTINGS CENTER REPORT.
13:21-22, August 1983.

Seeking unity to save lives, by M. Meehan, et al. REGISTER.
59:1+, July 17, 1983.

Senate nixes Hatch, by M. Meehan. REGISTER. 59:1+,
July 10, 1983.

The senate threat to our lives [Hatch amendment], by L. C.

180

Wohl. MS. 10:21, June 1982.

Sixteen thousand, five hundred fetuses intensify fight in which they have no stake, by P. Edmonds. NATIONAL CATHOLIC REPORTER. 19:1+, January 21, 1983.

State can't prohibit first-trimester, nonlifesaving abortion on incompetent. THE FAMILY LAW REPORTER: COURT OPINIONS. 8(48):2728-2729, October 12, 1982.

State statutes regulating abortion leave unresolved issues, by J. S. Showalter, et al. HOSPITAL PROGRESS. 63(12): 60-64, December 1982.

Stop signs and detours in the way of abortion, by L. McQuaig. MACLEANS. 96:36-37, July 25, 1985.

Strategy, please? NATIONAL REVIEW. 35:856-857, July 22, 1983.

Student refusal to pay abortion-related fees—a first amendment right? SAN DIEGO LAW REVIEW. 20:837-857, August 1983.

Support—Ohio. JUVENILE AND FAMILY LAW DIGEST. 14(3):122, March 1982.

Supreme court clarifies abortion rules, by A. H. Bernstein. HOSPITALS. 57(17):93, September 1, 1983.

Supreme court faces the family, by H. H. Clark, Jr. CHILDREN TODAY. 11(6):18-21, November-December 1982.

Supreme court reaffirms abortion rights [rulings on separate cases from Missouri, Virginia, and Akron, Ohio, testing the validity of state and local government efforts to regulate abortion, by E. Witt. CONGRESSIONAL QUARTERLY WEEKLY REPORT. 41:1247-1249, June 18, 1983.

Supreme court report: six justices stand firm on abortion

decision, by R. L. Young. AMERICAN BAR ASSOCIATION JOURNAL. 69:1290, 1292, September 1983.

Supreme court: rulings limit nonprofit groups' lobbying . . . remove restrictions on abortion, by P. R. McGinn. NATIONAL CATHOLIC REPORTER. 19:6, July 1, 1983.

Supreme court strikes Akron abortion provisions, by L. F. Powell. ORIGINS. 13:149+, July 21, 1983.

Supreme court abortion decisions: a critical study of the shaping of a major American public policy and a basis for change, by S. M. Krason. DISSERTATION ABSTRACTS INTERNATIONAL: A. 44(1), July 1983.

Sustaining the prolife momentun: legal and political strategies, by G. D. Wendel, et al. HOSPITAL PROGRESS. 63(12): 70-73, December 1982.

Technological advances and Roe v. Wade: the need to rethink abortion law, by K. Martyn. UCLA LAW REVIEW. 29(5-6):1194-1215, June-August 1982.

Ten years of abortion, by J. G. Deedy. TABLET. 237:148-150, February 19, 1983.

Three supreme court rulings nullify several abortion restrictions, by, J. S. Showalter, et al. HOSPITAL PROGRESS. 64(7): 20-21, 1983.

Trials on mistrial. NATURE. 304(5923):198, July 21-27, 1983.

Trying to slam the door [vote in favor of constitutional amendment banning abortions]. TIME. 122:42, September 19, 1983.

The U. S. supreme court 1982-83 term: abortion. THE CRIMINAL LAW REPORTER: SUPREME COURT PROCEEDINGS. 34(1):4024, October 5, 1983.

Verbal war of morality [Ireland], by B. Keenan. MACLEANS. 96:53, September 19, 1983.

AFRICA

Abortion laws in African commonwealth countries, by R. J. Cook, et al. JOURNAL OF AFRICAN LAW. 25:60-79, Autumn 1981.

CANADA

Abortion goes to trial, by D. Eisler. MACLEANS. 96:50, May 23, 1983.

Canada court helps, hurts prolife cause, by J. Rasmussen. REGISTER. 59:1+, October 30, 1983.

Civil law and common law traditions: judicial review and legislative supremacy in West Germany and Canada, by S. G. Mezey. INTERNATIONAL AND COMPARATIVE LAW QUARTERLY. 32:689-707, July 1983.

The meaning and implications of "unlawful" in Canada's abortion law, by P. J. Micallef. CAHIERS DE DROIT. 88:1029-1046, December 1982.

To rescue the unborn: two courtroom avenues offer new hope [Alberta], by R. Dolphin, et al. ALBERTA REPORT. 9:34-35, November 8, 1982.

DENMARK

The impact of legal termination of pregnancy and of prenatal diagnosis on the birth prevalence of down syndrome in Denmark, by M. Mikkelsen, et al. ANNALS OF HUMAN

CHINA

A doctoral says Chinese force women to have abortions [dismissal of S. Mosher from Stanford University]. CHRISTIANITY TODAY. 27:36, October 21, 1983.

GREAT BRITAIN
Abortion and the doctors, by M. Kenny. TABLET. 237:
942-943, October 1, 1983.

Conditions for abortion, by J. Finch. NURSING MIRROR
AND MIDWIVE'S JOURNAL. 156(17):38, April 27, 1983.

Down's syndrome, by R. Brandon. OBSERVER. June 12,
1983, p. 26.

A moral dilemma for the doctors, by R. Butt. TIMES.
September 29, 1983, p. 14.

Participate or not? . . . how nurses have become increasingly
involved in carrying out pregnancy terminations, by J.
Finch. NURSING MIRROR AND MIDWIVE'S JOURNAL.
156(18):38, May 4, 1983.

Protection of the unborn child . . . legal principles which
relate to the preservation of human life, by J. Finch.
NURSING MIRROR AND MIDWIVE'S JOURNAL.
156(16):33, April 20, 1983.

IRELAND
Abortion: Ireland divided once more, by R. Ford. TIMES.
August 26, 1983, p. 6.

Birth rights in Ireland, by S. Hoggart. OBSERVER. January 23,
1983, p. 43.

Ireland's abortion vote: the bishops and the press, by T. P.
O'Mahony. AMERICA. 149:329-330, November 26, 1983.

Irish abortion bill criticized. REGISTER. 59:3, April 17, 1983.

Irish voters and their new antiabortion amendment, by J. P.
McCarthy. AMERICA. 149:209-211, October 15, 1983.

The Irish will vote for life or death on September 7, by L. H.
Pumphrey. OUR SUNDAY VISITOR. 72:5, September 4,
1983.

Misbegotten referendum. ECONOMIST. 288:13, September 3, 1983.

Priests and politics, by M. Holland. NEW STATESMAN. September 2, 1983, p. 13-14.

Pyrrhic victory: the Irish abortion referendum, by O. O'Leary. SPECTATOR. September 17, 1983, p. 12, 14.

A pyrrhic victory [vote on abortion clause in constitution], by P. Kirby. COMMONWEAL. 110:517-519, October 7, 1983.

Rights for the unborn. ECONOMIST. 288:55-56, September 3, 1983.

An unfortunate amendment on abortion. TABLET. 237: 887, September 17, 1983.

An unpopular referendum, by L. McRedmond. TABLET. 237:816-818, August 27, 1983.

ITALY
Legal abortion in Italy, 1978-1980 [letter to the editor], by T. Landucci, et al. THE NEW ENGLAND JOURNAL OF MEDICINE. 308(1):51-52, 1982.

Right of the adolescent to health protection according to Italian legislation, by T. L. Schwarzenberg. MINERVA PEDIATRICA. 35(8):363-371, April 30, 1983.

JAPAN
Abortion in Japan, interview with A. Zimmerman, by M. Meehan. REGISTER. 59:1+, January 23, 1983.

Japanese ceremonies show private doubts over use of abortion, by U. C. Lehner. WALL STREET JOURNAL. January 6, 1983, p. 1.

GENETICS. 47(pt 2):123-131, May 1983.

RUMANIA
The unintended consequences of policy change: the effect of
a restrictive abortion policy [on maternal deaths in
Rumania], by J. S. Legge, Jr. ADMINISTRATION AND
SOCIETY. 15:243-256, August 1983.

SPAIN
Via Dolorosa. ECONOMIST. 286:62, February 5, 1983.

UNITED STATES
Abortion choice and the law in Vermont: a recent study.
VERMONT LAW REVIEW. 7:281-313, Fall 1982.

Abortion in America: ABC's of a raging battle; come January 22,
it will be a decade since the supreme court's landmark
ruling, by T. Gest. U. S. NEWS. 94:47-49, January 24, 1983.

Abortion trial tests limit of necessity defense, by J. Orso.
REGISTER. 59:1+, February 13, 1983.

Before the velvet curtain: the Connecticut contraceptive
cases as a study in constitutional law and supreme court
behavior, by R. J. Fiscus. DISSERTATION ABSTRACTS
INTERNATIONAL: A. 43(12), June 1983.

Big-boss government. ECONOMIST. 286:35, January 29, 1983.

Calling for prolife unity. REGISTER. 59:1+, January 23, 1983.

Can congress settle the abortion issue?, by M. C. Segers.
HASTINGS CENTER REPORT. 12:20-28, June 1982.

Court unmoved. ECONOMIST. 287:42-43, June 25, 1983.

The dilemma of an anti-abortion democrat, by D. R. Carlin, Jr.
COMMONWEAL. 110:626-628, November 18, 1983.

The fallacy of legalized abortion as a lesser evil, by C. De Celles.

SOCIAL JUSTICE REVIEW. 74:3-5, January-February 1983.

Fertility-related state laws enacted in 1982, by D. Bush. FAMILY PLANNING PERSPECTIVES. 15(3):111-116, May-June 1983.

Human life federalism amendment: 1. legal aspects; 2. legislative update, by W. R. Caron, et al. CATHOLIC LAWYER. 28:111-128, September 1983.

Kentucky's new abortion law: searching for the outer limits of permissible regulation, by K. Moorman. KENTUCKY LAW JOURNAL. 1982-1983, p. 617-646.

New prolife initiatives, by M. Meehan. REGISTER. 59:1+, February 20, 1983.

Parental notification and abortion: a review and recommendation to West Virginia's legislature. WEST VIRGINIA LAW RE- VIEW. 85:943-968, Summer 1983.

Re-examining Roe v. Wade, by C. De Celles. REGISTER. 59:1+, January 23, 1983; 59:1+, January 30, 1983.

Religion, law and public policy in America, by C. E. Curran. JURIST. 42:14-28, 1982.

Toward constitutional abortion control legislation: the Pennsylvania approach. DICKINSON LAW REVIEW. 87:373-406, Winter 1983.

WEST GERMANY
Civil law and common law traditions: judicial review and legislative supremacy in West Germany and Canada, by S. G. Mezey. INTERNATIONAL AND COMPARATIVE LAW QUARTERLY. 32:689-707, July 1983.

Acute collapse after administration of prostaglandin F2-alpha for induction of missed abortion, by O. Okland, et al. TIDSSKRIFT FOR DEN NORSKE LAEGEFORENING. 102(34-36):1855-1857, December 10, 1982.

Diagnosis and treatment of missed abortion, by M. A. Omarov, et al. AKUSHERSTVO I GINEKOLOGIIA. (5):57-59, May 1983.

Drug treatment of retained abortion, intrauterine death of the fetus and of vesicular mole with 15-ME-PGF2 alpha, by D. Granese, et al. MINERVA GINECOLOGIA. 34(6): 467-474, June 1982.

Formation of kidney stones in mummified extrauterine pregnancy, by H. J. Hertkens. ZEITSCHRIFT FUR UROLOGIE AND NEPHROLOGIE. 75(7):501-502, July 1982.

Induction of internal abortion and vesicular mole with intramuscular administration of 15(S)15-methyl-prostaglandin F2 alpha, by A. Nasi, et al. MINERVA GINECOLOGIA. 34(6):461-466, June 1982.

Management of missed abortion by intramuscular administration of 15(S) 15 methyl prostaglandin F2 alpha, by M. K. Mapa, et al. ASIA-OCEANIA JOURNAL OF OBSTETRICS AND GYNAECOLOGY. 8(4):369-372, December 1982.

Maternal deaths associated with antepartum fetal death in utero, United States, 1972 to 1978, by S. F. Dorfman, et al. SOUTHER MEDICAL JOURNAL. 76(7):838-843, July 1983.

Principles of examination and treatment in missed abortion, missed labor, by L. V. Timoshenko, et al. AKUSHERSTVO I GINEKOLOGIIA. (1):56-57, 1983.

Serum levels of polychlorinated biphenyls and some organo-chlorine insecticides in women with recent and former missed abortions, by B. Bercovici, et al. ENVIRONMENTAL RESEARCH. 30(1):169-174, February 1983.

Termination of pregnancy in cases of intrauterine fetal death, missed abortion, molar and anencephalic pregnancy with intramuscular administration of 2a 2b dihomo 15(S) 15 methyl PGF2 alpha methyl ester—a multicentre study, by S. M. Karim, et al. ANNALS OF THE ACADEMY OF MEDICINE, SINGAPORE. 11(4):508-512, October 1982.

Use of 15(S)-15-methyl PGF 2-alpha in the treatment of internal abortion and intrauterine death of the fetus, by G. B. Melis, et al. MINERVA GINECOLOGIA. 34(9):729-734, September 1982.

ABORTION: MORTALITY AND MORTALITY STATISTICS

Abortion mortality [letter], by K. Augensen, et al. AMERICAN JOURNAL OF OBSTETRICS AND GYNECOLOGY. 144(6):740-741, November 15, 1982.

Mortality from abortion and childbirth [letter], by A. R. Hansen. JOURNAL OF THE AMERICAN MEDICAL ASSOCIATION. 249(2):194, January 14, 1983.

Mortality from abortion and childbirth [letter], by M. J. Lanska, et al. JOURNAL OF THE AMERICAN MEDICAL ASSOCIATION. 250(3):361-362, July 15, 1983.

Perinatal mortality: changes in the diagnostic panorama 1974-1980, by O. Lofgren, et al. ACTA PAEDIATRICA SCANDINAVICA. 72(3):327-332, May 1983.

Researchers confirm induced abortion to be safer for women than childbirth: refute claims of critics. FAMILY PLANNING PERSPECTIVES. 14:271-272, September-October 1982.

ABORTION: OUTPATIENT TREATMENT

Foetus papyraceus, by U. Thakkar, et al. MEDICAL JOURNAL
OF ZAMBIA. 15(3):72-74, May-July 1981.

A foetus papyraceus in twin birth at term, by H. Gocke, et al.
GERBURTSHILFE UND FRAUENHEILKUNDE. 42(8):
605-608, August 1982.

ABORTION: PSYCHOLOGY AND PSYCHIATRY

Abortion: the morning after, by C. L. Mithers.
MADEMOISELLE. 89:66, September 1983.

Age of consent. ECONOMIST. 288:22, August 6, 1983.

All life is blessed, by J. Sammon. CATHOLIC WORKER. 50:
1-2, January-February 1983.

American childbirth educators in China: a transcultural
exchange, by D. Williamson, et al. JOURNAL OF NURSE-
MIDWIFERY. 27(5):15-22, September-October 1982.

Cellular immunity factors in the physiological course of
pregnancy and abortion, by P. I. Fogel. AKUSHERSTVO I
GINEKOLOGIIA. (12):28-30, 1982.

Characteristics of abortion patients in the United States, 1979
and 1980, by S. K. Henshaw, et al. FAMILY PLANNING
PERSPECTIVES. 15:5+, January-February 1983.

Child psychiatry and the law; developmental rights to privacy
and independent decisionmaking, by M. J. Guyer, et al.
JOURNAL OF THE AMERICAN ACADEMY OF CHILD
PSYCHIATRY. 21:298-302, May 1982.

A consideration of abortion survivors, by P. G. Ney. CHILD
PSYCHIATRY AND HUMAN DEVELOPMENT. 13(3):
168-179, Spring 1983.

Conversion disorder following termination of pregnancy, by
G. D. Tollefson, et al. JOURNAL OF FAMILY PRACTICE.

16(1):73-77, January 1983.

An 'epidemic' of spontaneous abortion: psychosocial factors, by M. Kaffman, et al. ISRAEL JOURNAL OF PSYCHIATRY AND RELATED SCIENCES. 19(3):239-246, 1982.

Grieving after termination of pregnancy [letter], by M. Ryan, et al. MEDICAL JOURNAL OF AUSTRALIA. 1(4):155, February 19, 1983.

A highly emotional decision . . . abortion, by J. Thompson. NURSING MIRROR AND MIDWIVE'S JOURNAL. 157(4):41, July 27, 1983.

The loss of baby Elizabeth . . . how Mary—a girl with down's syndrome—coped with the loss of her baby, by H. Hughes, et al. NURSING MIRROR AND MIDWIVE'S JOURNAL. 155(12):67-68, September 22, 1982.

Medicalized killing in Auschwitz, by R. J. Lifton. PSYCHIATRY. 45(4):283-297, November 1982.

Nobody wants an abortion, by M. B. Gordon. COMMONWEAL. 110:557-558, October 21, 1983.

Problems in indications for abortion in psychiatry, by J. Pogady, et al. BRATISLAVSKE LEKARSKE LISTY. 79(3):353-359, 1983.

Psychic disorders following induced abortions, by D. Langer. POLSKI TYGODNIK LEKARSKI. 37(11):305-308, May 10, 1982.

Psychologic approach to voluntary termination of pregnancy, by M. T. Aussilloux, et al. ANNALES MEDICO-PSYCHOLOGIQUES. 140(8):896-923, September-October 1982.

Psychological problems of pregnant women under special medical care, by M. Beisert, et al. GINEKOLOGIA POLSKA.

53(11):721-732, 1982.

Psychological sequelae from induced abortion: a follow-up study of women who seek postabortion counseling, by M. K. Hendricks-Matthews. DISSERTATION ABSTRACTS INTERNATIONAL: B. 44(5), November 1983.

Psychopathologic dynamics following abortion, or the Niobe syndrome of modern times, by R. Peltonen, et al. PRAXIS DER KINDERPSYCHOLOGIE UND KINDERPSYCHIATRIE. 32(4):125-128, May-June 1983.

Public opinion reflects secularization, rationalization, by W. J. Monahan. HOSPITAL PROGRESS. 63(12):65-69, December 1982.

Relative body weight as a factor in the decision to abort, by T. H. Thelen, et al. PSYCHOLOGICAL REPORTS. 52(3): 763-775, June 1983.

Relevance of early psychic development to pregnancy and abortion, by D. Pines. INTERNATIONAL JOURNAL OF PSYCHOANALYSIS. 63(3):311-319, 1982.

Response to requests for abortion: the influence of guilt and knowledge, by A. R. Allgeier, et al. JOURNAL OF APPLIED SOCIAL PSYCHOLOGY. 12(4):281-291, 1982.

Sharing the pain of abortion [impact on men], by J. Leo. TIME. 122:78, September 26, 1983.

Therapeutic abortion on psychiatric grounds. Part III. Implementing the abortion and sterilization act (1975-1981), by E. S. Nash, et al. SOUTH AFRICAN MEDICAL JOURNAL. 63(17):639-644, April 23, 1983.

The unwanted pregnancy and its termination—a possibility for unconscious introjection of grief, by A. E. Benz. PSYCHE. 37(2):130-138, 1983.

Unwanted pregnancy: a neurotic attempt at conflictsolving?
An analysis of the conflict-situations of 228 women
immediately before legal abortion, by P. Goebel.
ZEITSCHRIFT FUR PSYCHOSOMATISCHE MEDIZIN
UND PSYCHOANALYSE. 28(3):280-299, 1982.

ABORTION: REPEATED

Case study of the reproductive experience of women who
have had three or more induced abortions, by E. Lincoln.
DISSERTATION ABSTRACTS INTERNATIONAL: A.
44(4), October 1983.

Cervical cerclage: an aggressive approach to threatened or
recurrent pregnancy wastage, by W. R. Crombleholme, et al.
AMERICAN JOURNAL OF OBSTETRICS AND GYNE-
COLOGY. 146(2):168-174, May 15, 1983.

Chromosome heteromorphism in couples with repeated
spontaneous abortions, by P. K. Ghosh, et al. INDIAN
JOURNAL OF MEDICAL RESEARCH. 77:272-277,
April 1983.

A paracentric chromosomal inversion associated with repeated
early pregnancy wastage, by G. Stetten, et al. FERTILITY
AND STERILITY. 40(1):124-126, July 1983.

Personality factors, self-concept, and family variables related
to first time and repeat abortion-seekers behavior in
adolescent women, by M. B. Deutsch. DISSERTATION
ABSTRACTS INTERNATIONAL: A. 43(10), April 1983.

Repeat abortion in the United States: new insights, by C.
Tietze, et al. STUDIES IN FAMILY PLANNING. 13(pt 1):
373-379, December 1982.

Repeat abortion-seeking behaviour in Queensland, Australia:
knowledge and use of contraception and reasons for
terminating the pregnancy, by V. J. Callan. JOURNAL OF
BIOSOCIAL SCIENCE. 15(1):1-8, January 1983.

ABORTION: REPEATED (continued)

Repeat and first abortion seekers: single women in Brisbane, Australia, by V. J. Callan. JOURNAL OF BIOSOCIAL SCIENCE. 15:217-222, April 1983.

ABORTION: RESEARCH

Aborted fetus as source of information about the reproduction prospects of the family and population, by J. Dejmek, et al. CASOPIS LEKARU CESKYCH. 121(48):1485-1489, December 1982.

The abortifacient effect of synthetic androstane derivatives in the baboon, by V. Z. Pope. CONTRACEPTION. 27(2): 201-210, February 1983.

Abortifacient effects of the roots of Momordica angustisepala, by C. N. Aguwa, et al. JOURNAL OF ETHNOPARMACOL-OGY. 7(2):169-173, March 1983.

Abortion and M. T. P. cases—a study of hospital admissions from 1971 to 1979, by B. Mehta, et al. INDIAN JOURNAL OF PUBLIC HEALTH. 26(1):38-42, January-March 1982.

Abortion following the immigration of an adult male baboon (papio cynocephalus), by M. E. Pereira. AMERICAN JOURNAL OF PRIMATOLOGY. 4(1):93-98, 1983.

Abortion in mice induced by intravenous injections of anti-bodies to type IV collagen or laminin, by J. M. Foidart, et al. AMERICAN JOURNAL OF PATHOLOGY. 110(3): 346-357, March 1983.

Age at menarche and unsuccessful pregnancy outcome, by G. Wyshak. ANNALS OF HUMAN BIOLOGY. 10(1): 69-73, January-February 1983.

Anti-PP1Pk and early abortion, by G. Cantin, et al. TRANS-FUSION. 23(4):350-351, July-August 1983.

Benefits of the pill, by N. Mallory. HOME MAGAZINE.

18:92BB, May 1983.

Changes in uterine phosphatase levels in mice treated with
aristolic acid during early pregnancy, by A. Pakrashi, et al.
CONTRACEPTION. 26(6):635-643, December 1982.

Clinical efficacy of extracts of radix teichosanthis and
wikstroemia chamaedaphne meisn on mid-term labor
induction—analysis of 248 cases, by M. Z. Wu, et al.
CHUNG KUO I HSUEH KO HSUEH YUAN HSUEH
PAO. 4(4):241-242, August 1982.

Cytogenetic investigations on patients with difficulties in
reproducing, by S. Adzic, et al. JOURNAL DE
GYNECOLOGIE, ET BIOLOGIE DE LA REPRODUCTION.
11(3):371-374, 1982.

Cytotoxicity of anti-PP1Pk antibodies and possible relationship with early abortions of p mothers, by M. Lopez, et al.
CLINICAL IMMUNOLOGY AND IMMUNOPATHOLOGY.
28(2):296-303, August 1983.

Differences in the pregnancy-terminating effectiveness of an
LH-RH analogue by subcutaneous, vaginal, rectal, and
nasal routes in rats, by I. Yamazaki. ENDOCRINOLOGIA
JAPONICA. 29(4):415-421, August 1982.

Does protactin influence first trimester abortion? A preliminary
clinical observation, by E. Peer, et al. GYNECOLOGIC AND
OBSTETRIC INVESTIGATION. 15(6):362-364, 1983.

Effect of centchroman on ovarian responsiveness to exogenous
gonadotropins in immature female rats, by M. M. Singh,
et al. INDIAN JOURNAL OF EXPERIMENTAL BIOLOGY.
20(6):448-451, 1982.

Effect of influenza on pregnancy, the fetus and the newborn,
by V. Arnaudova, et al. AKUSHERSTVO I GINEKOLOGIIA.
21(4):278-284, 1982.

Effect of the toxic agents of pseudomonas aeruginosa culture on the course of pregnancy and fetal development in porton mice, by M. Bilinska, et al. MEDYCYNA DOSWIADCZALNA I MIKROBIOLOGIA. 34(3-4):145-148, 1982.

Effects of carbon monoxide exposure on pregnant sows and their fetuses, by M. A. Dominick, et al. AMERICAN JOURNAL OF VETERINARY RESEARCH. 44:35-40, January 1983.

Frozen embryo aborts, by V. Sarma. NATURE. 304(5924): 301, July 28-August 3, 1983.

HLA system antigens in abortion, by V. V. Grigor'eva, et al. AKUSHERSTVO I GINEKOLOGIIA. (12):26-28, 1982.

In utero selection against fetuses with trisomy [letter], by D. Warburton, et al. AMERICAN JOURNAL OF HUMAN GENETICS. 35(5):1059-1064, September 1983.

Induced abortion and social factors in wild horses, by J. Berger. NATURE. 303(5912):59-61, May 1983.

Methylmercury toxicity: in vivo evaluation of teratogenesis and cytogenetic changes, by D. C. Curle, et al. ANATO-MISCHER ANZEIGER. 153(1):69-82, 1983.

Morphologic and cytogenetic findings in early abortions, by H. Gocke, et al. VERHANDLUNGEN DER DEUTSCHEN GESELLSCHAFT FUR PATHOLOGIE. 66:141-146, 1982.

Practical contribution of examination of the products of abortion, by E. Philippe. ANNALES DE PATHOLOGIE. 3(1):73-78, 1983.

Pregnancy interception with a combination of prostaglandins: studies in monkeys, by J. W. Wilks. SCIENCE. 221(4618): 1407-1409, September 30, 1983.

Pregnancy termination by prostaglandin F2a stimulates maternal behavior in the rat, by J. F. Rodriguez-Sierva, et al. HOR-MONES AND BEHAVIOR. 16(3):343-351, September 1982.

Progesterone and testosterone: contraception and immuno-suppressive effects in mice, by Z. Pokorna, et al. ENDOKRINOLOGIE. 79(2):185-189, 1982.

Studies on the agent of bovine chlamydial abortion: serology, microbiology and cell culture, by T. Homma. DIS-SERTATION ABSTRACTS INTERNATIONAL: B. 44(5), November 1983.

Surveillance of pregnancy loss in human populations, by A. J. Wilcox. AMERICAN JOURNAL OF INDUSTRIAL MEDICINE. 4(1-2):285-291, 1983.

The use of prostaglandins for regulation of the estrous cycle and as an abortifacient in cattle, by J. G. Manns. VETERINARY CLINICS OF NORTH AMERICA. 5(1):169-181, March 1983.

ABORTION: SEPTIC: COMPLICATIONS

The bacteriology of septic abortion, by W. S. Callahan. AMERICAN JOURNAL OF MEDICAL TECHNOLOGY. 45(4):161-171, July-August 1983.

Bilateral tubal pregnancy with vaginal delivery, by H. M. Foster, et al. OBSTETRICS AND GYNECOLOGY. 60(5): 664-666, November 1982.

Campylobacter sp. isolated from the cervix during septic abortion, case report, by S. E. West, et al. BRITISH JOURNAL OF OBSTETRICS AND GYNAECOLOGY. 89(9):771-772, September 1982.

Conservative vs. surgical management of septic abortion with renal failure, by P. C. Singhal, et al. INTERNATIONAL

JOURNAL OF GYNAECOLOGY AND OBSTETRICS. 20(3):189-194, June 1982.

Criminal abortions as seen in the university teaching hospital, Lusaka, by J. N. Narone, et al. MEDICAL JOURNAL OF ZAMBIA. 15(3):80-84, May-July 1981.

Other milestones [letter], by L. G. Keith, et al. FERTILITY AND STERILITY. 40(2):272-273, August 1983.

Septic abortion in an IUCD user [letter], by C. J. Conaghan, et al. NEW ZEALAND MEDICAL JOURNAL. 95(720): 826-827, November 24, 1982.

Septic induced abortion—a report of 100 cases in Sarawak, by M. Teo Yu Keng, et al. MEDICAL JOURNAL OF MALAYSIA. 37(4):322-325, December 1982.

Septic shock in obstetrics, by B. V. Molodkin. FEL'DSHER I AKUSHERKA. 48(3):23-27, 1983.

ABORTION: SPONTANEOUS

Analysis of multiple birth rates in Japan. VII. Rates of spontaneous and induced terminations of pregnancy in twins, by Y. Imaizumi, et al. JINRUI IDENGAKU ZASSHI. 27(3): 235-242, September 1982.

Assessment of methods and results of reproductive occupational epidemiology: spontaneous abortions and malformations in the offspring of working women, by K. Hemminki, et al. AMERICAN JOURNAL OF INDUSTRIAL MEDICINE. 4(1-2):293-307, 1983.

Birth order, maternal age and spontaneous abortion [letter], by W. H. James. EARLY HUMAN DEVELOPMENT. 8(2): 179-180, July 1983.

Breast cancer and spontaneous abortion [letter], by W. H. James. AMERICAN JOURNAL OF EPIDEMIOLOGY.

117(5):641-642, May 1983.

Cervical resistance in patients with previous spontaneous mid-trimester abortion, by G. S. Anthony, et al. BRITISH JOURNAL OF OBSTETRICS AND GYNAECOLOGY. 89(12):1046-1049, December 1982.

Chromosome anomalies in spontaneous abortions, by M. Tsancheva. AKUSHERSTVO I GINEKOLOGIIA. 22(1): 7-13, 1983.

Chromosome heteromorphism in couples with repeated spontaneous abortions, by P. K. Ghosh, et al. INDIAN JOURNAL OF MEDICAL RESEARCH. 77:472-477, April 1983.

Community study of spontaneous abortions: relation to occupation and air pollution by sulfur dioxide, hydrogen sulfide, and carbon disulfide, by K. Hemminki, et al. INTERNATIONAL ARCHIVES OF OCCUPATIONAL AND ENVIRONMENTAL HEALTH. 51(1):55-63, 1982.

Cytogenetic surveillance of spontaneous abortions, by N. E. Morton, et al. CYTOGENETICS AND CELL GENETICS. 33(3):232-239, 1982.

Dynamic evaluation of the incidence of hereditary pathology by an accounting of spontaneous abortions and congenital developmental defects, by N. P. Bochkov, et al. TSITOL I GENETIKA. 16(6):33-37, November-December 1982.

Efficacy of antibiotic therapy in preventing spontaneous pregnancy loss among couples colonized with genital mycoplasmas, by P. A. Quinn, et al. AMERICAN JOURNAL OF OBSTETRICS AND GYNECOLOGY. 145(2):239-244, January 15, 1983.

IUD insertion following spontaneous abortion: a clinical trial of the TCu 220C, liuppes loop D, and copper 7.

STUDIES IN FAMILY PLANNING. 14(4):109-114, April 1983.

Idiopathic spontaneous abortions, by W. P. Faulk. AMERICAN JOURNAL OF REPRODUCTIVE IMMUNOLOGY. 3(1): 48-49, January-February 1983.

Immunogenetics of spontaneous abortions in humans, by T. J. Gill, 3rd. TRANSPLANTATION. 35(1):1-6, January 1983.

Immunohistochemical study of SP1, HPL and HCG in chorionic tissue with early spontaneous and induced abortions, by M. Ito, et al. NIPPON SANKA FUJINKA GAKKAI ZASSHI. 34(12):2115-2122, December 1982.

Initial results on spontaneous abortion from July 1976 to June 1978 in a TCDD-polluted area of Seveso, by G. Remotti, et al. ANNALI DI OSTETRICIA GINECOLOGIA, MEDICINA PERINATALE. 103(4):249-253, July-August 1982.

Maternal smoking and trisomy among spontaneously aborted conceptions, by J. Kline, et al. AMERICAN JOURNAL OF HUMAN GENETICS. 35(3):421-431, May 1983.

Menarcheal age and spontaneous abortion: a casual connection? [letter], by M. J. Mayaux, et al. AMERICAN JOURNAL OF EPIDEMIOLOGY. 117(3):377-378, March 1983.

Mycoplasma hominis and spontaneous abortion, by E. Damianova, et al. AKUSHERSTVO I GINEKOLOGIIA. 21(6):447-451, 1982.

Normal pregnancy with circulating anticoagulant after spontaneous abortion. Soulier—Boffa syndrome [letter], by J. H. Cohen, et al. NOUVELLE PRESSE MEDICALE. 11(51):3795, December 18, 1982.

Oxidative deamination of different amines in the placenta in spontaneous abortions and premature labor, by N. I. Miskevich, et al. AKUSHERSTVO I GINEKOLOGIIA. (3):41-43, 1983.

Parental origin of chromosome abnormalities in spontaneous abortions, by G. H. Meulenbroek, et al. HUMAN GENETICS. 62(2):129-133, 1982.

Pericentric inversion of chromosome 6 in women with spontaneous abortions, by A. Andreev, et al. AKUSHERSTVO I GINEKOLOGIIA. 22(1):14-16, 1983.

Prospects of pregnancy following induced and spontaneous abortion of primigravidae and assessment of fertility, by G. Schott, et al. ZENTRALBLATT FUR GYNAEKOLOGIE. 104(7):397-404, 1982.

Reciprocal translocations in couples with spontaneous abortions, by P. Alicata, et al. ACTA EUROPAEA FERTILITATIS. 13(2):73-78, June 1982.

The relationship of endometriosis to spontaneous abortion, by J. M. Wheeler, et al. FERTILITY AND STERILITY. 39(5):656-660, May 1983.

The relationship between spontaneous and induced abortion and the occurrence of second-trimester abortion in subsequent pregnancies, by J. I. Puyenbroek, et al. EUROPEAN JOURNAL OF OBSTETRICS, GYNECOLOGY AND REPRODUCTIVE MEDICINE. 14(5):299-309, February 1983.

Role of genetic anomalies in the etiology of spontaneous abortion, by B. Stambolov, et al. AKUSHERSTVO I GINEKOLOGIIA. 21(5):371-373, 1982.

Serologic evidence of ureaplasma urealyticum infection in women with spontaneous pregnancy loss, by P. A. Quinn, et al. AMERICAN JOURNAL OF OBSTETRICS AND GYNECOLOGY. 145(2):245-250, January 15, 1983.

Sex ratio in spontaneous abortions, by T. Hassold, et al.
ANNALS OF HUMAN GENETICS. 47(pt 1):39-47,
January 1983.

Smoking and the occurrence of congenital malformations
and spontaneous abortions: multivariate analysis, by K.
Hemminki, et al. AMERICAN JOURNAL OF OBSTETRICS
AND GYNECOLOGY. 145(1):61-66, January 1, 1983.

Spontaneous abortion and birth order [letter], by W. H.
James. EARLY HUMAN DEVELOPMENT. 7(2):195,
November 1982.

Spontaneous abortion and diabetes mellitus, by A. D.
Wright, et al. POSTGRADUATE MEDICAL JOURNAL.
59(691):295-298, May 1983.

Spontaneous abortion and induced abortion: an adjustment
for the presence of induced abortion when estimating
the rate of spontaneous abortion from cross-sectional
studies, by E. Susser. AMERICAN JOURNAL OF
EPIDEMIOLOGY. 117(3):305-308, March 1983.

Spontaneous abortion incidence in the treatment of infertility:
addendum on in vitro fertilization [letter], by R. P.
Jansen. AMERICAN JOURNAL OF OBSTETRICS AND
GYNECOLOGY. 144(6):738-739, November 15, 1982.

Spontaneous abortion: the role of heterogenous risk and
selective fertility, by A. J. Wilcox, et al. EARLY HUMAN
DEVELOPMENT. 7(2):165-178, November 1982.

Spontaneous abortions after the three mile island nuclear
accident: a life table analysis, by M. K. Goldhaber, et al.
AMERICAN JOURNAL OF PUBLIC HEALTH. 73(7):
752-759, July 1983.

Spontaneous abortions and reproductive selection mechanisms
in the rubber and leather industry in Finland, by K.
Hemminki, et al. BRITISH JOURNAL OF INDUSTRIAL

ABORTION: SPONTANEOUS (continued)

MEDICINE. 40(1):81-86, February 1983.

Spontaneous abortions in hospital staff engaged in sterilising instruments with chemical agents, by K. Hemminki, et al. BRITISH MEDICAL JOURNAL. 285(6353):1461-1463, November 20, 1982.

Spontaneous abortions in hospital sterilising staff [letter]. BRITISH MEDICAL JOURNAL. 286(6382):1976-1977, June 18, 1983.

Spontaneous abortions in an industrialized community in Finland, by K. Hemminki, et al. AMERICAN JOURNAL OF PUBLIC HEALTH. 73(1):32-37, January 1983.

Twinning rate in spontaneous abortions, by I. A. Uchida, et al. AMERICAN JOURNAL OF HUMAN GENETICS. 35(5):987-993, September 1983.

Ultrasonic placental localization in relation to spontaneous abortion after mid-trimester amniocentesis, by J. A. Hill, et al. PRENATAL DIAGNOSIS. 2(4):289-295, October 1982.

ABORTION: SPONTANEOUS: COMPLICATIONS (continued)

Cytogenetic studies in couples with multiple spontaneous abortions, by S. Schwartz. DISSERTATION ABSTRACTS INTERNATIONAL: B. 43(9), March 1983.

An 'epidemic' of spontaneous abortion: psychosocial factors, by M. Kaffman, et al. ISRAEL JOURNAL OF PSYCHIATRY AND RELATED SCIENCES. 19(3):239-246, 1982.

Exposure to anaesthetic gases and spontaneous abortion: response bias in a postal questionnaire study, by G. Axelsson, et al. INTERNATIONAL JOURNAL OF EPIDEMIOLOGY. 11(3):250-256, September 1982.

Genetic polymorphisms and human reproduction: a study of

phosphoglucomutase in spontaneous abortion, by M. Nicotra, et al. INTERNATIONAL JOURNAL OF FERTILITY. 27(4):229-233, 1982.

The incidence of intrauterine adhesions following spontaneous abortion, by Z. Adoni, et al. INTERNATIONAL JOURNAL OF FERTILITY. 27(2):117-118, 1982.

Morphological evaluation of human fetal kidneys from spontaneous abortions, by T. Kozielec, et al. FOLIA MORPHOLOGICA. 40(2):113-121, 1981.

Mosaic trisomies in human spontaneous abortions, by T. Hassold. HUMAN GENETICS. 61(1):31-35, 1982.

Spontaneous abortion and ectopic pregnancy, by R. F. Avant. PRIMARY CARE. 10(2):161-172, June 1983.

Spontaneous abortion and subsequent down syndrome live-birth, by E. B. Hook, et al. HUMAN GENETICS. 64(3): 267-270, 1983.

ABORTION: STATISTICS

Abortion and M. T. P. cases—a study of hospital admissions from 1971 to 1979, by B. Mehta, et al. INDIAN JOURNAL OF PUBLIC HEALTH. 26(1):38-42, January-March 1982.

Abortion surveillance: preliminary analysis, 1979-1980, United States. MORBIDITY AND MORTALITY WEEKLY REPORT. 32(5):62-64, February 11, 1983.

Abortion ten years later—1.5 million yearly; backers, foes polarized, by J. T. Beifuss. NATIONAL CATHOLIC RE-PORTER. 19:1+, January 21, 1983.

Australian attitudes towards abortion: recent complementary surveys, by S. E. Fraser, et al. AUSTRALIAN JOURNAL OF SEX, MARRIAGE AND FAMILY. 3(4):171-180, November 1982.

Characteristics of abortion patients in the United States, 1979 and 1980, by S. K. Henshaw, et al. FAMILY PLANNING PERSPECTIVES. 15(1):5-8, 10-16, January-February 1983.

Demographic implications of the biological determinants of female fecundity, by R. E. Frisch. SOCIAL BIOLOGY. 29:187, Spring-Summer 1982.

Differentials in the planning status of most recent live births to Mexican Americans and Anglos, by C. W. Warren, et al. PUBLIC HEALTH REPORTS. 98(2):152-160, 1983.

Expectation—threshold model of reproductive decision making, by L. R. Beach, et al. POPULATION AND ENVIRONMENT: BEHAVIORAL AND SOCIAL ISSUES. 5(2):95-108, Summer 1982.

Maternal deaths associated with antepartum fetal death in utero, United States, 1972 to 1978, by S. F. Dorfman, et al. SOUTHERN MEDICAL JOURNAL. 76(7):838-843, July 1983.

Mid-trimester abortions: a decade in review, by M. C. Martin, et al. CANADIAN JOURNAL OF SURGERY. 25(6): 641-643, November 1982.

Problem of unmarried mothers (a study of sociopsychological aspects of 100 women seeking MTP), by K. T. Mandal. JOURNAL OF THE INDIAN MEDICAL ASSOCIATION. 79(5-6):81-86, September 1982.

Reproductive rights 1983: an international survey, by S. L. Isaacs. COLUMBIA HUMAN RIGHTS LAW REVIEW. 311:353, Fall-Winter 1982-1983.

Researchers confirm induced abortion to be safer for women than childbirth: refute claims of critics. FAMILY PLANNING PERSPECTIVES. 14(5):271-272, September-October 1982.

Results of ten years of performing abortions at the gynecologic clinic of the Dresden medical academy, by F. Rossel, et al. ZENTRALBLATT FUR GYNAEKOLOGIE. 105(11): 700-709, 1983.

Role of abortion on demand and contraception in the reproductive process in a population, I. Dimitrov. AKUSHERSTVO I GINEKOLOGIIA. 21(3):234-238, 1982.

Social, spatial and political determinants of U. S. abortion rates, by N. F. Henry, et al. SOCIAL SCIENCE AND MEDICINE. 16(9):987-996, 1982.

Socio-demographic correlates of the decision process for medical termination of pregnancy and family planning, by A. R. Chaurasia, et al. INDIAN JOURNAL OF PUBLIC HEALTH. 26(1):4-9, January-March 1982.

Third-trimester induced abortion in Georgia, 1979 and 1980, by A. M. Spitz, et al. AMERICAN JOURNAL OF PUBLIC HEALTH. 73:594-595, May 1983.

Trends in induced abortion in England and Wales, by J. R. Ashton, et al. JOURNAL OF EPIDEMIOLOGY AND COMMUNITY HEALTH. 37(2):105-110, June 1983.

ABORTION: TECHNIQUES

Cephalothin prophylaxis for midtrimester abortion, by M. R. Spence, et al. OBSTETRICS AND GYNECOLOGY. 60(4):502-505, October 1982.

Clinical test for placenta in 300 consecutive menstrual aspirations, by R. A. Munsick. OBSTETRICS AND GYNE-COLOGY. 60(6):738-741, December 1982.

Coagulation studies following mid-trimester intra-amniotic urea injection, by M. A. Deshmukh, et al. JOURNAL OF POSTGRADUATE MEDICINE. 28(4):210-213, 1982.

D and E midtrimester abortion: a medical innovation, by
S. Lewit. WOMEN AND HEALTH. 7(1):49-55, Spring
1982.

Dilatation and evacuation [letter], by W. M. Hern. OBSTETRICS
AND GYNECOLOGY. 60(5):667-668, November 1982.

Early office termination of pregnancy by soft cannula
vacuum aspiration, by J. H. Meyer, Jr. AMERICAN JOUR-
NAL OF OBSTETRICS AND GYNECOLOGY. 147(2):
202-207, September 15, 1983.

Effectiveness and complications of interrupting pregnancy
during the second trimester with the Hungarian preparation
ensaprost F, by Ts. Despodova, et al. AKUSHERSTVO I
GINEKOLOGIIA. 21(5):373-377, 1982.

Evaluation of intramuscular 15 (S) 15 methyl prostaglandin
F2 alpha for menstrual regulation and preoperative cervical
dilatation, by S. Jain, et al. INDIAN JOURNAL OF
MEDICAL RESEARCH. 77:49-53, January 1983.

Experience with 16-phenoxy-omega-tetranor-PGE2-methyl-
sulfonamide (sulprostone) for termination of second trimester
pregnancy, by P. Fylling. CONTRACEPTION. 26(3):279-
283, September 1982.

Experiences with sulproston for cervical priming in pregnancy
termination in the first trimester, by S. Heinzl, et al.
GYNAEKOLOGISCHE RUNDSCHAU. 22(4):233-240,
1982.

Hypertonic saline as an abortifacient in a select group of patients,
by J. A. Garbaciak, Jr., et al. OBSTETRICS AND GYNE-
COLOGY. 61(1):37-41, January 1983.

Impact of vacuum aspiration abortion on future childbearing:
a review, by C. J. R. Hogue, et al. FAMILY PLANNING
PERSPECTIVES. 15(3):119-126, May-June 1983.

Incomplete and inevitable abortion: treatment by suction curettage in the emergency department, by R. G. Farrell, et al. ANNALS OF EMERGENCY MEDICINE. 11(12): 652-658, December 1982.

Midtrimester abortion by ethacridine lactate, by B. K. Goswami, et al. JOURNAL OF THE INDIAN MEDICAL ASSOCIATION. 79(1-2):7-9, July 1982.

Midtrimester abortion by hypertonic saline instillation experience in Ramathibodi hospital, by S. Suthutvoravut, et al. JOURNAL OF THE MEDICAL ASSOCIATION OF THAILAND. 66(3):176-182, March 1983.

New synthetic laminaria, by M. Chvapil, et al. OBSTETRICS AND GYNECOLOGY. 60(6):729-733, December 1982.

Our experiences with early vacuum aspiration (miniinterruption), by K. Poradovsky, et al. BRATISLAVSKE LEKARSKE LISTY. 78(1):74-78, July 1982.

Plasma lidocaine levels following paracervical infiltration for aspiration abortion, by L. J. Blanco, et al. OBSTETRICS AND GYNECOLOGY. 60(4):506-508, October 1982.

Second trimester abortion by dilatation and evacuation: an analysis of 11,747 cases, by W. F. Peterson, et al. OBSTET-RICS AND GYNECOLOGY. 62(2):185-190, August 1983.

Spontaneous abortions in hospital staff engaged in sterilising instruments with chemical agents, by K. Hemminki, et al. BRITISH MEDICAL JOURNAL. 285(6353):1461-1463, November 20, 1982.

Suction curettage for incomplete and inevitable abortion an emergency medicine procedure?, by M. C. Tomlanovich. ANNALS OF EMERGENCY MEDICINE. 11(12):695-696, December 1982.

Termination of early first trimester pregnancy by vaginal

administration of 16, 16-dimethyl-trans-delta 2-PGE1 methyl ester. ASIA-OCEANIA JOURNAL OF OBSTETRICS AND GYNAECOLOGY. 8(3):263-268, September 1982.

Termination of early gestation with 9-deoxo-16, 16-dimethyl-9-methylene prostaglandin E2, by P. F. Brenner, et al. CONTRACEPTION. 26(3):261-277, September 1982.

Termination of second trimester pregnancy by intramuscular injection of 16-phenoxy-omega-17,18,19,20-tetranor-PGE2 methyl sulphonylamide. INTERNATIONAL JOURNAL OF GYNAECOLOGY AND OBSTETRICS. 20(5):383-386, October 1982.

Termination of second trimester pregnancy with a long-acting vaginal pessary containing 15-methyl-PGF2 alpha methyl ester. INTERNATIONAL JOURNAL OF GYNAECOLOGY AND OBSTETRICS. 21(2):159-165, April 1983.

Ultrasonic diagnosis of retained tissues after artifical abortion on demand, by K. Ilieva, et al. AKUSHERSTVO I GINEKOLOGIIA. 22(1):45-48, 1983.

Uterine activity and placental histology in abortion at mid-trimester by rivanol and catheter, by Y. Manabe, et al. ACTA OBSTETRICIA ET GYNECOLOGICA SCANDI-NAVICA. 61(5):433-437, 1982.

ABORTION: THERAPEUTIC

Abortion in tumor patients from a legal viewpoint, by W. Spann. MUENCHENER MEDIZINISCHE WOCHENSCHRIFT. 124(44):957-958, November 5, 1982.

Anti-Jk B alloimmunization and abortion, by G. Noia, et al. HAEMATOLOGICA. 67(5):775-780, October 1982.

Antiserum to LH reverses the abortifacient effect of Bromergocryptine treatment in early rat pregnancy, by M. Tabarelli, et al. JOURNAL OF REPRODUCTIVE

IMMUNOLOGY. 4(6):325-335, December 1982.

CMA abortion survey. CANADIAN MEDICAL ASSOCIATION JOURNAL. 129(3):262-272, August 1, 1983.

Disseminated intravascular coagulation following midtrimester abortions, by P. F. White, et al. ANESTHESIOLOGY. 58(1):99-101, January 1983.

Effects of intracervical PGE2-gel on myometrial activity and cervical state in first trimester pregnancy, by A. Forman, et al. PROSTAGLANDINS. 24(3):303-312, September 1982.

Experience with prostaglandins for therapeutic abortion in Norway. Their need and their benefits, by P. Fylling, et al. ACTA OBSTETRICIA ET GYNECOLOGICA SCANDI-NAVICA, SUPPLEMENT. 113:113-116, 1983.

Fetal Rh blood group determination in pregnancy termination by dilatation and evacuation, by J. J. LaFerla, et al. TRANSFUSION. 23(1):67-68, January-February 1983.

Induction of therapeutic abortion by intra-amniotic and intravenous administration of prostaglandin F2-alpha in the second trimester of pregnancy, by A. Otoka, et al. WIADOMOSCI LEKARSKIE. 35(15-16):969-972, September 15, 1982.

Pelvic inflammatory disease associated with chlamydia trachomatis infection after therapeutic abortion. A prospective study, by E. Qvigstad, et al. BRITISH JOURNAL OF VENEREAL DISEASE. 59(3):189-192, June 1983.

Plasma creatine kinase and myoglobin levels, before and after abortion, in human fetuses at risk for Duchene muscular dystrophy, by R. J. Edwards, et al. AMERICAN JOURNAL OF MEDICAL GENETICS. 15(3):475-482, July 1983.

Plasma levels of 9-deoxo-16, 16-dimethyl-9-methylene-PGE2 in connection with its development as an abortifacient, by

K. Green, et al. PROSTAGLANDINS. 24(4):451-466, October 1982.

Pregnancy complicated by periateritis nodosa: induced abortion as an alternative, by D. A. Nagey, et al. AMERICAN JOURNAL OF OBSTETRICS AND GYNECOLOGY. 147(1):103-105, September 1, 1983.

Pregnancy interruption from the pediatric viewpoint, by A. Rett. GEBURTSHILFE UND FRAUENHEILKUNDE. 43(4):259-262, April 1983.

Therapeutic abortion and chlamydial infection, by G. L. Ridgway, et al. BRITISH MEDICAL JOURNAL. 286(6376): 1478-1479, May 7, 1983.

Therapeutic abortion and chlamydial infection [letter], by A. Mills. BRITISH MEDICAL JOURNAL. 286(6378):1649, May 21, 1983.

Therapeutic abortion and chlamydia trachomatis infection, by E. Qvigstad, et al. BRITISH JOURNAL OF VENEREAL DISEASE. 58(3):182-183.

Therapeutic abortion in life-threatening pregnancies [letter], by J. Aznar, et al. LANCET. 1(8336):1280-1281, June 4, 1983.

Therapeutic abortion: the medical argument, by J. F. Murphy, et al. IRISH MEDICAL JOURNAL. 75(8):304-306, August 1982.

Therapeutic abortion on psychiatric grounds. Part III. Implementing the abortion and sterilization act (1975-1981), by E. S. Nash, et al. SOUTH AFRICAN MEDICAL JOURNAL. 63(17):639-644, April 23, 1983.

Vacuum aspiration in therapeutic abortions, by G. Frick. ACTA OBSTETRICIA ET GYNECOLOGICA SCANDI-NAVICA. 61(6):523-524, 1982.

Water intoxication following oxytocin perfusion, by G. Borg, et al. JOURNAL DE GYNECOLOGIE, OBSTETRIQUE ET BIOLOGIE DE LA REPRODUCTION. 12(1):51-53, 1983.

Why is the number of pregnancies among teenagers decreasing?, by M. G. Powell, et al. CANADIAN MEDICAL ASSOCIATION JOURNAL. 127(6):493-495, September 15, 1982.

ABORTION: THREATENED

B, T and null lymphocytes in threatened abortion, by T. Bartoszewicz, et al. GINEKOLOGIA POLSKA. 53(5-6): 307-310, 1982.

Cellular immunity factors in the physiological course of pregnancy and abortion, by P. I. Fogel. AKUSHERSTVO I GINEKOLOGIIA. (12):28-30, 1982.

Cervical cerclage: an aggressive approach to threatened or recurrent pregnancy wastage, by W. R. Crombleholme, et al. AMERICAN JOURNAL OF OBSTETRICS AND GYNE-COLOGY. 146(2):168-174, May 15, 1983.

Cervical and serum IgA and serum IgG antibodies to chlamydia trachomatis and herpes simplex virus in threatened abortion: a prospective study, by M. Gronroos, et al. BRITISH JOURNAL OF OBSTETRICS AND GYNAECOLOGY. 90(2):167-170, February 1983.

Changes in the blood level of alpha-fetoprotein in threatened abortion, by D. Berlingieri, et al. ARCHIVIO DI OSTETRICIA E GINECOLOGIA. 87(1-2):21-32, January-April 1982.

Clinical significance of the determination of the plasma concentration of progesterone in threatened abortions during the first half of pregnancy, by I. Misinger, et al. CESKOSLOVENSKA GYNEKOLOGIE. 48(1):18-21, February 1983.

Comparison of serum and urine hCG levels with SP1 and PAPP-A levels in patients with first-trimester vaginal bleeding, by G. M. Masson, et al. OBSTETRICS AND GYNECOLOGY. 61(2):223-226, February 1983.

Correlation between hormonal levels and ultrasound in patients with threatened abortion, by R. Dessaive, et al. GYNE-COLOGIC AND OBSTETRIC INVESTIGATION. 14(1): 65-78, 1982.

HCG and SP-1 in normal pregnancy and in high-risk early pregnancy, by K. Vetter, et al. GEBURTSHILFE UND FRAUNHEILKUNDE. 42(12):868-870, December 1982.

Human placental lactogen, pregnancy-specific beta-1-glycoprotein and alpha-fetoprotein in serum in threatened abortion, by J. B. Hertz, et al. INTERNATIONAL JOUR-NAL OF GYNAECOLOGY AND OBSTETRICS. 21(2): 111-117, April 1983.

Incidence of obstetrical-risk pregnancies in the Wloclawek region—prenatal and intrapartum risk and the state of the newborn infant, by B. Bilyk, et al. GINEKOLOGIA POLSKA. 53(12):869-873, December 1982.

Intake of estroprogestins in pregnancy and hypospadias, by S. Milia, et al. MINERVA GINECOLOGIA. 34(12):1023-1027, December 1982.

Justification of the monitoring of early pregnancy under conditions of restricted fertility, by W. Gromadzki, et al. GINEKOLOGIA POLSKA. 53(5-6):311-320, 1982.

Landmarks during the first forty-two days of gestation demonstrated by the beta-subunit of human chorionic gonadotropin and ultrasound, by F. R. Batzer, et al. AMERICAN JOURNAL OF OBSTETRICS AND GYNE-COLOGY. 146(8):973-979, August 15, 1983.

Occurrence of IgM antibodies against cytomeglaovirusinduced late antigens in women with imminent abortion in comparison to women with normal pregnancy, by L. Gartner, et al. ZENTRALBLATT FUR GYNAEKOLOGIE. 104(16):1005-1008, 1982.

Pregnancy-associated plasma protein A in the prediction of early pregnancy failure, by J. G. Westergaard, et al. AMERICAN JOURNAL OF OBSTETRICS AND GYNE-COLOGY. 145(1):67-69, January 1, 1983.

Prognostic value of plasma progesterone—R. I. A. in threatened abortion, by D. Marchesoni, et al. CLINICAL AND EX-PERIMENTAL OBSTETRICS AND GYNECOLOGY. 9(1): 42-45, 1982.

Psychological problems of pregnant women under special medical care, by M. Beisert, et al. GINEKOLOGIA POLSKA. 53(11):721-732, 1982.

Re-evaluation of measurements of maternal serum hCG, hPL and progesterone as prognostic markers of abortion in early pregnancy, by N. Sugita, et al. ASIA-OCEANIA JOURNAL OF OBSTETRICS AND GYNAECOLOGY. 9(1):49-54, March 1983.

Serum copper and ceruloplasmin as an index of foetal well being in abortions, by A. Singhal, et al. INDIAN JOURNAL OF PATHOLOGY AND MICROBIOLOGY. 25(4):242-244, October 1982.

Use of hormonal preparations on women with threatened abortion, by R. N. Stepanova. AKUSHERSTVO I GINE-KOLOGIIA. (12):40-42, 1982.

Usefulness of cytohormonal vaginal smears for monitoring threatened early pregnancy, by M. Myskow, et al. WIADOMOSCI LEKARSKIE. 35(15-16):973-977, September 15, 1982.

Value of schwangerschaftprotein 1 (SP1) and pregnancy-

ABORTION: THREATENED (continued)

associated plasma protein-A (PAPP-A) in the clinical
management of threatened abortion, by G. M. Masson, et al.
BRITISH JOURNAL OF OBSTETRICS AND GYNAE-
COLOGY. 90(2):146-149, February 1983.

ABORTION: VOLUNTARY

Contraceptive use and perceptions of chance and ability of
conceiving in women electing abortion, by P. M. Klein.
JOURNAL OF OBSTETRIC, GYNECOLOGIC AND
NEONATAL NURSING. 12(3):167-171, May-June 1983.

The hidden grief of abortion, by J. Upton. PASTORAL
PSYCHOLOGY. 31(1):19-25, 1982.

Medico-social aspects of the voluntary interruption of
pregnancy: reflections on routine data from an outpatient
center, by C. Humblet, et al. REVUE DE L'INSTITUT DE
SOCIOLOGIE. (3):477-508, 1982.

ABORTION: ACUPUNCTURE

Acupuncture reflexotherapy in abortion, by A. I. Liubimova,
et al. AKUSHERSTVO I GINEKOLOGIIA. (12):31-34,
1982.

ABORTION: ADOLESCENTS

Personality factors, self-concept and family variables related
to first time and repeat abortion-seeking behavior in
adolescent women, by M. B. Deutsch. DISSERTATION
ABSTRACTS INTERNATIONAL: A. 43(10), April 1983.

Pregnancy in early and late adolescence, by D. de Anda.
JOURNAL OF YOUTH AND ADOLESCENCE. 12:33-
42, February 1983.

Quality of object relations in abortion seeking, in teleo-
cyesis and never-pregnant adolescents, by E. D. Hibbs.
DISSERTATION ABSTRACTS INTERNATIONAL: B.

ABORTION: ADOLESCENTS (continued)

44(3):September 1983.

ABORTION: ANESTHESIA

Exposure to anaesthetic gases and spontaneous abortion: response bias in a postal questionnaire study, by G. Axelsson, et al. INTERNATIONAL JOURNAL OF EPIDEMIOLOGY. 11(3):250-256, September 1982.

Safety: anaesthetic hazard in operating theatres, by S. Barnes, et al. OCCUPATIONAL HEALTH. 34(8):370-372, August 1982.

Trace anesthetic gases: an unproven health hazard, by L. F. Walts. ASSOCIATION OF OPERATING ROOM NURSES. 37(4):728-729, 732, 736+, March 1983.

ABORTION AND COLLEGE STUDENTS

College students' attitudes toward shared responsibility in decisions about abortion: implications for counseling, by I. J. Ryan, et al. JOURNAL OF THE AMERICAN COLLEGE HEALTH ASSOCIATION. 31(6):231-235, June 1983.

ABORTION AND CRIMINALS

Criminal abortions as seen in the university teaching hospital, Lusaka, Zambia, by J. N. Narone, et al. MEDICAL JOURNAL OF ZAMBIA. 15(3):80-84, 1981.

ABORTION AND ECONOMICS

Abortion and fertility in economic perspective: a theoretical and empirical analysis with special reference to New York City, 1969-1972, by M. J. Kramer. DISSERTATION AB-STRACTS INTERNATIONAL: A. 43(9), March 1983.

Attitudes toward abortion among Catholic Mexican-American women: the effects of religiosity and education, by S. Rosenhouse-Persson, et al. DEMOGRAPHY. 20:87-98, February 1983.

ABORTION AND ECONOMICS (continued)

Economic issues, not abortion, are the primary concern of the electorate. FAMILY PLANNING PERSPECTIVES. 15:35-36, January-February 1983.

ABORTION AND ERA

Feminists against abortion: the prolife movement is broadening, by B. Spring. CHRISTIANITY TODAY. 27:35-36, April 22, 1983.

Lesbian feminism and the pro-choice movement, by W. Kolasinska. RESOURCES FOR FEMINIST RESEARCH. 12:61-62, March 1983.

Prolife clause heats ERA debate. REGISTER. 59:2, September 4, 1983.

ABORTION AND FERTILITY

A sponge contraceptive, by C. A. Helwick. HEALTH. 14:13, April 1982.

ABORTION AND HORMONES

A bacterial mutagenicity study of rivanol, an acridine derivative used as an abortifacient, by M. Wugmeister, et al. YALE JOURNAL OF BIOLOGY AND MEDICINE. 56(1):9-13, January-February 1983.

Biophysical studies on molecular mechanisms of abortifacient action of prostaglandins. V. CNDO/2 estimation of the relative affinities of the cations Na+, Mg2+ and Ca2+ to the carboxylic group, by V. Kothekar, et al. JOURNAL OF THEORETICAL BIOLOGY. 101(2):225-231, March 21, 1983.

—. VI. Conformation energy calculation on PGE2, PGF2 alpha and 15-(s)-methyl PGF2 alpha, by V. Kothekar. JOURNAL OF THEORETICAL BIOLOGY. 101(2):233-240, March 21, 1983.

Changes in intraocular pressure during prostaglandin-induced abortion, by M. Ober, et al. KLINISCHE MONATS- BLAETTER FUR AUGENHEILKUNDE. 180(3):230-231, 1982.

Clinical applications of prostaglandins in obstetrics and gynaecology, by S. M. Karim. ANNALS OF THE ACADEMY OF MEDICINE, SINGAPORE. 11(4):493-502, October 1982.

Clinical significance of the determination of the plasma con- centration of progesterone in threatened abortions during the first half of pregnancy, by I. Misinger, et al. CESKOSLOVENSKA GYNEKOLOGIE. 48(1):18-21, February 1983.

Coagulation studies following mid-trimester intra-amniotic urea injection, by M. A. Deshmukh, et al. JOURNAL OF POSTGRADUATE MEDICINE. 28(4):210-213, 1982.

Comparison of natural and synthetic prostaglandin E2 tablets in labour induction, by E. R. Luther, et al. CANADIAN MEDICAL ASSOCIATION JOURNAL. 128(10):1189- 1191, May 15, 1983.

Comparison of three subcutaneous modes of prostaglandin F2 alpha administration for pregnancy termination in the hamster, by J. W. Wilks. PROSTAGLANDINS. 24(6):837- 842, December 1982.

Continuous extra-amniotic intracavitary application of prostaglandin F2 alpha for medicamentous induction of labour in high-risk cases of pregnancy interruption, by E. Ehrig, et al. ZENTRALBLATT FUR GYNAEKOLOGIE. 104(13):769-776, 1982.

Correlation between hormonal levels and ultrasound in patients with threatened abortion, by R. Dessaive, et al. GYNE- COLOGIC AND OBSTETRIC INVESTIGATION. 14(1): 65-78, 1982.

Determination of 15-methyl prostaglandin F2a by derivatization high pressure liquid chromatography, by Z. S. Wang, et al. YAO HSUEH HSUEH PAO. 17(8):603-608, August 1982.

Early midtrimester pregnancy termination: a comparison of dilatation and evacuation and intravaginal prostaglandin E2, by J. Robins, et al. JOURNAL OF REPRODUCTIVE MEDICINE. 27(7):415-419, 1982.

Effect of 15-me-prostaglandin F2 alpha on the release of endogenous prostaglandin F2 alpha and the concentration of estrogen and progesterone receptors in the human endometrium, by I. A. Manuilova, et al. AKUSHERSTVO I GINEKOLOGIIA. (1):54-55, 1983.

The effects of an antiprogesterone steroid in women: interruption of the menstrual cycle and of early pregnancy, by W. Herrmann, et al. COMPTE RENDUE DES SEANCES DE L'ACADEMIE DES SCIENCES. 294(18):933-938, May 17, 1982.

Experience with prostaglandins for therapeutic abortion in Norway. Their need and their benefits, by P. Fylling, et al. ACTA OBSTETRICIA ET GYNECOLOGICA, SCANDINAVICA. SUPPLEMENT. 113:113-116, 1983.

Extra-amniotic prostaglandin gel in the management of fetal death and fetal abnormality, by M. A. Quinn, et al. AUSTRALIAN AND NEW ZEALAND JOURNAL OF OBSTETRICS AND GYNAECOLOGY. 22(2):76-77, May 1982.

Hormonal profile of the second trimester of normal and pathologic pregnancies, by D. Tsenov, et al. AKUSHERSTVO I GINEKOLOGIIA. 21(3):184-188, 1982.

Induction of internal abortion and vesicular mole with intramuscular adminsitration of 15(S)15-methyl-prostaglandin F2 alpha, by A. Nasi, et al. MINERVA GINECOLOGIA. 34(6):461-466, June 1982.

219

Intake of estroprogestins in pregnancy and hypospadias, by S. Milia, et al. MINERVA GINECOLOGIA. 34(12):1023-1027, December 1982.

Local application of prostaglandin F2 alpha to primigravid interruption patients in first trimester, by M. Heinz, et al. ZENTRALBLATT FUR GYNAEKOLOGIE. 104(13):784-790, 1982.

Menses induction and second-trimester pregnancy termination using a polymeric controlled release vaginal delivery system containing (15S)15-methyl PGF2 alpha methyl ester, by M. Bygdeman, et al. CONTRACEPTION. 27(2):141-151, February 1983.

Midtrimester pregnancy termination by intravaginal administration of prostaglandin E2, by E. J. Surrago, et al. CONTRACEPTION. 26(3):285-294, September 1982.

A new class of nonhormonal pregnancy-terminating agents. Synthesis and contragestational activity of 3,5-diaryl-s-triazoles, by A. Omodei-Sale, et al. JOURNAL OF MEDICINAL CHEMISTRY. 26(8):1187-1192, August 1983.

Pregnancy interception with a combination of prostaglandins: studies in monkeys, by J. W. Wilks. SCIENCE. 221:1407-1409, September 30, 1983.

Pregnancy-terminating action of a luteinizing hormone-releasing hormone agonist D-Ser(But)6desGly10ProEA in baboons, by C. Das, et al. FERTILITY AND STERILITY. 39(2):218-223, February 1983.

Pregnancy termination by prostaglandin F2a stimulates maternal behavior in the rat, by J. F. Rodriguez-Sierva, et al. HORMONES AND BEHAVIOR. 16(3):343-351, September 1982.

Preoperative cervical dilatation by vaginal pessaries containing prostaglandin E1 analogue, by J. K. Chen, et al. OBSTETRICS

AND GYNECOLOGY. 62(3):339-342, September 1983.

Pre-operative cervical dilatation in termination of first trimester pregnancies using 16, 16-dimethyl-trans-delta 2 PGE1
methyl ester vaginal pessaries, by P. C. Ho, et al. CONTRA-
CEPTION. 27(4):339-346, April 1983.

Progesterone and testosterone: contraception and immuno-
suppressive effects in mice, by Z. Pokorna, et al. EN-
DOKRINOLOGIE. 79(2):185-189, 1982.

Prognostic value of plasma prosgesterone-R. I. A. in threatened
abortion, by D. Marchesoni, et al. CLINICAL AND EX-
PERIMENTAL OBSTETRICS AND GYNECOLOGY. 9(1):
42-45, 1982.

Re-evaluation of measurements of maternal serum hCG, hPL
and progesterone as prognostic markers of abortion in early
pregnancy, by N. Sugita, et al. ASIA-OCEANIA JOURNAL
OF OBSTETRICS AND GYNAECOLOGY. 9(1):49-54,
March 1983.

Side effects and early complications following cervical priming
with prostaglandin F2 alpha (PGF2 alpha) in inducing
abortion in young women in their first pregnancy, by B.
Seifert, et al. ZENTRALBLATT FUR GYNAEKOLOGIE.
105(11):710-714, 1983.

Systemic adverse reactions to prostaglandin F2 (PGF2 alpha,
dinoprostone, prostin F2 alpha, prostalmon F), by L.
Wislicki. INTERNATIONAL JOURNAL OF BIOLOGICAL
RESEARCH IN PREGNANCY. 3(4):158-160, 1982.

Synthesis and antifertility activity of 13-aza 14-oxo-
prostaglandins, by D. Favara, et al. PROSTAGLANDINS.
25(3):311-320, March 1983.

Termination of second trimester pregnancy with a long-acting
vaginal pessary containing 15-methyl-PGF2 alpha methyl
ester. INTERNATIONAL JOURNAL OF GYNAECO-

ABORTION AND HORMONES (continued)

LOGICAL OBSTETRICS. 21(2):159-165, April 1983.

Urea-prostaglandin versus hypertonic saline for instillation abortion, by N. J. Binkin, et al. AMERICAN JOURNAL OF OBSTETRICS AND GYNECOLOGY. 146(8):947-952, August 15, 1983.

The use of prostaglandins for termination of abnormal pregnancy, by N. J. Christensen, et al. ACTA OBSTETRICIA ET GYNECOLOGICA SCANDINAVICA. SUPPLEMENT. 113:153-157, 1983.

Will a do-it-yourself abortion drug hit the market soon? [Upjohn's research on prostaglandins], by R. Frame. CHRISTIANITY TODAY. 27:71-72, October 7, 1983.

ABORTION AND HOSPITALS

Abortion and M. T. P. cases—a study of hospital admissions from 1971 to 1979, by B. Mehta, et al. INDIAN JOURNAL OF PUBLIC HEALTH. 26(1):38-42, January-March 1982.

Hospitalization requirements for second trimester abortions: for the purpose of health or hindrance?, by M. C. Foley. THE GEORGETOWN LAW JOURNAL. 71(3):991-1021, 1983.

Policy implementation and community linkages: hospital abortion services after Roe v. Wade, by C. A. Johnson, et al. WESTERN POLITICAL QUARTERLY. 35(3):385-405, 1982.

Policy implementation and responsiveness in nongovernmental institutions: hospital abortion services after Roe v. Wade, by C. A. Johnson, et al. WESTERN POLITICAL QUARTERLY. 35:385-405, September 1982.

Use of hormonal preparations on women with threatened abortion, by R. N. Stepanova. AKUSHERSTVO I GINE-KOLOGIIA. (12):40-42, 1982.

ABORTION AND INSURANCE

Abortion—waiting period—hospitalization—insurance. THE FAMILY LAW REPORTER: COURT OPINIONS. 9(10): 2150, January 11, 1983.

Bill may ban abortion in unemployed health coverage. OUR SUNDAY VISITOR. 72:8, June 12, 1983.

New insurance law could mandate abortion coverage. OUR SUNDAY VISITOR. 72:8, May 29, 1983.

ABORTION AND MALES

Abortion—husband's consent—jurisdiction and procedure—mootness. THE FAMILY LAW REPORTER: COURT OPINIONS. 9(17):2267, March 1, 1983.

Abortion—notice to husband. THE FAMILY LAW REPORTER: TEXT NO. 1. 9(6):3001-3026, December 7, 1982.

Men and abortion: three neglected ethical aspects, by A. B. Shostak. HUMANITY AND SOCIETY. 7(1):66-85, February 1983.

Sharing the pain of abortion [impact on men], by J. Leo. TIME. 122:78, September 26, 1983.

Spousal notice—weighing the burden on a woman's abortion decision: Scheinberg v. Smith. STETSON LAW REVIEW. 12:250-264, Fall, 1982.

Spousal notification and consent in abortion situations: Scheinberg v. Smith. HOUSTON LAW REVIEW. 19:1025-1039, 1982.

ABORTION AND THE MENTALLY RETARDED

Commentary on making up her mind: consent, pregnancy and mental handicap, by M. Lockwood. JOURNAL OF MEDICAL ETHICS. 9:224-226, December 1983.

ABORTION AND NURSES

Abortion explained by a nurse, by M. A. Bastit i Costa. REVISTA DE ENFERMAGEN. 6(58-59):36-39, May-June 1983.

Determination of essential content as the basis for development of a curriculum model on care of the induced abortion patient for baccalaureate nursing faculty, by M. L. Olson. DISSERTATION ABSTRACTS INTERNATIONAL: A. 43(12), June 1983.

Open to debate . . . abortion . . . nurses should be involved in open debate, by A. Webber. NURSING MIRROR AND MIDWIVE'S JOURNAL. 157(4):38-40, July 27, 1983.

ABORTION AND PARENTAL CONSENT

Parental notification and abortion: a review and recommendation to West Virginia's legislature. WEST VIRGINIA LAW RE-VIEW. 85:943-968, Summer 1983.

Right to abortion limited: the supreme court upholds the consitutionality of parental notification statutes. LOYOLA LAW REVIEW. 28:281-296, Winter 1982.

Title X parental notification regulation—a different prognosis, by E. F. Diamond. LINACRE QUARTERLY. 50:56-63, February 1983.

ABORTION AND PHYSICIANS

Abortion. Doctors, pro and/or con. REVISTA DE ENFER-MAGEN. 6(58-59):28-31, May-June 1983.

Abortion and the doctors, by M. Kenny. TABLET. 237:942-943, October 1, 1983.

Abortion from the legal viewpoint for the physician, by H. D. Hiersche. GYNAKOLOGE. 15(2):72-79, June 1982.

Catholic doctor who fought for the pill (John Rock), by L.

McLaughlin. DISCOVER. 4:82+, February 1982.

Doctors and abortion, by J. Van Dusen. MACLEANS. 96:43, August 8, 1983.

The doctors defy antiabortion tides [abortions resume at Moncton hospital, N. B.], by D. Folster. MACLEANS. 96:15, January 10, 1983.

Doctors' dilemma, by D. Gollob. NEW STATESMAN. 105:18, February 4, 1983.

The judicial portrayal of the physician in abortion and sterilization decisions: the useand abuse of medical discretion, by A. Asaro. HARVARD WOMEN'S LAW JOURNAL. 6:51-102, Spring 1983.

Patient, physician, society: whose rights control 'life' issues?, by R. A. Carlson. HOSPITAL PROGRESS. 63(12):53-59, December 1982.

The real abortion issue, by S. G. Cole. THIS MAGAZINE. 17:4-8, June 1983.

Should a doctor tell? TABLET. 237:743, August 6, 1983.

ABORTION AND POLITICS

Abortion: the debate continues. ENGAGE/SOCIAL ACTION FORUM. 91(11):9-40, March 1983.

Abortion issues still raging after ten years, by N. Thimmesch. HEALTH EDUCATION. 43:16, February 26, 1983.

Abortion: a national security issue, by S. D. Mumford. HUMANIST. 42:12+, September-October 1982.

Abortion 1982: the supreme court once again, by J. M. Healey. CONNECTICUT MEDICINE. 46(11):681, November 1982.

Abortion pioneer now a top pro-life advocate: interview with Bernard Nathanson. HEALTH EDUCATION. 43:13, May 7, 1983.

Abortion politics and public policy, by P. R. Lee, et al. MOBIUS. 2(4):66-74, October 1982.

Abortion rights rescued: the triumph of coalition politics, by S. Caudle. MS. 11:40+, January 1983.

Attitude extremism in the abortion controversy: a test of social judgment, cognitive dissonance and attribution theories, by S. L. Goettsch. DISSERTATION ABSTRACTS INTERNATIONAL: A. 44(3), September 1983.

Attitudes towards abortion among Catholic Mexican-American women: the effects of religiosity and education, by S. Rosenhouse-Persson, et al. DEMOGRAPHY. 20(1):87-98, February 1983.

The battle over abortion , by G. Kopecky. GLAMOUR. 81:218+, June 1983.

Before the velvet curtain: the Connecticut contraceptive cases as a study in constitutional law and supreme court behavior, by R. J. Fiscus. DISSERTATION ABSTRACTS INTER-NATIONAL: A. 43(12), June 1983.

Bishop's pawns. ECONOMIST. 287:46+, April 9, 1983.

Can congress settle the abortion issue?, by M. C. Segers. HASTINGS CENTER REPORT. 12(3):20-28, 1982.

Carter holdover promotes foreign abortions, by D. Lambro. CATHOLIC DIGEST. 9:6, March 1983.

Church and state [Protestant backlash] , by M. Holland. NEW STATESMAN. 105:16-17, May 13, 1983.

The coathanger and the rose, by D. Granberg, et al. SOCIETY.

19(4):39-46, 1982.

Comparison of members of pro- and anti-abortion organizations in Missouri, by D. Granberg. SOCIAL BIOLOGY. 28:239-252, Fall-Winter 1981.

In congress: repeal Roe to senate floor, by M. B. Welch. OFF OUR BACKS. 13:9, June 1983.

Consistency, welfare rights and abortion: a reply to Perry, by J. P. Sterba. METAPHILOSOPHY. 14:162-165, April 1983.

The court stands by abortion, by A. Press, et al. NEWSWEEK. 101(26):62-63, June 27, 1983.

Dearth of contraception fuels world abortion rate. NATIONAL CATHOLIC REPORTER. 19:10, January 21, 1983.

Defining battle lines; rules for debate, by K. Himes. NATIONAL CATHOLIC REPORTER. 19:7, January 21, 1983.

The dilemma of an anti-abortion democrat, by D. R. Carlin, Jr. COMMONWEAL. 110:626-628, November 18, 1983.

Fifteen million lives snuffed out; President Ronald Reagan reports, by R. W. Reagan. COLUMBIA. 63:4-9, August 1983.

Growing conservatism in the United States? An examination of trends in political opinion between 1972 and 1980, by J. Saltzman-Chafetz, et al. SOCIOBIOLOGICAL PERSPECTIVES. 26(3):275-298, 1983.

Ireland's abortion vote: the bishops and the press, by T. P. O'Mahony. AMERICA. 149:329-330, November 26, 1983.

Irish voters and their new antiabortion amendment, by J. P. McCarthy. AMERICA. 149:209-211, October 15, 1983.

ABORTION AND POLITICS (continued)

The liberal position on abortion and welfare rights, by C. Perry. METAPHILOSOPHY. 14:12-18, January 1983.

Lobbying for life, by C. Hays. REGISTER. 59:9, February 6, 1983.

Lore Maier's fight against abortion is real war story, by G. Pakulski. OUR SUNDAY VISITOR. 72:3, July 31, 1983.

"March for life" marks tenth anniversary (anti-abortion demonstration). HEALTH EDUCATION. 43:26, February 5, 1983.

Marketing anti-abortion as pro-life. NATIONAL CATHOLIC REPORTER. 19:3, January 21, 1983.

Normative boundaries and abortion policy: politics of morality, by S. L. Markson. RESEARCH IN SOCIAL PROBLEMS AND PUBLIC POLICY. 2:21-33, 1982.

On Gutmann, moral philosophy and political problems, by P. Abbott. POLITICAL THEORY. 10:606-609, November 1982.

Policy implementation and community linkages: hospital abortion services after Roe v. Wade, by C. A. Johnson, et al. WESTERN POLITICAL QUARTERLY. 35(3):385-405, September 1982.

Politics of abortion: a Morgentaler invitation embitters Calgary alderman, by C. Hayes, et al. ALBERTA REPORT. 10:11, 13, April 11, 1983.

Post-election reflections, by J. Sobran. CENTER JOURNAL. 2(1):115-120, Winter 1982.

Priests and politics, by M. Holland. NEW STATESMAN. September 2, 1983, p. 13-14.

The prolife agenda: converts or convicts?, by R. E. Burns.

U. S. CATHOLIC. 48:2, April 1983.

Prolife, prochoice groups claim midterm election victories, by J. Castelli. HOSPITAL PROGRESS. 63:18-19, December 1982.

Pro-lifers, foes clash at fair, by C. Fugere. NATIONAL CATHOLIC REPORTER. 20:4, November 11, 1983.

Public policies and family outcomes: empirical evidence or theology?, by S. L. Zimmerman. SOCIAL CASEWORK. 64(3):138-146, 1983.

A pyrrhic victory; disarray over abortion, by P. Kirby. COMMONWEAL. 110:517-519, October 7, 1983.

Reagan appoints an ardent prolifer to a cabinet position [M. Heckler at health and human services] . CHRISTIANITY TODAY. 27:48-50, April 8, 1983.

Sixteen thousand fetuses intensify fight in which they have no stake, by P. Edmonds. NATIONAL CATHOLIC RE-PORTER. 19:1, January 21, 1983.

Supreme court's abortion decisions: a critical study of the shaping of a major American public policy and a basis for change, by S. M. Krason. DISSERTATION ABSTRACTS INTERNATIONAL: A. 44(1), July 1983.

Supreme court and congress on abortion: an analysis of comparative institutional capacity, by C. D. Reedy. DISSERTATION ABSTRACTS INTERNATIONAL: A. 43(11), May 1983.

The survivor, by M. Masterson. OUR SUNDAY VISITOR. 72:4-5, July 31, 1983.

Sustaining the prolife momentum: legal and political strategies, by G. D. Wendel, et al. HOSPITAL PROGRESS. 63(12):70-73, December 1982.

ABORTION AND POLITICS (continued)

Why is pro-abortion AID official still there? (J. J. Speidel), by
D. Lambro. HEALTH EDUCATION. 43:16, February 12,
1983.

ABORTION AND RELIGION

Abortion and the bomb—life-related issues; Presidential address
to the National Conference of Catholic Bishops, by J. R.
Roach. PRIEST. 39:12-14, February 1983.

Abortion and honesty [discussion of September 14-21, 1983
article, Abortion: a question of Catholic honesty], by D.
C. Maguire. CHRISTIAN CENTURY. 100:1136-1138,
December 7, 1983.

Abortion—education—registration fees—religion. THE FAMILY
LAW REPORTER: COURT OPINIONS. 9(1):2011,
November 2, 1982.

Abortion in the '80?s: confrontation and crisis, by R. Collison.
CHATELAINE. 56:47, 118+, July 1983.

Abortion: a look at our Christian roots, by E. K. Jesaitis.
NATIONAL CATHOLIC REPORTER. 19:7, January 21,
1983.

The abortion mess in Los Angeles [controversy over disposition
of dead fetuses found at defunct private pathology lab], by
D. W. Pawley. CHRISTIANITY TODAY. 26:46+,
September 17, 1982.

Abortion: a question of Catholic honesty, by D. C. Maguire.
CHRISTIAN CENTURY. 100:803-807, September 14-21,
1983.

Abortion ten years later. COMMONWEAL. 110:35-37, January
28, 1983.

Archbishop and the abortions: the pro-life turn their fire on
the Catholic establishment, by V. Byfield. ALBERTA

REPORT. 9:50, October 25, 1982.

Archbishop calls for nun's resignation from state post, by E. C. Szoka. ORIGINS. 12:621-622, March 10, 1983.

Archbishop Szoka announces his decision, by E. C. Szoka. OUR SUNDAY VISITOR. 71:5, March 13, 1983.

Are Catholic hospitals morally responsible for surgical practices in associated office buildings? HOSPITAL PROGRESS. 64(5):61-62, May 1983.

The arguments in favor of abortion are strong—if you accept one all-important assumption, by L. B. Smedes. CHRISTIANITY TODAY. 27:62, July 15, 1983.

Bishop's pawns. ECONOMIST. 287:46+, April 9, 1983.

The Catholic church and social justice issues, by S. Mumford. HUMANIST. 43:5-14, July-August 1983.

Catholics waver on abortion, by C. Hayes, et al. ALBERTA REPORT. 10:21, May 30, 1983.

Ces choix qui font de nous ce que nous sommes, by J. R. Roach. LA DOCUMENTATION CATHOLIQUE. 80:99-102, January 16, 1983.

Christian action: third approach to abortion, by G. B. Wilson. NATIONAL CATHOLIC REPORTER. 19:4, January 21, 1983.

Church-state cases, by W. R. Caron. CATHOLIC LAWYER. 27:197-204, Summer 1982.

Church and state [Protestant backlash], by M. Holland. NEW STATESMAN. 105:16-17, May 13, 1983.

Controversial appointment [Sister A. Mansour appointed head of Dept. of Social Services in Michigan]. CHRISTIAN

CENTURY. 100:266-267, March 23-30, 1983.

Dissenting Catholics take pro-choice stand, by B. Yuill. NATIONAL CATHOLIC REPORTER. 19:25, February 11, 1983.

Excommunication over abortion, by R. Lee, et al. ALBERTA REPORT. 10:42-43, July 11, 1983.

Forgiveness for abortion, by Sister M. A. Walsh. CATHOLIC DIGEST. 47:83-84, July 1983.

From judge Dooling's decision [National Conference of Catholic Bishops' pro-life organizing campaign], by J. Dooling. HUMANIST. 43:10-11, July-August 1983.

Genetic decision making and pastoral care. Clergy involvement. by R. C. Baumiller. HOSPITAL PRACTICE. 18(4):38A, 38D-38F, April 1983.

If not abortion, what then? CHRISTIANITY TODAY. 27:14-23, May 20, 1983.

In search of a constituency for the new religious rights, by C. Mueller. PUBLIC OPINION QUARTERLY. 47(2):213-229, 1983.

Ireland's abortion vote: the bishops and the press, by T. P. O'Mahony. AMERICA. 149:329-330, November 26, 1983.

Jesse Helms in the dock, by B. Spring. CHRISTIANITY TODAY. 27:78+, March 4, 1983.

Marriage: the vision of humanae vitae, by G. D. Coleman. THOUGHT. 58:18-34, March 1983.

NFP services in Catholic hospitals, by J. T. McHugh. LINACRE QUARTERLY. 50:246-250, August 1983.

Nun defended as head of agency funding abortions, by T. Ewald.

OUR SUNDAY VISITOR. 71:8, January 30, 1982.

The nun's revolt: Sister Agnes Mary Mansour: her vow to the people, by M. K. Blakely. MS. 12:54+, September 1983.

Obey or leave [A. Mansour leaves Sisters of Mercy in order to remain director of Michigan's Dept. of Social Services]. TIME. 121:57, May 23, 1983.

On abortion: sorting out the questions—a Lutheran contribution to the public policy debate, by R. W. Jenson. LUTHERAN FORUM. 17(1):9+, 1983.

Pope's role in Mansour case tied to abortion issue. OUR SUNDAY VISITOR. 72:8, May 29, 1983.

Prenatal testing for tay-sachs disease in the light of Jewish views regarding abortion, by J. Baskin. ISSUES IN HEALTH CARE OF WOMEN. 4(1):41-56, January-February 1983.

Priest and politics, by M. Holland. NEW STATESMAN. September 2, 1983, p. 13-14.

Principles in conflict [appointment of Sister A. Mansour to the Dept. of Social Services in Michigan]. AMERICA. 148:409-410, May 28, 1983.

Prolife compassion or crusade?, by J. Evans. AMERICA. 147:373-374, December 11, 1982.

Reagan addresses religious broadcasters, condemns abortion. REGISTER. 59:2, February 13, 1983.

The real abortion issue, by S. G. Cole. THIS MAGAZINE. 17:4-8, June 1983.

Religion, beliefs about human life and the abortion decision, by D. G. Williams. REVIEW OF RELIGIOUS RESEARCH. 24(1):40-48, September 1982.

ABORTION AND RELIGION (continued)

Religion, law and public policy in America, by C. E. Curran. JURIST. 42:14-28, 1982.

Serenely silent no longer, two angry nuns battle their bishops over the issue of abortion [opposition to Hatch amendment]. PEOPLE WEEKLY. 18:90, August 16, 1982.

Sister Mansour is not alone [appointment to Michigan Dept. of Social Services], by M. Kolbenschlag. COMMONWEAL. 110:359-364, June 17, 1983.

Trying to understand the other side, by A. Nowlan. THE ATLANTIC ADVOCATE. 73:62, January 1983.

The vatican and population growth control: why an American confrontation, by S. D. Mumford. THE HUMANIST. 43(5):18-24, 34, September-October 1983.

Vatican backs Szoka, by F. Lilly. REGISTER. 59:1+, April 10, 1983.

Vatican veto [appointment of nun to Michigan's Dept. of Social Services]. CHRISTIAN CENTURY. 100:337, April 13, 1983.

War and abortion are twin targets for this veteran Christian activist, by M. Meehan. REGISTER. 59:1+, October 23, 1983.

When rebel nuns go public [views on abortion], by A. P. Ware. MS. 12:102-104, September 1983.

ABORTION AND YOUTH

Abortions to black teens helped stem increase in out-of-wedlock births. FAMILY PLANNING PERSPECTIVES. 15:84-85, March-April 1983.

Adolescents and abortion: a theoretical framework for decision making, by M. A. Brown. JOURNAL OF OBSTETRIC

GYNECOLOGIC AND NEONATAL NURSING. 12(4):241-247, July-August 1983.

Adolescent autonomy and minors' legal rights: contraception and abortion, by H. Rodman, et al. JOURNAL OF APPLIED DEVELOPMENTAL PSYCHOLOGY. 3(4):307-317, October-December 1982.

Constitution and the anomaly of the pregnant teenager, by E. Buchanan. ARIZONA LAW REVIEW. 24:553-610, 1982.

Constitutional law—abortion—court focuses on husband's interest regarding spousal notification requirements to procure abortion. Scheinberg v. Smith. CUMBERLAND LAW REVIEW. 13:143-159, 1982-1983.

Constitutional law—a minor's abortion right under a parental notice statute. WAYNE LAW REVIEW. 28:1901-1928, Summer 1982.

Current legal trends regarding abortions for minors: a dilemma for counselors, by L. C. Talbutt. SCHOOL COUNSELOR. 31(2):120-124, November 1983.

Minor's right to abortion, by S. McCarthy, et al. ALBERTA REPORT. 10:38, November 14, 1983.

Pregnancy in teenagers—a comparative study, by D. Krishnamoni, et al. PSYCHIATRIC JOURNAL OF THE UNIVERSITY OF OTTAWA. 8(4):202-207, December 1983.

Race-specific patterns of abortion use by American teenagers, by N. V. Ezzard, et al. AMERICAN JOURNAL OF PUBLIC HEALTH. 72:809-814, August 1982.

Right of the adolescent to health protection according to Italian legislation, by T. L. Schwarzenberg. MINERVA PEDIATRICA. 35(8):363-371, April 30, 1983.

Unmarried black adolescent fathers attitudes toward abortion,

ABORTION AND YOUTH (continued)

contraception and sexuality: a preliminary report, by L. E.
Hendricks. JOURNAL OF ADOLESCENT HEALTH CARE.
2(3):199-204, 1982.

Why teens opt for abortion, by P. Craig. OKLAHOMA
OBSERVER. 14:12, November 10, 1982.

Young and dedicated, Ellen works for life, by V. Warner.
REGISTER. 59:1-2, June 26, 1983.

ABORTION CLINICS

Abortion: autonomy or isolation, M. O'Brien Steinfels.
CHRISTIANITY AND CRISIS. 43:192-194, May 16,
1983.

Beyond the abortion charges [H. Morgentaler's clinics], by
P. Carlyle-Gordge. MACLEANS. 96:17, September 12, 1983.

Fetal anatomical abnormalities and other associated factors
in middle-trimester abortion and their relevance to patient
counselling, by M. J. Haxton, et al. BRITISH JOURNAL OF
OBSTETRICS AND GYNAECOLOGY. 90(6):501-506,
June 1983.

Medical-social aspects of the voluntary interruption of pregnancy: reflections on the routine data of an outpatient
clinic, by C. Humblet, et al. REVUE DE L'INSTITUT DE
SOCIOLOGIE. (3-4):477-507, 1982.

The Morgentaler file, by E. Hillen. MACLEANS. 96:44,
July 18, 1983.

Morgentaler moves west [abortion clinic in Winnipeg], by P.
Carlyle-Gordge. MACLEANS. 96:42-43, May 16, 1983.

Morgentaler's crusade moves east [Toronto clinic opens], by
C. Bruman. MACLEANS. 96:44, June 27, 1983.

My visit to an abortion clinic, by A. Von Stamwitz.

ABORTION CLINICS (continued)

LIGUORIAN. 71:26-31, August 1983.

The nation's new agony over abortion. MACLEANS. 96:2,
32-38, July 25, 1983.

A raid in the abortion war [H. Morgentaler's clinic in
Winnipeg], by V. Ross. MACLEANS. 96:21, June 13,
1983.

Regional dimensions of abortion-facility services, by N. F.
Henry. PROFESSIONAL GEOGRAPHER. 34:65-70,
February 1982.

Service offers alternatives. NATIONAL CATHOLIC RE-
PORTER. 18:19, October 15, 1982.

ABORTION COUNSELING

The aborted abortion counselor, by A. Benz. PSYCHE.
37(5):470-473, May 1983.

Attitudes of abortion counselors and their work role, by A.
M. Jones. DISSERTATION ABSTRACTS INTERNATIONAL:
A. 43(7), January 1983.

College student's attitudes toward shared responsibility in
decisions about abortion: implications for counseling, by
I. J. Ryan, et al. JOURNAL OF AMERICAN COLLEGE
HEALTH. 31:231-235, June 1983.

Current legal trends regarding abortions for minors: a dilemma
for counselors, by L. C. Talbutt. SCHOOL COUNSELOR.
31(2):120-124, November 1983.

From discussion to normalization: the counselor's role in the
interview prior to a voluntary interruption of pregnancy, by
A. M. Devreux. REVUE FRANCAISE DE SOCIOLOGIE.
23(3):455-471, July-September 1982.

Post-abortion counselling, by G. Cooper. NURSING MIRROR

ABORTION COUNSELING (continued)

AND MIDWIVE'S JOURNAL. 157(8):Midwifery forum 8:
i-xi, August 24, 1983.

Psychological sequelae form induced abortion: a follow-up
study of women who seek postabortion counseling, by
M. K. Hendricks-Matthews. DISSERTATION ABSTRACTS
INTERNATIONAL: B. 44(5), November 1983.

Setting up the project . . . to determine a patient's needs after
an abortion, by S. Anthony. NURSING MIRROR AND
MIDWIVE'S JOURNAL. 156(4):Clinical forum 1:32,
January 26, 1983.

Sidewalk counselors are voice of the unborn, by S. Settle.
REGISTER. 59:1+, September 11, 1983.

Towards a better service . . . women would appreciate a
postabortion counselling service. NURSING MIRROR AND
MIDWIVE'S JOURNAL. 156(4):Clinical forum 1:37,
January 26, 1983.

ABORTION FUNDING

Abortion fuding restrictions: state constitutional protections
exceed federal safeguards. WASHINGTON AND LEE LAW
REVIEW. 39:1469-1489, Fall 1982.

Campaign to overturn ban on abortion funding begun, by N.
Cohodas. CONGRESSIONAL QUARTERLY WEEKLY
REPORT. 41:1689-1693, August 20, 1983.

Constitutional law—equal protection—abortion funding—state
constitution requires New Jersey to fund health preserving
but not elective abortions—Right to Choose v. Byrne.
SETON HALL LAW REVIEW. 13:779-802, 1983.

Foetuses, famous violinists and the right to continued aid, by
M. Davis. PHILOSOPHICAL QUARTERLY. 33:259-278,
July 1983.

ABORTION FUNDING (continued)

New Jersey limit on medicaid for abortions is held unconstitutional. THE FAMILY LAW REPORTER:
COURT OPINIONS. 8(44):2660-2661, September
14, 1982.

Nun defended as head of agency funding abortions, by T.
Ewald. OUR SUNDAY VISITOR. 71:8, January 30,
1982.

The nuns' revolt: Sister Agnes Mary Mansour: her vow to
the people, by M. K. Blakely. MS. 12:54+, September
1983.

Oregon rule permitting state funding of only some abortions
found invalid. THE FAMILY LAW REPORTER: COURT
OPINIONS. 9(32):2488-2489, June 14, 1983.

Restricting federal funds for abortion: another look, by P. M.
Sommers, et al. SOCIAL SCIENCE QUARTERLY. 64:340-
346, June 1983.

Sex discrimination: title VII burdens of proof, comparable
worth, and sexual harassment; abortion funding and notice
and consent requirements. ANNUAL SURVEY OF
AMERICAN LAW. December 1982, p. 1-47.

Six in ten Americans now support medicaid funding of abortions.
FAMILY PLANNING PERSPECTIVES. 15:201, July-
August 1983.

BIRTH CONTROL: GENERAL

All people are shocked by the birth control policy calamity:
the Chinese communists are facing an impasse of the problem
of population, by J. Wang. ASIAN OUTLOOK. 18:25-30,
April 1983.

Birth control, by M. McAdoo. MS. 11:113-114, May 1983.

Birth-control decisions, by J. Lederer. PSYCHOLOGY TODAY.

17:32-38, June 1983.

Birth-control myths and facts, by K. McCoy. SEVENTEEN.
42:52+, October 1983.

Birth control overseas, by J. C. Cazenave, et al. MEDECINE
TROPICALE. 43(1):93-97, January-February 1983.

Birth control update. HARPERS BAZAAR. 116:208+, October
1983.

Chick's in the male, by D. Lessem. BOSTON. 74:19, October
1982.

Child support—birth control. THE FAMILY LAW REPORTER:
COURT OPINIONS. 9(30):2462-2463, May 31, 1983.

Childlessness and partner selection, by V. J. Callan. JOURNAL
OF MARRIAGE AND THE FAMILY. 45:181-186, February
1983.

Conception and the concept of harm, by E. H. Morreim.
JOURNAL OF MEDICINE AND PHILOSOPHY. 8:137-
157, May 1983.

Empty cradles, by C. MacDonald. CANADA AND THE WORLD.
49:18-20, October 1983.

Genocide fears in a rural black community: an empirical
examination, by W. C. Farrell, Jr. JOURNAL OF BLACK
STUDIES. 14(1):49-67, September 1983.

How startups buck the odds in birth control, by M. McAdoo.
VENTURE. 4:56+, October 1982.

Know your organizations: the birth control trust, by J. Roe.
HEALTH VISITOR. 55(4):179, April 1982.

Know your organizations: British pregnancy advisory service,
by D. Munday. HEALTH VISITOR. 55(4):179, April 1982.

The man who would be anthropologist [S. Mosher dismissed from Stanford for article on birth control], by W. Herbert. SCIENCE NEWS. 123:252-253, April 16, 1983.

The mysterious expulsion of Steven Mosher [dismissal from Stanford University for article on birth control], by M. Sun. SCIENCE. 220:692-694, May 13, 1983.

1980 synod: about birth control, some compassion, by P. Hebblethwaite. NATIONAL CATHOLIC REPORTER. 20:18, October 28, 1983.

People and resources: a reappraisal, by A. Nevett. MONTH. 16:163-167, May 1983.

Planning for people, by R. Lawton. GEOGRAPHICAL MAGAZINE. 55:390-392, August 1983.

Questions women ask about birth control, by L. J. Sarrel, et al. REDBOOK. 161:35, June 1983.

The threat of numbers, by R. W. Peterson. AUDUBON. 84:107, July 1982.

What price children? [expensive years of parenthood], by C. Tuhy. MONEY. 12:77-84, March 1983.

When the pill is not first choice, by L. Edmunds. DAILY TELEGRAPH. August 31, 1983, p. 13.

AFRICA
The use of traditional and modern methods of fertility control in Kinshasa, Zaire, by J. T. Bertrand, et al. POPULATION STUDIES. 37:129-136, March 1983.

ASIA
The timing of entry into motherhood in Asia: a comparative perspective, by R. Rindfuss, et al. POPULATION STUDIES.

37:253-272, July 1983.

BANGLADESH
Life table analysis of birth intervals for Bangladesh, by M. Kabir, et al. JOURNAL OF FAMILY WELFARE. 29:21-32, March 1983.

CANADA
The Canadian birth control movement on trial, 1936-1937, by D. Dodd. HISTOIRE SOCIALE—SOCIAL HISTORY. 16(32):411-428, 1983.

Teen sex-clinic furore [Calgary], by F. Orr. ALBERTA REPORT. 10:32-33, September 26, 1983.

"What has this to do with working class women?": birth control and the Canadian left, 1900-1939, by A. McLaren. SOCIAL HISTORY. 14(28):435-454, 1981.

CHINA
Battle in the scholarly world [S. Mosher dismissed from Stanford for article on mandatory birth control], by E. McGrath. TIME. 121:72, March 14, 1983.

Battle of the bulge, by D. Bonavia, et al. FAR EASTERN ECONOMIC REVIEW. 117:18-19, July 9-15, 1982.

Battle of the bulge is no easy fight, by V. G. Kulkarni. FAR EASTERN ECONOMIC REVIEW. 120:50-51, April 28, 1983.

The China solution, by L. Lader. SCIENCE DIGEST. 91:78, April 1983.

China: two's a crowd and it's illegal. ECONOMIST. 286:31+, January 29, 1983.

China's population policy, by K. I. Chen. CURRENT HISTORY. 81:251+, September 1982.

China's she-baby cull. ECONOMIST. 287:36, April 16, 1983.

The ethics of anthropology, by J. Lincoln. NATION. 237:226, September 24, 1983.

The infantcide tragedy in China, by J. Mirsky. NATION. 237:12-14, July 2, 1983.

Marxism and Chinese population policies, by R. Wiltgen, et al. REVIEW OF RADICAL POLITICAL ECONOMY. 14:18-28, Winter 1982.

Mosher's expulsion from Stanford [discussion of May 13, 1983 article, The mysterious expulsion of Steven Mosher]. SCIENCE. 220:1334+, June 24, 1983.

New look at happiness. BEIJING REVIEW. 26:27-28, February 14, 1983.

One-fourth of the world is large enough. BEIJING REVIEW. 25:8, December 6, 1982.

One's good, two's enough, by S. Fraser. FAR EASTERN ECONOMIC REVIEW. 117:18-19, July 9-15, 1982.

Panel upholds dismissal of Mosher [alleged misconduct while conducting field research], by M. Sun. SCIENCE. 221: 348, July 22, 1983.

Planned fertility of one-couple/one-child policy in the people's republic of China, by L. J. Huang. JOURNAL OF MARRIAGE AND THE FAMILY. 44:775-784, August 1982.

Population lid: China cajoles families and offers incentives to reduce birth rate; but one-child policy stirs resistance, hasn't ended the preference for sons, by A. Bennett. WALL STREET JOURNAL. 202:1+, July 6, 1983.

Production versus reproduction: a threat to China's development strategy, by E. J. Croll. WORLD DEVELOPMENT. 11:467-481, June 1983.

Refusing the pill "no argument to those who want or need it," by J. Gomez. DAILY TELEGRAPH. August 17, 1983, p. 11.

Slaughter of the innocents still goes on [China], by V. G. Kulkarni. FAR EASTERN ECONOMIC REVIEW. 120:50-53, April 28, 1983.

Steven Mosher and the politics of cultural exchange, by J. Lincoln. NATION. 237:176+, September 3-10, 1983.

Struggling for the soul of social science [case of S. Mosher], by I. L. Horowitz. SOCIETY. 20:4-15, July-August 1983.

Two's a crowd and it's illegal. ECONOMIST. 286:47, 50, January 29, 1983.

COSTA RICA
Probability of another child in Costa Rica, by M. P. Shields, et al. ECONOMIC DEVELOPMENT AND CULTURAL CHANGE. 31:787-807, July 1983.

GREAT BRITAIN
The decline of marital fertility in the late nineteenth century: the case of England and Wales, by R. Woods, et al. POPULATION STUDIES. 37:207-225, July 1983.

INDIA
Compulsory birth control and fertility measures in India, by S. S. Halli. SIMULATION AND GAMES. 14(4):429-444, December 1983.

An equal-opportunity destroyer [use of amniocentesis as sex determinant], by J. McGowan. U. S. CATHOLIC. 48:27-29, April 1983.

BIRTH CONTROL: GENERAL (continued)

PHILIPPINES
Physicians vs. auxiliary nurse-midwives as providers of IUD services—a study in Turkey and the Philippines, by N. Eren, et al. STUDIES IN FAMILY PLANNING. 14:43-47, February 1983.

SOUTH PACIFIC
Toward a new understanding of population change in Bali, by M. Poffenberger. POPULATION STUDIES. 37:43-59, March 1983.

TURKEY
Physicians vs. auxiliary nurse-midwives as providers of IUD services—a study in Turkey and the Philippines, by N. Eren, et al. STUDIES IN FAMILY PLANNING. 14:43-47, February 1983.

UNITED STATES
Adolescent family life program as a prevention measure, by M. E. Mecklenburg, et al. PUBLIC HEALTH REPORTS. 98:21-29, January-February 1983.

Childlessness in a transitional population: the United States at the turn of the century, by S. E. Tolnay, et al. JOURNAL OF FAMILY HISTORY. 7:200-219, Summer 1982.

What U. S. women think and do about contraception, by J. D. Forrest, et al. FAMILY PLANNING PERSPECTIVES. 15(4):157-158, 160-166, July-August 1983.

BIRTH CONTROL: ATTITUDES

Birth control: different conceptions, by R. V. Wells. JOURNAL OF INTERDISCIPLINARY HISTORY. 10(3):511-516, 1979.

Chronic schizophrenic women's attitudes toward sex, pregnancy, birth control, and childrearing, by J. P. McEvoy, et al. HOSPITAL AND COMMUNITY PSYCHIATRY. 34(6):536-539, June 1983.

BIRTH CONTROL: ATTITUDES (continued)

Comparative study of the attitude of married and unmarried
women towards religion, equality of women and birth
control in relation to their adjustment, by M. A. Shah,
et al. ASIAN JOURNAL OF PSYCHOLOGY AND
EDUCATION. 9(1):15-20, January 1982.

Malthusianism, socialism and feminism in the United States,
by L. Gordon. HISTORY OF EUROPEAN IDEAS.
4:203-214, 1983.

Orientations toward voluntary childlessness, by F. E. Baum.
JOURNAL OF BIOSOCIAL SCIENCE. 15:153-164,
April 1983.

BIRTH CONTROL: COMPLICATIONS

Birth control and disease, by S. Katz. CHATELAINE. 56:20,
January 1983.

BIRTH CONTROL: EDUCATION

Birth control movie, by E. Mandell. BOOKLIST. 79(6):45,
November 15, 1982.

Birth control movie. LANDERS HERALD. 27(2):53,
November-December 1982.

Children by choice, not chance. FAMILY RELATIONS.
31(1):165, January 1982.

Economic analyses of the spacing of births, by J. L. Newman.
AMERICAN ECONOMIC REVIEW. 73:33-37, May 1983.

Male role in contraception: implications for health education,
by C. L. Chng. JOURNAL OF SCHOOL HEALTH. 53(3):
197-201, March 1983.

Self-help birth control study, by T. Land. TIMES HIGHER
EDUCATIONAL SUPPLEMENT. 498:7, May 21, 1982.

BIRTH CONTROL: EDUCATION (continued)

Simultaneity in the birth rate equation:the effects of education, labor force participation, income and health, by D. J. Conger, et al. ECONOMETRICA. 46:631-641, May 1978.

—. Discussion. ECONOMETRICA. 50:1585-1590, November 1982.

BIRTH CONTROL: HISTORY

Childlessness in a transitional population: the United States at the turn of the century, by S. E. Tolnay, et al. JOURNAL OF FAMILY HISTORY. 7:200-219, Summer 1982.

The decline of marital fertility in the late nineteenth century: the case of England and Wales, by R. Woods, et al. POPULA-TION STUDIES. 37:207-225, July 1983.

Elimination of medieval birth control and the witch trials of modern times, by G. Heinsohn, et al. INTERNATIONAL JOURNAL OF WOMEN'S STUDIES. 5(3):193-214, 1982.

Hamilton birth control clinic of the 1930's, by D. Dodd. ONTARIO HISTORY. 75(1):71-86, 1983.

BIRTH CONTROL: METHODS

Calculator for birth control, by S. Katz. CHATELAINE. 56:22, April 1983.

Elimination of medieval birth control and witch trials of modern times, by G. Heinsohn, et al. INTERNATIONAL JOURNAL OF WOMEN'S STUDIES. 5(3):193-214, 1982.

Hoechst conceives new birth control drug. CHEMISTRY AND INDUSTRY. January 3, 1983, p. 4.

BIRTH CONTROL: RESEARCH

LHRH and rat avoidance behavior: influence of castration and testosterone, by S. Mora, et al. PHYSIOLOGY AND

BIRTH CONTROL: RESEARCH (continued)

BEHAVIOR. 30(1):19-22, January 1983.

Reproductive state modulates ethanol intake in rats: effects of ovariectomys ethanol concentration, estrous cycle and pregnancy, by N. G. Forger, et al. PHARMACOLOGY, BIOCHEMISTRY AND BEHAVIOR. 17(2):323-331, August 1982.

BIRTH CONTROL: STATISTICS

A bibliography of publications based on the U. S. National Survey of Family Growth [on fertility, birth control and family formation]. POPULATION INDEX. 49:14-19, Spring 1983.

Correcting contraceptive failure rates for sample composition and sample selection bias, by J. Trussell, et al. SOCIAL BIOLOGY. 28:293-298, Fall-Winter 1981.

Typical AFDC family smaller than ten years ago: average number of children fell from three to two. FAMILY PLANNING PERSPECTIVES. 15:31-32, January-February 1983.

BIRTH CONTROL AND ERA

Malthusianism, socialism and feminism in the United States, by L. Gordon. HISTORY OF EUROPEAN IDEAS. 4:203-214, 1983.

BIRTH CONTROL AND FUNDING

Birth control is not the main issue: parental notification (federal funding and delivery of birth control devices is an illegitimate function of the government), by W. E. Williams. HUMAN EVENTS. 43:6+, March 12, 1983.

Third world family planning programs: measuring the costs, by N. Yinger, et al. POPULATION BULLETIN. 38:2-35, February 1983.

BIRTH CONTROL AND HORMONES

LHRH and rat avoidance behavior: influence of castration and testosterone, by S. Mora, et al. PHYSIOLOGY AND BEHAVIOR. 30(1):19-22, January 1983.

BIRTH CONTROL AND MALES

This is what you though about . . . men's rights. GLAMOUR. 80:21, July 1982.

BIRTH CONTROL AND MARRIAGE

Comparative study of the attitude of married and unmarried women towards religion, equality of women and birth control in relation to their adjustment, by M. A. Shah, et al. ASIAN JOURNAL OF PSYCHOLOGY AND EDUCATION. 9(1):15-20, January 1982.

BIRTH CONTROL AND THE MILITARY

Active duty pregnancy, by N. S. Stewart. MARINE CORPS GAZETTE. 67:19-20, February 1983.

Women in the sea services: 1972-1982, by G. C. Sadler. UNITED STATES NAVAL INSTITUTE PROCEEDINGS. 109:140-155, May 1983.

BIRTH CONTROL AND PARENTAL CONSENT

Birth control is not the main issue: parental notification (federal funding and delivery of birth control devices is an illegitimate function of the government), by W. E. Williams. HUMAN EVENTS. 43:6+, March 12, 1983.

D. C. federal district court enjoins enforcement of HHS "squeal rule." THE FAMILY LAW REPORTER: COURT OPINIONS. 9(18):2282, March 8, 1983.

Notice to parents not required when minors seek contraceptives. THE FAMILY LAW REPORTER: COURT OPINIONS. 9(37):2552, July 28, 1983.

BIRTH CONTROL AND PARENTAL CONSENT (continued)

Parents must be notified after minors receive birth control pills or devices. THE FAMILY LAW REPORTER: COURT OPINIONS. 9(14):2223-2224, February 8, 1983.

What's new: kiss and tell—squeal rule enjoined, by A. Ashman. AMERICAN BAR ASSOCIATION JOURNAL. 69:829-830, June 1983.

Your opinion [teen-age birth control squeal rule], by L. A. Sullivan, et al. SEVENTEEN. 42:42+, November 1983.

BIRTH CONTROL AND PHYSICIANS

N. Y. federal district court enjoins enforcement of HHS "squeal rule." THE FAMILY LAW REPORTER: COURT OPINIONS. 9(18):2281, March 8, 1983.

The provision of birth control services to unwed minors: a national survey of physician attitudes and practices, by E. D. Boldt, et al. CANADIAN JOURNAL OF PUBLIC HEALTH. 73(6):392-395, November-December 1982.

BIRTH CONTROL AND POLITICS

The Mumford affair [firing of population control researcher from Family Health International for anti-Catholic criticism]. HUMANIST. 43:5-10, November-December 1983.

President Reagan authors anti-abortion article. CHRISTIANITY TODAY. 27:42-43, June 17, 1983.

Presidential pen [R. Reagan's anti-abortion article published in Human Life review]. TIME. 121:36, May 9, 1983.

Steven Mosher and the politics of cultural exchange, by J. Lincoln. NATION. 237:176+, September 3-10, 1983.

After fifteen years humanae vitae called prophetic, by Sister M. A. Walsh. OUR SUNDAY VISITOR. 72:3, July 24, 1983.

Civil liberties: big-boss government. ECONOMIST. 286:21, January 29, 1983.

The covenant theology of sex, by J. F. Kippley. HOMILETIC AND PASTORAL REVIEW. 83:22-32, August-September 1983.

Humanae vitae, fifteen years later, by R. Bautch. REGISTER. 59:1+, July 24, 1983.

Marriage: the vision of humanae vitae, by G. D. Coleman. THOUGHT. 58:18-34, March 1983.

The Mumford affair [firing of population control researcher from Family Health International for anti-Catholic criticism]. HUMANIST. 43:5-10, November-December 1983.

Survey discloses NFP practices, preferences in U. S. Catholic hospitals, by M. C. Martin, et al. HOSPITAL PROGRESS. 64:52-58, February 1983.

The vatican and population growth control: why an American confrontation?, by S. D. Mumford. HUMANIST. 43:18+, September-October 1983.

BIRTH CONTROL AND YOUTH

Adolescent family life program as a prevention measure, by M. E. Mecklenburg, et al. PUBLIC HEALTH REPORTS. 98:21-29, January-February 1983.

The provision of birth control services to unwed minors: a national survey of physician attitudes and practices, by E. D. Boldt. CANADIAN JOURNAL OF PUBLIC HEALTH. 73(6):392-395, November-December 1982.

BIRTH CONTROL AND YOUTH (continued)

Sexually active teenager, by S. J. Emans. JOURNAL OF
DEVELOPMENTAL AND BEHAVIORAL PEDIATRICS.
4(1):37-42, March 1983.

Teenager's guide to sex safety, by A. K. Richards, et al. MS.
12:81-84, July 1983.

BIRTH CONTROL CLINICS

Birth-control rule: clinics ponder effects, by N. Brozan.
NEW YORK TIMES. January 29, 1983, p. 11.

Hamilton birth control clinic of the 1930's, by D. Dodd.
ONTARIO HISTORY. 75:71-86, March 1983.

Patterns of contraceptive use among female adolescents: method
consistency in a clinic setting, by M. Gorush. JOURNAL OF
ADOLESCENT HEALTH CARE. 3(2):96-102, September
1982.

CASTRATION

Anxieties of the castrator, by G. Devereux. ETHOS. 10(3):
279-297, Fall 1982.

Castration, clinging, shame: three Hermannian models, by B.
Dalle, et al. PERSPECTIVES PSYCHIATRIQUES. 19(4):
291-295, 1981.

Castration or incarceration?, by M. S. Serrill. TIME. 122:70,
December 12, 1983.

Comparative effects of castration and chlorpromazine in the
arcuate nucleus of the hypothalamus of the rat, by A.
Ledesma-Jimeno, et al. ACTAS LUSO-ESPANOLAS DE
NEUROLOGIA Y PSIQUIATRIA Y CIENCIAS AFINES.
10(6):351-358, November-December 1982.

Decisions, decisions [South Carolina judge sentences rapists
to choice of thirty years in prison or castration]. NEW

CASTRATION (continued)

REPUBLIC. 189:4+, December 26, 1983.

Effects of castration on aggressive and defensive-escape components of agonistic behaviour in male mice, by A. Sulcova, et al. ACTIVITAS NERVOSA SUPERIOR. 23(4):317-318, December 1981.

Sexual imprinting in male Japanese quail: effects of castration at hatching, by R. E. Hutchison, et al. DEVELOPMENTAL PSYCHOBIOLOGY. 15(5):471-477, September 1982.

CASTRATION AND CONTRACEPTIVE RESEARCH

Comparative effects of castration and chlorpromazine in the arcuate nucleus of the hypothalamus of the rat, by A. Ledesma-Jimeno, et al. ACTAS LUSO-ESPANOLAS DE DE NEUROLOGIA Y PSIQUIATRIA Y CIENCIAS AFINES. 10(6):351-358, November-December 1982.

CONTRACEPTION AND CONTRACEPTIVES: GENERAL

Basal body temperature [letter], by E. F. Keefe. FERTILITY AND STERILITY. 38(4):502-503, October 1982.

The careless streetwalker [failure of prostitutes to use contraceptives], by J. C. Horn. PSYCHOLOGY TODAY. 17:69, March 1983.

Contraception, marital fertility and breast-feeding in the Yemen Arab republic, by H. I. Goldberg, et al. JOURNAL OF BIOSOCIAL SCIENCE. 15:67-82, January 1983.

Contraceptive choices for lactating women: suggestions for postpartum family planning, by V. H. Laukaran. STUDIES IN FAMILY PLANNING. 12(4):156-163, April 1981.

The contraceptive mentality, by D. T. De Marco. HOMILETIC AND PASTORAL REVIEW. 83:56-63, July 1983.

Don't take a chance on love: the latest and safest in birth

CONTRACEPTION AND CONTRACEPTIVES: GENERAL
(continued)
> control. MADEMOISELLE. 89:38+, November 1983.

Everybody wants in, by J. Merwin. FORBES. 132:52-53, July 4, 1983.

The extent of contraceptive use and the social paradigm of modern demography, by G. S. Douglas. SOCIOLOGY. 17:380-387, August 1983.

Family lifeline—an aid for family life planning, by S. F. Weis. ILLINOIS TEACHER OF HOME ECONOMICS. 26(1): 29-30, September-October 1982.

Family planning update, by H. Martins. HEALTH VISITOR. 56(5):166-169, May 1983.

Getting the message across [combining family planning and parasite control], by M. Jones. WORLD HEALTH. February-March 1983, p. 22-24.

The goods [visit to the Trojan manufacturing plant], by B. Greene. ESQUIRE. 100:24+, July 1983.

Half our pregnancies are unintentional. NEWSWEEK. 102:37, October 10, 1983.

Indicators of contraceptive policy for nations at three levels of development [comparison of the use of condoms, birth control pills, and intrauterine devices], by I. M. Wasserman, et al. SOCIAL INDICATORS RESEARCH. 12:153-168, February 1983.

An interactive model program of care for diabetic women before and during pregnancy part 2, by D. L. McCoy, et al. DIABETES EDUCATOR. 9(2):suppl: 11S-20S, Summer 1983.

Maybe you should think twice about your contraceptive. RED-BOOK. 159:58+, May 1982.

CONTRACEPTION AND CONTRACEPTIVES: GENERAL
(continued)
The moral disarmament of Betty Coed, by G. Steinem. ESQUIRE. 99:243+, June 1983.

More reading, less breeding. ECONOMIST. 284:30, August 28-September 3, 1982.

Prostitutes and contraceptives. SOCIETY. 20:2-3, May-June 1983.

Society anxiety, sexual behavior and contraceptive use, by M. R. Leary, et al. JOURNAL OF PERSONALITY AND SOCIAL PSYCHOLOGY. 45:1347-1354, December 1983.

Today's contraceptives: what's new? What's best?, by W. S. Ross. READER'S DIGEST. 123:217+, November 1983.

Update on contraceptives: what's safe? Effective? Convenient? CHANGING TIMES. 37:72+, October 1983.

What you should know about over-the-counter contraceptives, by E. Rodgers. SEVENTEEN. 42:26+, April 1983.

AUSTRALIA
Repeat abortion-seeking behaviour in Queensland, Australia: knowledge and use of contraception and reasons for terminating the pregnancy, by V. J. Callan. JOURNAL OF BIOSOCIAL SCIENCE. 15:1-8, January 1983.

Testing times for women in body lab . . . depo provera, by W. Bacon. LAMP. 40(3):38-40, May 1983.

BANGLADESH
Contraceptive users in rural Bangladesh: a time trend analysis, by S. Bhatia. STUDIES IN FAMILY PLANNING. 14:20-28, January 1983.

Policy analysis of fertility and contraceptive behavior in Bangladesh. WORLD BANK RESEARCH NEWS. 4(1):

CONTRACEPTION AND CONTRACEPTIVES: GENERAL
(continued)
24-25, Spring 1983.

CHINA
Family planning [Shanghai], by Z. Wei-sen, et al. AMERICAN
JOURNAL OF PUBLICH HEALTH. 72:24-25, September
1982.

Glimpses of health programs in the people's republic of China:
family planning education, by M. V. Hamburg. JOURNAL
OF SCHOOL HEALTH. 53:108-111, February 1983.

The Sino-Stanford scandal [dismissal of S. Mosher for article
on mandatory birth control], by A. Dubro. SCIENCE
DIGEST. 91:98-101, August 1983.

COLUMBIA
Effect of child mortality on contraceptive use and fertility in
Columbia, Costa Rica and Korea, by B. S. Mensch.
DISSERTATION ABSTRACTS INTERNATIONAL: A.
44(3), September 1983.

Use of contraceptive for delaying and spacing births in Columbia,
Costa Rica and Korea, by J. S. Grigsby. DISSERTATION
ABSTRACTS INTERNATIONAL: A. 44(3), September
1983.

COSTA RICA
Effect of child mortality on contraceptive use and fertility in
Columbia, Costa Rica and Korea, by B. S. Mensch.
DISSERTATION ABSTRACTS INTERNATIONAL: A.
44(3), September 1983.

Use of contraceptive for delaying and spacing births in Columbia,
Costa Rica and Korea, by J. S. Grigsby. DISSERTATION
ABSTRACTS INTERNATIONAL: A. 44(3), September
1983.

DEVELOPING COUNTRIES
Family planning incentives in developing nations and Western
Europe, by N. Fincancioglu, et al. PEOPLE. 9(4):3, 1982.

CONTRACEPTION AND CONTRACEPTIVES: GENERAL
(continued)
Measuring the unmet need for contraception to space and limit
births: the findings suggest a sizable unsaturated market for
contraceptive services and supplies [developing countries],
by D. L. Nortman. INTERNATIONAL FAMILY PLANNING
PERSPECTIVES. 8:125-134, December 1982.

The relationship of contraceptive availability to contraceptive
use [based on a study of seven developing countries], by A.
R. Pebley, et al. INTERNATIONAL FAMILY PLANNING
PERSPECTIVES. 8:84-92, September 1982.

DOMINICAN REPUBLIC
Female employment and fertility in the Dominican Republic:
a dynamic perspective, by D. T. Gurak, et al. AMERICAN
SOCIOLOGICAL REVIEW. 47:810-818, December 1982.

EGYPT
Contraception and community in Egypt: a preliminary
evaluation of the population/development mix, by J. M.
Stycos, et al. STUDIES IN FAMILY PLANNING. 13(12):
365, December 1982.

Note of desired family size and contraceptive use in rural Egypt,
by C. S. Stokes, et al. JOURNAL OF BIOSOCIAL SCIENCES.
15(1):59-65, January 1983.

One from Egypt [disposable contraceptive sponge]. TIME.
121:48-49, March 28, 1983.

EUROPE
WFS surveys show that wester, eastern Europe differ greatly
in use of modern contraceptives. FAMILY PLANNING
PERSPECTIVES. 15(2):82-84, March-April 1983.

GREAT BRITAIN
Britain bites the bullet over depo-provera. NEW SCIENTIST.
98:136, April 21, 1983.

Contraception in ethnic minority groups in Bedford, by P.
Beard. HEALTH VISITOR. 55(8):417-421, August 1982.

CONTRACEPTION AND CONTRACEPTIVES: GENERAL
(continued)

Depo-provera: on trial again [injectable contraceptive, Britain].
ECONOMIST. 287:116, April 30, 1983.

The family planning association. HEALTH VISITOR. 56(5):
165-166, May 1983.

Family planning, cost benefits and the nursing role, by A.
Leathard. MIDWIFE, HEALTH VISITOR AND COMMUNITY
NURSE. 18(12):526-527, 536, December 1982.

Marriage, sexuality and contraception in the British middle
class, 1918-1939. The correspondence of Marie Stopes, by
E. M. Holtzman. DISSERTATION ABSTRACTS INTER-
NATIONAL: A. 43(10), April 1983.

The "pill scare" and fertility in England and Wales, by M.
Bone. INTERNATIONAL PLANNED PARENTHOOD
FEDERATION MEDICAL BULLETIN. 16(4):2, August
1982.

Sex and sympathy: contraceptive advice for under-16-year-olds,
by F. Hutchinson. SUNDAY TIMES. July 31, 1983, p. 16.

GREECE
A household study of the pattern of utilization of mother and
child health services in rural Greece and variation by
socioeconomic status, by C. G. Tzoumaka-Bakoula, et al.
CHILD CARE, HEALTH AND DEVELOPMENT. 9(2):
85-95, March-April 1983.

GUATEMALA
Increasing the effectiveness of community workers through
training of spouses: a family planning experiment in
Guatemala, by M. A. Pineda, et al. PUBLIC HEALTH
REPORTS. 98(3):273-277, May-June 1983.

HAITI
Evaluation of a continuing education program in sex therapy,
by P. M. Sarrel, et al. AMERICAN JOURNAL OF PUBLIC
HEALTH. 72(8):839-843, 1982.

CONTRACEPTION AND CONTRACEPTIVES: GENERAL
(continued)
INDIA
Family planning and health: the Narangwal experiment, by
R. Faruqee. FINANCE AND DEVELOPMENT. 20(2):
43-46, June 1983.

Family welfare as health need in Indian population policy,
by S. Bergstrom. TROPICAL DOCTOR. 12(4 pt 1):182-
184, October 1982.

IRAN
Family health by Women's Health Corps (WHC) in Iran, by
S. Amidi. JOURNAL OF TROPICAL PEDIATRICS.
28(3):149-152, June 1982.

JAMAICA
Patterns of contraceptive use in Kingston and St. Andrew,
Jamaica, 1970-1977, by W. Bailey, et al. SOCIAL SCIENCE
AND MEDICINE. 16(19):1675-1683, 1982.

KOREA
Effect of child mortality on contraceptive use and fertility
in Columbia, Costa Rica and Korea, by B. S. Mensch.
DISSERTATION ABSTRACTS INTERNATIONAL: A.
44(3), September 1983.

Use of contraceptive for delaying and spacing births in
Columbia, Costa Rica and Korea, by J. S. Grigsby.
DISSERTATION ABSTRACTS INTERNATIONAL: A.
44(3), September 1983.

MALAYSIA
A family planning study in Kuala Pilah, Peninsular Malaysia,
by V. Thambypillai. MEDICAL JOURNAL OF MALAYSIA.
37(4):326-335, December 1982.

MEXICO
Menstrual bleeding expectations and short-term contraceptive
discontinuation in Mexico, by G. Zetina-Lozano. STUDIES
IN FAMILY PLANNING. 14(5):127, May 1983.

CONTRACEPTION AND CONTRACEPTIVES: GENERAL
(continued)
NETHERLANDS
Contraception and fertility in the Netherlands, by E. Ketting.
FAMILY PLANNING PERSPECTIVES. 15(1):19-25,
January-February 1983.

Contraception and fertility in the Netherlands, by E. Ketting.
INTERNATIONAL FAMILY PLANNING PERSPECTIVES.
8:141-147, December 1982.

NORWAY
Contraceptive use high in Norway, where IUD is most popular
method. FAMILY PLANNING PERSPECTIVES. 15:87-88,
March-April 1983.

SWITZERLAND
Family formation, desire for children and birth control of
Swiss married couples—results of a representative survey.
II. Contraception in Switzerland—knowledge and practice
of Swiss married couples, by F. Kuhne, et al. GYNAE-
KOLOGISCHE RUNDSCHAU. 23(2):77-87, 1983.

Family planning, wish for children and birth control of Swiss
couples—results of a representative survey. I. Family planning
and wish for children, by F. Hopflinger, et al. GYNAE-
KOLOGISCHE RUNDSCHAU. 23(1):25-34, 1983.

THAILAND
Thailand's reproductive revolution: an update, by P.
Kamnuansilpa, et al. INTERNATIONAL FAMILY
PLANNING PERSPECTIVES. 8:51-56, June 1982.

The user perspective in northern Thailand: a series of case
studies, by N. Iddhichiracharas, et al. STUDIES IN FAMILY
PLANNING. 14:48-56, February 1983.

UNITED STATES
Contraceptive failure and continuation among married women
in the United States, 1970-1975, by W. R. Grady, et al.
STUDIES IN FAMILY PLANNING. 14:9-19, January
1983.

CONTRACEPTION AND CONTRACEPTIVES: GENERAL
(continued)
    The costs of contraception . . . one factor that affects the choice
        of a birth control method, by A. Torres, et al. FAMILY
        PLANNING PERSPECTIVES. 15(2):70-72, March-April
        1983.

    Ectopic pregnancies: rising incidence rates in northern California,
        by P. H. Shiono, et al. AMERICAN JOURNAL OF PUBLIC
        HEALTH. 72:173-175, February 1982.

    Fertility-related state laws enacted in 1982, by D. Bush.
        FAMILY PLANNING PERSPECTIVES. 15:111-116, May-
        June 1983.

    Never-pregnant teenagers more effective users of contraceptives
        than those previously pregnant. FAMILY PLANNING
        PERSPECTIVES. 15(3):137-138, May-June 1983.

    Survey discloses NFP practices, preferences in U. S. Catholic
        hospitals, by M. C. Martin, et al. HOSPITAL PROGRESS.
        64(2):52-58, February 1983.

CONTRACEPTION AND CONTRACEPTIVES: HISTORY

    Who is still afraid of the pill today? The development of
        hormonal contraception ('the pill') in the last 20 years.
        Current status, by M. van Vliet. TIJDSCHRIFT VOR
        ZIEKENVERPLEGING. 35(20):659-663, October 5, 1982.

CONTRACEPTION AND CONTRACEPTIVES: LAWS AND
LEGISLATION
    Challenging the teenage regulations: the legal battle, by P.
        Donovan. FAMILY PLANNING PERSPECTIVES. 15(3):
        126-130, May-June 1983.

    The courts, congress, parents, kids and the pill, by E. Kennedy
        Shriver. OUR SUNDAY VISITOR. 72:4, May 8, 1983.

    A cross-national comparison of contraception and abortion laws,
        by I. M. Wasserman. SOCIAL INDICATORS RESEARCH.
        13(3):281-309, October 1983.

CONTRACEPTION AND CONTRACEPTIVES: LAWS AND
LEGISLATION (continued)
Depo-provera: FDA hearings raise questions, by J. Skurnik.
OFF OUR BACKS. 13:5-6, February 1983.

Depo-provera: the jury still out, by R. B. Gold. FAMILY
PLANNING PERSPECTIVES. 15(2):78-81, March-April
1983.

FDA assails safety of depo-provera, by R. J. Smith. SCIENCE.
219:371, January 28, 1983.

Fertility-related state laws enacted in 1982, by D. Bush.
FAMILY PLANNING PERSPECTIVES. 15(3):111-116,
May-June 1983.

On trial again: depo-provera. ECONOMIST. 287:116, April 30-
May 6, 1983.

Personhood and the contraceptive right. INDIANA LAW
JOURNAL. 57:579-604, Fall 1982.

Reproductive rights 1983: an international survey, by S. L.
Isaacs. COLUMBIA HUMAN RIGHTS LAW REVIEW.
14:311-353, Fall-Winter 1982-1983.

Supreme court faces the family, by H. H. Clark, Jr. CHILDREN
TODAY. 11(6):18-21, November-December 1982.

CONTRACEPTION AND CONTRACEPTIVES: MORTALITY AND
MORTALITY STATISTICS
Consumer demand and household production: the relationship
between fertility and child mortality, by M. R. Rosenzeig,
et al. AMERICAN ECONOMIC REVIEW. 73:38-42, May
1983.

The effect of chromosome constitution on growth in culture
of human spontaneous abortions, by T. Hassold, et al.
HUMAN GENETICS. 63(2):166-170, 1983.

Infant and child survival and contraceptive use in the closed
pregnancy interval, by B. Janowitz, et al. SOCIAL SCIENCE

    AND MEDICINE. 17(2):113-118, 1983.

    Mortality associated with fertility and fertility control: 1983,
      by H. W. Ory. FAMILY PLANNING PERSPECTIVES.
      15(2):57-63, March-April 1983.

    Mortality rates, mortality events and the number of births, by
      R. J. Olsen. AMERICAN ECONOMIC REVIEW. 73:29-
      32, May 1983.

CONTRACEPTION AND CONTRACEPTIVES: RESEARCH

    Action mechanisms of gossypol as a male contraceptive agent:
      in vitro study (leydig cell of rats), by H. Hoshiai, et al.
      JAPANESE JOURNAL OF FERTILITY AND STERILITY.
      27(2):156-160.

    Attack directed by groups of male mice towards lactating
      intruders: involvement of hormones and neurotransmitters,
      by M. Haug, et al. AGGRESSIVE BEHAVIOR. 8(2):188-
      190, 1982.

    Changes in physiological, electroencephalographic and
      psychological parameters in women during the spontaneous
      menstrual cycle and following oral contraceptives, by D.
      Becker, et al. PSYCHONEUROENDOCRINOLOGY.
      7(1):75-90, 1982.

    Contraceptive versus pregnancy risks, by P. M. Layde, et al.
      SCIENCE NEWS. 121:375, June 5, 1982.

    Development of tolerance to the effects of morphine on
      luteinizing hormone secretion as a function of castration
      in the male rat, by T. J. Cicero, et al. JOURNAL OF
      PHARMACOLOGY AND EXPERIMENTAL THERA-
      PEUTICS. 223(3):784-789, December 1983.

    Effects of androgen treatment of full-grown puverally
      castrated rats upon male sexual behavior, intermale aggressive
      behavior and the sequential patterning of aggressive inter-

CONTRACEPTION AND CONTRACEPTIVES: RESEARCH
(continued)
    actions, by B. Bermond. BEHAVIOUR. 80(3-4):143-
    173, 1982.

  Effects of delta-9-THC and castration on behavior and plasma
    hormone levels in male mice, by S. L. Dalterio, et al.
    PHARMACOLOGY, BIOCHEMISTRY AND BEHAVIOR.
    18(1):81-86, January 1983.

  Effects of marking with preputial gland material on the attack
    directed towards long-term castrates by isolated males, by
    M. H. Homady, et al. AGGRESSIVE BEHAVIOR. 8(2):
    137-140, 1982.

  Implantation of dihydrotestosterone propionate into the
    lateral septum or medial amygdala facilitates copulation
    in castrated male rats given estradiol systemically, by
    M. J. Baum, et al. HORMONES AND BEHAVIOR. 16(2):
    208-223, June 1982.

  In vitro fertilization system of the rat: influence of rat
    spermatozoal antibodies: an experiment in the allogenic
    system, by L. Mettler, et al. ZUCHTHYGIENE. 17(1):
    19-28, 1982.

  Induction of female sexual behavior by GTP in ovariectomized
    estrogen primed rats, by C. Beyer, et al. PHYSIOLOGY AND
    BEHAVIOR. 28(6):1073-1076, June 1982.

  Infertility in bitches induced by active immunization with
    porcine zonae pellucidae, by C. A. Mahi-Brown, et al.
    JOURNAL OF EXPERIMENTAL ZOOLOGY. 222:89-
    95, July 20, 1982.

  Inhibition of human placental progesterone synthesis and
    aromatase activity by synthetic steroidogenic inhibitors
    in vitro, by T. Rabe, et al. FERTILITY AND STERILITY.
    39(6):829-835, June 1983.

  Maintenance of mating-induced, regulatory patterns in castrated,
    testosterone-treated male rats, by F. A. Weizenbaum, et al.

APPETITE. 3(3):191-202, September 1982.

Monthly birth control? [synthetic inhibitory analog of luteinizing hormone-releasing hormone]. SCIENCE DIGEST. 91:89, July 1983.

Natural or hormone-induced sexual and social behaviors in the female brown lemming (lemmus trimucronatus), by W. U. Huck, et al. HORMONES AND BEHAVIOR. 16(2): 199-207, June 1982.

A new contraceptive borrows an ancient idea. BUSINESS WEEK. April 18, 1983, p. 42.

New data on reproductive deaths. SCIENCE DIGEST. 91:91, March 1983.

Oral contraceptives and fibrinolysis among female cyclists before and after exercise, by I. A. Huisveld, et al. JOURNAL OF APPLIED PHYSIOLOGY. 53:330-334, August 1982.

Some effects of ovariectomy and estrogen replacement on body composition in the rat, by R. G. Clark, et al. PHYSIOLOGY AND BEHAVIOR. 28(6):963-969, June 1982.

Testing a better birth-control pill, by M. Clark. NEWSWEEK. 99:85, May 3, 1982.

Variation of fat intake with estrous cycle, ovariectomy and estradiol replacement in hamsters, by M. O. Miceli, et al. PHYSIOLOGY AND BEHAVIOR. 30(3):415-420, March 1983.

When patients ask . . . about . . . the latest and safest oral contraceptive, by E. Trimmer. MIDWIVE, HEALTH VISITOR AND COMMUNITY NURSE. 18(11):484, November 1982.

CONTRACEPTIVE AGENTS

FDA considers depo-provera as contraceptive, by M. F. Docksai. TRIAL. 19:15-16, March 1983.

CONTRACEPTIVE AGENTS: FEMALE

A case for concern?, by A. Gartland. NURSING TIMES. 79(18): 10-11, May 4-10, 1983.

Spermicide effect on unborn in question. SCIENCE NEWS. 121:326, May 15, 1982.

Vaginal spermicides, chromosomal abnormalities and limb reduction defects, by J. F. Cordero, et al. FAMILY PLANNING PERSPECTIVES. 15:16-18, January-February 1983.

CONTRACEPTIVE AGENTS: FEMALE: ORAL: COMPLICATIONS

The effect of fecundity of pill acceptance during postpartum amenorrhea: a comment, by R. Gray, et al. STUDIES IN FAMILY PLANNING. 14(5):150-155, May 1983.

CONTRACEPTIVE AGENTS: MALE

High court clears up any doubts on abortion; justices disallow limit on contraceptive ads, by L. Greenhouse. NEW YORK TIMES. June 19, 1983, news section 4, p. E7.

CONTRACEPTIVES: GENERAL

Abortion, contraception, infanticide, by P. E. Devine. PHILOSOPHY. 58:513-520, October 1983.

Buyer beware. CANADIAN NURSE. 79:62, June 1983.

MEXICO
Old age pensions and fertility in rural areas of less developed countries: some evidence from Mexico, by J. B. Nugent, et al.

ECONOMIC DEVELOPMENT AND CULTURAL CHANGE. 31:809-829, July 1983.

NIGERIA

Religious identity and attitudes toward contraceptives among university students in Nigeria, by I. Owie. SOCIAL BIOLOGY. 30(1):101-105, Spring 1983.

UNITED STATES

An analysis of access to contraceptive care in western Pennsylvania, by S. E. Milligan, et al. SOCIAL WORK, RE-SEARCH AND ABSTRACTS. 20:3, Fall 1984.

CONTRACEPTIVES: ADVERTISING

A delicate balance: not everything goes in the marketing of unmentionables [condoms], by J. Alter. ADVERTISING AGE. 53(sec 2):M2-M3+, July 12, 1982.

Fraud between partners regarding the use of contraceptives, by D. M. Carlton. KENTUCKY LAW JOURNAL. 71(3): 593-615, 1982-1983.

Morality of contraception, by H. Rodrigues. AUSTRALASIAN NURSES JOURNAL. 11(6):28-29, July 1982.

Oh, those filthy spots (laws banning advertising of contraceptives on television). PROGRESSIVE. 46:9-10, April 1982.

CONTRACEPTIVES: ATTITUDES

Attitude of the university student to contraceptive methods, by G. Escarcega Rivera, et al. GINECOLOGIA Y OBSTET-RICIA DE MEXICO. 50(304):205-212, 1982.

Changes in attitudes toward contraceptives concomitant with instructional activities in physiology, by I. Owie. JOURNAL OF RESEARCH AND SCIENCE TEACHING. 20(6):571-575, September 1983.

CONTRACEPTIVES: ATTITUDES (continued)

Chronic schizophrenic women's attitudes toward sex, pregnancy, birth control, and childrearing, by J. P. McEvoy, et al. HOSPITAL AND COMMUNITY PSYCHIATRY. 34(6): 536-539, June 1983.

Descriptive study of the attitudes of males involved in abortion, by D. A. Cornelio. DISSERTATION ABSTRACTS INTERNATIONAL: A. 44(5), November 1983.

Ethical considerations concerning adolescents consulting for contraceptive services, by T. J. Silber. JOURNAL OF FAMILY PRACTICE. 15(5):909-911, November 1982.

Factors affecting sexual and contraceptive attitudes and behaviors among adolescents, by R. S. Sterns. DISSERTATION ABSTRACTS INTERNATIONAL: A. 43(10), April 1983.

Morality of contraception, by H. Rodrigues. AUSTRALASIAN NURSES JOURNAL. 11(6):28-29, July 1982.

Religious identity and attitudes toward contraceptives among university students in Nigeria, by I. Owie. SOCIAL BIOLOGY. 30(1):101-105, Spring 1983.

Should courts curb mail they consider too direct [prophylactics], by T. J. McGrew. AD FORUM. 4:41, February 1983.

Socialization for sexual and contraception behavior: moral absolutes versus relative consequences, by E. Thompson. YOUTH AND SOCIETY. 14(1):103-128, September 1982.

A survey of attitudes concerning contraception and the resolution of teenage pregnancy, by C. Rinck, et al. ADOLESCENCE. 18(72):923-929, Winter 1983.

CONTRACEPTIVES: COMPLICATIONS

Contraception: yes, but at what cost?, by D. Grenon-Plante.

CONTRACEPTIVES: COMPLICATIONS (continued)

INFIRMIERE CANADIENNE. 24(10):27-31, November 1982.

CONTRACEPTIVES: COUNSELING

Ethical considerations concerning adolescents consulting for contraceptive services, by T. J. Silber. JOURNAL OF FAMILY PRACTICE. 15(5):909-911, November 1982.

CONTRACEPTIVES: ECONOMICS

The costs of contraception, by A. Torres, et al. FAMILY PLANNING PERSPECTIVES. 15:70-72, March-April 1983.

CONTRACEPTIVES: EDUCATION

A comparison of responses to adolescent-oriented and traditional contraceptive programs, by S. G. Philliber, et al. JOURNAL OF AMBULATORY CARE MANAGEMENT. 6(2):32-42, May 1983.

The male role in contraception: implications for health education, by C. L. Chng. JOURNAL OF SCHOOL HEALTH. 53(3):197-201, March 1983.

Sex education and contraceptive education in U. S. public high schools, by M. T. Orr. FAMILY PLANNING PERSPECTIVES. 14:304+, November-December 1982.

CONTRACEPTIVES: FEMALE

Contraception—are women getting a fair deal?, by J. Spray. HEALTH VISITOR. 56(5):163-164, May 1983.

Contraceptive failure and continuation among married women in the United States, 1970-1975, by W. R. Grady, et al. STUDIES IN FAMILY PLANNING. 14(1):9, January 1983.

Infant and child survival and contraceptive use in the closed pregnancy interval, by B. Janowitz, et al. SOCIAL SCIENCE

CONTRACEPTIVES: FEMALE (continued)

AND MEDICINE. 17(2):113-118, 1983.

Model of premarital coitus and contraceptive behavior among female adolescents, by W. M. Strahle. ARCHIVES OF SEXUAL BEHAVIOR. 12(1):67-94, 1983.

Religiosity, sexual behavior and contraceptive use of college females, by M. Young. JOURNAL OF THE AMERICAN COLLEGE HEALTH ASSOCIATION. 30:216-220, April 1982.

Young adult women's contraceptive decision: a comparison of two predictive models of choice, by E. J. Herz. DISSERTATION ABSTRACTS INTERNATIONAL: B. 44(3), September 1983.

CONTRACEPTIVES: FEMALE: BARRIER

Artifical insemination with fresh donor semen using the cervical cap technique: a review of 278 cases, by C. A. Bergquist, et al. OBSTETRICS AND GYNECOLOGY. 60(2):195-199, 1982.

A California scientist remodels a perpetual problem's ancient solution: the contraceptive sponge, by M. A. Fischer. PEOPLE WEEKLY. 19:57-58, May 2, 1983.

The cervical cap: a barrier contraceptive, by M. T. Hastings-Tolsma. AMERICAN JOURNAL OF MATERNAL CHILD NURSING. 7(6):382-386, November-December 1982.

The cervical cap: effectiveness as a contraceptive, by D. Boehm. JOURNAL OF NURSE-MIDWIFERY. 28(1):3-6, January-February 1983.

Contraceptive choices may soon include convenient OTC sponge . . ., but animal cancers till hold up FDA approval of depo-provera. MEDICAL WORLD NEWS. 24:24-26, February 14, 1983.

Contraceptive sponges. CANADIAN CONSUMER. 13:3, September 1983.

Counting on condoms . . . a CAC test. CANADIAN CONSUMER. November 1982, p. 116A-116B, 116D+.

Dalkon shield class action overturned, by S. Sherwood. BUSINESS INSURANCE. 16:1+, June 28, 1982.

Everybody wants in [sponge contraceptive coming to market makes VLI Corp. a hot stock], by J. Merwin. FORBES. 132:52-53, July 4, 1983.

Food and Drug Administration approves vaginal sponge, by D. Kafka, et al. FAMILY PLANNING PERSPECTIVES. 15(3):146-148, May-June 1983.

A new contraceptive borrows an ancient idea [vaginal polyurethane sponge saturated with spermicide]. BUSINESS WEEK. April 18, 1983, p. 42.

The new contraceptive sponge, by J. Ralston. MCCALLS. 110:48+, July 1983.

The new contraceptives [triphasic pill and sponge], by L. J. Sarrel, et al. REDBOOK. 161:20, August 1983.

One from Egypt [disposable contraceptive sponge]. TIME. 121:48-49, March 28, 1983.

Relationship of weight change to required size of vaginal diaphragm, by K. Fiscella. NURSE PRACTITIONER. 7(7):21, 25, July-August 1982.

The sponge, by K. Freifeld, et al. HEALTH. 15(7):56, July 1983.

Spray a day keeps babies away. NEW SCIENTIST. 96:293, November 4, 1982.

Taking the plunge and trying the sponge, by A. Diamant. REDBOOK. 161:29, September 1983.

CONTRACEPTIVES: FEMALE: BARRIER (continued)

Tests of a forgotten barrier [cervical cap]. SCIENCE NEWS. 123:236, April 9, 1983.

A throw-away diaphragm, by R. Kall. HEALTH. 14:18, March 1982.

Women who use barrier methods less likely to be hospitalized for PID [pelivc inflammatory disease]. FAMILY PLANNING PERSPECTIVES. 14:331-332, November-December 1982.

CONTRACEPTIVES: FEMALE: BARRIER: COMPLICATIONS

Dalkon shield warning. FDA CONSUMER. 17:2, July-August 1983.

Vaginal spermicides and miscarriage seen primarily in the emergency room, by H. Jick, et al. TERATOGENESIS, CARCINOGENESIS AND MUTAGENESIS. 2(2):205-210, 1982.

Vaginal spermicides, chromosomal abnormalities and limb reduction defects, by J. F. Cordero, et al. FAMILY PLANNING PERSPECTIVES. 15(1):16-18, January-February 1983.

CONTRACEPTIVES: FEMALE: COMPLICATIONS

Cardiovascular disease: risks and prognosis for women as compared with men, by S. R. Winternitz, et al. CONSULTANT. 23(2):118-120, 123, 126+, February 1983.

Menstrual bleeding expectations and short-term contraceptive discontuation in Mexico, by G. Zetina-Lozano. STUDIES IN FAMILY PLANNING. 14(5):127, May 1983.

CONTRACEPTIVES: FEMALE: IUD

Awkward questions about IUCDs, by E. Trimmer. MIDWIFE, HEALTH VISITOR AND COMMUNITY NURSE. 19(2): 66, February 1983.

A comparative study of the effectiveness of the lippes loop, the Copper-T-200 and the Nova-T intrauterine contraceptive devices in Lagos, Nigeria, by M. A. Oyediran, et al. INTERNATIONAL JOURNAL OF FERTILITY. 27(2):109-112, 1982.

Contraceptive use high in Norway, where IUD is most popular method. FAMILY PLANNING PERSPECTIVES. 15:87-88, March-April 1983.

Effects of breastfeeding on IUD performance, by L. P. Cole, et al. AMERICAN JOURNAL OF PUBLIC HEALTH. 73: 384-388, April 1983.

IUDS: an appropriate contraceptive for many women. POPULATION REPORTS. 10(4), July 1982.

IUD insertion following spontaneous abortion: a clinical trial of the TCu 220C, liuppes loop D, and copper 7. STUDIES IN FAMILY PLANNING. 14(4):109-114, April 1983.

Interval IUD insertion in parous women: a randomized multi-centre comparative trial of the lippes loop D TCu220C and the copper 7. CONTRACEPTION. 26(1):1-22, July 1982.

Medicine and the law. The postcoital pill and intrauterine device: contraceptive or abortifacient?, by D. Brahams. LANCET. 1(8332):1039, May 7, 1983.

Physicians vs. auxiliary nurse-midwives as providers of IUD services—a study in Turkey and the Philippines, by N. Eren, et al. STUDIES IN FAMILY PLANNING. 14:43-47, February 1983.

CONTRACEPTIVES: FEMALE: IUD: COMPLICATIONS

Effects of breastfeeding on IUD performance, by L. P. Cole, et al. AMERICAN JOURNAL OF PUBLIC HEALTH. 73(4): 384-388, April 1983.

CONTRACEPTIVES: FEMALE: IUD: COMPLICATIONS
(continued)
   IUD dangers: are you a potential victim?, by M. Engel.
      GLAMOUR. 81:254, November 1983.

   IUDS and ectopic pregnancy, by I. Sivin. STUDIES IN FAMILY
      PLANNING. 14(2):57, February 1983.

   Perforation risk greater when IUDs are inserted in breastfeeding
      women. FAMILY PLANNING PERSPECTIVES. 15(3):
      138-140, May-June 1983.

CONTRACEPTIVES: FEMALE: IMPLANTED

   A five-year clinical trial of levonorgestrel silastic implants
      (Norplant), by S. Diaz, et al. CONTRACEPTION. 25(5):
      447-456, 1982.

   Slow-release contraceptive systems [implants that release
      levonorgestrel]. SCIENCE NEWS. 123:236, April 9, 1983.

CONTRACEPTIVES: FEMALE: INJECTED

   A case for concern? . . . depo-provera, by A. Gartland. NURSING
      TIMES. 79(18):10-11, May 4-10, 1983.

   Contraceptive choices may soon include convenient OTC
      sponge . . ., but animal cancers still hold up FDA approval
      of depo-provera. MEDICAL WORLD NEWS. 24:24-26,
      February 14, 1983.

   The depo-provera debate, by M. Clark, et al. NEWSWEEK.
      101(4):70, January 24, 1983.

   Depo-provera: a drug on trial, by J. Bryan. TIMES. April 13,
      1983, p. 8.

   Depo-provera: the jury still out, by R. Gold. FAMILY
      PLANNING PERSPECTIVES. 15(2):78, March-April 1983.

   Depo-provera: a new offensive [issues in the marketing for
      human use of this long-acting, injectable contraceptive and

in its possible approval for use in the United States], by J. Norsigian. HEALTH AND MEDICINE. 1:3-5, Winter-Spring 1983.

Depo-provera: on trial again [injectable contraceptive, Britain]. ECONOMIST. 287:116, April 30, 1983.

Depo-provera under scrutiny, by A. Chen. SCIENCE NEWS. 123:122-123, February 19, 1983.

A drug on trial, by E. Potter, et al. SUNDAY TIMES. April 10, 1983, p. 17.

Effective, but how safe? [depo-provera]. TIME. 121:67, January 24, 1983.

Evaluating DMPA [medroxyprogesterone acetate], by A. Henry. OFF OUR BACKS. 13:7+, February 1983.

FDA considers depo-provera as contraceptive, by M. F. Docksai. TRIAL. 19(3):15-16, March 1983.

Is this drug dangerous? [depo-provera]. ESSENCE. 14:42, July 1983.

On trial again. Depo-provera. ECONOMIST. 287:110, April 30, 1983.

One shot too many [depo-provera]. PROGRESSIVE. 47:11-12, March 1983.

A prescription for concern: depo-provera. GUARDIAN. April 29, 1983, p. 15.

Questioning the ideal [depo-provera]. CONSUMER'S RE-SEARCH MAGAZINE. 66:4, March 1983.

Testing times for women in body lab . . . depo-provera, by W. Bacon. LAMP. 40(3):38-40, May 1983.

CONTRACEPTIVES: FEMALE: INJECTED (continued)

Trials of a contraceptive [depo-provera], by A. Kerr.
MACLEANS. 96:46, January 24, 1983.

CONTRACEPTIVES: FEMALE: METHODS

Factors influencing choice of contraceptive method among
married fecund women who intend no additional births:
health belief model and economic perspectives, by N. M.
MacDowell, Jr. DISSERTATION ABSTRACTS INTER-
NATIONAL: B. 43(11), May 1983.

Genito-urinary symptoms and signs in women using different
contraceptive methods, by N. B. Loudon, et al. BRITISH
JOURNAL OF FAMILY PLANNING. 8(1):3-6, 1982.

CONTRACEPTIVES: FEMALE: ORAL

Behavioral tests in monkey infants exposed embryonically to
an oral contraceptive, by M. S. Golub, et al. NEURO-
BEHAVIORAL TOXICOLOGY AND TERATOLOGY.
5(3):301-304, 1983.

Case for concern?, by A. Gartland. NURSING TIMES. 79(18):
10-11, May 4, 1983.

Contraceptive versus pregnancy risks, by P. M. Layde, et al.
SCIENCE NEWS. 121:375, June 5, 1982.

The courts, congress, parents, kids and the pill, by E. Kennedy
Shriver. OUR SUNDAY VISITOR. 72:4, May 8, 1983.

Depo-provera under scrutiny, by A. Chen. SCIENCE NEWS.
123(8):122, February 19, 1983.

Dr. Rock's magic pill, by S. Davidson. ESQUIRE. 100:100+,
December 1983.

Glycohemoglobin (hemoglobin A1) levels in oral contraceptive
users, by M. Blum, et al. EUROPEAN JOURNAL OF
OBSTETRICS AND GYNECOLOGY. 15(2):97-102, 1983.

In defence of the pill. EMERGENCY MEDICINE. 14(17): 205, October 15, 1982.

Medical update on the pill, by M. B. Gardner. GOOD HOUSE-KEEPING. 196:89-92, June 1983.

The new contraceptives [triphasic pill and sponge], by L. J. Sarrel, et al. REDBOOK. 161:20, August 1983.

Oral contraception, coital frequency and the time required to conceive, by C. F. Westoff, et al. SOCIAL BIOLOGY. 29:157-167, Spring-Summer 1982.

Oral contraceptive medication in prevention of psychotic exacerbations associated with phases of the menstrual cycle, by A. R. Felthons, et al. JOURNAL OF PREVENTIVE PSYCHOLOGY. 1(1):5-15, 1981.

POP . . . progestogen-only pill, by L. Pyle, et al. NURSING TIMES. 79(4):64-66, January 26-February 1, 1983.

The pill: a closer look, by J. Dickerson. AMERICAN JOURNAL OF NURSING. 83(10):1392-1398, October 1983.

The pill in various countries, by P. D. Bardis. REVUE INTERNATIONALE DE SOCIOLOGIE. 18(1-3):128-135, April-December 1982.

The pill: what's a woman to do?, by M. Wallace, et al. SUNDAY TIMES. October 23, 1983, p. 15, 18.

Some good news about the pill (cancer risks disputed). NEWS-WEEK. 101:84, April 4, 1983.

Sponge gets OK. SCIENCE NEWS. 123:261, April 23, 1983.

Toledo doctor wages campaign against the pill, by A. Jones. NATIONAL CATHOLIC REPORTER. 18:1+, October 15, 1982.

Behavioral tests in monkey infants exposed embryonically to an oral contraceptive, by M. S. Golub, et al. NEURO-BEHAVIORAL TOXICOLOGY AND TERATOLOGY. 5(3):301-304, May-June 1983.

Biosynthesis of platelet lipids in relation to aggregation in women using oral contraceptives, by M. Ciavatti, et al. CONTRACEPTION. 25(6):629-638, 1982.

Changes in physiological, electroencaphalographic and psychological parameters in women during the spontaneous menstrual cycle and following oral contraceptives, by D. Becker, et al. PSYCHONEUROENDOCRINOLOGY. 7(1):75-90, 1982.

Comparative effects of the oral contraceptive combinations 0;150 milligram desogestrel plus 0.030 milligram ethynylestradiol and 0.150 milligram levonorgestrel plus 0.030 milligram ethynylestradiol on lipid and lipoprotein metabolism in healthy female volunteers, by G. Samsioe. CONTRACEPTION. 25(5):487-504, 1982.

Effective, but how safe? TIME. 121(4):67, January 24, 1983.

Effects of desogestrel and levonorgestrel in low-dose estrogen oral contraceptives on serum lipoproteins, by E. W. Bergink, et al. CONTRACEPTION. 25(5):477-486, 1982.

Factors affecting the association of oral contraceptives and ovarian cancer, by D. W. Cramer, et al. NEW ENGLAND JOURNAL OF MEDICINE. 307:1047-1051, October 21, 1982.

Genito-urinary symptoms and signs in women using different contraceptive methods, by N. B. Loudon, et al. BRITISH JOURNAL OF FAMILY PLANNING. 8(1):3-6, 1982.

Immune reactivity among women on oral contraceptives, by H. D. Zane. DISSERTATION ABSTRACTS INTERNATIONAL: B. 44(4), October 1983.

Linking cancer with the pill [oral contraceptives containing synthetic progesterone]. NEWSWEEK. 102:78, October 31, 1983.

Long-term oral contraceptive use and the risk of breast cancer: the Centers for Disease Control Cancer and Steroid Hormone study. JOURNAL OF THE AMERICAN MEDICAL AS-SOCIATION. 249:1591-1595, March 25, 1983.

Managing drug interactions with oral contraceptives, by G. P. Stoehr, et al. JOURNAL OF OBSTETRIC GYNECOLOGIC AND NEONATAL NURSING. 12(5):327-331, September-October 1983.

The oral contraceptive pill: use, user satisfaction, side effects and fears among Manawatu women, by A. D. Trlin, et al. NEW ZEALAND MEDICAL JOURNAL. 95(717):700-703, October 13, 1982.

Oral contraceptive use and the risk of endometrial cancer: the Centers for Disease Control Cancer and Steroid Hormone study, by B. S. Hulka. JOURNAL OF THE AMERICAN MEDICAL ASSOCIATION. 249:1600-1604, March 25, 1983.

Oral contraceptive use and the risk of ovarian cancer: the Centers for Disease Control Cancer and Steroid Hormone study. JOURNAL OF THE AMERICAN MEDICAL ASSOCIATION. 249:1596-1599, March 25, 1983.

Oral contraceptives and rheumatoid arthritis: further epidemiologic evidence for a protective effect, by J. P. Vandenbroncke. DISSERTATION ABSTRACTS INTER-NATIONAL: B. 44(1), July 1983.

Oral contraceptives can increase the potency of diazepam. NURSES DRUG ALERT. 7(3):17, March 1983.

Oral contraceptives: the good news. JOURNAL OF THE AMERICAN MEDICAL ASSOCIATION. 249:1624-1625, March 25, 1983.

CONTRACEPTIVES: FEMALE: ORAL: COMPLICATIONS
(continued)

Pill cuts arthritis, ovarian cancer risk, doesn't cause gallbladder disease, raises stroke risk slightly. FAMILY PLANNING PERSPECTIVES. 15:36-37, January-February 1983.

The pill revisited: new cancer link?, by J. Silberner. SCIENCE NEWS. 124:279, October 29, 1983.

The "pill scare" and fertility in England and Wales, by M. Bone. INTERNATIONAL PLANNED PARENTHOOD FEDER-ATION MEDICAL BULLETIN. 16(4):2, August 1982.

Progestogen implicated in slight blood pressure rise among pill users. FAMILY PLANNING PERSPECTIVES. 15:88-89, March-April 1983.

Redefining risks: the good news about the pill [cancer risks], by M. Weber. VOGUE. 173:414, September 1983.

Trials of a contraceptive [depo-provera], by A. Kerr. MACLEANS. 96:46, January 24, 1983.

Ventilatory response of humans to chronic contraceptive pill administration, by C. A. Smith, et al. RESPIRATION. 43(3):179-185, 1982.

CONTRACEPTIVES: FEMALE: POST-COITAL

Behavioural patterns in women requesting postcoital contra-ception, by S. Rowlands, et al. JOURNAL OF BIOSOCIAL SCIENCE. 15:145-152, April 1983.

Better late than never? Post-coital contraception, by J. Naughton. OBSERVER. May 15, 1983, p. 25.

Matters of conscience: the morning after, the night before, by B. Bardsley. NURSING MIRROR. 156(21):12-13, May 25, 1983.

Medicine and the law. The postcoital pill and intrauterine device: contraceptive or abortifacient?, by D. Brahams. LANCET.

CONTRACEPTIVES: FEMALE: POST-COITAL (continued)

1(8332):1039, May 7, 1983.

Postcoital antifertility effect of piperine, by P. Piyachaturawat, et al. CONTRACEPTION. 26(6):625-633, December 1982.

Postcoital contraception or abortion? [letter]. LANCET. 2(8343):223, July 23, 1983.

CONTRACEPTIVES: FEMALE: SUPPOSITORY

New vaginal [suppository] contraceptive, by S. Katz. CHATELAINE. 56:16, May 1983.

CONTRACEPTIVES: FEMALE: TECHNIQUES

Contraception and the rhythm method (logical inconsistencies), by P. Clifion. RELIGIOUS HUMANISM. 17:36-39, Winter 1983.

CONTRACEPTIVES: MALE

Action mechanisms of gossypol as a male contraceptive agent: in vitro study (leydig cell of rats), by H. Hoshiai, et al. JAPANESE JOURNAL OF FERTILITY AND STERILITY. 27(2):156-160.

Cardiovascular disease: risks and prognosis for women as compared with men, by S. R. Winternitz, et al. CONSULTANT. 23(2):118-120, 123, 126+, February 1983.

Descriptive study of the attitudes of males involved in abortion, by D. A. Cornelio. DISSERTATION ABSTRACTS INTERNATIONAL: A. 44(5), November 1983.

Gossypol, an effective male contraceptive, was not mutagenic in sperm head abnormality assay in mice, by S. K. Majumdar, et al. CANADIAN JOURNAL OF GENETIC CYTOLOGY. 24(6):777-780, 1982.

Male contraceptive in stomach salve, by S. Steinberg. SCIENCE

CONTRACEPTIVES: MALE (continued)

NEWS. 124:117, August 20, 1983.

The male role in contraception: implications for health education, by C. L. Chng. JOURNAL OF SCHOOL HEALTH. 53:197-201, March 1983.

New male contraceptive, by S. Katz. CHATELAINE. 56:18, December 1983.

The pill for men: bad news, good news—or no news?, by J. Kelly. MADEMOISELLE. 89:210+, September 1983.

CONTRACEPTIVES: MALE: BARRIER

Question: I've recently heard that you can buy condoms coated with spermicide. CANADIAN CONSUMER. 13:6, May 1983.

CONTRACEPTIVES: MALE: ORAL

The quest for the male pill, by J. Langone. DISCOVER. 3(10): 26, October 1982.

The quest for the male pill, by G. Youcha. SCIENCE DIGEST. 90:33+, March 1982.

What's holding up the male birth-control pill?, by L. Lader. MCCALLS. 110:158, May 1983.

CONTRACEPTIVES: METHODS

Contraception, by R. Herbert. NURSING. 2(14):405, 408-409, 412-414, June 1983.

Contraception and the rhythm method, by C. Perry. RELIGIOUS HUMANISM. 17(1):36-39, 1983.

Contraception: yes, but at what price?, by D. Grenon-Plante. KRANKENPFLEGE. (5):38-41, May 1983.

Efficacy of the Billings' method, by W. Fijalkowski.

CONTRACEPTIVES: METHODS (continued)

PIELEGNIARKA I POLOZNA. (6):6-7, 1982.

LHRH found to inhibit ovulation successfully with few side effects. FAMILY PLANNING PERSPECTIVES. 15:32-34, January-February 1983.

Vaginal colonization of escherichia coli and its relation to contraceptive methods, by A. W. Chow. CONTRACEPTION. 27(5):497-504, 1983.

CONTRACEPTIVES: ORAL

Britain bites the bullet over depo-provera. NEW SCIENTIST. 98:136, April 21, 1983.

Effect of supply source on oral contraceptive use in Mexico, by J. Bailey, et al. STUDIES IN FAMILY PLANNING. 13(11):343, November 1982.

New oral contraceptive [triphasil], by S. Katz. CHATELAINE. 56:16, June 1983.

Oral contraception: selection and management, by J. C. Bartosch. NURSE PRACTITIONER. 8(5):56-63, 79, May 1983.

Oral contraceptives: the latest facts on their benefits and risks, by D. R. Mishell, Jr. CONSULTANT. 23(4):139-143, April 1983.

POP, by L. Pyle, et al. NURSING TIMES. 79(4):64-66, January 26-February 1, 1983.

Testing a better birth-control pill, by M. Clark. NEWSWEEK. 99:85, May 3, 1982.

When patients ask about the latest and safest oral contraceptive, by E. Trimmer. MIDWIFE, HEALTH VISITOR AND COMMUNITY NURSE. 18(11):484, November 1982.

CONTRACEPTIVES: ORAL (continued)

Will a do-it-yourself abortion drug hit the market soon: Upjohn Co. denies plans, but salesman resigns [G. Schimming; prostaglandins], by R. Frame. CHRISTIANITY TODAY. 27:71-72, October 7, 1983.

CONTRACEPTIVES: PARENTAL CONSENT

As I see it . . . parents', teenagers' rights clash in 'squeal' rule, by R. Mortimer, et al. AMERICAN NURSE. 15(6):5, 19, June 1983.

The courts, congress, parents, kids and the pill, by E. Kennedy Shriver. OUR SUNDAY VISITOR. 72:4, May 8, 1983.

A family affair [regulation requiring facilities receiving federal funding to notify parents after supplying contraceptive devices to minor children]. AMERICA. 148:102-103, February 12, 1983.

Family plan [squeal law providing for notification of parents when children receive contraceptives from clinics]. TIME. 121:41, February 7, 1983.

NFP center reaches couples, teens, physicians, parents; St. Francis Regional Medical Center, Inc., Wichita, KS. HOSPITAL PROGRESS. 64:28+, April 1983.

A new squeal rule, by C. Leslie. NEWSWEEK. 101:24, February 7, 1983.

Planned parenthood attacks a parent's need to know [regulation requiring that parents be informed if clinics give minors contraceptives], by K. S. Kantzer. CHRISTIANITY TODAY. 27:11-13, May 20, 1983.

Right of minors to confidential access to contraceptives. ALBANY LAW REVIEW. 47:214-240, Fall 1982.

The sex police [law requiring birth-control clinics to notify parents]. NATION. 236:164-165, February 12, 1983.

CONTRACEPTIVES: PARENTAL CONSENT (continued)

Should parents be told when teens get contraceptives?
CHRISTIANITY TODAY. 27:22, March 18, 1983.

The squeal rule and Lolita rights, by D. R. Carlin, Jr.
COMMONWEAL. 110:465-467, September 9, 1983.

The squeal rule: halt! [federal regulation that would require
health clinics to notify parents of any girl who applied
for prescription contraceptives]. NEWSWEEK. 101:17,
February 28, 1983.

Stifled squeal [injunction blocking requirement that federally
funded clinics notify parents if their teenagers receive
contraceptives]. TIME. 121:24, February 28, 1983.

There oughta be a law fantasy [regulations requiring birth
control clinics to notify parents when minors receive
contraceptives], by J. M. Wall. CHRISTIAN CENTURY.
100:171, March 2, 1983.

This bitter pill for parents: rule of professional secrecy over
contraception, by R. Butt. TIMES. July 7, 1983, p. 12.

CONTRACEPTIVES: PSYCHOLOGY AND PSYCHIATRY

Investigation of the relationship between sex role orientation,
level of assertiveness, affective orientation to sexuality and
a model of contraceptive behavior, by M. J. Hynes.
DISSERTATION ABSTRACTS INTERNATIONAL: B.
43(9), 1982.

Male adolescent psychosexual development: the influence of
significant others on contraceptive behavior, by D. D.
Cohen. DISSERTATION ABSTRACTS INTERNATIONAL:
A. 43(11), May 1983.

Psychological correlates of contraceptive behavior in late
adolescent women, by R. J. Ma. DISSERTATION
ABSTRACTS INTERNATIONAL: B. 44(5), November
1983.

CONTRACEPTIVES: PSYCHOLOGY AND PSYCHIATRY
(continued)
> Psychological issues arising from the development of new male contraceptives, by A. E. Reading, et al. BULLETIN OF THE BRITISH PSYCHOLOGICAL SOCIETY. 35: 369-371, October 1982.

> Relationship between psychological characteristics and contraceptive behaviors among university women, by C. N. Roper. DISSERTATION ABSTRACTS INTERNATIONAL: B. 44(4), October 1983.

CONTRACEPTIVES: STATISTICS

> Comparison of results of contraceptive prevalence surveys in five countries with particular emphasis on knowledge, use and availability, by T. Wardlaw, et al. WESTINGHOUSE HEALTH SYSTEMS REPORT. 2(35), March 1982.

> Contraceptive failure and continuation among married women in the United States, 1970-1975, by W. R. Grady, et al. STUDIES IN FAMILY PLANNING. 14:9-19, January 1983.

> Correcting contraceptive failure rates for sample composition and sample selection bias, by J. Trussell, et al. SOCIAL BIOLOGY. 28:293-298, Fall-Winter 1981.

> The extent of contraceptive use and the social paradigm of modern demography, by D. G. Sloan. SOCIOLOGY. 17(3):380-387, August 1983.

> Factor structure of the menstrual sympton questionnaire: relationship to oral contraceptives, neuroticism and life stress, by L. A. Stephenson, et al. BEHAVIOUR RESEARCH AND THERAPY. 21(2):129-135.

> Indicators of contraceptive policy for nations at three levels of development [comparison of the use of condoms, birth control pills, and intrauterine devices], by I. M. Wasserman, et al. SOCIAL INDICATORS RESEARCH. 12:153-168, February 1983.

CONTRACEPTIVES: STATISTICS (continued)

Measuring the unmet need for contraception to space and limit
births: the findings suggest a sizable unsaturated market for
contraceptive services and supplies [developing countries],
by D. L. Nortman. INTERNATIONAL FAMILY PLANNING
PERSPECTIVES. 8:125-134, December 1982.

Never-pregnant teenagers more effective users of contraceptives
than those previously pregnant. FAMILY PLANNING
PERSPECTIVES. 15(3):137-138, May-June 1983.

Patterns of contraceptive use in Kingston and St. Andrew,
Jamaica, 1970-1977, by W. Bailey, et al. SOCIAL SCIENCE
AND MEDICINE. 16:1675, 1982.

The risk of premarital first pregnancy among metropolitan-
area teenagers: 1976 and 1979, by M. A. Koenig, et al.
FAMILY PLANNING PERSPECTIVES. 14(5):239-241,
243-247, September-October 1982.

WFS surveys show that western, eastern Europe differ greatly
in use of modern contraceptives. FAMILY PLANNING
PERSPECTIVES. 15:82-83, March-April 1983.

CONTRACEPTIVES AND COLLEGE STUDENTS

Attitude of the university student to contraceptive methods,
by G. Escarcega Rivera, et al. GINECOLOGIA Y OBSTET-
RICA DE MEXICO. 50(304):205-212, 1982.

Contraceptive use by college dating couples: a comparison of
men's and women's reports, by C. T. Hill, et al. POPULA-
TION AND ENVIRONMENT: BEHAVIORAL AND
SOCIAL ISSUES. 6(1):60-69, Spring 1983.

Relationship between psychological characteristics and
contraceptive behaviors among university women, by
C. N. Roper. DISSERTATION ABSTRACTS INTER-
NATIONAL: B. 44(4), October 1983.

Relationships of selected variables to the use/nonuse of

CONTRACEPTIVES AND COLLEGE STUDENTS (continued)

contraceptives among undergraduate college and university students, by C. A. S. Ellis. DISSERTATION ABSTRACTS INTERNATIONAL: A. 43(9), March 1983.

Relative weight, smoking and contraceptive pills: interrelations to blood pressure in students, by A. Lehtonen. JOURNAL OF THE AMERICAN COLLEGE HEALTH ASSOCIATION. 31(3):105-108, December 1982.

Religious identity and attitudes toward contraceptives among university students in Nigeria, by I. Owie. SOCIAL BIOLOGY. 30(1):101-105, Spring 1983.

Religiosity, sexual behavior and contraceptive use of college females, by M. Young. JOURNAL OF THE AMERICAN COLLEGE HEALTH ASSOCIATION. 30(5):216-220, April 1982.

Self-care/health maintenance and contraceptive use, information needs, and knowledge of a selected group of university women, by J. W. Hawkins, et al. ISSUES IN HEALTH CARE OF WOMEN. 3(5-6):287-305, September-December 1981.

CONTRACEPTIVES AND FUNDING

Economic model of fertility, sex and contraception, by H. Brunborg. DISSERTATION ABSTRACTS INTER-NATIONAL: A. 44(6), December 1983.

CONTRACEPTIVES AND HORMONES

Development of tolerance to the effects of morphine on luteinizing hormone secretion as a function of castration in the male rat, by T. J. Cicero, et al. JOURNAL OF PHARMACOLOGY AND EXPERIMENTAL THERA-PEUTICS. 223(3):784-789, December 1983.

Effects of delta-9-THC and castration on behavior and plasma hormone levels in male mice, by S. L. Dalterio, et al.

288

PHARMACOLOGY, BIOCHEMISTRY AND BEHAVIOR. 18(1):81-86, January 1983.

Estroprogestative contraception, by A. Harlay. INFIRMIERE FRANCAISE. (244):20, April 1983.

Hormonal contraception for men: acceptability and effects on sexuality. STUDIES IN FAMILY PLANNING. 13(11): 328, November 1982.

Induction of female sexual behavior by GTP in ovariectomized estrogen primed rats, by C. Beyer, et al. PHYSIOLOGY AND BEHAVIOR. 28(6):1073-1076, June 1982.

LHRH found to inhibit ovulation successfully with few side effects . . . a nasal spray containing luteinizing hormone-releasing hormone. FAMILY PLANNING PERSPECTIVES. 15(1):32, 35, January-February 1983.

Maintenance of mating-induced, regulatory patterns in castrated, testosterone-treated male rats, by F. A. Weizenbaum, et al. APPETITE. 3(3):191-202, September 1982.

Monthly birth control? [synthetic inhibitory analog of luteinizing hormone-releasing hormone] . SCIENCE DIGEST. 91:89, July 1983.

Natural or hormone-induced sexual and social behaviors in the female brown lemming (lemmus trimucronatus), by U. W. Huck, et al. HORMONES AND BEHAVIOR. 16(2): 199-207, June 1982.

New prospects for luteinising hormone releasing hormone as a contraceptive and therapeutic agent, by H. M. Fraser. BRITISH MEDICAL JOURNAL. 6347:990-991, October 9, 1982.

POP . . . progestogen-only pill, by L. Pyle, et al. NURSING TIMES. 79(4):64-66, January 26-February 1, 1983.

CONTRACEPTIVES AND HORMONES (continued)

Variation of fat intake with estrous cycle, ovariectomy and estradiol replacement in hamsters, by M. O. Miceli, et al. PHYSIOLOGY AND BEHAVIOR. 30(3):415-420, March 1983.

CONTRACEPTIVES AND NURSING

Postpartum tubal ligation by nurse—midwives in Thailand: a field trial, by S. Satyapan, et al. STUDIES IN FAMILY PLANNING. 14(4):115-118, April 1983.

The role of the midwife in permanent contraception, by J. K. Gall, et al. JOURNAL OF NURSE-MIDWIFERY. 28(4): 13-17, July-August 1983.

CONTRACEPTIVES AND PHYSICIANS

NFP center reaches couples, teens, physicians, parents; St. Francis Regional Medical Center, Inc., Wichita, KS. HOSPITAL PROGRESS. 64:28+, April 1983.

Toledo doctor wages campaign against the pill, by A. Jones. NATIONAL CATHOLIC REPORTER. 18:1+, October 15, 1982.

CONTRACEPTIVES AND POLITICS

Dearth of contraception fuels world abortion debate. NATIONAL CATHOLIC REPORTER. 19:10, January 21, 1983.

CONTRACEPTIVES AND RELIGION

Catholic doctor who fought for the pill (John Rock), by L. McLaughlin. DISCOVER. 4:82+, February 1982.

Contraception and the rejection of God, by L. Ciccone. L'OSSERVATORE ROMANO. 50(813):9-10, December 12, 1983.

Contraception and the rhythm method, by C. Perry. RELIGIOUS HUMANISM. 17:36-39, Winter 1983.

Family size and contraceptive use among Mormons: 1965-1975, by T. B. Heaton, et al. REVIEW OF RELIGIOUS RESEARCH. 25(2):102-113, December 1983.

Moral dilemmas that are acute within a religious tradition. A Jewish perspective, by I. Franck. HOSPITAL PRACTICE. 18(7):192-196, July 1983.

Religiosity, sexual behavior and contraceptive use of college females, by M. Young. JOURNAL OF THE AMERICAN COLLEGE HEALTH ASSOCIATION. 30(5):216-220, April 1982.

CONTRACEPTIVES AND SEXUAL BEHAVIOR

Effects of androgen treatment of full-grown puberally castrated rats upon male sexual behavior, intermale aggressive behavior and the sequential patterning of aggressive interactions, by B. Bermond. BEHAVIOUR. 80(3-4):143-173, 1982.

Sex, sex guilt and contraceptive use, by M. Gerrard. JOURNAL OF PERSONALITY AND SOCIAL PSYCHOLOGY. 42:153-158, January 1982.

Sexual practice and the use of contraception, by J. Bell. HIGH SCHOOL JOURNAL. 65:241-244, April 1982.

CONTRACEPTIVES AND YOUTH

Adolescent autonomy and minors' legal rights: contraception and abortion, by H. Rodman, et al. JOURNAL OF APPLIED DEVELOPMENTAL PSYCHOLOGY. 3(4): 307-317, October-December 1982.

Adolescent development and its effects on sexual and contraceptive behavior: development and evaluation of a training design for health professionals, by C. D. Brindis. DISSERTATION ABSTRACTS INTERNATIONAL: A. 43(8), February 1983.

Adolescent sexuality, contraceptive and fertility decisions, by K. M. Charnowski. DISSERTATION ABSTRACTS INTERNATIONAL: A. 43(7), January 1983.

Challenging the teenage regulations: the legal battle, by P. Donovan. FAMILY PLANNING PERSPECTIVES. 15(3): 126-130, May-June 1983.

A comparison of responses to adolescent-oriented and traditional contraceptive programs, by S. G. Philliber, et al. JOURNAL OF AMBULATORY CARE MANAGEMENT. 6(2):32-42, May 1983.

Contraception is less risky for teenagers than is pregnancy. FAMILY PLANNING PERSPECTIVES. 14(5):274-276, September-October 1982.

Contraceptive practices of teenage mothers, by A. C. Washington, et al. JOURNAL OF THE NATIONAL MEDICAL ASSOCIATION. 75(11):1059-1063, November 1983.

Ethnic variation in adolescent use of a contraceptive service, by P. B. Namerow, et al. JOURNAL OF ADOLESCENT HEALTH CARE. 3(3):165-172, December 1982.

Ethical considerations concerning adolescents consulting for contraceptive services, by T. J. Silber. JOURNAL OF FAMILY PRACTICE. 15(5):909-911, November 1982.

An explanatory model of contraceptive use among young single women, by E. S. Herold, et al. JOURNAL OF SEX RESEARCH. 18:289-304, November 1982.

Factors affecting perception of pregnancy risk-in the adolescent, by P. B. Smith, et al. JOURNAL OF YOUTH AND ADOLESCENCE. 11(3):207-215, June 1982.

CONTRACEPTIVES AND YOUTH (continued)

Factors affecting sexual and contraceptive attitudes and
behaviors among adolescents, by R. S. Sterns. DIS-
SERTATION ABSTRACTS INTERNATIONAL: A.
43(10), April 1983.

Factors related to effective contraceptive use in adolescent
women, by D. M. Morrison. DISSERTATION ABSTRACTS
INTERNATIONAL: B. 43(12), June 1983.

First intercourse among young Americans, by M. Zelnik, et al.
FAMILY PLANNING PERSPECTIVES. 15(2):64-70,
March-April 1983.

The health belief model: can it help us to understand
contraceptive use among adolescents?, by E. S. Herold.
JOURNAL OF SCHOOL HEALTH. 53:19-21, January 1983.

Locus of control and the use of contraception among unmarried
black adolescent fathers and their controls: a preliminary
report, by L. E. Hendricks, et al. JOURNAL OF YOUTH
AND ADOLESCENCE. 12:225-233, June 1983.

Male adolescent psychosexual development: the influence of
significant others on contraceptive behavior, by D. D.
Cohen. DISSERTATION ABSTRACTS INTERNATIONAL:
A. 43(11), May 1983.

A model of premarital coitus and contraceptive behavior among
female adolescents, by W. M. Strahle. ARCHIVES OF
SEXUAL BEHAVIOR. 12:67, February 1983.

NFP center reaches couples, teens, physicians, parents; St.
Francis Regional Medical Center, Inc., Wichita, KS.
HOSPITAL PROGRESS. 64:28+, April 1983.

The need to know: recalled adolescent sources of sexual and
contraceptive information and sexual behavior, by D. J.
Kallen, et al. JOURNAL OF SEX RESEARCH. 19(2):
137-159, May 1983.

The nurse-midwife in a contraceptive program for adolescents, by G. Callender-Green, et al. JOURNAL OF AMBULATORY CARE MANAGEMENT. 6(2):57-65, May 1983.

Patterns of contraceptive use among female adolescents: method consistency in a clinic setting, by M. Gorosh. JOURNAL OF ADOLESCENT HEALTH CARE. 3(2): 96-102, September 1982.

Planned parenthood attacks a parent's need to know [regulation requiring that parents be informed if clinics give minors contraceptives], by K. S. Kantzer. CHRISTIANITY TODAY. 27:11-13, May 20, 1983.

Prior contraceptive attempts among pregnant black adolescents, by B. H. Wade. DISSERTATION ABSTRACTS INTER-NATIONAL: A. 44(6), December 1983.

Psychological correlates of contraceptive behavior in late adolescent women, by R. J. Ma. DISSERTATION AB-STRACTS INTERNATIONAL: B. 44(5), November 1983.

Repeat pregnancies among metropolitan-area teenagers: 1971-1979, by M. A. Koenig, et al. FAMILY PLANNING PERSPECTIVES. 14(6):341-344, November-December 1982.

The right of minors to confidential access to contraceptives, by A. L. Morano. ALBANY LAW REVIEW. 47(1):214-240, 1982.

Sex and sympathy: contraceptive advice for under-16-year olds, by F. Hutchinson. SUNDAY TIMES. July 31, 1983, p. 16.

Sex education and contraceptive education in U. S. public high schools, by M. T. Orr. FAMILY PLANNING PER-SPECTIVES. 14(6):304-307, 309-313, November-December 1982.

Sexually active but not pregnant: a comparison of teens who

plan, by J. B. Jones, et al. JOURNAL OF YOUTH AND ADOLESCENCE. 12:235-251, June 1983.

A study on the use of contraceptives by adolescents, by M. A. Requillart. REVUE FRANCAISE DE SOCIOLOGIE. 24:81-96, January-March 1983.

A survey of attitudes concerning contraception and the resolution of teenage pregnancy, by C. Rinck, et al. ADOLESCENCE. 18(72):923-929, Winter 1983.

Talking to parents about sex, birth control does not have an impact on teenagers' contraceptive use. FAMILY PLANNING PERSPECTIVES. 14(5):279-280, September-October 1982.

Teen-agers and birth control, by G. F. Will. NEWSWEEK. 101:80, February 28, 1983.

Teenagers' assessment of reproductive health-care services . . . designed to prevent first adolescent pregnancies, by S. W. Nenney, et al. PATIENT COUNSELLING AND HEALTH EDUCATION. 4(3):152-155, 1983.

The risk of premarital first pregnancy among metropolitan-area teenagers: 1976 and 1979, by M. A. Koenig, et al. FAMILY PLANNING PERSPECTIVES. 14(5):239-241, 243-247, September-October 1982.

Theoretical framework for studying adolescent contraceptive use, by K. A. Urberg. ADOLESCENCE. 17(67):527-540, 1982.

Unwanted pregnancies amongst teenagers, by C. Francome. JOURNAL OF BIOSOCIAL SCIENCE. 15:139-144, April 1983.

Why teenagers get pregnant [failure to use contraceptives due to erotophobia (fear of sex)], by W. A. Fisher. PSYCHOLOGY TODAY. 17:70-71, March 1983.

CONTRACEPTIVES AND YOUTH (continued)

Young adult women's contraceptive decision: a comparison
of two predictive models of choice, by E. J. Herz.
DISSERTATION ABSTRACTS INTERNATIONAL: B.
44(3), September 1983.

FAMILY PLANNING: GENERAL

Birth rate status. Number of children desired and actual
situation, by M. Ritamies. KATILOLEHTI. 88(4):85-89,
April 1983.

Breastfeeding and family planning: meaningful integration
of services, by E. C. Baer. STUDIES IN FAMILY
PLANNING. 12(4):164-166, April 1981.

Commentary from Coeur d'Alene: one baby—or two?, by E.
R. Fox. WESTERN JOURNAL OF MEDICINE. 138(6):
894-895, June 1983.

Communication factors and their influence on family planning
behaviour among non-adopters, by M. M. Reddy. JOURNAL
OF FAMILY WELFARE. 29:12-20, March 1983.

Determinants of national family planning effort, by W. R.
Kelly, et al. POPULATION RESEARCH AND POLICY
REVIEW. 2(2):111-130, May 1983.

Differential childlessness by color: a further examination, by
J. E. Veevers. SOCIAL BIOLOGY. 29:180-186, Spring-
Summer 1982.

Genocide fears in a rural black community: an empirical
examination, by W. C. Farrell, et al. JOURNAL OF BLACK
STUDIES. 14(1):49-67, September 1983.

Modernity value orientations, fertility and family planning,
by K. P. Singh. JOURNAL OF FAMILY WELFARE. 29:84,
December 1982.

NFP center reaches couples, teens, physicians, parents.

HOSPITAL PROGRESS. 64(4):28, 30, 32, April 1983.

New population policies, by L. R. Brown. ENVIRONMENT. 25:32-33, July-August 1983.

Value scaling of family planning conditions, by B. Maspfuhl. ZENTRALBLATT FUR GYNAKOLOGIE. 104(15): 980-987, 1982.

Why now?, by J. I. Rosoff. FAMILY PLANNING PER-SPECTIVES. 14(4):180, July-August 1982.

AFRICA
Marital sexual relationships and birth spacing among two Yoruba sub-groups, by L. A. Adeokun. AFRICA. 52(4): 1-14, 1982.

Perceptions of family planning among rural Kenyan women, by T. E. Dow, et'al. STUDIES IN FAMILY PLANNING. 14:35-42, February 1983.

Postpartum lactational amenorrhoea as a means of family planning in the Sudan: a study of 500 cases, by A. D. Adnan, et al. JOURNAL OF BIOSOCIAL SCIENCE. 15:9-24, January 1983.

Promotion of birth spacing on Idjwi Island, Zaire, by M. Carael, et al. STUDIES IN FAMILY PLANNING. 14(5): 134-142, May 1983.

U. S. population policies, development, and the rural poor of Africa, by E. Green. JOURNAL OF MODERN AFRICAN STUDIES. 20:45-67, March 1982.

The use of traditional and modern methods of fertility control in Kinshasa, Zaire, by J. Bertrand, et al. POPULATION STUDIES. 37(1):129, March 1983.

FAMILY PLANNING: GENERAL (continued)

ASIA
Progress in controlling population growth in Asia, by G. Jones.
AUSTRALIAN FOREIGN AFFAIRS RECORD. 53:760-
763, December 1982.

AUSTRALIA
Australian family planning surveys: some problems of com-
parability, by D. Lucas. JOURNAL OF BIOSOCIAL
SCIENCE. 15(3):357-366, July 1983.

CANADA
Ontario law on family planning classes causes uproar. OUR
SUNDAY VISITOR. 71:8, March 6, 1983.

CHINA
An approach to family planning for Indochinese refugee women,
by N. J. Presswell. AUSTRALIAN FAMILY PHYSICIAN.
11(8):644-645, 647-648, August 1982.

China's population crisis, by P. R. Ehrlich, et al. MOTHER
EARTH NEWS. 81:150-151, May-June 1983.

DEVELOPING COUNTRIES
The decline in the birth rate and its consequences for planning
in different sectors in developed capitalized countries, by J.
C. Chesnais. POPULATION. 37:1133-1158, November-
December 1982.

Perspectives on family and fertility in developing countries,
by M. Cain. POPULATION STUDIES. 36(2):159, July 1982.

Population growth and the policy of nations [developing
countries; emphasis on India] , by R. E. Benedick. DE-
PARTMENT OF STATE BULLETIN. 82:53-56, December
1982.

Third world family planning programs: measuring the costs,
by N. Yinger, et al. POPULATION BULLETIN. February
1983.

EGYPT

Marriage, fertility and family planning: summary of the major findings of the Egyptian rural fertility survey 1979. POPULATION STUDIES. 9:37-49, January-March 1982.

EUROPE

Low fertility in Europe: a report from the 1981 IUSSP meeting [International Union for the Scientific Study of Population], by D. Wulf. FAMILY PLANNING PERSPECTIVES. 14: 264-270, September-October 1982.

GREAT BRITAIN

Do we need a domiciliary family planning service?, by A. Arnheim. HEALTH VISITOR. 56(5):162-163, May 1983.

INDIA

Changing conceptions of family regulation among the Hindu East Indians in rural Trinidad, by J. Nevadomsky. ANTHROPOLOGICAL QUARTERLY. 55:189-198, October 1982.

Coercion in a soft state: the family planning program of India, by M. Vicziany. PACIFIC AFFAIRS. 55:373-402, Fall 1982-1983; 557-592, Winter 1982-1983.

Influence of background and programme factors on the family programme in India, by K. B. Pathak, et al. JOURNAL OF FAMILY WELFARE. 29:3-11, March 1983.

Population growth and the policy of nations [developing countries; emphasis on India], by R. E. Benedick. DEPARTMENT OF STATE BULLETIN. 82:53-56, December 1982.

Quantitative effect of family planning programme in India (1965-1976), by A. S. Mohammad, et al. INDIAN JOURNAL OF PUBLIC HEALTH. 25(3):111-116, July-September 1981.

INDONESIA

Technology transfer aids Indonesian family planning program

FAMILY PLANNING: GENERAL (continued)

[Japan] , by M. Tanaka. BUSINESS JAPAN. 27:61+,
November 1982.

IRELAND
Components of period fertility in the Irish Republic, 1962-
1977, by K. Wilson-Davis. JOURNAL OF BIOSOCIAL
SCIENCE. 15:95-106, January 1983.

ISRAEL
Coping with fertility in Israel: a case study of culture clash,
by E. Basker. CULTURE, MEDICINE AND PSYCHIATRY.
7(2):199-211, June 1983.

JAMAICA
Patterns of contraceptive use in Kingston and St. Andrew,
Jamaica, 1970-1977, by W. Bailey, et al. SOCIAL SCIENCE
AND MEDICINE. 16(19):1675-1683, 1982.

The Women's Centre in Jamaica: an innovative project for
adolescent mothers, by P. McNeill, et al. STUDIES IN
FAMILY PLANNING. 14(5):143-149, 1983.

KOREA
Intermediate variables and educational differentials in fertility
in Korea and the Philippines, by L. Bumpass, et al. DEMOG-
RAPHY. 19:241-260, May 1982.

The transition in Korean family planning behavior, 1935-1976:
a retrospective cohort analysis, by J. R. Foreit. STUDIES
IN FAMILY PLANNING. 13(8-9):227-236, 1982.

MEXICO
Demographic characteristics, wish and intent to procreate, and
the use of contraception in a group of women in Mexico
City, by E. Casanueva, et al. REVISTA DE INVESTIGACION
CLINICA. 35(1):21-26, January-March 1983.

Mass communication, cosmopolite channels, and family planning
among villagers in Mexico, by F. Korzenny, et al. DEVELOP-
MENT AND CHANGE. 14(2):237-253, April 1983.

Modern and traditional fertility regulation in a Mexican community: the process of decision making, by M. G. Shedlin, et al. STUDIES IN FAMILY PLANNING. 12(6-7):278-296, June-July 1981.

Population and family planning in Mexico: progress and problems, by D. Wulf. INTERNATIONAL FAMILY PLANNING PERSPECTIVES. 8:135-140, December 1982.

MIDDLE EAST

Successful family planning based on humanistic approach [Japanese Organization for International Cooperation in Family Planning], by C. Kunii. BUSINESS JAPAN. 27:69-70, November 1982.

PHILIPPINES

Intermediate variables and educational differentials in fertility in Korea and the Philippines, by L. Bumpass, et al. DEMOG-RAPHY. 19:241-260, May 1982.

The Philippine population program. NEWSETTE. 21(4):18-20, October-December 1981.

Providing maternal and child health-family planning services to a large rural population: results of the Bohol Project, Philippines, by N. E. Williamson, et al. AMERICAN JOURNAL OF PUBLIC HEALTH. 73(1):62-71, January 1983.

PUERTO RICO

A model of fertility control in a Puerto Rican community, by S. L. Schensul, et al. URBAN ANTHROPOLOGY. 11(1): 81-99, Spring 1982.

TAIWAN

Modernity and fertility preference in Taiwan, by K. Yamanaka, et al. SOCIOLOGICAL QUARTERLY. 23:539-552, August 1982.

FAMILY PLANNING: GENERAL (continued)

Trends in fertility, family size preferences, and family planning practice: Taiwan, 1961-1980, by M. C. Chang, et al. STUDIES IN FAMILY PLANNING. 12(5):211-228, May 1981.

THAILAND
Thailand's family planning program: an Asian success story, by A. Rosenfield, et al. INTERNATIONAL FAMILY PLANNING PERSPECTIVES. 8:43-51, June 1982.

TURKEY
Scholarship report of a 1982 study trip in western and middle Turkey, by A. L. Ericsson. JORDEMODERN. 95(10):337-340, October 1982.

UNITED STATES
Assessing the impact of copayment on family planning services: a preliminary analysis in California, by B. M. Aved, et al. AMERICAN JOURNAL OF PUBLIC HEALTH. 73(7): 763-765, July 1983.

The effect of administration family planning policy on maternal and child health, by L. S. Zabin. JOURNAL OF PUBLIC HEALTH POLICY. 4:268-278, September 1983.

Family planning and female sterilization in the United States, by T. M. Shapiro, et al. SOCIAL SCIENCE AND MEDICINE. 17(23):1847-1855, 1983.

Family planning clinic services in the United States, 1981, by A. Torres, et al. FAMILY PLANNING PERSPECTIVES. 15(6):272-278, November-December 1983.

Patient profile, national reporting system for family planning services: United States, 1978, by J. E. Foster. ADVANCE DATA. (73):1-6, June 24, 1981.

Subsidized family planning services in Texas, by L. W. Mondy. TEXAS MEDICINE. 78(11):58-62, November 1982.

FAMILY PLANNING: ATTITUDES

Attitudes of college males toward parenthood timing, by
D. B. Eversoll, et al. JOURNAL OF HOME ECONOMICS.
75(4):25-29, 49, Winter 1983.

Family planning among the Urban poor: sexual politics and
social policy, by M. Cummings, et al. FAMILY RELATIONS.
32(1):47-58, January 1983.

FAMILY PLANNING: ECONOMICS

Assessing the impact of copayment on family planning services:
a preliminary analysis in California, by B. M. Aved, et al.
AMERICAN JOURNAL OF PUBLIC HEALTH. 73(7):
763-765, July 1983.

Family planning, cost benefits and the nursing role, by A.
Leathard. MIDWIFE, HEALTH VISITOR AND COMMUNITY
NURSE. 18(12):526-527, 536, December 1982.

Relationship between socio-economic-status and attitude towards
family planning, by Mrs. S. Pratap, et al. PERSPECTIVES IN
PSYCHOLOGICAL RESEARCHES. 5(2):31, October 1982.

FAMILY PLANNING: HISTORY

Clinical research work of the Institute for Family Planning in
the area of intrauterine contraception from 1964-1980, by
M. Kozuh-Novak. JUGOSLAVENSKA GINEKOLOGIJA
I OPSTETRICIJA. 21(1-2):54-57, January-April 1981.

The development of the Institute for Family Planning in
Ljubljana, by Z. Ograjensek. JUGOSLAVENSKA GINE-
KOLOGIJA I OPSTETRICIJA. 21(1-2):50-53, January-
April 1981.

FAMILY PLANNING: LAWS AND LEGISLATION

Fertility-related state laws enacted in 1982 [laws affecting
sterilization, abortion, insurance benefits for pregnancy-
related health care, family planning services and information,

FAMILY PLANNING: LAWS AND LEGISLATION (continued)

and maternal and infant health; United States] , by D.
Bush. FAMILY PLANNING PERSPECTIVES. 15:111-
116, May-June 1983.

Some areas of the law relevant to family planning in medical
practice: an analysis from a comparative perspective, by
D. C. Jayasuriya. CEYLON MEDICAL JOURNAL. 24(3-4):
58-64, September-December 1979.

FAMILY PLANNING: METHODS

Complications of sickle cell disease, by I. Walters, et al.
NURSING CLINICS OF NORTH AMERICA. 18(1):
139-184, March 1983.

FAMILY PLANNING: NATURAL

Couple computerizes NFP. REGISTER. 59:2, August 28, 1983.

Couple to couple league, hospitals cooperate in teaching NFP,
by J. F. Kippley. HOSPITAL PROGRESS. 64:57, March
1983.

Faith, reason popularize natural family planning, by A. Jones.
NATIONAL CATHOLIC REPORTER. 19:1+, October 22,
1982.

For recognizing one's fertile period: Bioself. KRANKEN-
PFLEGE. (5):42, May 1983.

NFP center reaches couples, teens, physicians, parents. . . natural
family planning. HOSPITAL PROGRESS. 64(4):28, 30, 32,
April 1983.

NFP services in Catholic hospitals, by J. T. McHugh. LINACRE
QUARTERLY. 50:246-250, August 1983.

Natural family planning, by C. Bourdillon. CENTRAL AFRICAN
JOURNAL OF MEDICINE. 28(11):284-287, November
1982.

FAMILY PLANNING: NATURAL (continued)

Natural family planning: a birth control alternative, by N. Matis. JOURNAL OF NURSE-MIDWIFERY. 28(1):7-16, January-February 1983.

Natural family planning, an interview with Phyllis Jones, by G. Erlandson. REGISTER. 59:1+, July 24, 1983.

Natural family planning requires sexual maturity, by P. Cullen. OUR SUNDAY VISITOR. 72:5, November 6, 1983.

Natural means of birth control, by L. Dumas. INFIRMIERE CANADIENNE. 24(9):19-30, October 1982.

Psychological aspects of family planning, by K. D. Bledin. MIDWIFE, HEALTH VISITOR AND COMMUNITY NURSE. 18(12):518, 522-523, December 1982.

Survey discloses NFP practices, preferences in U. S. Catholic hospitals, by M. C. Martin, et al. HOSPITAL PROGRESS. 64:52-58, February 1983.

Technological marvel: not tonight, dear, the computer is beeping. NATIONAL CATHOLIC REPORTER. 19:1+, April 29, 1983.

FAMILY PLANNING: PLANNED PARENTHOOD

Planned parenthood affiliates served 1.5 million in 1981. FAMILY PLANNING PERSPECTIVES. 15(3):136, May-June 1983.

Planned parenthood, Shandong style. BEIJING REVIEW. 26:24-26, February 14, 1983.

FAMILY PLANNING: PSYCHOLOGY AND PSYCHIATRY

A survey of marital status and family planning of schizophrenics, by Y. Z. Fang. CHUNG HUA SHEN CHING CHING SHEN KO TSA CHIH. 15(4):204-206, November 1982.

Abortion in sows and the isolation of Pasteurella ureae, by J. D. Corkish, et al. VETERINARY RECORD. 110:582, June 19, 1982.

A critique of focus group and survey research: the machismo case, by J. M. Stycos. STUDIES IN FAMILY PLANNING. 12(12 pt 1):450-456, December 1981.

Family planning field research projects: balancing internal against external validity, by A. A. Fisher, et al. STUDIES IN FAMILY PLANNING. 14(1):3, January 1983.

Isolation of leptospira interrogans serovar hardjo from aborted bovine fetuses in England, by S. C. Hathaway, et al. VETERINARY RECORD. 111:58, July 17, 1982.

Pregnancy failure in the red-backed vole, clethrionomys gapperi, by F. V. Clulow, et al. JOURNAL OF MAMMALOGY. 63:499-500, August 1982.

Research in the area of family planning from the aspect of public health, by C. C. Standley, et al. JUGOSLAVENSKA GINEKOLOGIJA I OPSTETRICIJA. 21(1-2):3-5, January-April 1981.

Research in family planning: 1. WHO CHRONICLES. 36(4): 153-155, 1982.

Research in family planning: 2. WHO CHRONICLES. 36(5): 179, 1982.

Some biological insights into abortion, by G. Hardin. BIOSCIENCE. 32:720+, October 1982.

FAMILY PLANNING: RURAL

Acceptance of family planning practice among rural women clientele, by G. Kaur, et al. INDIAN JOURNAL OF PUBLIC HEALTH. 26(3):194-199, July-September 1982.

Changing conceptions of family regulation among the Hindu East Indians in rural Trinidad, by J. Nevadomsky. ANTHROPOLOGICAL QUARTERLY. 55:189-198, October 1982.

Perceptions of family planning among rural Kenyan women, by T. E. Dow, Jr., et al. STUDIES IN FAMILY PLANNING. 14(2):35, February 1983.

Providing maternal and child health-family planning services to a large rural population: results of the Bohol project, Philippines, by N. E. Williamson, et al. AMERICAN JOURNAL OF PUBLIC HEALTH. 73:62-71, January 1983.

U. S. population policies, development, and the rural poor of Africa, by E. Green. JOURNAL OF MODERN AFRICAN STUDIES. 20:45-67, March 1982.

Waiting times to first birth in a rural area, by L. Rosetta. ANNALS OF HUMAN BIOLOGY. 10(4):347-352, July-August 1983.

FAMILY PLANNING: STATISTICS

Population reports. Community-based health and family planning, by A. J. Kols, et al. POPULATION REPORTS SERIES L. (3):77-111, November-December 1982.

State of the world population [trends and family planning programs], by R. M. Salas. POPULI. 9(2):3-12, 1982.

Socio-demographic correlates of the decision process for medical termination of pregnancy and family planning, by A. R. Chaurasia, et al. INDIAN JOURNAL OF PUBLIC HEALTH. 26(1):4-9, January-March 1982.

FAMILY PLANNING: URBAN

Family planning among the urban poor: sexual politics and social policy, by M. Cummings, et al. FAMILY RELATIONS.

FAMILY PLANNING: URBAN (continued)

32:47-58, January 1983.

FAMILY PLANNING AND COLLEGE STUDENTS

Attitudes of college males toward parenthood timing, by D. B. Eversoll, et al. JOURNAL OF HOME ECONOMICS. 75(4):25-29, 49, Winter 1983.

FAMILY PLANNING AND THE HANDICAPPED

Family planning and the handicapped, by C. Welman. CURATIONIS. 5(3):54-56, September 1982.

FAMILY PLANNING AND HOSPITALS

The need for family planning in psychiatric hospitals, by G. Holloway. NURSING TIMES. 78(49):2087-2088, December 8-14, 1982.

Survey discloses NFP practices, preferences in U. S. Catholic hospitals, by M. C. Martin, et al. HOSPITAL PROGRESS. 64(2):52-58, February 1983.

FAMILY PLANNING AND NURSES

The nurse-midwife in a contraceptive program for adolescents, by G. Callender-Green, et al. JOURNAL OF AMBULATORY CARE MANAGEMENT. 6(2):57-65, May 1983.

On trial: nursing, by A. J. Kellett. MISSOURI NURSE. 51(3): 2-3, June-July 1982.

Vital aspects of nursing: the family planning component, by U. Bhandari, et al. NURSING JOURNAL OF INDIA. 73(5): 141-143, May 1982.

FAMILY PLANNING AND PARENTAL CONSENT

Planned parenthood attacks a parent's need to know, by K. S. Kantzer. CHRISTIANITY TODAY. 27:11-13, May 20, 1983.

FAMILY PLANNING AND PARENTAL CONSENT (continued)

Reagan wants parents to be told when teens get contraceptives. CHRISTIANITY TODAY. 26:41, April 23, 1982.

Should parents be told when teens get contraceptives: no, says the judge, that would be illegal. CHRISTIANITY TODAY. 27:22, March 18, 1983.

FAMILY PLANNING AND RELIGION

Family size and contraceptive use among Mormons: 1965-1975, by T. B. Heaton, et al. REVIEW OF RELIGIOUS RESEARCH. 25(2):102-113, December 1983.

Fertility and family planning behaviour among Muslims: a study in a village in Andhra Pradesh. HEALTH AND POPULATION: PERSPECTIVES AND ISSUES. 4(3): 151-162, July-September 1981.

Fertility and family planning in the 1970's, by W. D. Mosher. NATIONAL SURVEY OF FAMILY GROWTH. 14(6): 314-319, November-December 1982.

The Mumford affair. HUMANIST. 43(6):5-10, November-December 1983.

Survey discloses NFP practices, preferences in U. S. Catholic hospitals, by M. C. Martin, et al. HOSPITAL PROGRESS. 64(2):52-58, February 1983.

FAMILY PLANNING AND WOMEN

Nutritional status of women attending family planning clinics, by D. A. Roe, et al. JOURNAL OF AMERICAN DIETETIC ASSOCIATION. 81:682-687, December 1982.

FAMILY PLANNING AND YOUTH

A comparison of responses to adolescent-oriented and traditional contraceptive programs, by S. G. Philliber, et al. JOURNAL OF AMBULATORY CARE MANAGEMENT. 6(2):32-42, May 1983.

Developmental issues for adolescent parents and their children, by V. Washington, et al. EDUCATIONAL HORIZON'S. 61(4):195-199, Summer 1983.

Follow-up of adolescent family planning clinic users, by P. B. Namerow, et al. FAMILY PLANNING PERSPECTIVES. 15(4):172-176, July-August 1983.

Innovative approaches for reaching young people in health and family planning programs, by E. Vadies. BULLETIN OF THE PAN AMERICAN HEALTH ORGANIZATION. 16(4):323-328, 1982.

Institutional factors affecting teenagers choice and reasons for delay in attending a family planning clinic, by L. S. Zabin, et al. FAMILY PLANNING PERSPECTIVES. 15:25-29, January-February 1983.

The nurse-midwife in a contraceptive program for adolescents, by G. Callender-Green, et al. JOURNAL OF AMBULATORY CARE MANAGEMENT. 6(2):57-65, May 1983.

Project redirection results in better method use, fewer second pregnancies among teenage parents. FAMILY PLANNING PERSPECTIVES. 14(6):335-336, November-December 1982.

Selected family planning and general health profiles in a teen health clinic, by P. B. Smith, et al. JOURNAL OF ADOLESCENT HEALTH CARE. 2(4):267-272, June 1982.

Teenagers' assessment of reproductive health-care services, by S. W. Nenney, et al. PATIENT COUNSELLING AND HEALTH EDUCATION. 4(3):152-155, 1983.

The Women's Centre in Jamaica: an innovative project for adolescent mothers, by P. McNeil, et al. STUDIES IN FAMILY PLANNING. 14(5):143-149, May 1983.

Acceptability of medroxyprogesterone acetate among medical and paramedical personnel in family planning, by A. Cervantes, et al. GINECOLOGIA Y OBSTETRICIA DE MEXICO. 50(300):85-88, April 1982.

Acquaintance with the private clinic. Study of the use of a lay center, by G. Remotti, et al. ANNALI DI OBSTETRICIA GINECOLOGIA, MEDICINA PERINATALE. 103(3):237-240, May-June 1982.

Assessing the impact of copayment on family planning services: a preliminary analysis in California, by B. M. Aved, et al. AMERICAN JOURNAL OF PUBLIC HEALTH. 73:763-765, July 1983.

Assessment of reproductive knowledge in an inner-city clinic, by S. M. Johnson, et al. SOCIAL SCIENCE AND MEDICINE. 16(19):1657-1662, 1982.

Basic data on women who use family planning clinics: United States, 1980, by B. Bloom. VITAL HEALTH STATISTICS. 13(67):1-46, September 1982.

Community-based health and family planning. POPULATION REPORTS SERIES L. (3), 1982.

Community family planning clinics. An evaluation, by K. E. Schopflin. PRACTITIONER. 227(1379):829-831, May 1983.

Cutting the umbilical cord: can family planning clinics survive without government funding?, by L. A. Villadsen. REASON. 14:21-26, February 1983.

Family planning clinic services in the United States, 1981, by A. Torres, et al. FAMILY PLANNING PERSPECTIVES. 15(6):272-278, November-December 1983.

Institutional factors affecting teenagers' choice and reasons for delay in attending a family planning clinic, by L. Zabin,

et al. FAMILY PLANNING PERSPECTIVES. 15(1):25,
January-February 1983.

Nutritional status of women attending family planning clinics,
by D. A. Roe, et al. JOURNAL OF THE AMERICAN
DIETETIC ASSOCIATION. 81(6):682-687, December
1982.

Selected family planning and general health profiles in a teen
health clinic, by P. B. Smith, et al. JOURNAL OF ADO-
LESCENT HEALTH CARE. 2(4):267-272, June 1982.

Self-sustaining clinics: innovation or retreat?, by L. C. Landman.
FAMILY PLANNING PERSPECTIVES. 15(5):218-223,
September-October 1983.

FAMILY PLANNING PROGRAMS

Do we need a domiciliary family planning service?, by A.
Arnheim. HEALTH VISITOR. 56(5):162-163, May 1983.

Experiences in the treatment of childless couples in a family
service institute with special reference to andrologic problems,
by I. Aszodi. ZEITSCHRIFT FUER HAUTKRANKHEITEN
H UND G. 58(7):456-459, April 1, 1983.

The family planning association. HEALTH VISITOR. 56(5):
165-166, May 1983.

Family planning perspectives, by O. J. Sikes. POPULI. 9(2):
25, 1982.

The family planning service, by K. Arger. MIDWIFE, HEALTH
VISITOR AND COMMUNITY NURSE. 19(1):14-15,
January 1983.

Know your organizations: the Brook Advisory Centres. HEALTH
VISITOR. 55(4):177-178, April 1982.

Palaces of advice . . . results of a survey on where people obtain

FAMILY PLANNING PROGRAMS (continued)

family planning advice and reasons for their choice, by J. Bunting. NURSING MIRROR AND MIDWIVE'S JOURNAL. 156(3):Community Forum 1:34-36, January 19, 1983.

Primary health care and community-based family planning. POPULATION REPORTS. (3):79, November-December 1982.

Sources of population and family planning assistance. POPULATION REPORTS. (26):J621-655, January-February 1983.

Using model projects to introduce change into family planning programs, by M. H. Bernhart. STUDIES IN FAMILY PLANNING. 12(10):346-352, October 1981.

FAMILY PLANNING COUNSELLING

Community forum. 1. Family planning. Palaces of advice, by J. Bunting. NURSING MIRROR AND MIDWIVE'S JOURNAL. 156(3):34-36, January 19, 1983.

Experiences from a sex-counseling and birth control practice for adolescents, by H. J. Ahrendt. ZEITSCHRIFT FUR ARZTLICHE FORTBILDUNG. 77(5):201-205, 1983.

The health visitor, family planning and personal relationship, by H. Martins. HEALTH VISITOR. 56(5):161-162, May 1983.

New guidelines on counseling in family planning. KATILOLEHTI. 87(7-8):249-251, August 1982.

FAMILY PLANNING EDUCATION

Family planning education, by M. V. Hamburg. JOURNAL OF SCHOOL HEALTH. 53(2):108-111, February 1983.

Family-planning education in Michigan schools, by K. Sung. PUBLIC HEALTH REVIEWS. 10(2):199-212, April-June 1982.

FAMILY PLANNING EDUCATION (continued)

Glimpses of health programs in the people's republic of China: family planning education, by M. V. Hamburg. JOURNAL OF SCHOOL HEALTH. 53:108-111, February 1983.

Health practices: family planning and sex education, by C. Bailey. NURSING. 2(2):32-33, June 1982.

The health visitor, family planning and personal relationships . . . methods used to teach professional people, by H. Martins. HEALTH VISITOR. 56(5):161-162, May 1983.

Values clarification as a technique for family planning education, by J. V. Toohey, et al. JOURNAL OF SCHOOL HEALTH. 53(2):121-125, February 1983.

FAMILY PLANNING FUNDING

Assessing the impact of copayment on family planning services: a preliminary analysis in California, by B. M. Aved, et al. AMERICAN JOURNAL OF PUBLIC HEALTH. 73(7):763-765, July 1983.

An evaluation of the declaration method of eligibility determination, by G. T. Berns. ADMINISTRATION IN SOCIAL WORK. 7(2):23-36, Summer 1983.

Cutting the umbilical cord: can family planning clinics survive without government funding?, by L. A. Villadsen. REASON. 14:21-26, February 1983.

The family planning program and cuts in federal spending. Initial effects on the provision of services part 2, by A. Torres. FAMILY PLANNING PERSPECTIVES. 15(4):184-188, July-August 1983.

Subsidized family planning services in Texas credited with averting 56,000 pregnancies, saving 30 million dollars. FAMILY PLANNING PERSPECTIVES. 15:86-87, March-April 1983.

314

Third world family planning programs: measuring the costs, by N. Yinger, et al. POPULATION BULLETIN. February 1983.

FERTILITY AND FERTILITY CONTROL

Adolescent sexuality, contraceptive and fertility decisions, by K. M. Charnowski. DISSERTATION ABSTRACTS INTER-NATIONAL: A. 43(7), January 1983.

Age at menarche and fertility in Haiti, by J. Allman. HUMAN ORGANIZATION. 41:350-354, Winter 1982.

An analysis of factors affecting traditional family expectations and perceptions of ideal fertility, by W. J. Scott, et al. SEX ROLES. 9:901-914, August 1983.

An analysis of variations in U. S. fertility and female labor force participation trends, by B. Devaney. DEMOGRAPHY. 20:147-162, May 1983.

Breastfeeding and fertility control, by C. W. Tyler, Jr. AMERICAN JOURNAL OF PUBLIC HEALTH. 73: 364-365, April 1983.

Cohort fertility of Czech and Slovak women since 1930, by Y. Lesny. POPULATION. 38:267-282, March-April 1983.

Consumer demand and household production: the relationship between fertility and child mortality, by M. R. Rosenzeig, et al. AMERICAN ECONOMIC REVIEW. 73:38-42, May 1983.

Contraception and fertility in the Netherlands, by E. Ketting. FAMILY PLANNING PERSPECTIVES. 15(1):19-25, January-February 1983.

Coping with fertility in Israel: a case study of culture clash, by E. Basker. CULTURE, MEDICINE AND PSYCHIATRY. 7(2):199-211, June 1983.

The development of fertility in Romania: a longitudinal study, by V. Ghetau. POPULATION. 38:247-266, March-April 1983.

Do couples make fertility plans one birth at a time?, by J. R. Udry. DEMOGRAPHY. 20(2):117-128, May 1983.

Error patterns in the prediction of fertility behavior, by A. R. Davidson, et al. JOURNAL OF APPLIED SOCIAL PSYCHOLOGY. 11:475-488, November-December 1981.

Fertility and acquisition of property, by C. Bonvalet. POPULA-TION. 37:1198-1204, November-December 1982.

Fertility awareness: the University of California/Berkeley experience, by G. Kramer. JOURNAL OF THE AMERICAN COLLEGE HEALTH ASSOCIATION. 31(4):166-167, February 1983.

Fertility control, by M. J. Harper. MEDICINAL RESEARCH REVIEWS. 2(4):403-432, October-December 1982.

Fertility could plummet, if. U N CHRONICLE. 19:81-82, July 1982.

Fertility, development and family planning, by S. Menard. STUDIES IN COMPARATIVE INTERNATIONAL DEVELOPMENT. 17(3):77-100, Fall 1983.

Fertility rate slows in 1980, but large increases continue among older mothers, unmarried women. FAMILY PLANNING PERSPECTIVES. 15:38-39, January-February 1983.

Fertility-related state laws enacted in 1982, by D. Bush. FAMILY PLANNING PERSPECTIVES. 15(3):111-116, May-June 1983.

Modern and traditional fertility regulation in a Mexican community: the process of decision making, by M. G. Shedlin, et al. STUDIES IN FAMILY PLANNING.

12(6-7):278-296, June-July 1981.

Mortality associated with fertility and fertility control—1983, by H. W. Ory. FAMILY PLANNING PERSPECTIVES. 15:57-63, March-April 1983.

Principles to be considered in fertility control, by E. Donache. AUSTRALASIAN NURSES JOURNAL. 11(7):1, August 1982.

Safety of fertility control, by C. W. Tyler, Jr., et al. JUGO-SLAVENSKA GINEKOLOGIJA I OPSTETRICIJA. 21(1-2): 27-34, January-April 1981.

Sexuality, fertility and fertility control, by A. Woodhouse. WOMEN'S STUDIES INTERNATIONAL FORUM. 5(1): 1-15, 1982.

Socioeconomic determinants of fertility, by G. Arora. JOURNAL OF FAMILY WELFARE. 29:39-52, March 1983.

A spatial autocorrelation model of the effects of population density on fertility, by C. Loftin, et al. AMERICAN SOCIOLOGICAL REVIEW. 48:121-128, February 1983.

FERTILITY AND FERTILITY STATISTICS

Compulsory birth control and fertility measures in India, by S. S. Halli. SIMULATION AND GAMES. 14(4):429-444, December 1983.

Female employment and fertility in the Dominican Republic: a dynamic perspective, by D. T. Gurak, et al. AMERICAN SOCIOLOGICAL REVIEW. 47:810-818, December 1982.

Fertility and fertility planning behaviour among Muslims: a study in a village in Andhra Pradesh. HEALTH AND POPULATION: PERSPECTIVES AND ISSUES. 4(3): 151-162, July-September 1981.

317

A model of fertility control in a Puerto Rican community, by
S. L. Schensul, et al. URBAN ANTHROPOLOGY. 11(1):
81-99, Spring 1982.

The Mumford affair. HUMANIST. 43(6):5-10, November-
December 1983.

Spontaneous abortion: the role of heterogeneous risk and
selective fertility, by A. J. Wilcox, et al. EARLY HUMAN
DEVELOPMENT. 7(2):165-178, November 1982.

The use of traditional and modern methods of fertility control
in Kinshasa, Zaire, by J. Bertrand, et al. POPULATION
STUDIES. 37(1):129, March 1983.

HYSTERECTOMY

Effects of hysterectomy on sexual receptivity, food intake,
running wheel activity and hypothalanic ostrogen and
progestin receptors in rats, by H. B. Ahdieh, et al. JOURNAL
OF COMPARATIVE AND PHYSIOLOGICAL PSYCHOL-
OGY. 96(6):886-892, December 1982.

Hysterectomy and sexual counseling, by J. Ananth. PSYCHI-
ATRIC JOURNAL OF THE UNIVERSITY OF OTTAWA.
8(4):213-217, December 1983.

Hysterectomy and sterilisation rates. Regional variations, by
W. Savage. PRACTITIONER. 227(1379):839-845, May
1983.

Hysterectomy following sterilization, by A. A. Templeton, et al.
BRITISH JOURNAL OF OBSTETRICS AND GYNAE-
COLOGY. 89(10):845-848, October 1982.

Hysterectomy in six European countries, by P. A. Van Keep,
et al. MATURITAS. 5(2):69-76, 1983.

Post-hysterectomy adaptation: a review and report of two
follow-up studies, by B. Singh, et al. AUSTRALIAN AND

NEW ZEALAND JOURNAL OF PSYCHIATRY. 17:227-236, September 1983.

MISCARRIAGE

Early miscarriage: are we too quick to dismiss the pain?, by T. M. Stephany. RN. 45(11):89, November 1982.

Menarcheal age and miscarriage, by E. J. Martin, et al. AMERICAN JOURNAL OF EPIDEMIOLOGY. 117(5): 634-636, May 1983.

'Miscarriage': a diagnostic dilemma, by B. A. Buehler. NEBRASKA MEDICAL JOURNAL. 68(5):143-144, May 1983.

Psychological aspects of miscarriage, by G. B. Bjork. KATILOLEHIT. 88(3):108-111, March 1983.

Seventeenth century midwifery: the treatment of miscarriage, by R. K. Marshall. NURSING MIRROR AND MIDWIVE'S JOURNAL. 155(24):31-36, December 15, 1982.

Some questions of identity: late miscarriage, stillbirth and perinatal loss, by A. Lovell. SOCIAL SCIENCE AND MEDICINE. 17(11):755-761, 1983.

Treating early miscarriage in the ED. EMERGENCY MEDICINE. 15(13):148-152, July 15, 1983.

Ultrasonic and endocrinological aspects of first trimester miscarriage, by S. Sakamoto, et al. ASIA-OCEANIA JOURNAL OF OBSTETRICS AND GYNAECOLOGY. 8(2):105-116, June 1982.

Vaginal spermicides and miscarriage seen primarily in the emergency room, by H. Jick, et al. TERATOGENESIS, CARCINOGENESIS AND MUTAGENESIS. 2(2):205-210, 1982.

SEX AND SEXUALITY

Marriage, sexuality and contraception in the British middle class, 1918-1939. The correspondence of Marie Stopes, by E. M. Holtzman. DISSERTATIONS ABSTRACTS INTERNATIONAL: A. 43(10), April 1983.

Reduction of teenage pregnancy as a rationale for sex education, by P. Dunn. JOURNAL OF SCHOOL HEALTH. 52(10):611-613, December 1982.

Sexuality, fertility and fertility control, by A. Woodhouse. WOMEN'S STUDIES INTERNATIONAL FORUM. 5(1):1-51, 1982.

Society anxiety, sexual behavior and contraceptive use, by M. R. Leary, et al. JOURNAL OF PERSONALITY AND SOCIAL PSYCHOLOGY. 45:1347-1354, December 1983.

STERILIZATION: GENERAL

Late sequelae of sterilization in women, by E. Garner, et al. UGESKRIFT FOR LAEGER. 144(40):2935-2938, October 4, 1982.

Reproductive decisions· adolescents with down syndrome, by J. K. Williams. PEDIATRIC NURSING. 9(1):43-44, 58, January-February 1983.

Reversible methods of sterilization [letter], by G. W. Rosemann, et al. SOUTH AFRICAN MEDICAL JOURNAL. 62(18):635, October 23, 1982.

Sterilization by laparoscopy, by P. C. Pelland. CLINICAL OBSTETRICS AND GYNECOLOGY. 26(2):321-333, June 1983.

Sterilization: contraception for both men and women, by T. P. Reed, III. CONSULTANT. 22(10):240-242, October 1982.

Sterilization performed at the time of a probably fertilized but not yet nidated ovum, by K. D. Skyggebjerg, et al. UGESKRIFT FOR LAEGER. 145(27):2096, July 4, 1983.

Sterilization without surgery has promise, by N. Brozan. NEW YORK TIMES. September 6, 1982, p. 38.

Sterilization without surgery . . . several methods for plugging the fallopian tubes, by M. Klitsch. FAMILY PLANNING PERSPECTIVES. 14(6):324-327, November-December 1982.

Surgical sterilization. Analysis of 250 cases, by D. Campos Navarro, et al. GINECOLOGIA Y OBSTETRICIA DE MEXICO. 50(301):111-114, May 1982.

Three neuroleptanalgesia schedules for laparoscopic sterilization by electrocoagulation, by S. Koetsawang, et al. INTER-NATIONAL JOURNAL OF GYNAECOLOGY AND OBSTETRICS. 21(2):133-137, April 1983.

Trials with the Femcept method of female sterilization and experience with radiopaque methylcyanoacrylate, by R. S. Neuwirth, et al. AMERICAN JOURNAL OF OBSTETRICS AND GYNECOLOGY. 145(8):948-954, April 15, 1983.

Wrongful birth: how much is it worth not to be born?, by E. B. Goldman. MICHIGAN HOSPITALS. 19(3):25, 27-28, March 1983.

BANGLADESH

Deaths from contraceptive sterilization in Bangladesh: rates, causes, and prevention, by D. A. Grimes, et al. OBSTETRICS AND GYNECOLOGY. 60(5):635-640, November 1982.

Demographic consequences, client satisfaction, and reasons for selecting sterilization among vasectomy and tubectomy clients in Bangladesh, by I. Swenson, et al. CONTRA-

CEPTION. 25(6):573-590, June 1982.

Sterilization in Bangladesh: mortality, morbidity, and risk factors, by M. J. Rosenberg, et al. INTERNATIONAL JOURNAL OF GYNAECOLOGY AND OBSTETRICS. 20(4):283-291, August 1982.

BELGIUM
Voluntary sterilization in Flanders, by R. L. Cliquet, et al. JOURNAL OF BIOSOCIAL SCIENCE. 13(1):47-61, January 1981.

BRAZIL
Interval sterilizations. A substitute for postpartum procedures, an example from Southeast Brazil, by B. Janowitz, et al. SOCIAL SCIENCE AND MEDICINE. 16(22):1979-1983, 1982.

CANADA
Catholic hospitals in today's Canada, by E. J. MacNeil. CHAC REVIEW. 10(4-5):12-15, July-October 1982.

Sterilization in Quebec, by N. Marcil-Gratton, et al. FAMILY PLANNING PERSPECTIVES. 15:73-77, March-April 1983.

CHINA
Sterilization acceptance in China, by H. Y. Tien. STUDIES IN FAMILY PLANNING. 13:287-292, October 1982.

COSTA RICA
Public policy and female sterilization in Costa Rica, by M. Gomez Barrantes, et al. STUDIES IN FAMILY PLANNING. 14(10):246-252, 1983.

EL SALVADOR
Sterilization of Salvadorans promoted by U. S. agency, by C. Hedges. NATIONAL CATHOLIC REPORTER. 20:1, November 11, 1983.

STERILIZATION: GENERAL (continued)

GERMANY

Involuntary sterilization in Germany from 1933 to 1945 and some consequences for today, by F. Pafflin, et al. INTERNATIONAL JOURNAL OF LAW AND PSYCHIATRY. 5(3-4):419-423, 1982.

Racism and sexism in Nazi Germany: motherhood, compulsory sterilization and the state, by G. Bock. SIGNS. 8(3):400-421, 1983.

GUATEMALA

Sterilization of Salvadorans promoted by U. S. agency, by C. Hedges. NATIONAL CATHOLIC REPORTER. 20:1, November 11, 1983.

Voluntary sterilization in Guatemala: a comparison of men and women, by G. Roberto Santiso, et al. STUDIES IN FAMILY PLANNING. 14(3):73, March 1983.

INDIA

Two-year follow-up of 3,466 sterilizations in India, by S. Pachauri, et al. JOURNAL OF REPRODUCTIVE MEDICINE. 27(8):459-463, August 1982.

ITALY

Sterilization—forbidden by Rome, pushed by U. S., by R. J. McClory. NATIONAL CATHOLIC REPORTER. 20:1+, November 11, 1983.

MEXICO

Contraceptive sterilization: a comparison of Mexican-Americans and Anglos living in U. S. counties bordering Mexico, by C. W. Warren, et al. SOCIAL BIOLOGY. 28(3-4):265-280, Fall-Winter 1981.

THAILAND

Postpartum tubal ligation by nurse—midwives in Thailand: a field trial, by S. Satyapan, et al. STUDIES IN FAMILY PLANNING. 14(4):115-118, April 1983.

STERILIZATION: GENERAL (continued)

UNITED STATES
Eugenic sterilization in Virginia: Aubrey Strode and the case of
Buck vs. Bell, by P. A. Lombardo. DISSERTATION
ABSTRACTS INTERNATIONAL: A. 43(10), April 1983.

Family planning and female sterilization in the United States,
by T. M. Shapiro, et al. SOCIAL SCIENCE AND MEDICINE.
17(23):1847-1855, 1983.

Sterilization—forbidden by Rome, pushed by U. S., by R.
J. McClory. NATIONAL CATHOLIC REPORTER. 20:1+,
November 11, 1983.

STERILIZATION: ATTITUDES

Husband-wife communication, wife's employment and the
decision for male or female sterilization, by F. D. Bean,
et al. JOURNAL OF MARRIAGE AND THE FAMILY.
45(2):395-403, May 1983.

STERILIZATION: COMPLICATIONS

Changes in menstrual blood loss and libido after different
methods of tubal ligation, by A. Neri, et al. INTER-
NATIONAL SURGERY. 67(4 suppl):527-528, October-
December 1982.

Complications after abdominal and vaginal sterilization
operation, by J. Misra. JOURNAL OF THE INDIAN
MEDICAL ASSOCIATION. 80(2):25-27, January 16,
1983.

Complications of laparoscopic sterilization, by B. Gonik, et al.
JOURNAL OF REPRODUCTIVE MEDICINE. 27(8):
471-473, August 1982.

Ectopic pregnancy after sterilization [letter], by A. McCausland.
OBSTETRICS AND GYNECOLOGY. 61(6):766, June 1983.

Endoscopy and pelvic infection, by S. L. Corson. CLINICAL OBSTETRICS AND GYNECOLOGY. 26(2):334-338, June 1983.

Failures of laparoscopic sterilization by Hulka-Clemens clips, by A. Tadjerouni, et al. EUROPEAN JOURNAL OF OBSTETRICS, GYNECOLOGY AND REPRODUCTIVE BIOLOGY. 14(6):393-398, March 1983.

Metrorrhagia after sterilization, by C. Nickelsen, et al. UGESKRIFT FOR LAEGER. 144(40):2938-2940, October 4, 1982.

A rare complication following the insertion of a bleier-secu-clip, by W. Behrendt. GEBURTSHILFE UND FRAUENHEIL-KUNDE. 43(4):248-249, April 1983.

Reproductive hazards in the workplace: bearing the burden of fetal risk, by R. Bayer. MILBANK MEMORIAL FUND QUARTERLY. 60(4):633-656, Fall 1982.

Risk of ectopic pregnancy following tubal sterilization, by F. Destefano, et al. OBSTETRICS AND GYNECOLOGY. 60(3): 326-330, 1982.

Risk of hysterectomy after sterilization [letter], by P. J. Cooper. LANCET. 1(8314-8315):59, January 1, 1983.

STERILIZATION: EDUCATION

Question and answers about female sterilization . . . patient education aid. PATIENT CARE. 17(9):147-148, May 15, 1983.

STERILIZATION: FEMALE

Characteristics and follow-up of sterilized women, by R. Molina, et al. REVISTA MEDICA DE CHILE. 110(2):175-180, February 1982.

A comparison of definable traits in women requesting reversal of sterilization and women satisfied with sterilization, by A. Leader, et al. AMERICAN JOURNAL OF OBSTETRICS AND GYNECOLOGY. 145(2):198-202, January 15, 1983.

Damages for the birth of a child—some possible policy barriers, by G. Robertson. MEDICINE, SCIENCE AND LAW. 23(1):2-4, January 1983.

Early postnatal sterilization, by R. Ichnovsky, et al. CESKOSLOVENSKA GYNEKOLOGIE. 48(2):117-118, March 1983.

Fertility following reversal of male and female sterilization, by E. Weisberg, et al. CONTRACEPTION. 26(4):361-371, October 1982.

Husband-wife communication, wife's employment and the decision for male and female sterilization, by F. D. Bean, et al. JOURNAL OF MARRIAGE AND THE FAMILY. 45(2):395-410, May 1983.

Laparoscopic sterilization of women, by O. H. Jensen, et al. TIDSSKRIFT FOR DEN NORSKE LAEGEFORENING. 102(19-21):1008-1009, July 10, 1982.

Mini-incision for post-partum sterilization of women: a multi-centred, multinational prospective study. CONTRACEPTION. 26(5):495-503, November 1982.

Psychodynamics of the desire for refertilization in women after sexual sterilization, by S. Davies-Osterkamp, et al. GEBURTSHILFE UND FRAUENHEILKUNDE. 43(5): 313-320, May 1983.

Reversal of female sterilization by magnification lens, by S. Srivannaboon. JOURNAL OF THE MEDICAL ASSOCIATION OF THAILAND. 66(1):7-9, January 1983.

STERILIZATION: FEMALE (continued)

Reversal of female sterilization: a review, by G. P. Wood.
JOURNAL OF THE ARKANSAS MEDICAL SOCIETY.
79(12):443-444, May 1983.

Sterilization of mentally retarded women, by W. Heidenreich,
et al. GEBURTSHILFE UND FRAUENHEILKUNDE.
42(7):554-557, July 1982.

Sterilisation of women: prevalence and outcome, by A. F.
Wright. BRITISH MEDICAL JOURNAL. 285(6342):609-
611, August 28, 1982.

Tetanus complicating elective surgery. Two cases following
female sterilization, by J. M. Aubert, et al. TROPICAL
DOCTOR. 13(2):61-64, April 1983.

Tubal sterilization: characteristics of women most affected
by the option of reversibility, by R. N. Shain, et al. SOCIAL
SCIENCE AND MEDICINE. 16(10):1067-1077, 1982.

Voluntary sterilization in Guatemala: a comparison of men
and women, by G. Roberto Santiso, et al. STUDIES IN
FAMILY PLANNING. 14(3):73, March 1983.

What's new in female sterilization? The silicone tubal plug is,
by F. D. Loffer. ARIZONA MEDICINE. 39(7):442-445,
July 1982.

Women in toxic work environments: a case study of social
problem development, by D. M. Randall, et al. SOCIAL
PROBLEMS. 30:410-424, April 1983.

STERILIZATION: FEMALE: COMPLICATIONS

Women, work and reproductive hazards, by R. Bayer.
HASTINGS CENTER REPORT. 12:14-19, October 1982.

STERILIZATION: LAWS AND LEGISLATION

Damages for the birth of a child—some possible policy barriers, by G. Robertson. MEDICINE, SCIENCE AND LAW. 23(1): 2-4, January 1983.

Damages for wrongful birth, life and death, by A. H. Bernstein. HOSPITALS. 57(1):67, 70-72, January 1, 1983.

Developmental disability and human sexuality, by M. J. Krajicek. NURSING CLINICS OF NORTH AMERICA. 17(3):377-386, September 1982.

Dispositions—Indiana. JUVENILE AND FAMILY LAW DIGEST. 15(5):183-186, May 1983.

Dispositions—Maryland. JUVENILE AND FAMILY LAW DIGEST. 14(12):395-398, December 1982.

Eugenic sterilization in Virginia: Aubrey Strode and the case of Buck vs. Bell, by P. A. Lombardo. DISSERTATION ABSTRACTS INTERNATIONAL: A. 43(10), April 1983.

Fertility-related state laws enacted in 1982, by D. Bush. FAMILY PLANNING PERSPECTIVES. 15(3):111-116, May-June 1983.

In re guardianship of Eberhardy (Wis): the sterilization of the mentally retarded. WISCONSIN LAW REVIEW. 1982, p. 1199-1227.

Involuntary sterilization standard of evidence spelled out by court. THE FAMILY LAW REPORTER: COURT OPINIONS. 9(41):2623-2625, August 23, 1983.

Jurisdiction: the superior court possesses jurisdiction over petitions for sterilization of incompetents—in the matter of C. D. M. ALASKA LAW REVIEW. Spring 1982, p. 213-221.

Law: wrongful birth, by H. Creighton. NURSING MANAGE-MENT. 14(7):41-42, July 1983.

STERILIZATION: LAWS AND LEGISLATION (continued)

Sterilization—medical practices—life-endangering conditions.
THE FAMILY LAW REPORTER: COURT OPINIONS.
8(47):2717, October 5, 1982.

Sterilization petitions: developing judicial guidelines. MONTANA
LAW REVIEW. 44:127-136, Winter 1983.

Voluntary sterilization for persons with mental disabilities:
the need for legislation, by B. A. Burnett. SYRACUSE
LAW REVIEW. 32:913-955, Fall 1981.

STERILIZATION: MALE

Fertility following reversal of male and female sterilization,
by E. Weisberg, et al. CONTRACEPTION. 26(4):361-371,
October 1982.

Husband-wife communication, wife's employment and the
decision for male and female sterilization, by F. D. Bean,
et al. JOURNAL OF MARRIAGE AND THE FAMILY.
45:395-404, May 1983.

Reanastomosis of the vas deferens: techniques and results,
by S. S. Schmidt. CLINICAL OBSTETRICS AND
GYNECOLOGY. 25(3):533-540, September 1982.

Voluntary sterilization in Guatemala: a comparison of men
and women, by G. Roberto Santiso, et al. STUDIES IN
FAMILY PLANNING. 14(3):73, March 1983.

STERILIZATION: METHODS

A nonsurgical method for sterilization [plastic-like plug], by
D. Winston. VENTURE. 5:19+, September 1983.

STERILIZATION: PSYCHOLOGY OF

Psychological conditions in pregnancy and the puerperium and
their relevance to postpartum sterilization: a review, by K.
D. Bledin, et al. BULLETIN OF THE WORLD HEALTH

STERILIZATION: PSYCHOLOGY OF (continued)

ORGANIZATION. 61(3):533-544, 1983.

STERILIZATION: RESEARCH

Boll weevil (coleoptera: curculionidae): field competitiveness of diflubenzuron-fed, irradiated males—1980, 1981, by E. J. Villavaso. JOURNAL OF ECONOMIC ENTOMOLOGY. 75:662-664, August 1982.

Chemical sterilization in the male part 1: rats, by M. S. Fahim, et al. ARCHIVES OF ANDROLOGY. 9(3):261-265, November 1982.

Contraceptive sterilization: a comparison of Mexican-American and Anglos living in U. S. counties bordering Mexico, by C. W. Warren, et al. SOCIAL BIOLOGY. 28(3-4):265-280, Fall-Winter 1981.

Conventional versus laser reanastomosis of rabbit ligated uterine horns, by J. K. Choe, et al. OBSTETRICS AND GYNECOLOGY. 61(6):689-694, June 1983.

Effects of benzylphenol and benzyl-1,3-benzodioxole derivatives on fertility and longevity of the yellow fever mosquito (diptera: culicidae), by F. R. S. Nelson, et al. JOURNAL OF ECONOMIC ENTOMOLOGY. 75:877-878, October 1982.

Evaluation the sterile male method on red-winged blackbirds: effects of the chemosterilant thiotepa on the reproduction of clinically treated birds under field conditions, by N. Potvin, et al. CANADIAN JOURNAL OF ZOOLOGY. 60:2337-2343, October 1982.

A field evaluation of the sexual competitiveness of sterile melon flies, dacus (zeugodacus) cucurbitae, by O. Iwahashi, et al. ECOLOGICAL ENTOMOLOGY. 8:43-48, February 1983.

Mating competitiveness of irradiation-substerilized males of

the tobacco moth, by J. H. Brower. JOURNAL OF
ECONOMIC ENTOMOLOGY. 75:454-457, June 1982.

Prospects for autosterilisation of tsetse flies, glossina ssp.
(diptera: glossinidae), using sex pheromone and bisazir in
the field, by P. A. Langley, et al. BULLETIN OF
ENTOMOLOGICAL RESEARCH. 72:319-327, June
1982.

Sterilising effects of benzyl-1,3-benzodioxoles in the tsetse
fly glossina morsitans morsitans Westwood (diptera:
glossinidae), by P. A. Langley, et al. ENTOMOLIGICAL
REVIEW. 72:473-481, September 1982.

Sterilising effects of tepa, hempa, and N,N'-hexamethylenebis
(1-aziridinecarboxamide) on the smaller European elm
bark beetle, by W. N. Cannon, Jr. JOURNAL OF ECONOMIC
ENTOMOLOGY. 75:535-537, June 1982.

STERILIZATION: STATISTICS

Eleven million sterilizations from 1971 to 1981, but rate is
now declining. FAMILY PLANNING PERSPECTIVES.
15:89-90, March-April 1983.

Microsurgical reversal of sterilization: experiences and results
in 119 cases, by H. W. Schlosser, et al. GEBURTSHILFE
UND FRAUENHEILKUNDE. 43(4):213-216, April 1983.

STERILIZATION: TECHNIQUES

Ambulatory sterilization by minilaparotomy, by S. Melander.
LAKARTIDNINGEN. 79(38):3310-3314, September 22,
1982.

Choice of sterilization procedure [letter], by R. L. Anderson.
JOURNAL OF FAMILY PRACTICE. 16(2):238, February
1983.

A comparison of different laparoscopic sterilization occlusion techniques in 24,439 procedures, by P. P. Bhiwandiwala, et al. AMERICAN JOURNAL OF OBSTETRICS AND GYNECOLOGY. 144(3):319-331, October 1, 1982.

Conventional versus laser reanastomosis of rabbit ligated uterine horns, by J. K. Choe, et al. OBSTETRICS AND GYNECOLOGY. 61(6):689-694, June 1983.

Cryocauterization of the vas deferens, by P. L. Dias. JOURNA JOURNAL OF THE ROYAL SOCIETY OF MEDICINE. 75(11):868-870, November 1982.

Cumulative prevalence rates and corrected incidence rates of surgical sterilization among women in the United States, 1971-1978, by T. F. Nolan, et al. AMERICAN JOURNAL OF EPIDEMIOLOGY. 116(5):776-781, November 1982.

Deaths associated with laparoscopic sterilization in the United States, 1977-1979, by H. B. Peterson, et al. JOURNAL OF REPRODUCTIVE MEDICINE. 27(6):345-347, June 1982.

Effect of anaesthesia and surgery on the pre-S-phase cell cycle kinetics of mitogen-stimulated lymphocytes of previously healthy people, by A. J. Robertson, et al. BRITISH JOURNAL OF ANAESTHESIOLOGY. 55(4):339-347, April 1983.

Emotional consequences of sterilization. Clinical comments on the methodology of psychological studies, by P. Petersen. GEBURTSHILFE UND FRAUENHEILKUNDE. 43(4): 253-258, April 1983.

Epididymo-deferens anastomosis. Experimental study in the rat, by P. Hacker, et al. JOURNAL OF UROLOGY. 89(3): 193-199, 1983.

Examinations of various coagulation techniques, by H. H. Riedel, et al. PROGRESS IN CLINICAL AND BIOLOGICAL RESEARCH. 112(pt B):119-126, 1982.

STERILIZATION: TECHNIQUES (continued)

Fallopian tube microsurgery, by B. G. Bateman, et al. VIRGINIA MEDICAL. 110(3):171-173, 176, March 1983.

Fallopian tube occlusion rings: a consideration in the differential diagnosis of ureteral calculi, by D. B. Spring. RADIOLOGY. 145(1):51-52, October 1982.

Female sterilization with Hulka clips—initial experience at the University Hospital, Kuala Lumpur, by A. A. Rahman, et al. MEDICAL JOURNAL OF MALAYSIA. 37(3):276-280, September 1982.

A five year experience with laparoscopic falope ring sterilization, by J. H. Meyer, Jr. INTERNATIONAL JOURNAL OF GYNAECOLOGY AND OBSTETRICS. 20(3):183-187, June 1982.

Hysteroscopic sterilization: silicone elastic plugs, by T. P. Reed. CLINICAL OBSTETRICS AND GYNECOLOGY. 26(2):313-320, June 1983.

Hysteroscopic tubal occlusion with formed-in-place silicone plugs, by R. M. Houck, et al. OBSTETRICS AND GYNE-COLOGY. 60(5):641-648, November 1982.

Inferior epigastric haemorrhage, an avoidable complication of laparoscopic clip sterilization, by D. W. Pring. BRITISH JOURNAL OF OBSTETRICS AND GYNAECOLOGY. 90(5):480-482, May 1983.

Laparoscopic sterilization with the Falope-ring. Peroperative and late complications, method safety and a randomized investigation of immediate postoperative abdominal pain, by K. E. Larsen, et al. ACTA OBSTETRICIA ET GYNE-COLOGICA SCANDINAVICA. 62(2):125-130, 1983.

Laparoscopic sterilisation with the Filshie clip under local anaesthesia, by P. Paterson. MEDICAL JOURNAL OF AUSTRALIA. 2(10):476-477, November 13, 1982.

STERILIZATION: TECHNIQUES (continued)

Laparoscopic sterilizations (16,803) without vaginal manipulation, by P. V. Mehta. INTERNATIONAL JOURNAL OF GYNAECOLOGY AND OBSTETRICS. 20(4):323-325, August 1982.

Macroscopic and microscopic changes in the fallopian tube after bipolar cauterization, by K. D. Gunston, et al. SOUTH AFRICAN MEDICAL JOURNAL. 63(14): 518-519, April 2, 1983.

Menstrual pattern changes following laparoscopic sterilization [letter], by P. A. Poma. JOURNAL OF REPRODUCTIVE MEDICINE. 28(3):115-116, March 1983.

Menstrual pattern changes following laparoscopic sterilization with different occlusion techniques: a review of 10,004 cases, by P. P. Bhiwandiwala, et al. AMERICAN JOURNAL OF OBSTETRICS AND GYNECOLOGY. 145(6):684-694, March 15, 1983.

Method of sterilization using surgery of the fallopian tubes, Mkh. Iakhv'iaeva-Urunova. AKUSHERSTVO I GINEKOLOGIIA. (11):25-26, November 1982.

Minilaparatomy sterilization by Valtchev's uterine mobilization, by S. Grunstein, et al. HAREFUAH. 102(7):275-276, April 1, 1982.

Minor complications relevant to anaesthetic technique following bilateral tubal ligation, by J. P. Jayasuriya, et al. CEYLON MEDICAL JOURNAL. 26(2):71-76, June 1981.

An original method of reversible surgical sterilization of women: salpingodeviation, by I. Terzi, et al. MINERVA GINECOLOGICA. 34(10):797-802, October 1982.

Post-cesarean ovarian transposition as a method of reversible sterilization: initial study, by V. Ruiz Velasco, et al. GINECOLOGIA Y OBSTETRICIA DE MEXICO. 50(297): 1-3, January 1982.

Postsalpingectomy endometriosis: a reassessment, by R. J. Stock. OBSTETRICS AND GYNECOLOGY. 60(5):560-570, November 1982.

Pregnancy after tubal occlusion. A five-year study, by K. D. Gunston, et al. SOUTH AFRICAN MEDICAL JOURNAL. 63(14):517-518, April 2, 1983.

Randomized comparative study of culdoscopy and mini-laparotomy for surgical contraception in women. CONTRA-CEPTION. 26(6):587-593, December 1982.

Reopening of the tubes after surgical sterilization, by B. Lanciaux, et al. LARC MEDICAL. 2(11):927-931, December 1982.

Reversibility of clip sterilizations [letter], by J. F. Hulka, et al. LANCET. 2(8304):927, October 23, 1982.

Spring clip technique for sterilization [letter], by J. F. Hulka. OBSTETRICS AND GYNECOLOGY. 60(6):760, December 1982.

STERILIZATION: TUBAL

Advising women on sterilization options, by C. B. Demarest. PATIENT CARE. 17(9):128-131, 134-135, 139+, May 15, 1983.

Analysis of failure of microsurgical anastomosis after mid-segment, non-coagulation tubal ligation, by A. H. De-Cherney, et al. FERTILITY AND STERILITY. 39(5): 618-622, May 1983.

Catamnestic examinations performed after the utilization of two different sterilization techniques, by H. H. Riedel, et al. GYNECOLOGIC AND OBSTETRIC INVESTIGATION. 15(2):119-126, 1983.

Complications of interval laparoscopic tubal sterilization, by

STERILIZATION: TUBAL (continued)

F. Destefano, et al. OBSTETRICS AND GYNECOLOGY.
61(2):153-158, February 1983.

Deaths attributable to tubal sterilization in the United States,
1977 to 1981, by H. B. Peterson, et al. AMERICAN
JOURNAL OF OBSTETRICS AND GYNECOLOGY.
146(2):131-136, May 15, 1983.

Deaths attributable to tubal sterilization—United States, 1977-
1981. MORBIDITY AND MORALITY WEEKLY REPORT.
32(19):249-250, May 20, 1983.

The doing and undoing of surgical sterilization: a psychosocial
profile of the tubal reimplantation patient, by J. Ballou,
et al. PSYCHIATRY. 46(2):161-171, May 1983.

Ectopic pregnancy after tubal sterilization, by I. T. Jones.
MEDICAL JOURNAL OF AUSTRALIA. 1(6):279-280,
March 19, 1983.

Ectopic pregnancy after tubal sterilization: mechanism of
recanalization: a case, by P. Rimdusit. JOURNAL OF
THE MEDICAL ASSOCIATION OF THAILAND. 65(2):
101-105, 1982.

Ectopic pregnancy following tubal sterilization, by E. Qvigstad,
et al. INTERNATIONAL JOURNAL OF GYNAECOLOGY
AND OBSTETRICS. 20(4):279-281, August 1982.

Evaluation of ovarian function after tubal sterilization, by
E. Radwanska, et al. JOURNAL OF REPRODUCTIVE
MEDICINE. 27(7):376-384, July 1982.

Factors influencing the outcome of microsurgical tubal
ligation reversals, by J. C. Seiler. AMERICAN JOURNAL
OF OBSTETRICS AND GYNECOLOGY. 146(3):292-
298, June 1, 1983.

For safety and efficacy, most methods of tubal sterilization
are similar. FAMILY PLANNING PERSPECTIVES.

15(3):141-142, May-June 1983.

Histopathologic changes in fallopian tubes subsequent to
sterilization procedures, by R. J. Stock. INTERNATIONAL
JOURNAL OF GYNECOLOGICAL PATHOLOGY. 2(1):
13-27, 1983.

Hysteroscopic findings in 100 women requesting reversal of
a previously performed voluntary tubal sterilization, by J.
L. Goerzen, et al. FERTILITY AND STERILITY. 39(1):
103-104, January 1983.

Hysteroscopic tubal occlusion with silicone rubber, by T. P.
Reed, III, et al. OBSTETRICS AND GYNECOLOGY.
61(3):388-392, March 1983.

Is tubal sterilization with the Tupla-clip a reversible method?,
by B. Henkel, et al. GEBURTSHILFE UND FRAUENHEIL-
KUNDE. 43(2):127-130, February 1983.

Laparoscopic tubal coagulation—technic and follow-up results,
by H. Hopp, et al. ZENTRALBLATT FUR GYNAE-
KOLOGIE. 105(1):19-25, 1983.

Laparoscopic tubal sterilisation using Yoon's rings. The
technique and psychological effects, by M. Dubois, et al.
JOURNAL DE GYNECOLOGIE, OBSTETRIQUE ET
BIOLOGIE DE LA REPRODUCTION. 11(5):611-618,
1982.

Leads from the MMWR. Tubal sterilization-related deaths
in U. S., 1977-1981. JOURNAL OF THE AMERICAN
MEDICAL ASSOCIATION. 249(22):3011, June 10, 1983.

Long-term effects of tubal sterilization [letter], by P. A.
Poma. AMERICAN JOURNAL OF OBSTETRICS AND
GYNECOLOGY. 146(1):119-120, May 1, 1983.

Medical aspects of tubal sterilization in modern planning
of human reproduction, by B. M. Beric. JUGOSLAVENSKA

337

STERILIZATION: TUBAL (continued)

GINEKOLOGIJA I OPSTETRICIJA. 21(1-2):45-50, January-April 1981.

Microscopic tubal reversal, by C. Fleming, et al. ASSOCIATION OF OPERATING ROOM NURSES. 37(2):199-204, February 1983.

Microsurgical repair of the fallopian tubes, by B. M. O'Brien, et al. AUSTRALIAN AND NEW ZEALAND JOURNAL OF SURGERY. 53(2):161-167, April 1983.

Microsurgical reversal of tubal sterilization: a review, by N. Perone. TEXAS MEDICINE. 78(11):47-54, November 1982.

Microsurgical tubal reanastomosis in a community hospital: report of a three-year study, by A. C. Wittich. JOURNAL OF THE AMERICAN OSTEOPATHIC ASSOCIATION. 82(9 suppl):695-703, May 1983.

Moving the tubing: "parking" the fallopian tubes in the pelvic membrane makes for reversible sterilization, by V. Hewitt. HEALTH. 15(6):14, June 1983.

Pharmacokinetics and pharmacodynamics of local analgesia for laparoscopic tubal ligations, by F. J. Spielman, et al. AMERICAN JOURNAL OF OBSTETRICS AND GYNECOLOGY. 146(7):821-824, August 1, 1983.

Progesterone levels before and after laparoscopic tubal sterilization using endotherm coagulation, by G. Helm, et al. ACTA OBSTETRICIA ET GYNECOLOGICA SCANDINAVICA. 62(1):63-66, 1983.

Psychological issues in contraceptive sterilisation, by K. D. Bledin. MIDWIFE, HEALTH VISITOR AND COMMUNITY NURSE. 19(1):6, 10-11, January 1983.

Rabbit oviduct microvascular architecture after tubal ligation, by C. J. Verco, et al. FERTILITY AND STERILITY.

40(1):127-130, July 1983.

Risk of ectopic pregnancy following tubal sterilization, by F. Destefano, et al. OBSTETRICS AND GYNECOLOGY. 60(3):326-330, 1982.

Risk factors for complications of interval tubal sterilization by laparotomy, by P. M. Layde, et al. OBSTETRICS AND GYNECOLOGY. 62(2):180-184, August 1983.

Risk of wound and pelvic infection after laparoscopic and sterilization: instrument disinfection versus sterilization, by C. M. Huezo, et al. OBSTETRICS AND GYNECOLOGY. 61(5):598-602, May 1983.

The safety and efficacy of tubal sterilization: an international overview, by H. B. Peterson, et al. INTERNATIONAL JOURNAL OF GYNAECOLOGY AND OBSTETRICS. 21(2):139-144, April 1983.

Study of Bleier tubal clip for fertility control, by C. S. Vear. AUSTRALIAN AND NEW ZEALAND JOURNAL OF OBSTETRICS AND GYNAECOLOGY. 22(4):234-236, November 1982.

Trend of socio-demographic characteristics of tubectomy acceptors in a rural area of West Bengal (Singur), by S. P. Saha. INDIAN JOURNAL OF PUBLIC HEALTH. 25(3): 102-110, July-September 1981.

Tubal plugs bar pregnancy [tubal occlusion; silicone plugs block fallopian tubes]. SCIENCE DIGEST. 90:89, November 1982.

Tubal sterilization: characteristics of women most affected by the option of reversibility, by R. N. Shain, et al. SOCIAL SCIENCE AND MEDICINE. 16(10):1067-1077, 1982.

Tubal sterilization and menstrual dysfunction, by J. E.

339

STERILIZATION: TUBAL (continued)

Malick, et al. JOURNAL OF THE AMERICAN OSTEO-
PATHIC ASSOCIATION. 82(2):103-108, October 1982.

Tubal sterilization: findings in a large prospective study, by
M. Vessey, et al. BRITISH JOURNAL OF OBSTETRICS
AND GYNAECOLOGY. 90(3):203-209, March 1983.

Vasoplasty: flap operation, by H. Singh, et al. BRITISH
JOURNAL OF UROLOGY. 55(2):233-234, April 1983.

STERILIZATION: VOLUNTARY

Changes in sexual desire after voluntary sterilization, by F. D.
Bean, et al. SOCIAL BIOLOGY. 27:186-193, Fall 1980.

Husband or wife?: a multivariate analysis of decision making
for voluntary sterilization, by M. D. Clark, et al. JOURNAL
OF FAMILY ISSUES. 3(3):341-360, September 1982.

Husband-wife communication, wife's employment and the
decision for male or female sterilization, by F. D. Bean,
et al. JOURNAL OF MARRIAGE AND THE FAMILY.
45(2):395-403, May 1983.

Voluntary sterilization in Flanders, by R. L. Cliquet, et al.
JOURNAL OF BIOSOCIAL SCIENCE. 13:47-61, 1981.

Voluntary sterilization in Guatemala: a comparison of men
and women, by R. Santiso, et al. STUDIES IN FAMILY
PLANNING. 14(3):73-82, March 1983.

STERILIZATION AND CRIMINALS

Hormone treatments for sex offenders. CRIMINAL JUSTICE
NEWSLETTER. 14(7):3, March 28, 1983.

How to curb the fertility of the unfit: the feeble-minded in
Edwardian Britain, by D. Barker. OXFORD REVIEW OF
EDUCATION. 9(3):197-211, 223-225, 1983.

California conservator's petition to sterilize incompetent ward denied. THE FAMILY LAW REPORTER: COURT OPINIONS. 9(31):2471-2472, June 7, 1983.

In re guardianship of Eberhardy (Wis): the sterilization of the mentally retarded. WISCONSIN LAW REVIEW. 1982, p. 1199-1227.

Retardation and sterilization, by B. M. Dickens. INTERNATIONAL JOURNAL OF LAW AND PSYCHIATRY. 5(3-4):295-318, 1983.

Sterilization and the mentally handicapped person, by R. McManus. NORTH CAROLINA MEDICAL JOURNAL. 44(2):92-93, February 1983.

Sterilization and the mentally retarded, by K. L. Dickin, et al. CANADA'S MENTAL HEALTH. 31(1):4-8, March 1983.

Sterilization of the mentally retarded, by C. D. Davis. TEXAS HOSPITALS. 38(4):48-49, September 1982.

Sterilization of mentally retarded women, by W. Heidenreich, et al. GEBURTSHILFE UND FRAUENHEILKUNDE. 42(7):554-557, July 1982.

Sterilization of the retarded: a break in the impasse?, by H. C. Moss, et al. JOURNAL OF THE INDIANA STATE MEDICAL ASSOCIATION. 75(7):458-459, July 1982.

Voluntary sterilization for persons with mental disabilities: the need for legislation, by B. A. Burnett. SYRACUSE LAW REVIEW. 32:913-955, Fall 1981.

STERILIZATION AND PHYSICIANS

The judicial portrayal of the physician in abortion and sterilization decisions: the use and abuse of medical discretion, by A. Asaro. HARVARD WOMEN'S LAW JOURNAL. 6:51-102, Spring 1983.

STERILIZATION AND POLITICS

Compulsory sterilization statutes: public sentiment and public policy, by R. A. Cohen, et al. RESEARCH IN COMMUNITY AND MENTAL HEALTH. 2:327-357, 1981.

STERILIZATION AND RELIGION

Moral dilemmas that are acute within a religious tradition. A Jewish perspective, by I. Franck. HOSPITAL PRACTICE. 18(7):192-196, July 1983.

STERILIZATION COUNSELLING

Advising women on sterilization options, by C. B. Demarest. PATIENT CARE. 17(9):128-131, 134-135, 139+, May 15, 1983.

STERILIZATION FUNDING

Government funding for surgical reversal of voluntary female sterilization. Ethical points of reference, by B. Freedman, et al. JOURNAL OF REPRODUCTIVE MEDICINE. 27(6): 339-344, June 1982.

STERILIZATION INVOLUNTARY

Involuntary sterilization in Germany from 1933 to 1945 and some consequences for today, by F. Pfafflin, et al. INTERNATIONAL JOURNAL OF LAW AND PSYCHIATRY. 5(3-4):419-423, 1983.

VASECTOMY

Clinical immunology of vasectomy and vasovasostomy, by L. Linnet. UROLOGY. 22(2):101-114, August 1983.

Current concepts in vasectomy reversal, by E. F. Lizza, et al. WEST VIRGINIA MEDICAL JOURNAL. 78(11):283-285, November 1982.

Demographic consequences, client satisfaction and reasons for selecting sterilization among vasectomy and tubectomy clients in Bangladesh, by I. Swenson, et al. CONTRACEPTION. 25(6):573-590, 1982.

The effects of sperm antibodies on fertility after vasectomy reversal, by J. M. Parslow, et al. AMERICAN JOURNAL OF REPRODUCTIVE IMMUNOLOGY. 3(1):28-31, January-February 1983.

Fertilizing capacity and sperm antibodies in vasovasostomized men, by E. Requeda, et al. FERTILITY AND STERILITY. 39(2):197-203, February 1983.

Immunoglobulin in seminal fluid of fertile, infertile, vasectomy and vasectomy reversal patients, by J. E. Fowler, Jr., et al. JOURNAL OF UROLOGY. 129(4):869-872, April 1983.

Intraoperative observations during vasovasostomy in 334 patients, by A. M. Belker, et al. JOURNAL OF UROLOGY. 129(3):524-527, March 1983.

Masculinity-femininity and the desire for sexual intercourse after vasectomy: a longitudinal study, by D. Williams, et al. SOCIAL PSYCHOLOGY QUARTERLY. 43(3):347-352, September 1980.

Microsurgical reversal in a patient vasectomized ten years previously, by A. L. Gaspari, et al. MINERVA UROLOGICA. 35(1):49-52, March 1983.

Microsurgical vasovasostomy: an outpatient procedure under local anesthesia, by K. W. Kaye, et al. JOURNAL OF UROLOGY. 129(5):992-994, May 1983.

Micro-vasovasotomy: report of seven cases, by X. Li. CHUNG HUA WAI KO TSA CHIH. 21(3):180, March 1983.

Morphologic changes of the vas deferens after vasectomy and vasovasostomy in dogs, by A. Hamidinia, et al. SURGERY, GYNECOLOGY AND OBSTETRICS. 156(6):737-742, June 1983.

VASECTOMY (continued)

New technique for microscopic vasovasostomy, by S. A. Leonard, et al. UROLOGY. 22(2):188-189, August 1983.

Recovery of fertility following vasovasotomy, by S. R. Plymate, et al. ANDROLOGIA. 15(3):279-281, May-June 1983.

Reversal of vasectomy [letter], by O. N. Mehrotra. NEW ZEALAND MEDICAL JOURNAL. 95(717):710, October 13, 1982.

Sterilization by vas occlusion without transection does not reduce postvasectomy sperm-agglutinating antibodies in serum. A randomized trial of vas occlusion versus vasectomy, by T. C. Gerstenberg, et al. SCANDINAVIAN JOURNAL OF UROLOGY AND NEPHROLOGY. 17(2):149-151, 1983.

Study finds no rise in atherosclerosis symptoms in men vasectomized an average of fifteen years ago. FAMILY PLANNING PERSPECTIVES. 15(1):30-31, January-February 1983.

Termino-terminal vaso-vasostomy and spermatic granuloma. Experimental research in rats, by G. Cavallaro, et al. MINERVA CHIRURGICA. 37(23-24):2097-2103, December 15-31, 1982.

Vasectomy, by H. Brownlee, et al. JOURNAL OF FAMILY PRACTICE. 16(2):379-384, February 1983.

The vasectomy decision-making process, by S. D. Mumford. STUDIES IN FAMILY PLANNING. 14(3):83, March 1983.

Vasectomy, disease link refuted. SCIENCE NEWS. 124:377, December 10, 1983.

Vasectomy in Guatemala: a follow-up study of five-hundred acceptors, by R. Santiso, et al. SOCIAL BIOLOGY. 28(3-4): 253-264, Fall-Winter 1981.

Vasectomy: an international appraisal, by J. H. Johnson.
FAMILY PLANNING PERSPECTIVES. 15:45-48,
January-February 1983.

Vasectomy reversal: experience in Ramathibodi Hospital,
Thailand, by K. Ratana-olarn, et al. JOURNAL OF THE
MEDICAL ASSOCIATION OF THAILAND. 65(5):240-
245, May 1982.

Vasectomy reversal technique and results, by S. E. Denton,
et al. ARIZONA MEDICINE. 40(1):33-36, January 1983.

Vasovasostomy in the rat. Improved technique using
absorbable microsuture (polyglycolic acid), by S. Lee,
et al. UROLOGY. 20(4):418-421, October 1982.

Vasovasostomy: results 1975-1981 of reconstructive operations
following the sterilization of males, by H. J. Ubels, et al.
NEDERLANDS TIJDSCHRIFT VOOR GENEESKUNDE.
126(30):1359-1363, July 24, 1982.

AUTHOR INDEX

346

Eversoll, D. B. 19
Ewald, T. 90
Ezzard, N. V. 108

Faden, R. 101
Fahim, M. S. 28
Fang, Y. Z. 128
Farrell, R. G. 69
Farrell, W. C., Jr. 62
Faruqee, R. 57
Faulk, W. P. 67
Favara, D. 128
Felthons, A. R. 92
Ferrand-Picard, M. 80
Fibison, W. J. 44
Fijalkowski, W. 51
Fincancioglu, N. 57
Finch, J. 34, 75, 95, 105
Fiscella, K. 110
Fischer, M. A. 24
Fiseus, R. J. 21
Fisher, A. A. 57
Fisher, W. A. 141
Fleming, C. 82
Fogel, P. I. 26
Foidart, J. M. 11
Foley, M. C. 65
Folster, D. 12, 45, 88
Ford, N. 53
Ford, R. 11
Foreit, J. R. 133
Forger, N. G. 112
Forman, A. 50
Forrest, J. D. 140
Foster, H. M. 21
Foster, J. E. 95
Fowler, J. E., Jr. 68
Fox, E. R. 31
Fox, H. 18
Fox, T. C. 113
Frame, R. 142

Franck, I. 84
Francome, C. 136
Fraser, H. M. 89
Fraser, S. 92
Fraser, S. E. 20
Freedman, B. 63
Freifeld, K. 121
Frick, G. 137
Frisch, R. E. 42
Frohock, F. M. 2
Fugere, C. 104
Fylling, P. 54

Gall, J. K. 115
Gallegos, A. J. 143
Gangrade, K. D. 2
Garbaciak, J. A., Jr. 66
Gardner, M. B. 80
Garner, E. 75
Gartland, A. 25
Gartner, L. 91
Gaspari, A. L. 82
Gerrard, M. 102, 118
Gerstenberg, T. C. 124
Gest, T. 11
Geuras, D. 9
Ghetau, V. 43
Ghose, N. 84
Ghosh, P. K. 29
Gill, T. J., III. 68
Ginger, S. 11
Gluckin, D. S. 120
Gocke, H. 61, 85
Goebel, P. 136
Goerzen, J. L. 66
Goettsch, S. L. 19
Gold, R. 42
Goldberg, H. I. 36
Goldhaber, M. K. 122
Goldkamp, D. 31, 104
Goldman, E. B. 142

350

351

Matis, N. 87
Mayaux, M. J. 81
Mecklenburg, M. E. 15
Meehan, M. 13, 18, 64, 74, 78,
  88, 89, 103, 116, 132, 140
Mehrotra, O. N. 113
Mehta, B. 8
Mehta, P. V. 75
Melander, S. 16
Melis, G. B. 136
Menard, S. 59
Menke, A. 7
Mensch, B. S. 48
Merwin, J. 53
Mettler, L. 69
Meulenbroek, G. H. 94
Meyer, J. H., Jr. 46, 61
Mezey, S. G. 30
Micallef, P. J. 79
Miceli, M. O. 138
Mikkelsen, M. 68
Milbauer, B. 3
Milby, T. H. 88
Milia, S. 71
Milligan, S. E. 16
Mills, A. 131
Milnor, S. 4
Mirsky, J. 54, 70
Mirthy, N. 4
Mishell, D. R., Jr. 93
Misinger, I. 30
Miskevich, N. I. 94
Misra, J. 34
Mithers, C. L. 12
Mohammad, A. S. 107
Molina, R. 28
Molodkin, B. V. 117
Monahan, W. J. 106
Mondy, L. W. 126
Moorman, K. 74
Mora, S. 74

Morano, A. L. 114
Morgentaler, H. 4
Morreim, E. H. 34
Morrison, D. M. 55
Mortimer, R. 95
Morton, N. E. 40
Mosher, W. D. 59
Moss, H. C. 124
Mueller, C. 68
Mumford, S. D. 12, 26, 138,
  139
Munday, D. 74
Munsick, R. A. 30
Murchison, W. 19
Murphy, J. F. 131
Musto, M. 46
Myskow, M. 137

Nagey, D. A. 100
Namerow, P. B. 52, 61
Narone, J. N. 39
Nash, E. S. 131
Nasi, A. 70
Naughton, J. 21
Navarro, D. 127
Nelson, F. R. S. 49
Nenney, S. W. 129
Neri, A. 27
Neuhaus, R. J. 7
Neuwirth, R. S. 134
Nevadomsky, J. 28
Nevett, A. 95
Newman, J. L. 47
Ney, P. G. 35
Nickelsen, C. 82
Nicotra, M. 62
Noia, G. 17
Nolan, T. F. 39
Noonan, J. T., Jr. 64
Norback, J. 4
Norsigian, J. 43

355

360